The Study Skills Handbook

Palgrave Study Skills

Pocket Study Skills

Series Editor: Kate Williams

Palgrave Research Skills

Visit the book's companion website at http://us.macmillan.com/thestudyskillshandbook

The Study Skills Handbook

Stella Cottrell

palgrave
macmillan

First edition 1999
Second edition 2003
Third edition 2008
First United States edition 2012

Published by
PALGRAVE MACMILLAN

Palgrave Macmillan in the UK is an imprint of Macmillan Publishers Limited,
registered in England, company number 785998, of Houndmills, Basingstoke,
Hampshire RG21 6XS.

Palgrave Macmillan in the US is a division of St Martin's Press LLC,
175 Fifth Avenue, New York, NY 10010.

Palgrave Macmillan is the global academic imprint of the above companies
and has companies and representatives throughout the world.

Palgrave© and Macmillan© are registered trademarks in the United States,
the United Kingdom, Europe and other countries

ISBN 13: 978-0-230-36968-9

A catalogue record for this book is available
from the British Library.

A catalog record for this book is available
from the Library of Congress.

This book is printed on paper suitable for recycling and
made from fully managed and sustained forest sources.

10 9 8 7 6 5 4 3 2 1
21 20 19 18 17 16 15 14 13 12

Printed in the United States of America

Contents

Acknowledgments

The author would like to thank the following:

Lynn Chiswick, for her full encouragement and support for *Skills for Success* when all I had to show her were a few pencil-and-paper sketches and a lot of enthusiasm.

Robert Simpson, Pam Dixon and David Gosling for helpful comments on the first edition of the *Handbook.*

The many lecturers at University of East London who used *Skills for Success* and the other materials that have been incorporated into this *Handbook*, including the dyslexia support tutors who piloted some of the material with dyslexic students at the university—the feedback of all these staff on what to include, and on how to adapt some of the early material, has been invaluable.

Kate Williams, for reading through the original text and for her many useful suggestions on how to improve it, and the kindness, encouragement and sensitivity with which she offered these.

Lecturers from British and international universities for their constructive feedback on the first two editions. Wherever possible their suggestions have been incorporated into later editions. Special thanks to Mary Drury, Karry Omer and Andy Lloyd for specific suggestions for the third edition.

Margaret, Andrew, Claire, Rachael, Julie, Tina, C.E.D. and all those whose work behind the scenes made this book possible. Particular thanks to Suzannah Burywood for her support, her enthusiasm and her belief in the book over many years, and to Jennifer Schmidt, for her work on this edition.

The hundreds of students who were open to discussing with me what they found difficult about studying and willing to elaborate new and individual ways of approaching their study—to them, and to all future students who may struggle for even a day, this book is dedicated.

This book would not have been possible without the assistance from a number of reviewers. The publisher would like to thank Todd Campbell, Bonnie Devet, Trakenya Dobbins, Cora Dzubak, Arthur Ford, Soomie Han, Calley Hornbuckle, Shelia Jefferson, Ileka Leaks, Kelly Lid Stephens, Jaime Lynn Longo, Joel V. McGee, Mark Poisel, and Evanthia Rosati for their generous help and constructive feedback.

Introducing

The Study Skills Handbook

The study skills needed for college are ultimately gained only through studying at that level. Study skills don't hatch fully formed, any more than a grown hen pops from an egg. They evolve and mature through practice, trial and error, feedback from others, and reflection as you move through the different stages of your college career. You will be surprised at how your thinking and language skills develop simply through continued study.

However, there are some basic approaches which can start you off on a good footing, help you find shortcuts, and accelerate the learning process. This *Handbook* developed out of practical work under-taken with hundreds of students over twenty years.

The core of the book has been used by hundreds of thousands of students and instructors worldwide, whose varied comments have contributed to this edition of the *Handbook*.

Quick tips and deeper learning

A reflective, active, self-evaluating approach to learning develops deeper understanding in the long term. However, quick tips are also invaluable to students, especially in emergencies. This *Handbook* offers both approaches. To meet your immediate and long-term study needs, move flexibly between the two approaches.

LEARNING OUTCOMES

The Study Skills Handbook aims to help you to manage your own success as a student. It does this by:

- encouraging you to understand that success as a student is about more than being "smart"—good grades, as well as other kinds of successful outcome, are possible for any student

- preparing you for what to expect from college

- encouraging you to think about the skills you have already, which you will need both as a student and in your working life

- providing resources to help you evaluate, reflect upon and manage your own learning

- making suggestions on how to develop positive approaches and good study habits

- offering guidance on how to tackle activities that many students find difficult

- identifying how technology and e-resources can be used to support and personalize your study

- helping you to understand more about how learning, intelligence and memory work and how to develop critical and analytical thinking styles.

How to use *The Study Skills Handbook*

This is a guide that you can dip into as you need—or use by working through the chapters related to a particular aspect of study. You can do as little or as much as you find helpful. Of necessity, the *Handbook* focuses on a different aspect of study in each chapter. However, as your study progresses, you will notice that these skills are interconnected. Developing one area of your study will also help with other aspects.

Finding what you need

- Each chapter begins with an outline of the learning outcomes for that chapter. Browsing through this list may help you decide whether you need to read the chapter.
- Each chapter deals with several topics, and each topic is introduced by a heading like the one at the top of this page. These headings make it easier to browse through to find what you need quickly.
- The index (at the back) gives page references for specific topics.

Photocopyable pages

Pages containing self-evaluations, checklists, planners and record sheets may be photocopied for individual reuse. (You may like to enlarge some of them onto larger paper.) When you have used the photocopies, keep them with your journal for future reference.

 This symbol is used to indicate a page that can be used for self-evaluation or for planning.

Using the website

Additional free material can be found on the Palgrave website at http://us.macmillan.com/thestudyskillshandbook. You can also download some of the resource material rather than photocopying it from the book.

Cartoons and page layout

The cartoons and different layouts act primarily as visual memory-joggers. Even if you cannot draw

well, you can use visual prompts like these in your own notes. (This will also help you to find things more quickly.) The variety will encourage learning through different senses, too—see Chapter 8 for more details.

The self-evaluation questionnaires

The self-evaluation questionnaires will help you in two ways:

- by breaking down major study skills into their component subskills
- by enabling you to pinpoint which components make the study skill difficult for you and to notice steps or activities that you missed out in the past.

Sometimes just going through the questionnaire will be all you need to do to identify the missing link. Use the questionnaires to monitor your progress and identify your strengths.

Challenging material

If you are returning to study after a few years' absence, or if there are aspects of study that are new to you or that proved difficult in the past, don't let these put you off now.

It is very common for students to find that material which was difficult the first time around becomes comprehensible when they return to it after a gap. Even students who find academic language and methods unexpected or difficult usually adapt to these quite quickly.

Knowledge of specialized terms and of underlying theories empowers you as a student. It sharpens your thinking, allows you to describe things more accurately and improves your overall performance.

Keeping a journal

 This symbol reminds you to note down your reflections in your study journal. For details, see page 59.

Where to begin

- Read through the *Seven approaches to learning* used by *The Study Skills Handbook* (page 4). The *Handbook* will then make more sense to you.
- Complete the *What do I want from college?* questionnaire (page 6). This will help you to orient yourself as a student.
- Browse through the *Handbook* so you know roughly what is in it. You may not know what to use until you start assignments.
- Use the *Study skills: priorities* planner (page 27) to focus your thinking.
- If you are unsure where to begin with a study skill, do the *Self-evaluation* questionnaire in the appropriate chapter to clarify your thinking.
- Chapters 2–4 cover groundwork and approaches basic to the rest of the *Handbook*. You will probably find it helpful to work through these early on.

If you know little about college life ...

Start with Chapter 1, *Starting college*. This gives you an idea of what to expect from college and gives advice on how to prepare yourself for your freshman year. Chapter 4 is also likely to be useful.

You may also find it helpful if you:

- identify your current skills and qualities (see pages 23–26)
- look at your motivation (*What do I want from college?*, pages 6 and 87)
- develop confidence in your reading (pages 97–103) and writing (pages 232–237)
- check your computer skills (pages 124–125).

If you have recently graduated from high school ...

You may find that you can browse through the early sections of each chapter quite quickly. Chapters 4, 7, 10, 12, 14, and 15 may be the most useful for you. If you feel uncomfortable about a book that uses images as learning tools, read page 45 and Chapter 8 on *Memory* and the methods may make more sense.

Dyslexic students

There are now hundreds of thousands of dyslexic students studying in college. Many aspects of this book are designed with dyslexic students in mind, including:

- the contents
- the use of visual images
- the book's layout
- the emphasis on structure
- the use of varied and multisensory approaches to learning.

Pace yourself

If you have been away from study for a while, or if you are finding study difficult, be kind to yourself. It takes time and practice to orientate yourself to the college environment and to develop study habits, especially academic writing skills.

Everybody learns in their own way

There are many avenues to successful study. Experiment. Explore. Be creative. Find what suits *you* best.

Chapters 2–4 encourage you to look for your own learning patterns and make suggestions on how to experiment with your learning.

Seven approaches to learning

The Study Skills Handbook uses seven approaches to learning.

1 ▶ Learning can be an adventure

It is difficult to learn if you are stressed or bored. This *Handbook* encourages you to be effective rather than virtuous and to seek out ways of making your learning more fun. Degree programs take several years, so you need to find ways of making your learning enjoyable.

Small children learn extraordinary amounts without trying particularly hard—simply through being relaxed, observing, playing, role-playing, trying things out, making mistakes, and being interested in what they are doing. They don't regard setbacks as failures; they don't worry about what others think; and they don't tell themselves they might not be able to learn. When a child falls over, she or he just gets up and moves again, and eventually walking becomes easy. Adults can learn in this way too—if they allow themselves.

2 ▶ Use many senses

The more we use our senses of sight, hearing and touch, and the more we use fine muscle movements in looking, speaking, writing, typing, drawing, or moving the body, the more opportunities we give the brain to take in information using our preferred sense.

The use of several senses also gives the brain more connections and associations, making it easier to find information later, which assists memory and learning. This book encourages you to use your senses to the fullest and to incorporate movement into your study. This will make learning easier—and more interesting.

3 ▶ Identify what attracts you

It is easier to learn by keeping desirable outcomes in mind than by forcing ourselves to study out of duty. Some aspects of study may be less attractive to you, such as writing assignments, meeting deadlines or taking tests, and yet these also tend to bring the greatest satisfaction and rewards.

It is within your power to find in any aspect of study the gold that attracts you. For example, visualize yourself on a large movie screen enjoying your study—or your later rewards. Hear your own voice telling you what you are achieving now. Your imagination will catch hold of these incentives and find ways of making them happen.

4 ▶ Use active learning

We learn with a deeper understanding when we are both actively and personally engaged:

- juggling information
- struggling to make sense
- playing with different options
- making decisions
- linking information.

For this reason, most pages of this book require you to *do* something, however small, to increase your active engagement with the topic.

5 ▶ Take responsibility for your own learning

As you will see from Chapter 1, colleges generally expect you to be ready to study on your own, with minimum assistance, especially for basics such as spelling or grammar. As a college student, you are expected to be largely responsible for your own learning.

One way in which you can act responsibly towards yourself is to ensure that you *are* ready for the stage of study that you are entering. Many students enter college without adequate preparation. This can make study more stressful and difficult than it need be and undermine confidence. Make sure *you* are ready or are aware of the steps you need to take to get ready quickly.

6 ▶ Trust in your own intelligence

Many students worry in case they are not intelligent enough for college. Some did not do well in high school and worry that being a good student is "not in their genes." Panic about this

can, in itself, make it hard to learn. That is why this book considers ideas about intelligence (in Chapter 3) and stress (in Chapter 9). Many students who were not ideal pupils in high school do extremely well in college, following thorough preparation.

7 ▶ Recognize your own learning preferences

Each of us learns in an individual way—though we also have a lot in common. Some theorists divide people into "types" such as *visual*, *auditory* and *kinesthetic*, or *introverted* and *extroverted*— there are lots of ways of dividing people up. The important thing, however, is not to discover which "type" you are but rather to recognize the many different elements that contribute to how you yourself learn best.

If you regard yourself as a "type" you may over-identify yourself with that type. You may then get stuck with that image of yourself—and always consider yourself a "visual introverted" type, or a "chaotic extrovert." This may leave you with rigid views about the one way you learn. What you *need* to do is experiment with strategies and skills you currently underuse. The human brain is highly adaptable: Able learners move easily between different strategies and learning styles, depending on the task at hand.

The good thing about being aware of how *you* learn best is that you can adapt new learning to fit where you are now. You may also be able to see more clearly why you did well or badly in high school, depending on whether the teaching matched your personal learning preferences.

What do I want from college?

Our imaginations are extremely powerful. Just try *not* to think about something, such as whether you left the stove on, and you quickly discover how easy it is for your imagination to see your home burned to the ground! If you give your imagination any leads, it will act on them.

You can use this capacity of the imagination in many ways to help your study. Try using the following questionnaire to consider what, in five years' time, you would like to be saying to yourself about what you achieved in college. You may then find that your orientation towards your work and to different activities on campus starts to change, as your imagination goes to work.

You may also like to come back to this questionnaire at different times in the future, to see if your thinking about what really counts for you has changed.

Imagine yourself five years from now, thinking back on what you achieved in college. From your chair in the future, rate the following desirable outcomes (1, 2, 3, etc.) in their order of importance to you then.

☐ I made good friends
☐ I got a good degree
☐ I made full use of college facilities
☐ I developed new interests
☐ I developed skills which helped me find a good job
☐ I learned to work better with other people
☐ I learned to express myself better
☐ I really enjoyed myself
☐ I found out more about who I was as a person
☐ I learned to think and reason better
☐ I developed my creativity
☐ I took care of my health and well-being
☐ I took on positions of responsibility
☐ I learned to manage myself as an effective adult
☐ I stretched myself intellectually
☐ I learned to manage stressful situations with calm
☐ I learned how to balance work, friendship and family

What do these priorities suggest to you now about how you could best use your time in college?

Enjoy the book

Enjoy the rest of
The Study Skills Handbook—
and enjoy your time in college!

Chapter 1

Starting college

The big decision

Going to college can be a life-transforming experience. Most students look back on their days in college with great fondness. This is because college provides unique opportunities to:

- take on academic work that stretches you intellectually

- explore new ideas and consider the kind of person you want to be in the world

- find out a great deal about yourself, not least how you rise to the challenge of higher level study

- make friends that will last you for life.

While starting out in college is an exciting time, it can also raise many questions about what it will be like and what is expected of you. If you are eager to succeed, this can also be accompanied by some anxiety about if you are ready and what you can do to ensure that you give yourself the best chance of doing well.

Preparing the way

This chapter looks at ways to prepare yourself practically and mentally for your first semester in college. If you already know what to expect from higher education, you may wish to skip quite quickly over this chapter.

On the other hand, you may know little about college especially if you have been out of education for a few years or if you are the first member of your family to go to college. Some aspects of studying in college are very different from high school. The following pages will give you a general idea of what to expect. They also provide suggestions of things you can do to ease the transition to studying in college.

Choosing the right time for you

In general, colleges do not provide much support to help you "catch up." They expect you to be ready for higher level study from the outset. It pays to be well prepared before you start your program.

Even if you are eager to get started, it is best not to rush into going to college if you are not yet ready—it can be very expensive, in terms of money, stress, health and relationships. You could always start by taking courses at a local community college before progressing to a higher degree.

Help is available

If you have been out of education for more than a year or two since high school, you may find it helpful to speak first with the appropriate members of staff—your college may have advisors specifically for adult and returning students, transfer students, veterans or part-time students, for instance. These staff will be familiar with your needs and will know what services are available to you.

What to expect in college

Teaching methods

Teaching methods differ but you can expect at least some of the following.

Lectures

These vary according to program and subject area but in general, expect:

- size: 50–300 people
- length: 1–3 hours
- weekly: 5–15 hours
- no individual attention.

See also pages 115–116.

There is usually a set of lectures for each course. You are likely to study with different students for each class. Lectures are used to give an overview of the topic. Usually, students listen and take notes while professors speak or read from notes, write on a board, or present information using PowerPoint. Some professors encourage questions and include activities; others do not. Occasionally, lectures are delivered by video or transmitted from another campus.

Classes

These usually involve group discussion of material presented either in a lecture or in assigned reading.

Often a student (or a group of students) is asked to begin the discussion by making a presentation. It is important to prepare for classes by reading through lecture notes and background reading, even if you are not asked to make a presentation yourself. You may sometimes be asked to write a research paper based on your reading for the class.

- size: 12–30 people
- length: 1–3 hours
- weekly: varies (perhaps 1–3 each week).

See also Chapter 10 *Group work and presentations*.

Other teaching styles used in college

Colleges are becoming more flexible in the ways they teach, so you may experience a wide range of teaching styles, including some or all of the following.

Group work

This could be for discussion or mutual support, or to undertake a joint project. Students are often expected to form their own support groups. (See Chapter 10.)

Work-based learning and work placements

More vocational courses require students to be employed or on work placements. While there, they may be supervised by an instructor from the college or by somebody at the workplace—or a mixture of the two.

Laboratory work, studio work and practicals

Science students may spend most of their time doing practical work in laboratories; fine arts students may work predominantly in studio space they are allocated at the college. The amount of practical work of this kind will depend on your program. (See page 119.)

Distance learning

Students on some programs work mostly at home. Materials are sent either online or by mail. Contact with instructors may be by email, by video conferencing at a local center or in local meetings.

Independent study

This is the most common and possibly most challenging feature of studying in college. Apart from scheduled elements such as lectures, almost all programs expect students to work on their own for the rest of the week. (See pages 10–11 and 318–319.)

E-learning and technology

These are now used to enhance study on most programs. See Chapter 6.

Seeing your professors

College professors are likely to be much less available than your teachers in high school. Teaching is only one of their responsibilities. They may undertake research or teach at other colleges. They may also be consultants outside the college. Some are contracted for only a few hours a week.

A professor may have a great many students to see. For all of these reasons, you may need to book an appointment well in advance.

Instructors' varied approaches

College subject areas or departments have their own traditions, and even individual instructors may

Now let me get this straight. Mr. Jiff wants work on both sides of the paper, Dr. Lank on one. Ms. Snape wants everything word-processed. Mr. Kip wants papers sent by email. Ms. Snape wants sub-headings …

have strong personal tastes in how things should be done. You need to be alert to this and notice your instructors' preferences. (See page 263.)

The college week

Most full-time college programs are considered to be the equivalent of an average full-time working week. This means that you are expected to study for 35–40 hours a week, in a mixture of independent study, at home or in a library in and scheduled classes on campus.

The way that time is divided up varies greatly. Some programs require students to attend 15 hours of lectures a week and research around the subject, read, think and write assignments for the rest of the week. Practical courses may involve only 2 hours of lectures a week, with very few written assignments in the year and most of the time spent on work placements or in the studio.

> ### Will this suit you?
>
> If you have strong preferences about how you spend your time, investigate how your program breaks up the study week and the kinds of teaching methods used.

Independent study

Types of independent study

Independent study is a feature of *all* college programs. The amount and the kind varies from one program to another.

Independent study

You may be able to study all or part of your degree by negotiated independent study, designing your program according to given learning outcomes. With this approach, you agree the relevant title, approach, outputs, and resources with your advisor. Although you have some ongoing contact with your advisor, there may not be any designated taught sessions. See pages 318–319.

Individually designed degrees are subject to approval, or "validation," by the institution, to ensure that the degree is of the same standard and quality as other degrees. Usually, a learning contract of some kind is approved and updated on an agreed basis.

Activity

What does "independent study" suggest to you?

1 In pencil, underline all the words you associate with the phrase "independent study."

making my own success

freedom

going it alone   failure!

being in control   less help

maturity

isolation   good study management   responsibility

free time   pursuing my own interests

managing my time   less guidance

being left to my own devices

working on my own   enjoyment   finding support

2 Using a bright marker pen, circle all the words that describe how you would *like* independent study to be. Use the bubbles to add words of your own.

Independent study within a degree program

In most programs, "independent study" means working on your own between taught sessions. Early on you are given more guidance, though probably still less than you received in high school. As you move through the program, you are usually given more choices and greater personal management of the study process. The amount of independent study increases until you may be asked to undertake a final-year research project, which you do almost completely by independent study.

Levels of independence

Different levels of independence are involved for each program and for each year. This depends on how far you:

- have control over the content, design, and learning outcomes for your program or class

- study from resources rather than attend taught sessions
- have choices over the classes you take
- decide the pace of study
- are expected to study on your own each week
- can choose where and when you study
- can choose your assignment topics
- can choose how you will be assessed.

Independent learning can be all the things you would *like* it to be! College learning allows you a great deal of freedom to shape your learning experience to suit yourself. The better your study skills, the easier you will find managing that freedom so that you can enjoy yourself while undertaking independent study successfully. It is up to you to manage that process well.

Independent learning: taking control

A different approach to learning and teaching

In college, it is expected that you have sufficient maturity to work on your own for longer periods, without an instructor in the room to guide you. You are given a great deal more responsibility for your own success than is typical of high school. This *can* feel as if your study lacks structure. However, it can also feel very liberating—you have more freedom to study in ways that suit you. To take advantage of this, you need a deeper understanding of your own learning, so that you can study effectively (see pages 44–50 and Chapter 4).

Making choices

It is your responsibility to make sensible choices of options within your program, as well as to plan extracurricular activity. Your choices will affect your program and your future career. This can feel rather daunting. However, it can also feel exciting to be more in charge of your own life. The literature you are given usually tells you clearly how to go about making choices and finding help. Guidance will be available, but it is usually up to you to find out

where and when this guidance is delivered—and to read the materials provided.

Finding resources and support

You will receive recommendations for books, equipment and sources of support. Usually these will be given in a handbook or similar literature, either in print or online. These recommendations, however, are only part of what you need to know. You will need to find out for yourself what additional reading is needed, what resources are available, what support is available and when to use each of these.

In high school you may have received a great deal of guidance on what pages to read in books, how to interpret essay questions, how to interpret what you read, what information to include in an assignment and how to structure your answers. In college you will be expected to work out most of this on your own. You will need to set aside time to think through these sorts of issues.

Time management

You will spend only a small amount of your time in scheduled activity. You will be responsible for organizing your time around taught sessions and meeting assignment deadlines. This may seem hard at first—especially as excuses for missed deadlines are seldom acceptable. If you miss a deadline, you may have to retake part or all of the class. Good time management skills are therefore essential—see pages 63–79.

Keeping going

When you work on your own, it is important to stay focused and to maintain your motivation. It is quite natural for motivation to change over time. There is no need to worry about this, but it is good to give it some advance thought and planning. Most people find that it is useful to have the support of other people in maintaining their motivation. See *Motivated learning* (page 86) and *Study support networks* (page 225).

Skills and personal development

Key skills and skills development

Most colleges provide opportunities to develop a range of skills, but each college takes a different approach. For example, your college may:

- build on key skills developed in high school or work
- use its own skills set
- offer classes to develop specific skills
- build skills into each program
- deliver skills sessions through the Career Center
- assess skills as part of your program.

Making use of skills opportunities

College offers more opportunities to develop responsibilities and to gain experience and knowledge in a wide range of areas than almost any other setting. It is in your interest to make the most of these opportunities. When you apply for jobs, your employers will know that you have had these opportunities and will be interested to see how well you used them.

Find out the skills and experience that employers really want—and create opportunities to gain these. In particular, find ways of developing:

- "people skills"
- problem-solving skills
- creative thinking skills
- personal management skills.

These skills are in high demand for college graduate jobs.

Student records

Your college keeps records of your progress. Files may consist of several elements including a transcript and academic progress file.

Transcripts

When you leave college, you will be given a transcript that gives details of the aspects of your program you completed successfully. At some colleges, the transcript will also itemize the skills you have developed during the program.

Personal records

Keep your own records to track your progress and achievements in ways that are meaningful to you and for your future employers. Your personal records could contain:

- a reflective journal, log or blog
- a record or e-portfolio of the skills, knowledge, experience, qualities and attitudes you have developed through study, work, extracurricular activities and life generally
- certificates for courses you have taken. (See also Chapters 2 and 15.)

I've written my action plan. Would you check it out?

Career Center

Personal development planning

Your college will offer opportunities for career or personal development planning. This will be managed differently at each institution. Most will offer activities such as:

- work experience or placements
- mentoring in local high schools
- volunteer work
- career advice
- being a "student rep." for the program.

Some colleges will also structure the curriculum to increase opportunities for personal development. For example, they may offer academic credit for career planning, skills development or work-based learning. There will also be many opportunities through student clubs, the student union, and the local community.

Chapter 1

The student's year

Orientation

The academic year usually begins late in August or September with orientation programs for first-year students. Orientation may include tours of the campus, information sessions and skills workshops. You will also learn about social events, students clubs and activities and have the opportunity to meet professors and other students, to ask questions and socialize.

Orientation processes vary and may include events run throughout the first semester or year. They can make a great difference to how you settle in and succeed as a student. The people you meet in the first weeks can be a great source of support during your program. Attend as many course and social events as you can to build a network for study support and friendship.

Semesters

The academic year is divided into two "semesters" with the second semester starting in January. There may also be a "summer semester."

Choosing options

When the year begins, you may be asked to select options at different levels of study, which combine to make your program.

Instructors for the year

You are likely to have the same professors and teaching staff for one semester and sometimes for the whole year.

Academic advisors

You will probably have an academic advisor, who will be concerned with your study overall. Talk to this person if you experience life or study difficulties that could prevent you from completing your degree.

Assessment

Classes vary in how they assess your work. Some assess by papers only, some by tests and others by a mixture of papers and tests. Tests are usually taken at various times throughout the year, although some courses leave examinations until the end of the semester.

If tests do not play a central part in your assessment, you may be asked instead to submit research papers, reports, workbooks, case studies or project work, or to make an oral presentation to the class.

Deadlines and extensions

It is important that you keep to deadlines. Make sure you familiarize yourself with your instructors' policy on extensions and late submission. If something unforeseen happens, you may be able to ask for extenuating circumstances to be taken into consideration when your work is being graded.

Always speak to your instructors as soon as there is any possibility of a deadline being missed or in special circumstances such as family or health problems. The longer you leave it, the less likely it is that instructors will be able to take your circumstances into consideration.

Summer

Between May and August there is time to catch up on missed study, to take summer classes, to prepare for the next semester, to rest—and, for many students, to earn some money.

What is expected from you?

It's not like in high school where you were stuck in a classroom from 8 till 3 and teachers told you what you needed to do. —*Ade, first-year student*

As a college student you are expected to have the following characteristics.

To cope with a university environment, you need to be reasonably good at:

- adapting to new people and environments
- surviving in potentially very large groups
- being flexible in your learning style.

Independence

You must be able to "stand on your own two feet." However, there is help available. The student union and student services will have details.

Self-motivation

You have to be able to work on your own a lot.

Openness to working with others

You will need to organize study sessions with friends.

Ability to set goals to improve your work

Whoopee!! 75%! Next time I want 80!

Ability to organize your time

You need to keep track of time. You must:

- know when and where you should be for scheduled classes, events and tests
- know when work has to be handed in
- keep to deadlines for handing in work.

(See Chapter 4.)

	MONDAY	TUESDAY	WEDNESDAY
9-10	put notes in order	Ecology lecture Rm G10	prepare for botany seminar
10-11	lecture Dr Shah Rm X22		
11-12	do plan (Science Report)		Botany Seminar Rm R21

Ability to work things out for yourself

"How successful was the Higher Education Act of 1965?"

It's terrible! The professors expect us to tell them all the answers!

Ability to work out when, how and where you learn best

On second thoughts, maybe I do work better indoors, in the daytime.

Anxieties and resources

It is quite natural to feel some anxiety when you start something new, and many students have concerns about starting college.

It is easier to work out strategies for handling potential challenges and to manage your anxieties if you have:

- sorted out in your own mind what your worries are
- considered how serious they really are
- realized that many other people feel the same way.

On the right are listed some anxieties that are common among new students. Check the box beside any that apply to you, or add in others in the empty spaces.

Study and learning

- ☐ Keeping up with other people
- ☐ Finding the time to do everything
- ☐ Understanding academic language
- ☐ Having the confidence to speak
- ☐ Developing confidence in myself
- ☐ Writing assignments
- ☐ Getting used to college life
- ☐ Meeting deadlines
- ☐ ....
- ☐ ....

Personal, family, work commitments

- ☐ Making friends with other students
- ☐ oping with travel
- ☐ Organizing childcare
- ☐ People treating me differently/"fitting in"
- ☐ Coping with job requirements
- ☐ Family responsibilities
- ☐ ....
- ☐ ....

Look again at the items you have checked. Beside each, write the number of the statement below that most closely corresponds with your feeling. Then read the comments on the next page.

1 I expect this to be a minor difficulty: I will get around it easily or in time.

2 I expect this to be quite a serious difficulty: I will work on a solution.

3 I expect this to be a great difficulty: I may need to work hard at finding a solution.

4 I expect this to be a major difficulty: I may need to ask for help.

- What initial ideas do you have about how you could manage some of these anxieties?

- What strategies have you used in the past to deal with a new or difficult situation? Which of these strategies could be helpful now?

Managing anxieties

Study and learning anxieties

It is important to give yourself time to settle in and see what is required. Many colleges pace the first year more slowly, to give you time to find your feet.

Focus on planning your own activities rather than worrying about how well other students are doing. Some people play psychological games, claiming that they do no work and can write papers overnight. Very few people can really do this; it is certainly not expected of you, and it is not a sensible way to study.

Find support. Many students will be anxious about some aspect of their study and it helps to share concerns. Make time to meet other students in your classes. Once you have formed a bond with other students, you will have more confidence about joining in.

The following chapters make practical suggestions on ways of handling aspects of study such as speaking, writing assignments, meeting deadlines, managing stress and generally setting yourself up to succeed. Focus on your motivation for study, and be determined to enjoy your program. Think of yourself as being on an adventure—not on trial!

Managing other anxieties

There is pressure on students to juggle family and work commitments in ways that were not expected in the past. Students have to be more creative in problem-solving and very organized in their time management.

At many colleges, Student Services and the Student Union offer advice on managing your finances, finding work, financial aid, child care, healthcare, counseling, disability and many other issues that arise for students.

Talk to them early on if you experience problems that you find difficult to resolve. Advisors can help more successfully if problems are tackled before they become emergencies.

Make an action plan

Look back to the items you checked on page 15.

Set priorities

- What needs to be done immediately?
- Which things can wait?
- In which order do you need to deal with these anxieties?
- Use the *Priority organizer* (page 78).

Resources

- What sources of help are available? Contact the college and ask.
- Fill out *What are my personal resources?* (page 18).
- Talk to other students who may have the same worries. See if you can form a study or discussion or support group including other students with whom you feel comfortable.

Reflection

It helps if you write down and explore your anxieties.

- Note down your feelings.
- Write down your options and decide between them (see pages 88–90).
- Record how you dealt with each problem so you that can evaluate your progress later.

How do other students manage?

The short passages on the next page were written by students about their first semester. You may notice that their time seemed very pressurized; being organized is an important theme in these writings. However, these students made space for themselves to relax, meet others and use college facilities such as sports or drama clubs, which are also important to the overall college experience.

My first semester

After the terrible time I had in high school, I was very worried about what I might be putting myself through coming back to study as an adult. I was sure I wouldn't be able to keep up. When I got my first few assignments back, the grades were not very good, and I felt I ought to leave.

Luckily, I was talked out of leaving. I made an effort to meet other adult students and found many of them were having similar experiences to me. One of them encouraged me to ask my instructors for more detailed feedback on my work. I had not wanted to ask for any help in case the instructors thought I was not good enough for the program. Bit by bit my grades started to get better, and some were very good. This boosted my confidence.

I had expected study to be difficult. What I had not expected was that other aspects of being a student could be just as hard. It took me ages to build up the confidence to eat in the dining hall—it seemed so enormous and bustling. I used to rush away after classes rather than talking to strangers. My bus service is very erratic and I kept arriving late. My sister, who was going to look after my children, moved. Sorting out all these things has made me very skilled at problem-solving!

I have to say that there are many positive things about being a student. Now that I have got to know other people here, I look forward to coming in to study. I feel like I am escaping into time just for me. I like having the library to work in—and not being disturbed while I just get on with it.

I would recommend to new students that they give themselves a chance to settle in and not panic if anything seems to be going wrong. If they have children, I cannot overemphasize how important it has been to me to have plans to cover every eventuality. I wish I had had reserve plans for child care right from the beginning because that, more than anything else, had an effect on my studies. I also recommend that new students find other people who have similar experiences to themselves—talking to each other you can come up with good ideas about how to tackle problems and boost each other's morale.

You are bound to find you think differently about many things by the time you finish your degree—for me, discussing things with other people has become a very exciting activity. Above all, I think students have to think, "I might never get this chance again—how am I going to get the most out of it?" There are many facilities available and it is a very good opportunity to try things you might never have imagined yourself doing—starting your own group, karate, or going on an expedition. It is a wonderful opportunity—but you have to make it work for yourself.

Sasha

A typical day

On Tuesdays I have a lecture from 10 a.m. to 12 noon. This professor does not just talk at us: She breaks the time up into short tasks, discussions, videos, etc. When all 90 of us are discussing something in groups, it can be rather noisy, but you get used to it. The rest of the day is "free" but as I am already on the site, I go to the library and prepare for the next day's lectures or do some reading for the classes I have on every second Wednesday. Some Tuesday afternoons, I go to the gym and study in the evening instead.

Krishna

My Thursday as a student

Dash the kids to the day nursery. Dash into the labs for 10. Suddenly time changes. I am caught up in what I am doing—the project I am working on with two other people. I can spend hours mixing and measuring, comparing my findings with others'. We talk a lot about what we are doing, and why, and make suggestions on why our results are different. I always ask my instructors if I am unsure—some are very helpful, but some are not. In the afternoon, I have one lecture. Recently, I have arranged it so I can go to drama club on Thursday nights.

Charlie

What are my personal resources?

Have you considered all the resources that might be available to you? Try brainstorming (adding in your own ideas) around keywords on the pattern notes below. If you feel you have few resources, it may help if you speak to an academic advisor or learning center staff.

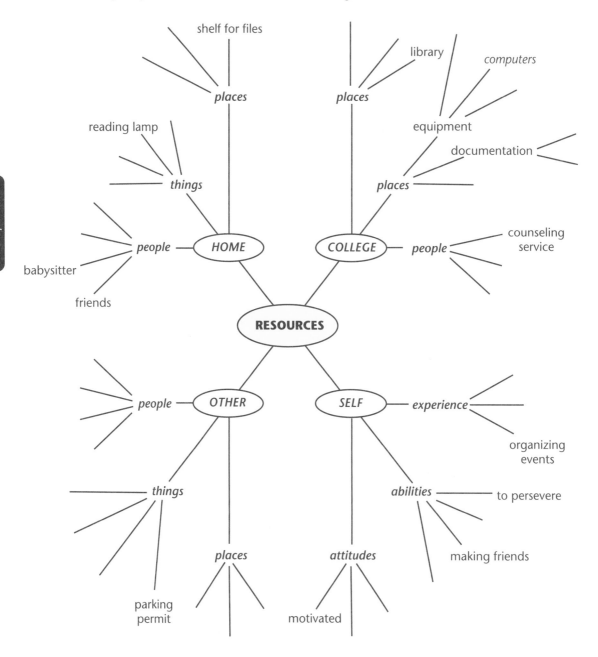

Chapter 1

Seven things you can do at the start of college

1 Familiarize yourself with this book

Browse through this book so that you know what it contains and roughly where to find it. Some items may be useful now; some may not be needed until you undertake certain aspects of study.

2 Reflect on your past learning

Start a reflective study journal

See pages 57–59. Make a start by doing the activity below.

College isn't like high school ...

Chapter 1

Activity

How do you learn best?

Think back to a time when you found something very easy or enjoyable to learn. It might have been something in high school, or at work, or even putting up shelves. In your journal, jot down any ideas about *why* this was the case. What made it into a good learning experience for you? The teaching? Your interest in the subject? Because it was visual, or used numbers? Or because each step was clear? You may find your notes for the activities in Chapter 2 (pages 23–24) can help with this activity.

Now think of a time when learning something was difficult or unpleasant.

- What happened on that occasion that was different from your first example?
- What could have made the experience more manageable?
- What do these two experiences tell you about the way that you learn best?

Write down your reflections.

3 Read the literature you are given

Read anything the college provides, such as handbooks and subject guides. These cover essential information on college regulations, sources of help, appeals and grievance procedures, and student clubs and facilities. Also check if this (or more!) information is provided online.

Read this information carefully— once your assignments start, you will probably be too busy. Set up a file to ensure you have it to hand when you need it.

Look out especially for:

- essential dates, such as for orientation, selecting options, deadlines, exam dates and dates when semesters begin and end— put these into your planner and don't double-book them: they are unlikely to be negotiable
- information about sources of help.

4 Familiarize yourself with libraries

Start getting used to the college library as soon as possible. Many students are fearful of appearing foolish in libraries, especially when using library technology such as online catalogs, consulting special collections or working out the numbering system.

It is best to get over these fears quickly. Librarians are used to people not being able to use libraries: If you need help, ask for it.

5 Know your bookstores

Visit the campus bookstore. Find out where the relevant books for your subjects are shelved, and browse the authors and titles for your major. Find out where new books are displayed and how long it takes to order books. Check bookstores regularly for new titles; this will give you a rough idea of what is topical in your subject areas.

6 Start to develop your study skills

If you have been out of education for a while, use some of the suggestions in this book to get you into the study habit. Pay particular attention to:

Writing

- Write in your journal (page 59) every day.

- Practice writing short passages from notes you take when reading.
- (See Chapter 11.)

Keyboard and computer skills

- Being able to use a computer, find your way around the Internet and type at a reasonable speed will be of great benefit.
- Develop these through practice or look for short training courses that may be available.

Reading

- When reading for class, try reading faster than you usually would.
- See if you can still grasp the gist of what is written. Jot down the key points using only a few key *words*, rather than writing in sentences or copying.

7 Be prepared

- See Chapter 4, *The C·R·E·A·M strategy for learning*, on organizing time and space.
- Organize child care before the semester starts. Have backup plans for emergencies.
- Contact the college if you are in doubt about any aspects of your program.
- Make sure you are free for all orientation sessions.

Review

In this chapter you have looked at a number of ways in which you can prepare yourself for college.

Your chances of getting a degree once in college depend crucially on whether you are *ready* for the program. This is a completely different question from whether you have the *ability*. In some countries almost the whole population studies at a higher level, so it seems that with sufficient preparation most people have the ability. Contact the learning center at your college if you feel you need support.

You now have an idea of what the college environment is like and what you can expect in terms of teaching methods, the college week and year, the way time is broken up and some of the terminology used. Being on campus and talking to

students who are already there will give you a clearer picture of what is involved.

As an undergraduate, you will be expected to take a lot more responsibility for your own learning than you may be used to from high school. This makes the study more exciting, but you do need to develop good study and coping strategies.

Finally, it can take time to orient yourself at the beginning of the first semester, especially as there are so many new people to meet and so many interesting things to do on a college campus. The better prepared you are for the semester, the easier it will be to settle into a study routine and the more time you will have to enjoy other aspects of college life.

Chapter 2

Identifying your skills

Chapter 2

LEARNING OUTCOMES

This chapter offers you opportunities to:

- reflect on what is meant by a "skill"

- consider the five main study skills components

- develop your awareness of skills and qualities you bring with you to college

- identify areas of strength in your current study skills and areas to be developed

- set priorities for developing your study skills

- consider the wider range of skills you can develop in college

- map out a profile of your own skills and qualities, in preparation for job applications

- monitor your own achievements and record these.

Skill

To be skilled is to be able to perform a learned activity well and at will.

A skill is a learned activity—something you can develop through practice and reflection. You can fine-tune skills, including study skills, just as runners perfect their movement, breathing and pacing.

Fine-tuning a skill involves developing personal qualities as well, such as:

- awareness
- commitment
- determination
- perseverance.
- self-motivation
- time management
- positive thinking

These qualities are also of key importance to successful study: The more obvious study skills, such as knowing how to write papers and use techniques to pass tests, are only part of the story.

Most undergraduates hope that their degree will lead to a good career. Many employers are more interested in your wider range of skills, qualities and experience than which degree you studied or your grades. This chapter looks at how academic study can be an opportunity to develop skills that are "transferable" to employment.

Subskills

Each skill consists of *subskills*—the component skills that make up the overall skill. A weakness in one subskill can affect what would otherwise be a good performance. For example, you might have the potential to be an excellent essay writer but have weaknesses in structuring your ideas or using paragraphs. This *Handbook* focuses on subskills to enable you to develop the wider study skills.

What are your own ideas about what a "skill" is and how skills are developed?

What are your own ideas about what a "skill" is and how skills are developed?

Five study-skills components

1 Self-awareness and self-evaluation

To develop a skill, you need first to know where you are starting from. What are your current strengths and weaknesses? What do you want to achieve? Where do you need to improve? How are you going to improve? What are your resources? What could obstruct your goals? Knowing more about yourself, your individual strengths and interests can help you to decide on a major as well as a future career path. This will also help you to identify which classes you need to take to pursue your goals, for example, pre-med or math if you wish to go to medical school. In turn, working towards your dream career will help keep you motivated and improve your chances of completing your degree.

Ways of developing this awareness include self-evaluation questionnaires, reflective journals, group discussion and using instructor feedback on your work.

2 Awareness of what is required

To score a goal, you need to know where the goalposts are. In an academic context, this means finding out what is expected of you and what your instructors are looking for.

Essential information on this is usually provided in course handbooks and handouts. For each class, find out about:

- the syllabus—the course content
- the outcomes or objectives—what you must know or be able to do by the end of the course
- how grades are allocated—what gets good grades? what loses points?
- the special preferences of each instructor—if in doubt, ask!

3 Methods, organization, strategies

It is easier to study and saves you time if you have a method for working and are well organized. A skilled student uses strategie—and with practice these strategies become nearly automatic.

4 Confidence and permission

To succeed without undue stress, you need to feel that you are *entitled* to learn and achieve. Many students, however, feel that academic success is for other people. This may be because of their experiences in school, or because nobody from their family has a degree. Often it is because they hold particular ideas about intelligence—and especially their own intelligence—so Chapter 3 focuses on what we mean by "intelligence" and "learning."

If you are to succeed as a student, it is very important that you believe that success is possible.

5 Familiarity: practice and habit

All skills improve through practice, feedback and monitoring. The more you study and reflect on your learning, the more you become:

- adept at finding shortcuts
- aware of subskills you need to improve
- able to see patterns in what you do
- able to focus on study for longer
- able to perform subskills automatically.

The way to study well and easily becomes a habit. It is important to develop regular study habits in the first year, especially if you have been away from study or are not used to managing so much unscheduled time.

You don't have to be "smart"!

When you consider these study-skills components, it is clear that good study skills have little to do with being "naturally smart." They owe much more to awareness, strategies, confidence and practice, leading to an overall development in your learning. Each of these aspects is covered in the various chapters of the *Handbook*.

Skills and qualities you have now

This section offers you the chance to undertake a skills audit. It looks at how your current subskills—such as observation, selection, and concern for others—may be transferable to *academic* skills, and how academic skills may later be transferable to *employment* skills. In the process you can identify your current study priorities and map out your skills and qualities within a personal profile or portfolio so that you can monitor your own progress. This record will also be useful when applying for work.

Skills audits

The most important aspects of making a skills audit are these:

- you can become used to self-evaluation rather than depending on the estimation of others
- you can become aware of your strengths, so that you can present yourself well to others
- you can develop the confidence and insight to identify areas of potential weakness
- you can learn to set your own priorities for developing new skills.

Identifying your current skills

Think about something you do well, a difficulty you overcame or a personal achievement, no matter how small. It might be success on your SATs or ACTs, skill in a particular sport, learning to drive or being accepted to college.

What did you do to create the conditions that led to success? Which skills, attitudes and qualities did you exhibit? Did you practice? Did you urge yourself on in a particular way? Did you find people to help? Or did you just believe you could do it? Look at the next example for some ideas.

Example: The beautiful garden

Suppose one year your garden or a window box was absolutely beautiful. How did that happen?

Many small things may have brought about a perfect outcome. For example, maybe you watered the plants very carefully, depending on the weather. If so, you used powers of *observation* and *deduction*. You may have weeded and pruned in the rain, when you wanted to stay indoors. Here you *kept in mind your long-term goal* for the garden, showing *dedication* and *perseverance*.

You may have *selected* some new plants from a wide range of options, to match your garden conditions. You *followed specific instructions* on how to grow them. You probably did *research* by reading gardeners' books and seed packets, talking to other gardeners or watching television programs. You may have purchased special fertilizer and pots, or prepared the ground in a certain way or pruned at particular times: Such care requires *attention to detail*, *time management* and *task management*.

All these skills are relevant to study. Whether your experience is in cooking, riding a bike, athletics or bringing up children, you are likely to have developed a range of strengths such as those described in the example above. The important thing is to recognize which qualities and abilities you already have so that you can draw on them when you need them.

Activity

Skills from experience

Write down all the elements that go into something you have done well, as in the example of the garden. Note the skills, qualities and attitudes you identify in yourself.

> Were you surprised to discover how many skills you have already? Do you tend to underestimate or overestimate your skills?

By doing the "Skills from experience" exercise, you probably discovered you have more skills than you thought. If not, go through the exercise with someone who knows you, or use the list as a prompt. Most people already have qualities and skills that they can adapt to study in higher education.

- Students who enter college directly from high school have the benefit of recent study experience and established study habits.
- Adult and returning students often have practice in managing time and responsibility, show perseverance and can evaluate other people's views. These are valuable assets when studying.

Keep your notes to the "Skills from experience" exercise near you for use in the following exercise.

If you did not check many items, you may need to search through your past experiences again for examples—or go through the list with a friend. You may be being too modest!

File your answers for use later in the chapter.

Evaluating skills and setting priorities

The following pages offer resource sheets to:

- help you to evaluate your current profile of strengths and weaknesses
- relate academic skills to life and employment skills
- set priorities for skills development
- monitor your progress.

Update your profile

Awareness of your current skills increases your confidence, which in turn increases your chances of success.

As you progress with your program, your skills profile and self-evaluation will change. Take time to update your skills profile or personal portfolio at least once every six months. (See Chapter 15.)

Activity

Current skills

1 Photocopy the list of *Current skills and qualities* on page 25 so that you can use it again.
2 On your photocopy, check all the items at which you are reasonably good.
3 Put stars by items at which you excel.
4 For each of the skills and qualities you have checked from the list, starting with the starred items, think of one example of an occasion when you demonstrated that skill or quality. Write down your examples. If you find it hard to remember, the "prompt box" on the right lists some situations in which you might have developed these skills.
5 Hang the list where you can see it. Congratulate yourself!

Where did I develop the skills and qualities that I have now?

High school	Weekend jobs
Employment	Unemployment
Applying for jobs	Voluntary work
Family life	Making a home
Domestic responsibility	Friendships
Caring for others	Travel/vacations
Interests and hobbies	Clubs/societies
Independent study	Personal setbacks
Emergency events	Ill-health
Personal development	Athletics

Current skills and qualities

People

- [ ] Ability to get on with people from different backgrounds
- [ ] Ability to see and understand other people's points of view
- [ ] Dealing with the general public
- [ ] Teamwork
- [ ] Managing other people
- [ ] Teaching or training others
- [ ] Negotiating
- [ ] Helping others to arrive at decisions
- [ ] Being sensitive to others' feelings
- [ ] Caring for others
- [ ] Ability to read other people's body language
- [ ] Dealing with others by phone
- [ ] Ability to cope with "difficult" people
- [ ] Speaking clearly and to the point
- [ ] Being able to take direction from others
- [ ] Courage to speak out against injustice
- [ ] Other:

Activities

- [ ] Creativity, design and layout
- [ ] Ability to see the "whole picture"
- [ ] Classifying and organizing information (e.g., filing)
- [ ] Being good at argument and debate
- [ ] Making decisions
- [ ] Managing change and transition
- [ ] Setting priorities

- [ ] Working out agendas
- [ ] Organizing work to meet deadlines
- [ ] Staying calm in a crisis
- [ ] Facilitating meetings
- [ ] Reading complex texts
- [ ] Word processing
- [ ] Computer literacy
- [ ] Working with numbers
- [ ] Selling
- [ ] Problem solving
- [ ] Practical things
- [ ] Seeing how things work
- [ ] Writing reports or official letters
- [ ] Other:

Personal qualities

- [ ] Ability to recognize my own needs and ask for help
- [ ] Ability to learn from mistakes
- [ ] Stress management
- [ ] Willingness to take risks and experiment
- [ ] Assertiveness
- [ ] Determination and perseverance
- [ ] Ability to set my own goals
- [ ] Maintaining a high level of motivation
- [ ] Ability to take responsibility for my own actions
- [ ] Trust in my own abilities
- [ ] Other:

Chapter **2**

Turning personal skills into academic skills

The *Current skills and qualities* exercise (page 25) includes specific skills that have more relevance to some courses than others. For example, "selling" is more relevant to marketing than to history.

The following exercise is an opportunity to map out your current skills in terms of the general (or "generic") skills required for most academic courses and to rate how well you already perform them. This will give you a better idea of how well you may cope with academic study.

Academic skills (skills used in everyday life that relate to academic skills)	Self-rating 5 = good; 1 = very weak	Examples: where or when you developed this skill
e.g. Managing deadlines	4	Get children to school on time Got college application in despite illness
1 Managing deadlines		
2 Being self-motivated and able to persevere with difficult tasks		
3 Having the confidence to "give it a try" and to express my own ideas		
4 Finding out information from different sources (research)		
5 Reading complicated texts or forms to find the gist of what they are saying		
6 Being able to select what is relevant from what is irrelevant		
7 Comparing different opinions and deciding what are the best grounds for judging who is right		
8 Being able to weigh up the "pros" and "cons", good points versus bad		
9 Writing things in my own words		
10 Being able to argue my point of view, giving good reasons		

Study skills: priorities, stage 1

Column A Check if the statement is generally true of you.
Column B Rate how important it is to acquire this skill: 6 = unimportant; 10 = essential.
Column C Rate how good you are at this skill now: 1 = very weak; 5 = excellent.
Column D Subtract the score in column C from that in column B (B – C). Items with the highest scores in column D are likely to be priorities. Then turn to page 28.

Later in the term, do this exercise again. Compare your ratings, then and now.

Study-skills statements	A This is true (✓)	B Skill needed? (scale 6–10)	C Current ability? (scale 1–5)	D Priority (B – C)
I am aware of how I learn best and how to reflect upon and evaluate my own work				
I am well motivated and know how to set myself manageable goals				
I have good time and space management skills, and am able to organize my workload				
I have strategies for getting going with a new task or assignment				
I am confident of my research skills				
I am confident about my reading strategies				
I am good with numbers				
I am able to take, organize, store, find and use my notes effectively (checklist, page 117)				
I am able to use lecture time effectively and get the best out of lectures				
I know how to prepare for and deliver oral presentations, playing to my strengths (page 229)				
I know how to make the most of group work and classes (subskills list, page 224)				
I am able to manage a range of writing tasks appropriately (subskills list, page 232)				
I know how to use IT to help in academic study				
I am able to think critically and analytically, and evaluate my own and other people's arguments				
I have good memory strategies				
I have good study techniques and test-taking strategies (subskills list, pages 188 and 204)				

Chapter **2**

Identifying your skills

Study skills: priorities, stage 2

Column A   Using the scoring from stage 1, decide if each item really is a priority, if it could wait, who else could do it or any other options you have.

Column B   Number your priorities in order. Highlight in yellow the one you are going to work on next. Highlight it in red once you have worked on it.

Column C   Shows the pages of this *Handbook* related to the given study skill.

Study skills statements	A Priority for action? Check or enter "can wait" or other options	B	C Pages
I am going to find out how I learn best and how to reflect upon/evaluate my work			57–62, 91
I am going to be better motivated and learn to set myself manageable goals			86–90
I am going to improve my organizational and time management skills			63–79, 107, 247
I am going to improve my research skills			Chs. 5, 7, 13–14
I am going to develop my reading skills			97–103
I will develop my skills and confidence in using numbers			Ch. 13
I am going to improve my note-taking and organize and use my notes effectively			104–14, 116–117
I am going to use lecture time effectively to get the best out of lectures			115–117
I am going to improve my oral presentations			227–230
I am going to make the most of working with others (groupwork, classes, etc.)			Ch. 10
I am going to develop my writing skills			Chs. 11, 12 and 14
I am going to make more use of IT to help my academic study			Ch. 6
I am going to develop my critical and analytical thinking skills			Ch. 7
I am going to improve my memory strategies			Ch. 8
I am going to develop good study techniques and test-taking strategies			Ch. 9

Chapter 2

Study skills: action plan

Go back over your answers to the different exercises and the self-evaluations you completed for Chapters 1 and 2. Bring together the different ideas about your current strengths, the areas you wish to develop and your priorities.

Date:
Summary of my current strengths, skills and qualities: What I have achieved so far
Summary of what I need to work on, develop or improve
My priorities: What I am going to do, when and how
How will I know that I have improved? (E.g., What changes would I expect in my work, in myself or in the attitudes of others?)

Chapter **2**

Monitoring skills development

Baseline (starting place)

Date: Skill being developed:

My current level of confidence in this skill (circle one):

1 very low   **2** low   **3** OK   **4** high   **5** very high

Aspects of this skill I have already demonstrated:

Goal

What I want to be able to do (aspects, subskills, qualities I want to develop):

Record of progress

Note down steps in your development of this skill. It is up to you to decide what progress means for you. It could be the achievement of a personal goal (such as getting a particular grade for an assignment) or a small step towards one of your goals (such as asking a question in class for the first time, or developing a successful strategy for arriving on time if you find time management is a challenge).

Date	Achievement	How you know
	(what I can do now that I couldn't before)	*(evidence or example)*

Personal profiles

What is a "profile"?

A profile is simply a snapshot of yourself as you are—your skills, qualities, attributes and achievements. It has several uses, of which these are especially important:

- it gives you a sense of where you are now, so that you can work to a personal development plan
- compiling it develops habits of reflection and self-analysis
- experience of evaluating and describing yourself is valuable preparation for job interviews.

In this chapter you have already started to put together your profile of strengths, qualities and priorities. If you photocopied the pages, you can use them again to update your profile as you progress with your program. The profile will help when drawing up a resume for job interviews. Add in your achievements and skills from other areas of your life.

What are recruiters looking for?

A report by Civic Enterprises and Corporate Voices for Working Families found that 53 percent of US business leaders say their companies face a very or fairly major challenge in recruiting nonmanagerial employees with the skills, training and education their company needs. Although employers still value academic and specialist skills, they also look for a wider range of experience and generic skills, especially "soft skills."

Which "soft" skills?

"Soft skills" are skills such as oral communication and teamwork, which are less easily quantifiable than academic qualifications. The "Soft skills" evaluation can be used to develop a skills profile (pages 32–33) for employment.

Employers value soft skills in the following areas:

1. Managing yourself: intrapersonal skills
Self-reliance, self-awareness and focus; the capacity to learn, plan action and take the initiative; resourcefulness, motivation and realism.

2. Managing people: people skills
Networking; teamwork; communication skills in negotiating, persuading and influencing; customer focus; leadership and ability to support and motivate others; cultural awareness; languages.

3. Managing projects: skills and qualities
Business awareness; a strong work ethic; being able to get on with a task and achieve a result; application of IT skills; numerical reasoning; problem solving; managing projects; versatility, flexibility and multiskilling; willingness to take risks; competitiveness; being logical, methodical and systematic; being practical and results-orientated.

Sources

- Civic Enterprises and Corporate Voices for Working Families (March 2011), *Across the Great Divide: Perspectives of CEOs and College Presidents on America's Higher Education and Skills Gap*, http://www.civicenterprises.net/pdfs/across-the-great-divide.pdf (accessed August 2011)
- The Conference Board et al., (2006) *Are they really ready to work? Employers' Perspectives on the Basic Knowledge and Applied Skills of New Entrants to the 21st Century U.S. Workforce*, http://p21.org/documents/FINAL_REPORT_PDF09-29-06.pdf (accessed August 2011)
- United States Department of Labor, "Soft Skills: The Competitive Edge," http://www.dol.gov/odep/pubs/fact/softskills.htm (accessed August 2011)

Additional resources

For more about developing soft skills, see:

- Stella Cottrell (2010), *Skills for Success: Personal Development and Employability*, 2nd edition (Basingstoke: Palgrave Macmillan)
- Free resources on http://us.macmillan.com/thestudyskillshandbook

Activity

- Browse advertisements for college graduate jobs. Also browse a website such as college.monster.com—note the skills for which employers say they are looking.
- Which of these skills could you develop while in college?

Transferable and soft employment skills

Just as you identified how the skills you brought to college could translate into academic skills, so you can see how academic skills translate into the "transferable" and "soft" skills required in employment. These skills are needed especially at "team leader" and other management levels.

On the chart below are some of the soft skills that you could develop as a student—you will be able to think of others. On the next page, map out for yourself the skills you actually develop as a student. This exercise is especially useful in your final year, but if you do it earlier as well you will be better prepared to make use of the various opportunities that college offers.

Area of academic activity	Examples of potential transferable and soft skills that could be developed
Personal development planning	Self-management; forward planning; taking responsibility for improving performance; increasing personal effectiveness; reflective skills; skills development
Attending lectures, classes, tutorials, etc.	Time management; working flexibly
Lectures	Listening skills; identifying and selecting relevant points; written communication; information management
Classes, group work, team projects	Teamwork; negotiating; oral communication; learning to take directions from others and to give directions; taking responsibility; problem-solving; listening; working with people from a variety of backgrounds; dealing with differences in opinion; relationship development; sharing knowledge
Oral presentation	Speaking in public; persuading and influencing others; making a case; time management; presentation skills; using audiovisual aids; planning; sharing knowledge; adapting communication style
Writing papers and other forms of academic writing	Written communication skills, developing an argument or putting a strong case; working to word limits; working to deadlines; task analysis; sharing knowledge; breaking tasks into component parts; attention to detail
Maths and statistics	Problem solving; presenting information; interpreting data; sharing knowledge
Observation	Listening skills; working with people from a variety of backgrounds; information management; attention to detail
Research	Time management; managing large amounts of information; working to deadlines; decision-making; project management
Studying for tests and test-taking	Working to deadlines; managing stress and crisis; planning

Turning academic skills into transferable and soft employment skills

Use the exercises you completed in Chapter 2 to complete the profile below, showing soft and transferable skills developed in college and elsewhere. Look especially at page 25, *Current skills and qualities*.

The first four items that often appear at the top of employers' lists are already written in. Add in others at which you are particularly good.

Skills, qualities, attributes and achievements	Specific examples
Self-awareness and self-reliance	
Verbal skills	
Teamwork	
Practical skills in managing projects	

Other transferable skills I can offer

☐ Driver's license   ☐ Computer literacy   ☐ Languages:

Chapter **2**

Recording achievement

Celebrate success

When you have achieved a goal or taken a significant step towards a goal:

- *Acknowledge your achievement* Give yourself credit for what you have done.
- *Celebrate* Give yourself a reward, appropriate to the significance of your achievement.
- *Record it* Note down what happened.
- *Use it* Use your success as an example of what you can achieve when you focus your energies. When applying for jobs, or to build personal motivation, use your records to find examples of different kinds of achievement.

Records of success and personal records

Records of achievement can vary from simple lists of qualifications to reflective logs or e-portfolios. Your college will give you a formal transcript that lists your academic achievements, such as classes taken and passed, but only *you* will know:

- how your levels of confidence have changed
- how you have developed as a person
- personal goals you have achieved
- how you did it—the steps you took and the personal qualities and resources you drew on in order to succeed
- how you kept yourself motivated
- what you learned about yourself in the process.

It is useful to have records of *how* you achieved your goals as well as *what* you achieved. These enable you to make use of your experience and to chart change over time. Records of this kind are sometimes referred to as "personal" or "reflective portfolios," "progress files," "records of achievement," or "personal records."

Maintaining a personal portfolio

A portfolio is a file in which you bring together diverse materials on a theme. A personal portfolio, for example, is a collection of key materials related to your own development. To keep the portfolio meaningful and easy to use:

- divide it into sections
- label everything, and use a contents page
- update it regularly, removing old materials
- include an updated personal statement.

Personal statements

A personal statement draws together details of where you are now, where you want to be and how you will get there. It can be brief. Include such things as:

- long-term and short-term objectives
- what you have done so far towards achieving these (in high school, college or work)
- the personal significance of those goals and achievements
- what you learned about yourself along the way (e.g. how to stay motivated, how you learn best, what you need in order to succeed)
- skills and qualities you have achieved, with examples that demonstrate these
- what you need to do next (current targets).

Academic portfolios

Some programs require you to hand in portfolios for instructors to monitor or grade. These portfolios are different from personal portfolios. When handing in a portfolio:

- Be selective: include only what is required.
- If possible, choose good examples rather than dumping everything in the file.
- Indicate exactly where instructors can find each piece of evidence to support the points you make in your personal statement or to meet assignment criteria. Annotate or highlight the evidence in the file.
- Remove or edit material that identifies other people by name or gives personal details.
- Number all pages and compile a contents page.

Developing a personal portfolio

What is the purpose of a personal portfolio?

A portfolio has several uses:

- it keeps related documents together
- it helps the process of reflection
- it gives the process of self-evaluation and personal development a higher focus in your life
- in some industries, you can take it to job interviews
- it can hold relevant examples and information for when you need them, such as when applying for work placements, work or other courses.

Do you have to keep a portfolio?

A portfolio may be required for your major. However, even if you don't *have* to keep a portfolio, you will probably find it *helpful* to do so—to organize your thinking about what you need to do and to monitor your progress.

Checking and updating your portfolio

Update your portfolio regularly—at least once or twice a year, and whenever you achieve something new. Rereading or rewording what you have written may refocus your energies.

What to put in your portfolio

1 Full contents list for each section.

2 Self-evaluation and profile sheets, planners and action plans.

3 A profile of vocational and technical skills you have developed.

4 An up-to-date list of courses and training.

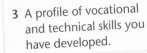

5 Certificates (tests, courses, achievements, etc.).

6 An up-to-date list of your work experience, with the dates, addresses of employers, brief job descriptions, your main responsibilities, skills or qualities you demonstrated, and what you learned from doing that work.

7 Your resumé. (A career guidance counselor can help you to compile this.)

8 Your ideas about where you would like to be in seven years' time and what you need to do to achieve this goal.

9 Examples of your work and interests, if relevant—but without breaching anyone else's confidentiality. Examples include a copy of a report undertaken during a work placement, slides of your artwork or a copy of an article you wrote for a student magazine.

10 Personal statement—see page 34.

11 Degree or course certificates; transcript.

Review

The term "study skills" is often used in a loose way. There is a temptation to look at the end product, the finished paper or the good assignment grade, and to imagine that knowing a few tips is all that is needed to achieve these. At the other extreme, people may think that high scores are something they can never achieve.

This chapter and Chapters 3 and 4 emphasize that real progress in study skills occurs when skills development is treated as part of a wider, general process of learning. At its best, this is a process in which you learn about yourself and how you perform to your potential under *any* circumstances, not just academically. It involves developing an understanding about how personal opinions, attitudes and states of mind influence your success. Fundamental to that process is self-awareness, based on reflection and self-evaluation, so that you know what you do well and why, and what needs to be improved and how.

This chapter has encouraged you to look at your current qualities and skills in a different way. The process of self-evaluation can begin in quite mechanistic ways, such as filling in questionnaires, rating yourself, setting priorities and assembling information about yourself. In time, however, this can develop into a deeper process of self-reflection and self-development that benefits any aspect of your life, including your study.

Some students feel as if they have no academic skills. Others, especially those who entered college straight from school, can be anxious about having the right skills to find employment when they leave. For this reason it is important to see the parallels between skills used in academic study and those used elsewhere. Everybody brings to college experiences and skills which contain subskills that are transferable to academic study. In turn, academic study develops skills and ways of thinking that can be of great benefit in employment. However, skills cannot usually be transferred from one situation to another unless the person concerned can *see* similarities in the two situations. This takes creative reflection, and may require help from others, but it is worth the effort. Graduates who do well in the job market are not necessarily more skilled than others, but they have learned to *identify* their skills and can therefore talk about them confidently and with examples of their application.

Students may also feel that they do not know where to begin to develop their study skills. The ideas of mapping or profiling skills, identifying weak points for improvement, setting priorities, and drawing up action plans, are themes that run throughout this book. However, the *Handbook* also encourages you to look at opinions, states of mind or belief systems that can affect learning. Chapters 3 and 4 focus on attitudes and approaches that can help or hinder study.

Chapter 3, *Intelligence and learning*, has been included because so many students consulted during the writing of this book expressed secret doubts about their ability to study or about their intelligence. Most of these students had had their confidence undermined in the past, sometimes by a chance comment. Earlier anxieties about failure can remain for years, eating away at self-esteem and preventing positive outcomes. Looking at underlying myths about intelligence and the realities about learning can enable some students to reevaluate their learning and go on to perform extremely well. If you feel this applies to you, you may find it helpful to read Chapter 3 now; if not, you may prefer to come back to the chapter later in the year.

Chapter 3

Intelligence and learning

LEARNING OUTCOMES

This chapter offers you opportunities to:

- develop awareness of your own views about intelligence and learning
- evaluate how these views, or the views of others, may have affected your previous learning
- consider different theories about intelligence
- reflect on varieties of learning and the conditions that facilitate learning
- put together a plan to optimise your learning
- reflect on how study skills fit more generally into your overall learning development.

When to read this chapter

This chapter is more theoretical than the others and requires you to reflect on your beliefs about learning. If you are in a mood to be more active, you may prefer to leave this chapter until another day.

The learning process

Study skills are important as an aspect of learning, and make the learning process easier. *Learning* is about more than just study skills, however. This chapter focuses on the learning process itself, looking at how intelligence develops through learning and the conditions that are necessary for learning to occur.

It is often taken for granted that "success" is the result of "being smart," and that this is something you are either blessed with at birth or not. For older

students especially, this was part of the educational doctrine with which they grew up.

Nevertheless, the world is full of successful people who did *not* do well in high school—and so are colleges, and sometimes even college teaching departments! Each of us has to discover for ourselves that the early opinions of others were not necessarily accurate—what they thought of us does not define our real potential or determine what we can become. None of us really knows what we are capable of achieving, but usually this is a great deal more than we suppose.

Self-belief and the right conditions for learning are both vital in developing as a learner. To develop confidence in yourself as a learner, it is important to understand your own learning history and become aware of any beliefs and practices arising from it that might constrict you in the present.

"Am I smart enough for college?"

This "ghost" question haunts many freshmen, even if their grades are excellent. They worry that "secretly" or "deep down" they are not smart enough to succeed.

"So far I've been lucky ..."

> Your grades were OK last time—but that was a fluke. This time you might fail, and you'll be so embarrassed because now everyone expects you to do well.

One reason for this anxiety is that students are rarely taught to evaluate their own work. They have no criteria for evaluating their own performance. Instead, they feel prey to the whims of chance: Good or bad results "just happen," or depend on luck (such as which instructor they have), or reflect their level of "natural smartness."

This can leave students feeling disempowered or adrift, even if their grades are good. Students can feel very vulnerable, and may worry about suddenly being exposed as stupid. Anxiety may create a vicious cycle: Such students can't settle down to study, can't focus attention, can't take in what they read, or can't remember what they learned, and this reinforces their suspicion that "really" they lack intelligence. This is very common, so it is important to look at what we mean by intelligence.

What is "intelligence"?

Check any response that you feel is true.

- [ ] 1 Intelligence is an underlying, general smartness that, because it depends on genetics, is fixed for life.
- [ ] 2 There are many kinds of intelligence.
- [ ] 3 Intelligence can be developed.
- [ ] 4 Intelligence depends on your life opportunities.
- [ ] 5 What is regarded as intelligence depends on the environment and the culture.
- [ ] 6 Intelligence is about applying what you know easily to new contexts.
- [ ] 7 Intelligence is a question of how much you know.
- [ ] 8 Intelligence is easy to measure.
- [ ] 9 Intelligence is a question of habit and practice.

Note down how your own views— and other people's views—of your intelligence might have affected your previous academic performance. Then read the following opinions about intelligence.

Afterwards, return to the notes you took and note down if your opinions about yourself or your intelligence have changed because of your reading and reflection.

Nine different views of intelligence

1 Intelligence is a general, underlying "smartness" that is fixed for life

Early psychologists such as Spearman (1927) and Terman (1916) believed that each individual has a general level of intelligence, known as the *intelligence quotient* or IQ. They regarded intelligence as a single, fixed, underlying capacity: A person who did well on one test would do well on all or most intelligence tests; and no matter what happened in life, those born "very intelligent" would remain generally more intelligent than those born "less intelligent." More recently, psychologists have used studies of identical twins to support this idea, arguing that some traits, including intelligence, are up to 80 percent dependent on genetic inheritance.

However, other psychologists, using the same data, argue that genetic influence is as little as 20 percent or even zero (Gardner 1993). Pairs of twins used in twin studies are often brought up in similar environments and, as they look the same, they may evoke similar responses in other people so that their experiences may be unusually alike.

There is also strong evidence to suggest that environment plays a great part in intellectual performance. For example, the *Raven's Progressive Matrices*—an intelligence test used to measure abstract reasoning ability—were designed for use with people of any language, age or culture. The person being tested has to choose a visual pattern from a selection of options, in order to complete a larger visual sequence. Scores are graded, according to age, to give an IQ score. Scores for Raven's correlated very well with those of other IQ tests, including language-based tests. So far, this supports the notion that intelligence is "general."

However, although Raven's is supposed to be culture-free and language-free, it was found that Asian children's scores, scaled according to age, went up by 15–20 points after they had lived for five years in Britain—a very significant change (Mackintosh and Mascie-Taylor 1985). This suggests that what is measured by an intelligence test is at best only a snapshot of a person's experiences and learning up to that moment. It is not an indication of the person's underlying intelligence or potential.

A snapshot of current performance

2 There are multiple intelligences, not one general intelligence

Thurstone (1960), after experiments involving hundreds of college students, concluded that there was no evidence of any *general* form of intelligence. Similarly, Gardner (1993) argues that intelligence consists of many separate, independent systems, which interact with each other. For Gardner, there are at least seven main "intelligences"; each consists of abilities to solve the problems or produce the objects that are relevant within the person's culture and environment.

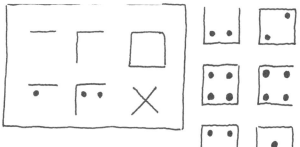

A Raven's-style question

Which option from a–f fits the space at x?

Gardner's multiple intelligences

1 **Linguistic**
   - such as reading, writing, talking, listening, or poetry

2 **Logical, mathematical**
   - such as ability with numbers, or legal or scientific thinking

3 **Spatial**
   - such as navigating a boat or plane, driving or architecture

4 **Musical**
   - such as singing, composing, playing an instrument or appreciating music

5 **Bodily-kinesthetic**
   - such as sports, drama, dance or making things

6 **Interpersonal**
   - such as counseling and teaching skills, or understanding others

7 **Intrapersonal**
   - such as self-understanding, self-management or reflection

Research in neuropsychology suggests that different cognitive abilities, such as speech, may be semiseparate "domains" of ability, controlled by different circuits within the brain (Karmiloff-Smith 1992). Some people show a weakness in one area, such as a complete inability to recognize faces. Other people show poor development for most skills but have an outstanding ability in one area, such as drawing or mathematical calculation. This supports Gardner's view that intelligence is "multiple" rather than "general."

It is obvious that most of the intelligences on Gardner's list can be developed. For example, people can attend workshops to develop interpersonal skills and counseling or meditation to develop intrapersonal awareness. A scientific way of thinking is formed through practice, training and exposure to the language and conventions of

scientific research (see pages 269–270). Skill in writing poetry or papers can also be developed through practice.

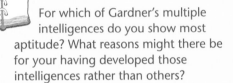

For which of Gardner's multiple intelligences do you show most aptitude? What reasons might there be for your having developed those intelligences rather than others?

3 Intelligence can be developed

In Japan, the Suzuki Violin Talent Education Program has trained many children to play the violin to virtuoso level. The program begins with exposure to music from soon after birth and involves daily practice from an early age. Even the less remarkable students perform to a level that in other cultures would be considered that of a child prodigy (Gardner 1993).

Similarly, children exposed to several languages from an early age tend to become multilingual quite naturally. People who start later in life can also develop into good violinists or linguists. The Suzuki Program suggests the importance of the belief that *anyone* can learn to a high standard, as well as showing the role of environment and practice in developing skills. Excellence need not be the preserve of the few.

Just as we would not, in general, expect excellent violin playing from somebody who rarely played the instrument, we would not expect outstanding intellectual performances from people whose minds are not regularly challenged by ideas and problems. College provides part of that necessary stimulation. As you progress with your program, the language and thinking styles of your subjects will become part of your own thinking processes and linguistic expression.

4 Intelligence depends on life opportunities

As the Suzuki example illustrates, life opportunities can make a significant difference. Academic intelligence may be fostered by opportunities such as these:

- easy access to books, equipment, and appropriate teaching

- sufficient time to study, think or practice
- stimulating conversations that require active engagement and reflection
- validation by people who are important to you of your specific learning interests, whether for geometry, philosophy or *cordon bleu* cookery
- being part of a culture that values academic intelligence.

There are ways in which you can increase these opportunities, such as making use of local libraries, taking courses at a local community college and even through your choice of newspaper and radio or TV programs. If you did not have ideal opportunities for learning when you were younger, or if you were not then ready for them, it may take some time to catch up. But it can be done—and it *is* done, every year, by thousands of adult students.

> In what ways could you make more use of the opportunities currently available to you?

5 Intelligence depends on what is needed and relevant within a culture

According to this view, intelligence is not just something that individuals carry around in their heads but includes the equipment and tools available to them—their filing systems, the amount of memory on their computers, the sophistication of the tools they can use, the lines of communication within their society, the people they meet. Intelligence is not cut off and measured in relation to individuals but regarded as a *social* phenomenon (Vygotsky 1978; Resnick, Levine and Teasley 1991).

For example, the intelligence needed in industrial settings may be very different from that required for a rural economy or for life in the mountains. Similarly, the education valued for girls, or for the youngest child within a family, may be different from that sought for boys or for older children. Children are skilled at adapting to what is expected of them.

Sternberg (1985) described intelligence as being, in part, a sensitivity to the environmental context. This can apply to learning contexts also. One learning environment may match what a person is

used to, making learning easy. For another person, the same teaching methods may not work. Some people learn best in quiet stillness; others find that sitting quietly is a torture. Some find it difficult to learn from books and learn better by ear. Some learn best when the curriculum is very structured; others when it is flexible and open.

If you did not do as well in high school as you might have done, it may be worth reflecting on how *you* learn best—then compare this to the way you were taught. You might also consider what you were good at when you were a child and what you valued as important. Were your interests shared and valued by the people around you—your teachers, parents and friends? If not, this may have made learning more difficult for you.

Are the things you value *today* shared by the people around you? Do they understand and support your desire to study? If not, as an adult, you can now take responsibility for setting up the right environment for yourself as a student. You may need to find a table you like in the library or set up a space to study that nobody else can use.

Similarly, you can organize information in a way that suits your learning preferences. For example, you could record your materials or convert information to images—whatever works for you.

On the whole, your instructors will not be able to create the ideal environment *for* you, as each person's needs will be different. So it's up to you to look after your own needs.

> How could you change your total learning environment so that you don't repeat earlier learning experiences? Do you need to surround yourself with more people who support your study ambitions? (Chapters 1, 4, 8 and 9 may give you some further ideas.)

6 Intelligence is about applying what you know to new contexts

Sternberg (1984) emphasized that any skill is made up of underlying processes and subskills; he saw intelligence as the ability to transfer those skills easily when confronted with a new task. What is important is not just that you are able to perform a given task, such as making a pancake or writing a paper, but that you are able to apply what you know to new situations, such as baking a cake or writing a report.

However, it is not necessarily an easy matter to transfer a skill from one learning situation to another. Research into mathematical problem-solving suggests that for skills to be transferred from one problem to another, the student has first to be helped to identify their common features and the underlying principles in solving that kind of problem. If students can recognize that two problems have similar underlying structures, they can apply the principles for solving one problem in solving the other. Unless the teacher makes the link between the old and the new learning explicit, the student may not realize that two problems are connected. Further, the new learning needs to be at around the same level of complexity as that already covered (Reed, Dempster and Ettinger 1985).

If teaching has not followed these lines, the student may feel lost and give up. In addition, the student may think that the fault lies with her or his intelligence rather than in the way the problem was presented. A good teacher will help students to see what they already know and to use this as the basis for the next step in their learning.

Applying multiple intelligences to study contexts

Gardner suggests that different intelligences interact. Students who work in a multisensory or a multidisciplinary way often find that learning in one area enhances learning in other areas. If you develop a sense of rhythm, this can improve not only music and dance but math and spelling. Similarly, students who are sensitive to shades of color can use these to structure and organize information visually and spatially, which in turn can help memory and understanding.

It is important to look for connections between the intelligences you have already developed and those in which you feel you are weak. You don't need to be a genius in music or art to harness music, color, shape and movement as learning tools. Croaky singing of chemical formulae, imagining your

relatives as courtroom personalities when preparing for law tests or using the rainbow to sequence paragraphs from pattern notes, are ways of using multiple intelligences to make studying easier—and more interesting.

> Look back to your answer on multiple intelligences (pages 39–40). How could you transfer abilities from your area of strength to help your learning?

7 ▸ Intelligence is a question of how much you know

The popular view of intelligence is that it is an ability to answer the type of closed questions set on *Who Wants to Be a Millionaire*. This does not take into consideration aspects of intelligence such as creativity or coping in real-life situations. Another view is that intelligence is a capacity for abstract reasoning, such as formulating general hypotheses, and that you don't need to *know* much at all to reason well.

Donaldson (1978) argued that the way we reason depends upon the particular context we are in and on what we already know. For example, she demonstrated that both children and adults interpret what they hear by attending not just to the meaning of words but also to their under-standing of those words based on their own thoughts and previous knowledge. It follows that the amount and kinds of background knowledge you bring to academic study will affect the ease with which you can process new information and reason with it.

Our ability to think in abstract ways about something may depend on having already had real-life experience of similar problems. Butterworth (1992) describes how abstract notions such as "generosity" are actually concrete social realities. The real-life, concrete experience allows us to develop a mental model, and this model later provides the basis for abstract thinking. If we have gaps in concrete experience—for example with manipulating.numbers—we are likely to find it harder to move on to more abstract examples until we have filled the gaps.

Butterworth suggests that when presented with a familiar problem in an unfamiliar context, we may be unable to recognize that the two are the same. This can make us look like complete beginners when we are not. We may need somebody to point out the similarity between what we already know and the new learning. When we see the link, we can do the problem.

Plastic brains

The brain has "plasticity": It is capable of change and development. When a person takes up a new skill, millions of fresh connections are set up between different neurons in the brain to deal with the new information—rather like a set of telephone wires relaying information. The more you develop an ability, the more elaborate the neural networks or wiring system, and the faster your brain can process information related to that skill.

When you begin to study a new subject, the speed at which you will be able to take things in and make sense of them will depend on how far your brain can use past learning experiences. If you have studied something very similar in the past, you may experience the new learning as quite easy.

If a subject is very new, however, there is little foundation for you to build upon. Your brain has fewer connections it can use to make sense of the new information. If the language used is also unfamiliar to you, the brain will need to build connections for this too. You may *experience* this as finding it harder to listen or harder to read: You may get tired more quickly, or you may feel that your brain is "dead" or that nothing makes sense. As you go over the same material from different angles, though, the new connections will get stronger and learning will become easier.

8 Intelligence can be measured

IQ tests only measure things that can be measured! Many areas of human excellence, however, cannot easily be measured—such as artistic and musical creativity, emotional maturity, intuition, sensitivity to the needs of others, keeping a cool head in emergencies, being able to impersonate other

people and inventiveness. Some people may excel in these areas and yet perform poorly in tests that are language-based. Students who have failed in language- or number-based subjects in high school often do very well in college art classes. Similarly, some people who are poor at languages are excellent at computer science.

Einstein's schoolwork was not very good—yet IQ tests are supposed to correlate well with school performance. Einstein claimed that his initial ideas on the relativity of time and space struck him in a moment of inspiration while he was daydreaming that he was riding on a sunbeam. This kind of imaginative thinking is difficult to measure using IQ tests.

9 Intelligence depends on study habits and study skills that can be learned

This book is based on the premise that what we regard as intelligence is often a question of good study habits, strategies and skills that you can develop. For example, research shows that students who do best at problem-solving spend longer than other students in working out exactly what the problem is before trying to solve it. Other students look at the surface of the problem and do not see the underlying structure that connects it to problems they already know how to solve. Some students fail because they don't spend enough time considering the examples and information they are given; others copy examples without reflecting on the underlying purpose of the activity (Keane, Kahney and Brayshaw 1989). Successful students use strategies that can be learned.

Although the research mentioned above referred to a particular *kind* of problem-solving, its findings apply to college-level study in general. Some students skim across the surface of their learning, copying a bit from one book and a line from another, without really looking at why the work was assigned, what the information means or its relevance to themselves. With most college assignments you will benefit from taking time to reflect, clarifying what is really being asked, the issues within the assignment prompt, the reasons for that piece of work being assigned and the best strategy to use. Over time, this way of working becomes a habit.

> With which of these nine views of intelligence are you most familiar? Which make most sense to you? Which best encourage learning?

What is "learning"?

Conscious learning   Unconscious learning

We have looked at how intelligence can be fostered though a learning process. At each new stage of study, it is important to reflect on *how* to learn at that level. Many people have never "learned how to learn" and most institutions now offer "learning to learn" classes.

So what is "learning"? It is clearly more than just study skills. It is a multifaceted process, involving each individual learner and her or his learning history, the current learning environment, and the interaction between these. We can say that learning has taken place when we both understand something and can explain, teach or demonstrate it to others.

The ways in which we can learn are very varied. Next are listed five dimensions along which learning activity can vary.

Five learning dimensions

1   *Conscious or unconscious*

Conscious learning

Learning is conscious when we are *aware* that we are learning, as when we set out to memorize a poem or a phone number, or when we recognize that we have understood new material. Typical methods of learning consciously are:

- repeating something
- writing it out
- checking that we have remembered it
- telling someone else what we know.

Unconscious learning

We are aware of only a small part of the information taken in by the senses, which the brain processes. Learning is unconscious when we are unaware of it happening. Occasionally, unconscious learning may emerge into consciousness later, as when we feel we "just know" something we didn't realize we had learned. You may have experienced suddenly recognizing which way to go on an unfamiliar car journey, or surprising yourself by answering a question without thinking and then wondering, "How did I know that?"

2   *With different levels of attention*

Our level of attention may vary, depending on:

- our mental or physical state for learning

- the way information is presented to us
- whether the material is completely new.

As we saw from the example of Einstein and the sunbeam (page 43), learning can take place in a relaxed, aware state—it does not always require effort and great concentration. You will be able to recall many occasions when you tried hard to remember something but forgot it quickly, such as a telephone number, while remembering easily something to which you had paid little attention, such as an advertisement on a billboard or a line from a song.

3 Via different sense sequences

Each of us has our own preferred order for seeing, hearing, speaking, writing and using information in order to learn it.

Experiment with your own preferences. Make a list of words that you have difficulty spelling (or some other information you need to learn). Try learning them using different sense sequences. For example:

- look at it; say it aloud; write it; check what you've written
- say it aloud; look at it; write it; check what you've written
- draw it; look at it; say it aloud; write it; check what you've written
- record it; listen to it; repeat it; write it; look at what you've written; check it.

Which sequence works best for you?

(For other visual, auditory and kinesthetic activities, see pages 176–178.)

4 By detail or by the whole picture

Some people learn best when they see the overall picture first; they are confused or overwhelmed by too much detail early on. Others learn best through

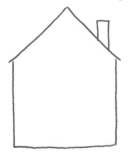

building up details, allowing the whole picture to emerge. This whole picture may be meaningless to them until they have a flavor of the specific details.

5 By fast track or by the scenic route

Some people find efficient "highway routes," learning exactly what they need and only that. Others take scenic routes, gathering material that may not be essential but that makes the learning more interesting. The scenic route can lead to deeper processing, and can be a richer experience. However, it can also generate a lot of information that is not essential to the task in hand. Which way is appropriate depends on what you have to learn, why you are learning it and how long you have in which to learn it.

Combined methods

Most of the time we change places along each of these five dimensions, depending on information from the environment and according to our needs and focus. It is easier to develop good study strategies when you are conscious of these dimensions and of your own individual approach to learning.

Some conditions are essential to learning, while others are desirable. Awareness of these allows you to create optimal learning conditions.

Six conditions for learning

For learning to occur at all, and for us then to know that the learning is complete, we need:

1 New experiences
2 Foundations
3 Rehearsal
4 Processing
5 Understanding
6 Demonstration

1 New experiences

In order to learn, we need to be exposed to novelty: to new ideas, new information, new situations, new challenges, new emotions.

Imagine, for example, discovering that when Hannah put her hand in a flame, she did not feel pain. This discovery might challenge your previous learning: That fire burns and is likely to cause pain. It might stimulate a series of questions about why and how this might *not* happen.

A new experience is an opportunity to learn—based on curiosity, a desire to know, a wish to see how everything fits together. Our brains try to fit new information into what we already know: To assimilate it. If that is not possible, the brain adapts previous knowledge to accommodate the new data.

2 Learning foundations

Learning is easier if it builds on earlier learning—if it can use similar or related experiences as a foundation to "make sense" of new information. Thus, if we look at the object in the diagram and are asked what we know about it, we can only describe what we see.

However, if we are told it is a *fruit*, we know how to react to it, what to expect from it: It can be eaten; it will probably be sweet; it is unlikely to move, make a noise, attack us or want to go for a walk. If on the other hand we are told it is an *animal* or a musical *instrument*, we will automatically call upon different sets of knowledge. Our knowledge provides models (or schemata) to help us to make sense of the world.

The same is true of academic learning. For example, it is easier to read when we have a good vocabulary. If we need to keep looking up words in the dictionary, our attention to what we are reading is continually interrupted—we lose the flow, which affects our comprehension. We also have to try to make sense of what we are reading while simultaneously remembering the meaning of the new words and fitting it all together. This leads to overload, and is often the point where people feel they "can't learn." In reality, they are learning a great deal—but too much at once.

Your brain will take time to assimilate new information, and may need to see how it all fits together, as well as what all the parts are individually, before it feels it "knows" what it is taking in. People who seem to learn things very quickly may simply have good foundations of information and practice in similar problems.

3 Rehearsal

Academic learning is similar to learning physical activities, such as dance or soccer. We generally need to repeat the action or the new information several times to take it in, and we need to come back to it or practice. Otherwise, we become "rusty" and forget. This is just as true of writing papers or reading academic books as it is of soccer, drawing, playing a violin or making a soufflé.

If you think back to what you learned in high school, you will probably be aware of a vague overall knowledge of some subjects even though the details may seem hazy. You would learn these subjects more quickly a second time around. Just glancing again at some old schoolbooks may bring whole areas of knowledge flooding back.

4 Processing new information

Superficial or "surface" processing

We may process new information at a superficial level. For example, we may just note and remember that Hannah (page 46) does not feel pain and then think no further about this. We may learn it by heart as a fact, like learning math tables, or record it as an entry in our notebooks.

Memory and recording are only part of learning, however. If we use only surface methods, we don't develop a sense of the underlying structure or the significance of what we learn. This makes it more difficult to apply the new knowledge in other situations.

Deep processing—making sense of what you learn

Alternatively, we may try to make sense of Hannah's experience, looking for explanations. We may ask ourselves questions to stimulate our thinking, exploring the problem from many angles. Perhaps Hannah is very good at exercising mind over matter? Maybe she has a neurological condition that prevents her from feeling pain? Maybe she *does* feel pain but hides this?

We may also start to wonder what pain really is. How does it work—is it regulated by the brain? Or chemicals in the body? Or our attitude? Or maybe the flame was different from the flames we are used to? Maybe the answer is not in Hannah but in chemistry?

As you analyze the experience from different angles, raising new questions and experimenting with possible answers, you process at a deeper level.

"No, I don't need to practice—I have a natural gift!"

5 ▶ Moving to another level of understanding

In order to understand a new phenomenon, such as what happens when Hannah's hand is in the fire, we may have to change our previous views of the world. We may have thought that everybody would feel pain from fire.

- When we realize that there are situations in which people don't feel pain in quite the same way as others, we move to a different level of knowledge.
- When we know *why* this occurs, we move to a deeper level of understanding.
- When we appreciate how we came to hold our previous set of beliefs and why we now hold a different set, we are learning at an even deeper level—understanding how knowledge is constructed, and how we come to know and understand at all.
- When we learn in this way we have to be prepared to open our minds to new ways of seeing and doing things, even to new ways of thinking about ourselves, looking at how we came to believe what we believe. This makes study exciting, and is one reason why so many students go to graduate school.

6 ▶ Demonstrating learning

We are not really sure of our knowledge until we have put it to the test—demonstrating to ourselves and others that we really do *know* it.

One way of testing our understanding of new material is to put it to use. In some cases there may be a practical use, such as fixing a piece of machinery or producing a new design. In other cases, such as understanding how pain works, we can demonstrate learning by explaining it to other people. If we can do this

- in writing, speech or a diagram, or by practical demonstration
- without checking the details during the presentation
- and in a way that is clear and makes sense to our audience

then our thinking is also likely to be clear and a stage in our learning is complete.

If we *cannot* demonstrate what we feel we know, then our thinking may be rather confused and our understanding incomplete. We may need to check back over what we have learned. It may help:

- to take a different angle on the issue
- to use a different book
- to see if we missed a step earlier.

The section on encoding information in *Memory* (Chapter 8) and *The C·R·E·A·M strategy for learning* (Chapter 4) may also help.

Learning in college

Some people think that memorizing "facts" is all there is to learning. Certainly it *is* always useful to have information readily available in your head for when you need it. For many college classes, however, what counts is not how many facts you can fit into your answers but how you *use* information.

You will be expected to demonstrate:

- that you can evaluate and select what is relevant and important, and what can be omitted
- that you know how ideas are linked and interconnected
- that you have made sense of your course
- that you can structure your ideas and knowledge to make a convincing argument.

Optimal learning

A number of factors determine whether or not you can learn effectively. Learning is easier when circumstances are favorable in the following ways.

When you are in a physical state to learn

- You can't learn easily if you are tired, stressed, hungry, dehydrated or on a high-sugar diet.

- A glass of plain water several times a day helps neural activity in the brain and releases energy. Other drinks do not have the same effect. If you tire easily when studying, or if your thinking is blurred, drink some water.

- Foods such as cereal-based products (rice, oats and wheat), which release natural sugars slowly, help balance your energies.

- Stress may put you into "survival mode," diverting your energies away from your brain to your muscles (see page 173). We learn best when relaxed, interested and motivated.

When you *believe* you can learn

- Believe in your intelligence (Chapter 3).
- Believe you have the right to learn.
- Create a positive state of mind for learning.

When the medium suits you

- Rewrite, draw, act, record or sculpt new information so that it is easier to absorb—whatever suits you best.
- Experiment with different layouts, colors, fonts, page sizes.
- Personalize information to make it your own.

When information is organized

Organize information so that your brain can structure it (see page 179).

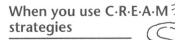

When you use C·R·E·A·M strategies

Be creative, reflective, effectively organized, active and highly motivated (see Chapter 4).

When you use your whole brain

Take full advantage of your brain. Use:

- both the "left" and "right" sides of your brain (pages 171–2)
- the triune brain (page 172)
- all your senses to encode information (see page 176).

Learning is easier when ...

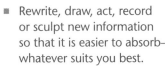

When the five study-skills components are in place

You need:

- self-awareness
- awareness of what is required of you
- methods and strategies
- confidence and permission
- familiarity, practice and habit.

See page 22.

When you enjoy what you learn

Make the learning fun. Make sure:

- that it has meaning for you
- that you really care about the outcome, attracted to success like a bee to honey
- that you are fully engaged in what you are learning.

When you work with others

See Chapter 10.

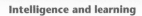

Look over the notes you took for each section about intelligence. In your journal, note your thoughts now in response to these questions.

- Have your ideas changed or been reinforced as you read through this chapter?

- What is your own learning history? As a child, were you encouraged or discouraged in learning? What effect did that have?

- Is your current learning affected by patterns from the past? If so, do you need to make any changes to improve your learning?

- What is necessary for you to achieve optimal learning? Based on what you have read in this chapter, list three things you could do now to enhance your own learning.

- How do your study skills needs fit with your other learning development needs?

Review

This chapter has provided an opportunity to reflect upon your attitude to intelligence and learning, and how your attitude could be affecting your ability to learn. It has considered the idea of study skills in a broad sense, looking at the relationship between intelligence, life experiences and learning.

There are many different views about intelligence. Some traditional attitudes have been limiting. They reduced people's self-esteem, making it more difficult for them to learn and overlooking their potential to develop new areas of ability.

Different cultures and different environments require, appreciate and develop different aspects of intelligence. How much early support individuals have for their own learning preferences and subject choices may have long-term effects on their performance and indeed their self-esteem. As an adult learner, you have much more control over your learning than you did as a child in high school. You can now decide to alter aspects of your environment, your social networks, your attitudes and your study habits, as well as personalizing your

study materials to support your own learning preferences. You can give yourself permission to succeed.

The chapter has also looked at how concrete experience and previous learning affect our performance in new areas of learning—including coping with academic information or writing papers. If these skills are underdeveloped through lack of adequate prior experience, study may seem difficult and we may feel less intelligent. On the other hand, as explained in Chapter 2, the subskills required for academic study are often similar to those used in other areas of life. No student begins from scratch.

Finally, the chapter has encouraged you to consider that there are different ways to approach learning. As you become more used to study at a higher level you will find that being flexible in your approaches to learning can make study both more efficient and more interesting. This idea is developed further in Chapter 4, *The C·R·E·A·M strategy for learning*.

Chapter 4

The C·R·E·A·M strategy for learning

LEARNING OUTCOMES

This chapter offers you opportunities to:

- become aware of the contribution of each aspect of the C·R·E·A·M strategy to the learning process—and know how to apply it to your own study

- develop ideas on how to take more creative and active approaches to your study

- build upon the reflective work started in Chapters 2 and 3

- understand the difference between being a *virtuous* student and being an *effective* student

- develop tools for organizing your space and time more effectively

- explore and clarify your motives for study, and learn how to set yourself clear and achievable goals.

C·R·E·A·M

C·R·E·A·M stands for:

C—Creative

Have the confidence to use your individual strategies and styles, applying imagination to your learning.

R—Reflective

Be able to sit with your experience, analyze and evaluate your own performance, and draw lessons from it.

A—Active

Be personally involved and doing things, physically and mentally, in order to make sense of what you learn.

E—Effective

Organize your space, time, priorities, state of mind and resources (including information technology, IT), to the maximum benefit.

M—Motivated

Be aware of your own desired outcomes; keep yourself on track using short- and long-term "goals."

Developing each of these aspects strengthens all the others. For example, being motivated involves reflection about what you really want. Active learning and creativity require motivation, and also help you stay motivated. Good organizational strategies benefit from imagination and reflection—and so on.

Creativity is especially important for generating ideas in the early stages of new assignments. You can use more logical approaches later, to evaluate which creative ideas to use.

Attitudes that prevent creativity

- "It's a waste of time."
- "It's childish."
- "There's a time for work and a time for play."
- "There's a right way of doing things."
- "It's not logical."
- "I'm not creative."
- "I can't."

> Do you express any of the above attitudes? Were you given any messages when you were younger that stifle your creativity now?

Approaches that foster creativity

Playtime: lateral thinking

Choose any two random objects, such as a cup and a plant. Think of as many ways as possible that they could be considered connected (e.g., by size, color, the way they break, if they are opposites, how they spin, when they were bought). How can you apply this type of play to your assignments?

You find what you are looking for

- Find three round things in the room.
- Find three things that "open."

You will probably find that the room is suddenly filled with these things. If you look for new ways of doing things, or for answers, you will find them too.

There's more than one right answer

Once you have come up with an answer, look for another one. It may be better—or give you a way of fine-tuning the first idea.

Combine things

Take the front half of one animal and the rear of another. What new animal have you invented? The essence of invention is mixing two different ideas or contexts to create a new variety. This helps in academic thinking too—such as comparing viewpoints.

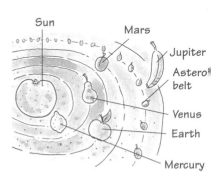

Metaphor

Let one thing stand for, or represent, another: This is using metaphor or analogy. Play at seeing an object, or a study problem, from different perspectives. Make problems visual or concrete. Take an issue out of the academic context

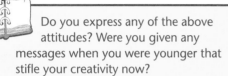

"Suppose this apple is the earth, this orange is the sun, and these other fruits are the rest of the solar system...."

and see what it looks like in the world of oranges and apples, or knives, forks, salt and pepper.

If something doesn't make sense, map it out with objects on a table—just as generals mapped out different strategies using "toy" soldiers.

Activity

Search for connections

See how many ideas you can generate by completing the sentences below.

- Writing a paper is like making cakes because ....
- Study is like a game of soccer because ....
- Being a student is like being a sandwich because ....

What other metaphors can you think of to describe what study or learning is like?

Chapter 4

Be a professor—and other ideas

Give yourself a new subpersonality

In our minds and even in our bodies, we carry various subpersonalities—an internal *critic* who tells us off, a *playful child* who sees the funny side of things, a *hero* who wades in to save the situation, and many others.

Listen to yourself think and you will gradually become aware of those different characters within.

Add to your dramatic cast and find a professor within you

Go through the ideas later to see which you can use. Many may lead nowhere— that's part of the creative process—but sometimes one will be just what you need.

Be curious about what you don't know

Creative people are curious. They want to know everything—just in case it fits together with something else one day.

It is difficult to be creative if you are frightened of what you don't know. Be open to the curious child in you who wants to give everything a try.

Create opportunities to break a routine

When you take a different route, even if it is not the quickest way, you discover new things of interest.

Examine your routines. Ask:
- Why am I doing it this way?
- Have the original reasons now changed?
- How else could I do things?

Imagine alternatives

Ask "what if ...?" questions

What if the weekend were three days long? What if this paper had to be in tomorrow? What if I were only allowed 100 words to write up my research— what would I include?

How would others do it?

Consider: How might Pablo Picasso approach this study problem? Or Nelson Mandela? Mahatma Gandhi? Agatha Christie? Mozart? Whoopi Goldberg? A politician? A choreographer? Your mother? Your internal professor? Whose approach would most help and inspire you?

Activity

You are the world's leading expert

When you cannot think of a way of doing a piece of work, imagine you are a professor or inventor, dealing with a world-important problem. Experts don't find problems easy, but they are more open to dealing with the seemingly impossible.

Those working at the forefront of research cannot look up the answer in a book—it isn't there yet! Like Einstein daydreaming on a sunbeam (page 43) they may play with ideas, juggle with options that seem crazy and go on flights of fancy, imagining "what if ...?," generating lots of possible answers and then examining them more closely to see if any could actually work.

You can do that too. What does your internal professor look like? Sound like? How do you move your hands and head when you are in "professor" mode? Let your professor come alive and talk to you about possible approaches to study problems.

Keep an ideas notebook

Value each passing idea, as writers and artists do. Jot ideas down at once in a notebook or on Post-it® notes. Keep paper and pen by your bed.

Creative learning

People devise many different strategies to help them to learn. Here are a few.
Check the box beside any *you* could use. What other methods can you think of?

☐ **1**
We like to argue with each other.

No—we discuss things, really.

It's a sort of argument, though.

☐ **2**
I make a big chart out of wallpaper—and link up all I learn on one subject.

☐ **3**
I organize my ideas while I vacuum—then no-one can hear me talking my ideas through.

☐ **4**
I record my ideas and play them back to myself.

☐ **5**
I have a notebook to jot down ideas as they come to me—I take it with me everywhere.

☐ **6**
We talk a lot …

… Share ideas …

… Work things out together.

☐ **7**
I like a method:
a I work out the main ideas;
b think of headings;
c summarize notes;
d summarize onto one page.

☐ **8**
"I write lots of draft outlines. I fit new information into one of the outlines."

☐ **9**
I try to imagine I am a lawyer—I always have to argue the other side of what I think.

"It is therefore clear, your Honor that …"

☐ **10**
Swahili Ibo Esperanto Farsee Chinese
I imagine crazy pictures to help me to remember things.

☐ **11**
I use "look and cover": I read or try to learn something; then I cover the page. I write down what I can remember. Then I check back to see what I got right. Then I try again.

☐ **12**
I scribble my ideas down as fast as I can and see where my mind takes me. I organize them later to see which bits I can use.

The C·R·E·A·M strategy for learning

What is my learning style?

Below are a range of approaches to learning. Identify which, if any, describes you best.
Note your learning strengths and things you could develop to broaden your study strengths.

The diver

Characteristics

- ☐ You tend to jump in and give it a try.
- ☐ You like to get things over with.
- ☐ You like to see if things work.
- ☐ You like to get onto the next thing quickly.
- ☐ You work well with short bursts of activity.

Learning strengths

- ☐ You don't waste time worrying.
- ☐ You start tasks early.
- ☐ You can motivate others.
- ☐ You are good in role-play activities, problem-solving, and crises.

Areas to develop

- Reflection and planning.
- Creative thinking.
- Considering alternatives.
- Listening to and working with others.
- Increasing your personal interest, so that you can work for longer periods.

The dreamer

Characteristics

- ☐ You think a lot about the subject.
- ☐ You like to research things thoroughly.
- ☐ You put off practical aspects, such as writing.
- ☐ You have no idea where time goes.
- ☐ You continually rewrite your planner.

Learning strengths

- ☐ You reflect and evaluate well.
- ☐ You are creative, with lots of ideas.
- ☐ You get to the root of things.
- ☐ You listen well and sensitively to others.

Areas to develop

- Effective learning strategies.
- Timekeeping and organizational skills.
- Taking responsibility for self and others.
- Participating.
- Setting priorities and taking decisions.
- Assertiveness and risk-taking.

The logician

Characteristics

- ☐ You like things to make sense.
- ☐ You like to know the reasons behind things.
- ☐ You are organized in your approach to study.
- ☐ You enjoy tackling complex problems.
- ☐ You are a perfectionist.

Learning strengths

- ☐ You are good at analytical and critical thinking.
- ☐ You have organizational skills.
- ☐ You are good at science, math, law, problem-solving.
- ☐ You have a questioning approach.

Areas to develop

- Creative and imaginative thinking.
- Sensitivity to the differences in others.
- Personal reflection.
- Working with others.
- Stress management.

The searchlight

Characteristics

- ☐ You find everything interesting.
- ☐ You like to see the big picture.
- ☐ You have bits of information on lots of things.
- ☐ You are fascinated by details but don't remember them.
- ☐ You find it hard to select what is relevant.

Learning strengths

- ☐ You have high motivation and interest.
- ☐ You have broad general knowledge.
- ☐ You can see connections between things.
- ☐ You are creative and inventive.

Areas to develop

- Setting goals and priorities.
- Analytical and critical thinking.
- Categorizing and selecting.
- Editing skills.
- Developing memory for detail.

Personalize your learning style

She says she's experimenting with her learning style.

You probably found that using general categories like these excluded some of your individual learning attributes. Invent a style that sums up just *you*.

- Consider if you prefer to
  - see, hear, speak or sing information
  - work alone or with others
  - have support or be independent
  - receive encouragement and feedback
  - involve physical movement of some kind
  - be at home or on campus
  - have guidance or work things out yourself.

- List your learning strengths.
- List areas you need to develop.
- Then choose a word, phrase, animal or object that best sums up how *you* learn.

You may use one set of learning styles for subjects you like and another set for those that bore you. If you are open, flexible and creative in trying new approaches, you will develop into a more rounded personality and a more effective learner and you will have more options and more strategies available to you in the long term.

Adapting your program to suit you

If your program is structured in a way that does not already match your learning preferences, you can "adapt" it through the way you choose to study.

Example 1

If you prefer to work with others, organize a study group or arrange to work with a friend. Work in libraries and get involved in student activities.

Example 2

If you like to work to your own agenda, focus on time management so that your time feels like your own. Look for articles that nobody else is likely to use. Find examples that others may not think of.

Example 3

If you prefer to work by ear, record lectures and extracts from books, listen to them while traveling, and record your own ideas. Form a support group so that you can learn through discussion. Find out what information is available that can be downloaded onto your MP3 player.

In your journal, note ways you could organize your approach to the program to suit your own learning style better. Try this exercise later in the year and compare your results and comments.

⚡Reflective learning

As a student in higher education, you are responsible for your own progress—for your development as an autonomous learner. Although you will receive formal assessment (grades and comments) from instructors, it is important not to be dependent upon the assessment and views of other people. You benefit from being able to work out for yourself, through a process of analysis and reflection, what you do well, what you need to improve and your priorities. You started work on this process in Chapter 2.

Developing the habit of reflection

Your performance as a student is likely to improve if you develop a habit of putting time aside to reflect on *how* you learn. You will find that you study more effectively if you consider, for example:

- your motivation
- changes in your attitudes and ideas
- the appropriateness of your current study strategies to the tasks you are undertaking
- which skills you need for different kinds of assignment
- what is blocking your learning
- any gaps there are in your knowledge or your skills audit.

Five methods of developing reflection

1 Keep a learning journal or blog (page 59).
2 Use the self-evaluation questionnaires.
3 Keep an updated profile or portfolio (page 35).
4 Make constructive use of feedback from instructors (page 282).
5 Fill in progress sheets regularly (page 58).

Evaluating your own progress

Questionnaires and checklists

- Use these as starting points to focus your thinking about your learning.
- Select a few points from each questionnaire to consider in your journal.

Be fair to yourself

When you decide that you are "good" or "bad" at something, consider your *reasons* for thinking that. What criteria are you using to assess yourself? Work out what is involved in the task, breaking it into smaller tasks or subskills. Are you better at some parts than others? What makes some parts more difficult than others?

People may easily underestimate themselves when:

- they have been out of formal education for a few years
- they learn more about a subject (the more we know, the more we are aware of what we don't know, and that can be unsettling).

Monitor your performance

- Photocopy the blank questionnaires and fill them in again later in the semester. Compare answers, looking for progress.
- Read through your journal regularly. Comment on your progress.

How well am I doing?

Class:	Date:
Level:	Year of study:
1a Generally, how well am I doing in this class?	**1b** On what am I basing this self-evaluation? (My grades? Instructor feedback? Self-monitoring? Other ways?)
2a In this class, I am best at: What makes me better at these aspects?	**2b** On what am I basing this self-evaluation?
3a To do better in this class, I need to improve: What prevents me from doing as well at present?	**3b** How will I bring about this improvement? My time scale for this improvement is:
4a What have I already learned, or improved, since I started taking this class?	**4b** How do I know this? How do I measure or monitor what I have learned? (How long it takes? My level of confidence? My understanding? My level of enjoyment?)

Chapter 4

The C·R·E·A·M strategy for learning

Reflective learning journals

In a sturdy notebook, or using your computer, start a reflective learning journal.

Start a reflective learning journal now!

Why?

- The act of writing things down helps you to clarify your thoughts and emotions, to work out strategies and to focus on your development and progress.
- A written record will help you see how you are progressing from week to week and from semester to semester.

Who is it for?

For yourself—to help you focus on your own development.

What do you write?

Anything that helps *you* to reflect on:

- your feelings about the class, the instructors, other students, your progress
- things you find difficult: challenges
- changes in your attitude or motivation
- how you tackle tasks—your strategies
- things you find out about yourself
- thoughts about how you learn best
- ideas that arise from your studies
- how different areas of study link up
- how your studies relate to real life.

Use the *How well am I doing?* sheet (page 58) to prompt ideas. Identify the criteria you are using to assess yourself.

> "... I can't believe the difference between my first essay (very bad!!!) and this one. Keeping an ideas book has helped."

> "I used to read the hardest books first—to be a 'real' student. Now I look for a simple overview first."

> "Why am I always late? I think it's because I always try to get somewhere on time, whereas I should think about getting there 5 minutes early—then I might be on time!"

Other uses of reflective learning journals

As a basis for discussion

It can be helpful to discuss your journal or blog entries with other students in your class. How does their experience of the class compare with your own? Have they worked out strategies that might help you?

Preparing for advisor meetings

Go through the journal and make a list of issues that you want to discuss in the next meeting with your academic advisor. Put these in order of priority. If you have any problems, think through some possible options, so that the discussion with your advisor will be more focused.

Risky writing

Keeping a private journal helps to develop your writing. You can experiment with different styles if you want to. You can take risks. The journal is for *your* benefit—and for your eyes only. This may make a welcome change from writing to the demands of your course or instructors!

This sign is used in the book at points where it may be useful to stop, think and write in your journal.

Start now

How do you feel about starting your program? What challenges do you anticipate? How can you use your experiences to help you to meet these challenges? (See Chapter 2.)

Virtue versus effectiveness

Studying hard is not the same as working efficiently. Consider the table below which shows the study strategies of one student, Leila. Leila feels she should get good grades because she works very hard. She studies 50 hours a week and gets all her work done by the deadline.

Can you see why Leila's grades are getting worse, even though she is working harder? Note your thoughts in your journal.

Leila's study strategies	
Leila feels virtuous ...	**... Yet her study strategy is inefficient**
1 Leila reads every book on the reading list and searches the Internet constantly.	■ The same information is repeated in several books. She does not select from one book to another.
2 She reads every book from cover to cover.	■ Not all of the book is equally relevant. She does not use a reading strategy (see pages 98–100).
3 She writes very detailed notes.	■ She has more information than she needs. ■ Her notes are repetitive and take a long time to read. ■ She doesn't think much about what she is noting down. ■ It takes her a long time to find things in her notes. ■ She has to rewrite her notes to study for tests. ■ She copies large sections—and copies these into her own work—which loses her points.
4 She writes her notes neatly, and in full sentences.	■ Using abbreviations would save time. ■ As long as she can read her notes and find information easily, they do not need to be neat.
5 She works long hours with few breaks.	■ She gets tired and cannot think as clearly. ■ She gets bored and loses interest easily. ■ Her mind wanders and she forgets what she has read. ■ Sometimes she takes notes without realizing she has done so—with no idea what they say.
6 She locks herself away to work solidly.	■ She misses out on other people's opinions, suggestions and perspectives.

Virtuous or effective?

Activity

Do you think the following examples are "virtuous" or "effective" or neither?

Write V for virtuous
E for effective
N for neither

1 ☐ Linking new information to what you already know or have studied.

2 ☐ Learning difficult information "by heart."

3 ☐ Copying chunks from textbooks—because the writer says it better than you could.

4 ☐ Questioning if what you have heard is really true or representative.

5 ☐ Writing fast so that you can take down almost everything the instructor says.

6 ☐ Reading your papers and assignments slowly and out loud before you hand them in.

Start tasks early …

- You only need a piece of paper and a pencil to get started. Don't wait until you have all your books, or tidied your desk (excuses to put off getting started).

- If you don't feel like studying, give yourself permission to study for only ten minutes. Quickly jot down questions to focus your ideas; write a list of things you need to do, etc. Attend to the "excuses" afterwards—if you still want to. You will probably find you are "hooked" into the study and want to keep going.

- Get your mind working on a problem as soon as you can. Your mind continues working on the problem even when you go on to do something else. This is why it pays to start looking at new assignments as soon as you receive them.

Answers to activity

1 *Effective*   This helps you to understand and remember your subject.

2 *Virtuous*   Whether or not it is effective depends on what you are learning and why. You may need to memorize formulas, equations, names and dates. For written text, however, this is an ineffective method. (See Chapter 8.)

3 *Neither*   You are expected to show that you understand your material and can write it in your own words. Even your notes should be in your own words: This also helps you to avoid plagiarism (see page 110).

4 *Effective*   You need to develop your knowledge and understanding by asking questions. (See Chapter 7.)

5 *Neither*   This is an ineffective strategy. You need to note the main points in your own words. You will also end up with more notes than you need and have to spend time editing them. (See Chapter 5.)

6 *Effective*   Reading out loud helps you spot mistakes that you need to correct.

Effective learning

Ineffective approaches

Do you:

- feel guilty if you are not working?
- feel you are cheating if you don't read a book from cover to cover?
- worry if you cannot remember every detail of what you have learned?
- worry that other people have taken far more notes than you?

Instead, work out a strategy for learning in the most effective way.

Examples of ineffective learning

Your learning is likely to be ineffective if you:

1 work when you are too tired to concentrate
2 listen or read without questioning and challenging what you hear or read
3 sit down to study but let your mind wander to other matters
4 learn things by heart without really understanding them
5 don't ask for help when you need it
6 don't make connections between what you learn in different subject areas
7 don't relate your studies to real life.

Jot down any other examples you can think of. Which ones apply to you?

Consider this 10-point "effective learning" checklist

1	☐	Do I need to be more reflective and aware in relation to my study habits?	*See pages 57–68, 91.*
2	☐	Am I in touch with my reasons for study? Do I need more motivation?	*See pages 87–90.*
3	☐	Are there anxieties and concerns I need to sort out first?	*See pages 15–18.*
4	☐	Am I being too virtuous rather than effective?	*See pages 60–61.*
5	☐	Am I working to my preferred learning style?	*See pages 54–56.*
6	☐	Are my time and space organized effectively?	*See pages 63–79.*
7	☐	Am I aware of my priorities for developing my study skills?	*See pages 27–29.*
8	☐	Am I in the best frame of mind for study?	*See page 63.*
9	☐	Is my learning active enough?	*See pages 83–85.*
10	☐	Do I need more support from others?	*See pages 215, 225.*

Settling down to study

Effective study depends on having your state of mind, space, time, and materials organized in the ways that best suit your learning.

Creating a state of mind for study

For many people, it is quite difficult to get into a study mood. Everyone has their own particular distracters: endless cups of coffee, chats on the phone, more laundry, watching TV—anything rather than settling down to study. Many people need to use "triggers" to start a study session.

Give yourself study triggers

One student clears his desk each time he finishes studying: His study trigger is a clear, inviting surface. Another student has a "ritual" of switching on the computer, bringing in a glass of water and then opening her books at the appropriate pages before she feels she is ready to begin. Another begins by making coffee while standing in the kitchen, brainstorming ideas onto paper. He feels he has already started to study before he sits down.

What actions or thoughts could trigger *you* into a study mode? If you don't know, make some up and try them out until you find the ones that suit you.

Create the right environment

What kind of study environment suits you best for different stages of the study process? Make a conscious note of what it is that enables you to begin study: Is there quiet or music or background noise? Do you need to be at home or in a library or with friends? Do you need a clear table? What else is needed?

Use your distractions to help you study

Study on the move

If your distractions involve movement (such as going to the store or housework), spend ten minutes browsing a chapter or going over notes first. Then give in to your distraction task if you still want to—but go over what you have just read as you do it. For example, rehearse information in your head as you walk or cook. See how much you remember. Plan what you will do next, or try to solve a study problem in your head as you move.

This can be especially helpful if your mind goes blank when you sit down to study. Some people learn better "on the move."

Deprive yourself of study

Begin by allowing yourself only ten minutes to study—maybe standing. Then do something else, but keep thinking about what you have just studied in that ten minutes. For example, consider if you agree with what you have read. Has the author or instructor given enough evidence to prove the case? As your ideas develop, jot them down.

If you come to a standstill or can't remember something, take a brief look—a mere moment or two, to refresh your memory—and then continue with the painting or ironing, and with your mental recall and study. Keep pen and paper nearby.

Use distractions as resources

If you tend to call your friends as a distraction, ask them to help you focus on your work. Tell them to ask you about the assignment or use them as a sounding board. Set time limits for calls.

Connect to your motivation

See pages 86–90.

When, how and where?

If you are finding it difficult to start a piece of work, it may be because you have not established the right conditions for study.

For each of the five aspects below, work out which conditions suit you best for starting and completing a piece of work. For example, do you know what kind of task you do best early in the morning or late at night? Do you know the best time and place for you to redraft a piece of writing? Or read difficult texts?

Experiment until you find which times and places suit you best for different types of task. Note these down. Whenever you find you cannot settle down to a piece of work, check this page and your own notes.

Organize your time, space and mind for study

For each of the five areas below, write at least one suggestion of some change you could make now to improve your studying.

Am I doing this for myself?

- [ ] Am I clear about my motivation for going to college?
- [ ] Have I thought about how to make this more interesting for myself?
- [ ] Have I thought about how to make this study as enjoyable as possible?

Are my expectations realistic?

- [ ] Am I taking things step by step?
- [ ] Am I setting myself manageable goals?
- [ ] Am I rewarding myself for meeting goals and for other achievements?
- [ ] Am I taking breaks, eating, relaxing and sleeping?
- [ ] Am I selecting particular aspects of my study for improvement today (and leaving others for another time)?

Am I in the right place?

Where do I work well?

- [ ] Do I have a good surface to write on?
- [ ] Do I feel comfortable?
- [ ] Do I have good light and ventilation?

- [ ] Do I have the equipment I need?
- [ ] Am I likely to be uninterrupted?

Am I working at the right time?

- [ ] Do I work productively at this time of day?
- [ ] Is this the best time for this activity?
- [ ] Am I completing tasks in order of priority?

Am I aware of my distractions?

- [ ] Do I know my excuses for putting off getting started ("First, I just need to …")?
  1 . . . .
  2 . . . .
  3 . . . .
- [ ] Do I know my weak points for getting distracted (e.g., cups of coffee, "quick" phone calls, chatting)?
  1 . . . .
  2 . . . .
  3 . . . .
- [ ] Am I taking steps to prevent such distractions?
- [ ] Do I use distractions creatively?

Chapter 4

Organizing space for study

Dedicated study space

Create a separate space for study where you can leave things and come back to them. If you don't have access to a desk or table, use a shelf or closet to keep all your study things together.

Light and comfort

It is good to work near a window, so that you have adequate light. Sitting with the window behind or to one side will cut down on distractions. A reading lamp and natural daylight bulbs are a good investment if you study in the evening.

Make the study area a pleasant one to come back to—preferably with a comfortable chair, so that it encourages you to return to study. As far as possible, keep surfaces clear and papers organized. This not only makes it easier to find things but is relaxing for study.

Study tools

You will probably need:

- lined, punched paper
- a ring binder for each subject —use different colors
- lots of file dividers
- plastic "envelopes" (for files)
- a smaller folder to carry your day's work—use file dividers to separate the contents by subject
- an attractive notebook for your reflective journal
- an organizer or planner— ideally with "a week to view"
- a dictionary and a thesaurus
- an address book in which to note spellings alphabetically
- a calculator
- essential books
- large sheets of paper or wallpaper (or backs of posters) for wall charts
- *lots* of colored pencils, markers, pens and highlighters, plus a ruler, correction fluid, glue, etc.

Note Make sure you know which of the books on your syllabus you are expected to buy.

A computer?

Consider this carefully.

- Do you really need your own, or will college facilities do?
- If you do need your own, must it be compatible with college software? If so, what does the college recommend?
- Do you need any special software?
- See page 142.

Filing notes

- See page 109.
- Ensure you file notes every few days.
- Cut-out cereal boxes make good holders for loose sheets and articles.
- Label everything!

Other items

- Flash drive.
- MP3 or MP4 player?
- Digital recorder.

Time management in college

Time management = study success

Your success as a student will be strongly affected by the combination of two time-related factors:

- how much time you spend in study
- how well you use that time.

If you spend both more time in study AND manage that time effectively, you are much more likely to do well.

Time management = all-around success

Good time management can make an enormous difference to:

- your grades
- your ability to meet, successfully, different sets of competing deadlines
- your confidence in coping with study
- your ability to juggle study with social life, work and other demands
- having time to do the basics, such as eating and sleeping properly and making friends
- your sense of well-being as a student and as a person.

Time management = positive choices

If you use time effectively, you then have choices about how you spend the time saved. You can choose one or more of the following:

- do more reading and thinking about a subject, developing your understanding so that your work stands out
- spend time reinforcing what you have learned, so that it makes more sense to you
- spend more time revisiting material and preparing for tests
- pursue some topics in more depth, so that you are more expert in these
- have more time for life beyond your studies.

Independent study and time management

No matter which major or classes you are pursuing, it is likely that:

- you will have to spend time in independent study
- much of that time will be spent in reading, writing, thinking and problem solving
- you will benefit from good management of the time you spend in independent study.

First steps in time management

Time management starts with three basic stages:

1 **Finding out about time requirements:** identifying what you have to do and how long these activities are expected to take.

2 **Observing current use of time:** how you actually spend your time now.

3 **Planning time:** how you intend to allocate your time from now on.

Finding out about time requirements

As a student, the first steps are to find out:

- how many hours study are required
- the pattern of study required for your program—especially the amount of independent study
- program time requirements, such as the amount of time expected for different types of study such as lectures, classes, practical work and independent study each week.

Managing your time

As only part of your week and year will be formally scheduled, you will be responsible for organizing most of your study time. This can be challenging when there are commitments such as work, family and friends to fit in.

Organize your time

To manage time well, it helps to do the following:

- be aware of your own time management
- be aware of how much time it takes you to complete each type of study task
- be aware that many aspects of study take much longer than expected
- schedule time for unforeseen events
- schedule time for relaxation and leisure
- be very specific in your time-planning.

Improve your time management

If your time management needs further improvement, you could:

- check the *Ten time-saving suggestions* (page 70)
- complete a *Study time* record sheet, so that you know exactly how you spend your time (page 71)
- do the *Where does the time go?* exercise (page 72)
- use the *Time management* sheet (page 77)
- use the *Priority organizer* (page 78)
- use the *Working backwards from deadlines* planner (page 79).

Set your priorities

You may find that you have more things to do than there is time to complete. If so, it will help if you think through what your priorities are, either for the day, or the week or the year. The *Priority organizer* (page 78) and the following checklist may help you to sort out what to do and when to do it.

How well do I manage my time now?

	yes / no
Do I usually arrive on time?	☐ ☐
Do I keep most appointments?	☐ ☐
Do I manage to fit in most of the things that I need to do?	☐ ☐
Do I find I often have to rush things at the last minute?	☐ ☐
Do I meet deadlines?	☐ ☐
Have I any time for myself and to relax?	☐ ☐
Do I use my time effectively?	☐ ☐

What do your answers to these questions suggest about how well you manage your time now? Do you need to change any of your attitudes to time in order to manage your studies well?

Priority-setting checklist

Have you:

- ☐ written a list of everything you have to do?
- ☐ underlined essential tasks in one color and items that can wait in another color?
- ☐ identified the most urgent item on the list?
- ☐ worked out the best order in which to do things?
- ☐ worked out how long you can spend on each?
- ☐ entered each essential task into your schedule and planner?

Effective planner-keeping

A "week-to view" planner for the academic year is ideal. Fill in all the important dates for the year, such as family vacations, medical appointments and study activities. Include everything you do.

What to put in about your study

To be effective, your organizer or planner needs to be a *complete* record of what you have to do:

- write in all study deadlines, test dates, field trips, etc.
- write in exactly where, and with whom, each appointment or class is
- add in very specific study tasks, such as "Read Chapters 2–4 of *Urban Ecology*"
- schedule some free time to be used in catching up on what got missed.

Map into the planner the times when you will:

- think about the subject
- prepare for lectures and classes
- prepare for other formal sessions
- plan your work
- organize and refile your notes
- reflect on your learning
- discuss work with others
- research each subject
- write early drafts
- edit and redraft your writing
- check your work.

Allow some time for emergencies and unforeseen events.

How to use your planner

Your planner will be effective only if you keep it up to date and *use* it:

- carry your planner with you at all times
- check it several times a day, especially at night and first thing in the morning
- add new appointments straight into it
- write inessential appointments in pencil, so you can make changes easily
- organize entries so you can see at a glance

which time is filled—to make sure you cannot double-book yourself

- also use the year planner included.

Color codes and symbols

Use colors and symbols to indicate different activities and subjects in your planner. If you use color and symbols consistently, you will find after a while that you don't need to "read" the entries: You will be able to see at a glance what is there. Use a positive or energizing symbol for activities you dislike.

Examples of symbols you could devise

socializing   writing   reading

lecture   library   class

final draft   test   travel

Planner entries

MONDAY, JULY 20

9–11	Rm 33, B Block. Dr Olafemi
11–11:30	Meet Dan in Pink Room
11:30–1	Read articles on urban wildlife
1–2	Jane & Linda—meet in Jet café
2–3	Travel home
3–5	Read Brown, Chs. 4–8
5–6:30	Shopping, swimming
6:30–7:30	Plan paper on fox habitats
7:30–8:15	Dinner
8:15–11	First draft of fox habitats paper

Planner lists

- Write a fresh list of things to do on a piece of paper or Post-it® note.
- Divide the list into "Today" and "Soon" (so you are aware of what you need to do long-term).
- Write items under headings so that they are easy to see: "Study," "Home," "Other" (or whatever headings suit you).
- Star or highlight the essential items.
- Attach or paper clip the list to the page opposite the current page of the planner.
- Cross out all completed items so that you are clear what is left to do.

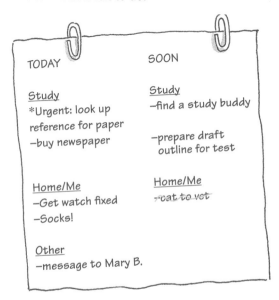

TODAY

SOON

Study
*Urgent: look up reference for paper
—buy newspaper

Study
—find a study buddy

—prepare draft outline for test

Home/Me
—Get watch fixed
—Socks!

Home/Me
—cat to vet

Other
—message to Mary B.

Time patterns

Look for time patterns that suit you. You may prefer to work in short spells of twenty minutes or find you are increasingly engrossed by study as the day progresses.

As far as possible, schedule study activities to suit your own time patterns. For example, if you begin slowly, schedule short activities, such as brainstorming ideas, early in the day. You may find it easier to write at night when it is quiet—or it may suit you to write in the mornings when you feel more alert.

Give yourself manageable short-term goals

Mini-goals

Set yourself mini-goals as milestones, so that you have a sense of achievement.

- Break larger assignments, such as writing a paper, into smaller tasks: "Read class notes," "Find resource materials," etc.
- Break each of *these* sections into smaller tasks: "Take notes on pp. 20–40 of *Business Management*."
- Set a realistic time allowance for each mini-goal: "Take notes on pages 25–45: 20 mins."
- Give yourself a start time—and stick to it!
- Set a target endtime. However, if you have not finished, keep going until you have.
- The important thing is not how long you spend studying but to *complete* each mini-goal.

Mini-goals work best when they are:

- *integrated:* clearly linked to a larger plan, such as your paper, project or your overall motivation for the course
- *manageable and realistic:* set yourself achievable goals
- *specific:* so you know precisely what you are going to tackle
- *measurable:* such as a set number of pages to read, or a specific section to write
- *flexible:* plan "empty" spaces into your schedule for emergencies, and be prepared to change things around if necessary.

Chapter 4

Ten time-saving suggestions

1 Save rewriting notes, and find more quickly what you have written

- Write on ready-punched note paper. (It can be moved more easily between files and rearranged as needs arise.) Notebooks are much less convenient.
- When taking notes, write each major point on a different sheet. Then, when you are writing papers or reports, you can shuffle pages as necessary. Make sure each page is adequately headed so that you can put it back in the right file afterwards.
- Write your notes on a laptop, computer or a digital notepad if you have one.

2 Save time writing notes

- Avoid writing notes in full sentences—use headings and keywords.
- Don't rewrite notes "neatly."
- Leave lots of space so you can add details later.
- Don't write the same information twice—if two writers make the same point, note in the margin a cross-reference to your earlier notes.

3 Save time looking for notes

- Keep them all in one place.
- File them as you go along.
- Number your pages, and label or color-code them by subject in the top outer corner, so that you can arrange and find information easily.
- Note where the information came from.
- Keep an (updated) guide to your files.

4 Save time reading

- Use "smart reading" strategies (*Am I a smart reader?*, page 98).
- Read only what is relevant for this paper or assignment.
- If something looks interesting for the future but is not relevant now, fill out an index card or make an electronic record, noting what looked worth reading.

5 Save time in writing and looking up your references

- In the margin of your notes, write the page reference from the book.
- For every book, article, etc. that you read, complete an index card (page 114).
- Alternatively, keep an updated file of your references on the computer—you will probably use some for more than one assignment. Some word processing packages have a card index facility.

6 Use word limits to focus your energies

- You need to research less, read less, note less and write less for an 8-page paper than for a 20-page paper. If you don't spend *less* time preparing and writing, you will take *extra* time later, reducing your notes and cutting text to meet the word limit.
- Plan your assignment to match the word limit (page 249).

7 Save time thinking

- Always carry a small book in which you can record ideas as they occur to you.
- Try "brainstorming" to get your mind working (see pages 106 and 237).

8 Save time organizing information

- Use numbers and highlighter pens to group information written on different pages, rather than writing it all out again.
- In the early stages of making pattern notes, use small Post-it® notes so that you can shuffle ideas around (see pages 106 and 247).

9 Save time writing

- Write assignments directly onto a computer.

10 Avoid duplicating effort

- Find a study partner to share research tasks and tactics and to bounce ideas off.

Study time

Use a photocopy of this sheet for each study period until you are happy with how you use your time.

Column 1 (fill out during study)	Column 2 (fill out after study)
Date: Where: Time I am starting: Study conditions:	Were the conditions, time and place the best possible? Could I improve anything?
How long am I going to study for in total?	How long did I study for?
How many breaks do I intend to take? Times of breaks (approx.)? Length of breaks?	When did I take breaks? Did I stick to the break time? If not, what do I need to do to get back to study?
Interruptions that occurred Type of interruption Length 1 2 3 4 5 Time finished: Total time worked:	How could I prevent these interruptions? Actual time spent really studying:
Thoughts and observations about my study habits and time management	

Chapter 4

Where does the time go?

If you are not sure where your time goes, for a few days pencil into your planner everything you do—roughly every hour. Be as accurate as you can—nobody will see this except you!

Work out approximately how many hours each day you spend on sleep, working out, lectures, etc. Make two photocopies of the *Time circle* (page 73), which is divided into a 24-hour day.

Circle 1: How I use time now

Using different colors or symbols for each type of activity, mark in where your time usually goes in a day. Treat each segment as roughly one hour.

Which activities are left out or don't receive enough time? Which activities take up too much time?

Example

- sleep—10 hr
- eating—2 hr
- socializing—3 hr
- personal/home—3 hr
- travel—1 hr
- lectures and classes—2 hr
- reading—2 hr
- writing—1 hr
- thinking—0 hr
- working out/relaxation—0 hr

Circle 2: How I want to use my time

On the second circle divide the day into how you would *prefer* to use your time so that your day is balanced between different activities. This is your goal to work towards.

Example

- sleep—8 hr
- eating and socializing—3 hr
- personal/home—2 hr
- travel—1 hr
- lectures and classes—2 hr
- reading—3½ hr
- writing—2 hr
- thinking—1 hr
- working out/relaxation—1½ hr

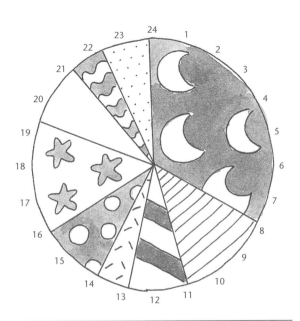

Time circle

Date:

Highlight one heading:

How I use time now   *or*   **How I want to use my time**

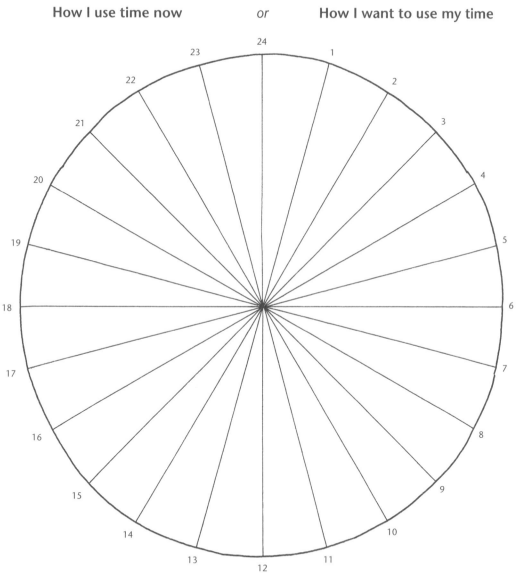

Chapter **4**

Key to shading

☐ _____   ☐ _____   ☐ _____

☐ _____   ☐ _____   ☐ _____

☐ _____   ☐ _____   ☐ _____

Strategies for managing online study time

Surfing, browsing and communicating online can be addictive and often take up much more time than we think.

Be rigorous in timing how long you spend online.

Monitor online study time

It can be useful and interesting to browse for material on a topic you are studying, watch online videos, listen to podcasts of whole lectures or send messages to students on matters related to your study.

- As these activities are for study, they can seem helpful even when they are not the best use of your study time. If you spend too long on any one of these, you can run out of time for other aspects of your study, such as reading or writing an assignment.
- Find out exactly how much time you spend on each type of online study activity.
- Consider if that time allocation is working well for your study.
- Use some of the suggestions on this page.

Plan online study

- Decide how much time to spend on each activity.
- Plan what time you will start each new activity. Put your list of start times where you can see it easily.
- Keep to your plan.

Use a timer

- Set an online timer or the alarm on your cell phone to go off a few minutes before the time you wish to start on your next activity.
- When the timer goes off, be strict in finishing your current activity so that you can get going on the next.
- It may take some time to work out realistic amounts of time to set for each type of activity.

Plan time for social networking and browsing

If you enjoy social networking and other non-study-related activity, then plan that into your day. You can then enjoy your leisure time online without the distraction of study—as well as studying without distractions or feelings of guilt.

Monitor online distractions

- When timing your online activities, be scrupulous in timing how much time you spend on things that distract you from your main study plan.
- Include distractions that take only a few moments.
- Note how much time it takes you to settle down to study after each distraction.
- Also note if the occasional minutes are really just that or if they add up to significant distractions.
- Add up the total amount of study time lost to these distractions over an hour, a day, a week, a year.
- Consider if that is how you still want to spend your time online.

2 hours for study

Minus 2 minutes logging on

Minus 10 minutes trying to find where I put the file

Minus 3 minutes answering a message from Sam

Minus 2 minutes on a quick email

Minus 10 minutes ordering a book

Minus 5 minutes online shopping …

Minus …

Total time spent studying: 17 minutes

Identifying and managing distractions

Time-eating "danger zones"

In terms of time management, our "danger zones" are those websites and e-resources that take up a disproportionate amount of our time. They can be useful sites that we overuse, sites that distract us too easily from our main purpose or sites that are launch pads to other sites. We tend to know our own "danger zones," as these are the ones we use the most or for longest, whether for entertainment, social networking or study.

- Take note of which sites, apps and tools take up a disproportionate amount of your time.
- Decide how much time you really want to spend on using these.
- How will you build reasonable use of your favorite sites or resources into your day?
- Consider how you will keep yourself to that amount: How will you monitor how long you are using each? How will you motivate yourself to close the site or app?

My "danger zone" websites and tools

The main websites and resources that take up too much of my time or distract me from study are:

1)
2)
3)
4)
5)
6)
7)

I'll manage my time using these by:

My "danger" apps

The apps that take up a disproportionate amount of my time or distract me from study are:

1)
2)
3)
4)
5)

I'll manage my time using these by:

Other distractions

You may find that you are also easily distracted by friends, family, personal interests, day dreaming, or a host of other things.

Other key personal distractions

The other main distractions that prevent me from settling down to study or draw me away from study once started.

1)
2)
3)
4)
5)

I'll manage my time using these by:

1. Know your weak points and don't pretend they don't matter! Mine is Twitter. I want to tweet all the time and I'm useless at doing bits of study between tweets so basically it is no tweeting for me when I am studying. It's just easier. I know I can send some smug tweets at the end of the day about how much work I have done!

2. I make myself study for 45 minutes and then I let myself "play"—play is looking at baseball scores, music videos, emails, games, anything I want. I need constant reward, so that is how I do it.

3. The thing about studying so much on your own is that you realize how you rely on other people, teachers or just others working around you to help stay concentrated yourself. When it is just you and the computer, you drift off more easily, so you need to give yourself ways of staying focused. I always start out by making a list of things I have to do—there's always more to add than I imagine, and that usually shocks me into getting down to it.

4. Emails are the worst. You can kid yourself that they are really urgent. You need to make yourself ignore the flashing signal that says there is a new email in the box.

5. I am very selective about which search engines I use—there isn't much point using lots of search tools when a really good one gives you as much as you are likely to need.

6. Sorting out how you use time—that is the one big thing to get right about study, especially if you go online a lot. In my first year, time just disappeared before I knew it and everything was rushed and my grades were OK but not great. This year I am the other extreme. I am constantly thinking about how I am using the time I have.

7. My advice to other students would be don't have your treats before you get down to work—study first or else it's much harder to make yourself do it!

8. When you are researching online there is always the temptation to look up just one more thing or to see what one more search engine turns up. You have to know when enough is enough.

9. I thought time management was a just a catchphrase, not something I should actually think about. I had no idea how much time I wasted until I actually started to take note of it. It made me realize all the things I could do if I was more disciplined in how I use time—so now I am!

10. I just don't waste time reading material on sites where I can't validate the source or the reliability of the information.

Reflection: Learning from others

Are any of these students' experiences similar to your own? What could you learn from their experiences and their strategies for managing time in online study?

Chapter **4**

Time management

	Analysis: How well do I spend my time?	Strategy: What I will do to improve
1 Do I use time efficiently? How do I waste time?		
2 What or who distracts me from study?		
3 Do I need to plan out my time for: – the year? – the semester? – the week? – the day? – each piece of work?		
4 Do I waste time getting started?		
5 Do I make the most of free time?		
6 Do I find time passes and I don't know what has happened? (See *Active learning*, pages 83–85.)		

Chapter **4**

PLANNER

Priority organizer

If you have difficulties in setting priorities, try using or adapting this sheet.

- *Column A*   Rate how important it is to do this at all. (6 = unimportant; 10 = essential.)

- *Column B*   If this is to be done at all, how important is it that you do it soon? (1 = must be done at once; 5 = it can wait.)

- *Column C*   Subtract the score in column B from

column A. The highest scores in column C are the most likely to be priorities.

- *Column D*   Number the order for completing the tasks and the time or date to do each.

- Highlight in yellow the thing you will do next. When it is complete, highlight it in red.

List of things to do	A need to do (scale 6–10)	B do now (scale 1–5)	C (A – B)	D order of priority/when

Chapter 4

The C·R·E·A·M strategy for learning

Working backwards from deadlines

	How long will it take?	When will I do it?	How long it actually took
Preliminaries			
■ Early brainstorming, reflection and discussion with others	_____		_____
■ Working out what is required	_____		_____
Research			
■ Working out which research methods to use	_____		_____
■ Working out what information/data I need	_____		_____
■ Assembling information (to read, watch videos, gather data, experiment, etc.)	_____		_____
■ Digesting and reflecting on the information collected	_____		_____
Organizing the content			
■ Grouping and organizing information	_____		_____
■ Selecting what to include	_____		_____
Writing draft versions			
■ Thinking about and improving each draft	_____		_____
■ Writing each draft	_____		_____
■ Likely number of drafts	——_expected_		___ _actual_
Completing the task			
■ Writing up the references	_____		_____
■ Writing the final draft	_____		_____
■ Checking your work	_____		_____
■ Final deadline	_____		_____

Use this information in planning your next assignment.

Chapter 4

Combining work and study effectively

Students may combine work and study in various ways and circumstances, such as:

- part-time students in paid employment
- students whose work is home-based, including family and care commitments
- full-time students who need to work for money or help out with a family business
- students whose programs include work placements or internships or are primarily work-based.

Benefits

Which of the following potential benefits of combining work and study are relevant to you?

- [ ] a broader range of experience and skills
- [ ] greater confidence in adult work settings
- [ ] increased maturity and self-reliance
- [ ] professional and/or business awareness
- [ ] understanding how academic theory relates to professional practice
- [ ] income from work
- [ ] networks and work contacts.

- What other benefits would work/study combinations bring for you?
- What arrangements would you need to make?

Before you start

If you want to combine study and work, it is worth investigating, early on, potential obstacles and ways of managing these. For example:

- [ ] Check that you can attend as required.
- [ ] Find out if there are classes, workshops, trips and other nonscheduled events you need to attend.
- [ ] Plan out typical weeks to see if your proposals are manageable.

- [ ] Check how your schedule might change from one semester or year to the next.
- [ ] Sort out your finances—study costs, loans and financial support can vary depending on what you earn and your mode of study.

Look for creative and efficient work/study synergies

If you are already employed and have sympathetic employers, talk to them about how best to manage your work with study:

- Can you undertake relevant work-based projects that could count towards your degree?
- Would your employer be willing to provide study leave, quiet space and time to study at work, or support towards costs?
- Are there ways your study could be counted as professional development as part of a work-related appraisal scheme?
- Some jobs lend themselves less easily to work/study combinations than others, but appropriate projects may still be possible.

Some jobs lend themselves more easily to work/study combinations …

Effective management of work-based projects

Most academic aspects of work-based projects use skills that are outlined elsewhere in this book. Such projects have specific logistical issues you must also learn to manage. Some key issues are identified on this page and the next.

Do you need your employer's consent?

Before undertaking a work-related project, check if you need your employer's consent. For assignments that are more theoretical in content, or that call on informal observations and your own experiences, often you will not need permission. On the other hand, you *will* need your employer's permission, for example:

- if you would be using work time or your employer's resources in carrying out an assignment
- if you would be making use of certain types of information acquired in the workplace (such as confidential or commercially sensitive information)
- if the nature of your assignment is such that you might lose the trust of your employer or your colleagues if they were unaware of it in advance
- if you are likely to produce work that could be published or stored, and in which your employer or clients might be identifiable.

Before giving you permission to carry out a work-based project, your employer may wish to impose conditions: If so, put these in writing so that you are both clear about what has been agreed.

Organize yourself for the project

- Check legal "data protection" requirements and consider how you will meet these.
- Gain permission for use of workplace data and information.
- If you are using observations, photographs, client material or the like, obtain written agreements from those concerned.
- Schedule interviews and observations early on to be sure that colleagues will be available when needed.
- Find out if you yourself need to undergo any

formal checks, such as criminal background checks, for example, if children are involved. Arrange such checks well in advance.

Workplace mentors

Students generally find it very helpful if they have a mentor to provide support. Ideally, this will be someone in the workplace who:

- knows the pressures the student might be under
- can help to negotiate access to data, relevant work tasks, study time or other resources
- can be a sounding board for ideas about what is feasible in the workplace
- can provide current professional and practical perspectives on issues.

Effective use of workplace mentors

- Build your relationship with your mentor. Show your appreciation for her or his time.
- Clarify what you need from your mentor, and when. Check before you start that he or she is able to provide these.
- To help your mentor support you as effectively as possible, identify what she or he will need from you for meetings, observations and at other times, and when this is needed.
- Arrange dates and outline agendas in advance for a series of meetings.
- Arrive prepared for each session. Ensure that you have completed whatever is asked of you.

Project-based skills: related sections

- *Working with others*, Chapter 10.
- *Research skills*, Chapter 5.
- *Managing an e-group project*, page 143.
- *Research projects*, Chapter 14.
- Recording your skills, pages 340–345.

Chapter 4

Effective management of study leave

Employers may offer flexible scheduling or time off to study at work or off-site. If managed well, this is a valuable resource.

Student comments

Half a day a week study leave made all the difference to me. It meant I could get onto campus to sort out administrative bits and pieces, meet instructors and so on, that would have been hard to do outside college hours.

For me, an afternoon a week was OK. I went to the library to read things that weren't online.

I didn't get much out of study leave. By the time I did the shopping and got home, the day was almost over and I had to start the family's dinner.

I tended to use the time to catch up on other things—not much on study.

I meant to take the half day but something always came up at work so it didn't happen.

I preferred taking a whole study day once every other week rather than a half day each week.

- What do the experiences of these students suggest to you about how best to approach and plan any time off you have to study?
- What kinds of circumstances might prevent you from making best use of study leave and what would you do to manage these?

Half-day or full-day leave?

Half-day leave can be the more difficult to manage effectively. It can mean time is wasted in travel, and provides less opportunity for consolidated study. It tends to suit people who:

- prefer short bursts of academic study
- like to study "little and often"
- have little travel to undertake
- manage study time well.

Making best use of time

If you prefer more concentrated bursts of study time, see if you can consolidate weekly study leave into longer, less frequent leave.

Making effective use of study leave

- Plan ahead so that you make most of the time available. For example, identify tasks that could be completed in the study time for that week, so that you gain a sense of achievement at the end of the study period.
- Check if there is a quiet room at work that could be used for study, to save travel time.
- If you have negotiated study time in the workplace, see if you can connect to appropriate online study resources from there. If not, would you study more effectively on campus?
- Plan use of your half-day study within the context of your overall working week. It may be more useful to rationalize certain activities at particular times. The specific time off given for studying might be best used for other activity if, for example, that cuts down on your overall travel time.
- If you find it better to use the time off for non-study purposes, ensure that you do put aside equivalent study time elsewhere in your schedule.

Active learning

Why is it important to develop the habit of active learning techniques?

1 Look at the illustrations on page 84.

2 Look at the characteristics of both passive and active learning, summarized in the chart below.

From these, you should be able to see for yourself why active learning methods make success more likely.

 What initial reflections and ideas do you have about whether your study habits are passive or active?

Characteristics of passive learning	Characteristics of active learning
1 You wait for directions and information to be fed to you.	1 You look for ways of being more involved in what you are learning.
2 Information is delivered to you—you just follow what is said or written and do as you are told.	2 You are engaged in the whole learning process (and in a position to see why information has been selected).
3 Different pieces of information are treated as separate units.	3 You look for links between different things that you discover.
4 You repeat information without understanding.	4 You make a conscious effort to make sense of, and find meaning in, what you learn. Understanding is usually deeper.
5 You don't reflect upon what you have learned.	5 You are involved in reflection and self-evaluation.
6 You may become bored and tired easily.	6 Your attention span is longer because your mind is more fully engaged.
7 You use surface processing (page 47), in which case you are less likely to understand or remember.	7 Long-term memory is assisted. If you understand what you learn, and keep relating what you learn to what you already know, you are more likely to remember what you have learned.
8 You are less likely to be able to use what you learn.	8 Linking information helps you to see how you can apply it to different situations.
9 What you study may seem irrelevant.	9 Learning is personalized and interesting.
10 You expect others to prompt you or to remind you of steps, stages and deadlines, so you often feel uncertain about what to do next.	10 You take charge of your learning and manage it like a project, so you feel confident that you know what to do, when and why.

Emphasis on action!

Consider the illustration below and the ideas on page 85. Jot down any ideas you have about making yourself a more active learner.

Inactive learning strategies (A)

A1

A2

A3

A4

A5

Active learning strategies (B)

B1 Prepare for lectures

B2 Set yourself questions

B3 Rework your notes

B4 Link ideas and information

B5 Discuss with others

B6 Mull things over

B7 Organize information

B8 Draft and redraft work

B9 Evaluate your own work

B10 Use feedback constructively

Chapter **4**

Active learning strategies

1 Check any of these active learning strategies you could try.
2 Select *two* to try this week.
3 Select *two more* to try later this month.

☐ Summarize a passage in 8–12 words. This makes you think about what you have read.

☐ Make spider diagrams—or other patterned notes. (See page 106.)

☐ Think of 3–5 real-life examples of what you have learned. This helps you to apply what you learn.

☐ Work out which is the best example, and why. This will help you to prioritize and evaluate.

☐ List 50 mini-questions about one aspect of the subject ("What, why, who, where, when, how did *x* happen?"). This helps you to explore the subject.

☐ Answer your own mini-questions. This helps you to research in an organized and focused way.

☐ Draw a diagram or a cartoon to illustrate a theory or concept.

☐ Write action plans—of things to do today, or this week or this semester.

☐ "Teach" what you have learned to a real or an imaginary person. Imagine you are giving a lecture or instructions.

☐ Keep a reflective study journal.

☐ Sum up the three most important points of a lecture. Which is the *one* most important point? This helps you to evaluate and select salient points.

☐ With other students, start a wiki.

☐ Make a wall chart or a large plan, linking all you have learned about an aspect of your studies.

☐ On your wall chart, in a different color ink, link information from another area of your studies.

☐ Which is the one best book for the subject you are studying now?

☐ Which section of the book you are reading is the most interesting or useful?

☐ Pretend you disagree with everything you are reading—how would you argue your case? What examples and evidence would you use?

☐ How does what you have learned link with your work or your everyday life?

☐ Invent essay questions for papers or essays. Give yourself 5 minutes to write a quick outline plan for one of these.

☐ List all the key points for one aspect of study.

☐ Draw a simple picture or symbol to remind you of each aspect.

☐ Discuss your ideas—or your difficulties— with other people.

☐ Contribute to your course chat room, or start one.

☐ Write key points on index cards or Post-it® notes. Juggle these around to see how many ways you could organize the same information.

Motivation and goal-setting

Your level of motivation will affect your success, especially in slow or difficult patches. It is likely that there will be times when you get bored, frustrated or anxious. You may feel as though you cannot be bothered with a piece of work or that you are struggling with your studies. You may even feel like giving up altogether. You will need clear motivation to keep yourself going even through such tough times.

Strengthen your motivation

Reflect upon your reasons for pursuing this course of study. Use the questionnaire (page 87) to help focus your thinking. Photocopy it so you can redo the exercise later and compare responses.

Decide which are the *two* most important factors for you.

Jot down your thoughts about why these are important to you.

If study becomes a struggle, look back over your answers to boost your motivation.

Keep setting yourself new goals and challenges

Set goals

Make tasks more manageable by breaking them down into mini-goals (see page 69). Set yourself small, short-term goals so that you are able to have lots of small successes. In time these add up to greater achievements.

Celebrate successes

Set targets and deadlines that are easy to meet—increase your chances of success. When you achieve a short-term goal (such as two hours' reading), reward yourself (for example, by taking a half-hour break).

Give yourself bigger rewards for completing whole tasks, to encourage yourself next time.

Mark success

Note down your achievements and successes in your reflective journal—it is important to identify what you do well, so that you can do it again!

After a few months, look back on your early work. Give yourself credit for any improvements you have made.

Aim for higher peaks

When you have met one set of goals, push yourself a bit harder. Make your next set of goals a little more challenging.

Find support

Find someone who encourages you and makes you feel good about yourself. Talk to this person about your goals and ambitions.

Attitude

Attitude is very important. Try to think of *difficulties* as *challenges*. If there is something you have to learn that seems threatening, consider the ways in which it can also be an opportunity to do something new.

Which aspects of being a student appear like "threats" or "problems" to you at the moment? How could these be seen as challenges and opportunities?

Chapter **4**

What do I aim to achieve in college?

What are the outcomes you hope to achieve by going to college? Circle the number that indicates how important each potential outcome is to you.

Outcome	Less important								Very important
Personal development									
To prove something to myself	1	2	3	4	5	6	7	8	9
To acquire more self-confidence	1	2	3	4	5	6	7	8	9
To broaden my horizons	1	2	3	4	5	6	7	8	9
To get my life out of a rut	1	2	3	4	5	6	7	8	9
To experience college life	1	2	3	4	5	6	7	8	9
Course-related									
To gain a higher education qualification	1	2	3	4	5	6	7	8	9
To learn more about a subject that interests me	1	2	3	4	5	6	7	8	9
To have the opportunity to study	1	2	3	4	5	6	7	8	9
To get a good grade	1	2	3	4	5	6	7	8	9
I just want to get through	1	2	3	4	5	6	7	8	9
Work-related									
To improve my career opportunities	1	2	3	4	5	6	7	8	9
To be better at my current job/employment	1	2	3	4	5	6	7	8	9
To improve my chance of promotion/higher salary	1	2	3	4	5	6	7	8	9
Other outcomes									
To show my family/friends that I can do it	1	2	3	4	5	6	7	8	9
To make up for having missed out on education when I was younger	1	2	3	4	5	6	7	8	9
To make new friends with similar interests	1	2	3	4	5	6	7	8	9

Chapter 4

Select two outcomes you have decided are important to you. Write in more detail about what you aim to achieve.

Look back at this from time to time to see if your aims and motivation for studying are changing. Use pages 88–90 to explore your desired outcomes further.

Using desired outcomes to guide study strategy

Your reasons for studying and your desired outcomes can guide the way you proceed with your study, as in the following examples.

Outcome A: to learn about the subject

If learning about the subject is the most important outcome for you, then reading around the subject and doing what interests you may be more important than following the curriculum.

Outcome B: to get a good grade

If your chief priority is getting a good grade, then it is likely to be important that you "play the game" and find out exactly what is required.

Outcome C: just to get through

If you have many other demands on your time or gaps in your education, you may have to limit yourself to covering essentials. What is important is that you know how to find and use information to get you through—you can fill gaps in your knowledge later in life.

Stating your desired outcomes

Outcomes are most motivating when stated in the present:

> I am able to achieve a 3.2 GPA!

It is also best to state them as positive objectives:

> I am able to gain a good job.

(Negatively formed outcomes, such as "A degree will help me to escape from my current job," are less effective in providing motivation.)

The effect of thinking negatively

Having a negative outcome is like going shopping with a list of what you are not going to buy.

O'Connor and McDermott (1996)

Analyze desired outcomes in detail

The following questions are based on an approach known as Neuro-Linguistic Programming (NLP). For each desired outcome, go through the following questions and the resource sheet on page 90.

Are your desired outcomes "well-formed"?

- Are the desired outcomes clear and specific?
- Are they at all limiting?
- Do they help you?
- Are they realistic?
- Are they sufficiently motivating?
- Are the outcomes worth it?
- Are they really desirable?
- How will you know you have achieved the outcomes—what will be different?

What are the implications of having these desired outcomes?

- Will you need to put everything else on hold?
- Will you have to change your study options?
- Who else will be affected?
- Are there other implications?

What are the potential gains?

- Will you feel more in control of your life?
- Will you have more respect for yourself?
- Are there other potential gains?

What are the potential losses?

- Will you see less of family and friends?
- What sacrifices are involved?
- Are there other potential losses?

Visualize yourself in the future, having achieved the outcome

- Where are you as a result of your achievement?
- Are there any good or bad consequences?
- What has changed for you?
- Are you as happy as you thought you would be?

What will you do to achieve the outcomes?

Visualize or consider exactly what you will do and when. For example, for an assignment, see the time laid out in your planner; watch yourself doing the required study. Ask yourself:

- Where am I?
- What am I writing on?
- What do I have available to drink or eat?

What obstacles might prevent you from achieving the outcomes?

Look at problems in advance.

- What could stop you achieving your desired outcomes?
- Have you set yourself too much to do?
- Are there people who would suffer?
- Who might try to stop you?
- What other obstacles might there be?
- How will you overcome each of these obstacles?
- Visualize yourself overcoming obstacles in the same way you did above, in relation to achieving the outcomes.

Fine-tune your outcomes

Keep modifying your outcomes until you have goals that feel, sound and look right for you.

- Use the chart on page 90 to clarify and focus your thinking about each of your desired outcomes.
- Do you need to reassess or reword the original outcomes so that they are more realistic and motivating?

Self-sabotage

It can be hard to accept that we may *achieve* our desired study outcomes. Many people have set patterns that they use in their daily life to sabotage their own best-laid plans.

It is not clear exactly why this happens. Sometimes it is simply hard to accept that we might now be successful where once we struggled. If we do succeed, we may start to feel that we should have

---

> ### Make a clear mental plan
>
> Create in advance the mental plan for as much of an activity as you can. Your mind will now orient you to achieve it.

tried harder in the past. If we fail now, however, this will "prove" that we were "right all along" in believing that we could not do something. At other times, we may fear failure so much that we just want it to happen quickly so that it is over with: Waiting to see if we can succeed may be too difficult.

Kinds of self-sabotage

Students sabotage their studies in all kinds of ways. Examples include:

- not going to lectures and classes
- not seeking help from their professors
- not using support services offered, for example, writing centers
- leaving work until the last minute and then missing deadlines
- not taking tests because they feel they will fail them
- filling their time with any activity *except* study
- refusing to enter a library
- spending all their time socializing.

There are many more to choose from!

- What kind of self-sabotage are you most likely to engage in?
- What kinds of events are most likely to trigger you into self-sabotage?
- How could you recognize that you had started to sabotage your studies?
- Is there anybody whom you would trust to point this out to you?
- What would you do to turn this around?

Chapter 4

Achieving desired outcomes

Desired outcome *State this with positive wording, in the present tense.*	
Potential gains	
Potential losses	
How I'll recognize when the outcomes have been achieved	
Targets (sub-goals)	
Possible obstacles	
Steps to overcoming obstacles	
How I'll celebrate success	

The C·R·E·A·M strategy for learning

Chapter 4

The C·R·E·A·M strategy

C·R·E·A·M strategy	How I will incorporate this strategy into my study
Giving more freedom to my imagination	
Finding ways to increase my enjoyment in study	
Personalizing what I learn and the way I study it	
Being flexible in study strategies and having plenty of variety	
Reflecting on my learning and evaluating my progress	
Organizing time and space, and being in the right state of mind for study	
Seeing where I waste effort by being overvirtuous	
Linking learning in one subject to other subjects and to real-life issues	
Increasing my motivation	
Formulating clear outcomes and subgoals	

Chapter 4

Review

This chapter has encouraged you to consider and to develop attitudes and approaches that make learning more interesting for you, as well as more effective. Successful study can be:

- personalized—through particular strategies, your learning preferences, your desired outcomes and your own motivations for study
- individual and varied
- creative, fun and enjoyable
- active and dynamic.

You will also have gained an insight into many ways in which you can study more effectively, through:

- your attitude to learning
- your organization of space
- an awareness of your time, such that you plan and monitor how you use it.

The attitudes and approaches covered in this chapter, and the personal qualities that these develop, are increasingly important features of the learning process at higher levels. As we will see in Chapter 6, new technologies also encourage personalized approaches to learning. This picture is also true for better jobs in the workplace— creativity, professional reflection, independence, self-reliance, self-motivation and evidence of personal effectiveness are valued and rewarded.

The C·R·E·A·M strategy is a general principle or "meta-strategy" that encourages you to consider your own attitudes and motivation and to apply strategy to any area of study or life. It encourages you to look for options and to identify for yourself how you could study more easily and successfully.

It is an open-ended strategy that you can adapt for yourself. How successful you are depends on your own creativity, your powers of self-observation and reflection, your personal effectiveness, your readiness to be actively involved in your learning process and your level of motivation.

Chapter 5

Reading, note-taking, and referencing

Informed opinions

In higher education you will often be told to use your own ideas and express your opinions. This means giving not just "commonsense" answers but your *informed* opinions, based on knowledge of recent or important texts in the subject area. You are expected to show a deeper understanding of the subject and to use more precise information than the average person in the street.

Chapter 5

The nature of research

Research, or "finding out," is something we do all the time. If we want to know more about a vacation resort, or about news we have heard, or where to get a good deal for a new purchase, we find out more—we do some basic research.

Depending on the topic we want to know about and how much detail we want to know, our methods will vary. The approaches we take will also differ according to whether a great deal of information is available easily or information is difficult to find.

Likewise, for academic study, there are different approaches, different methods, different levels of intensity and different degrees of systematic inquiry

depending on the subject discipline and the academic level. As you progress you will be introduced to specialized research skills, methods and approaches that are suited to your own particular academic discipline or major.

This chapter and the chapters that follow introduce you to some generic skills and approaches that underlie more advanced research skills. You may have well-established skills in some of these areas already, such as being skilled in reading or taking notes, but here you will learn how to apply those skills more effectively and in ways appropriate to a higher academic level of study.

Identifying the task

The nature of the task

We saw above (page 43) that successful students tend to spend more time in the early stages of an assignment, working out exactly what is required. Before launching into any piece of work you are set, take time to clarify in your own mind exactly what is required. Use this knowledge to plan how best to prepare for the work—being clearly focused at the outset will save you time later.

Survey the field

- *Organize and plan*   Plan your work and allocate your time according to what you are expected to produce.
- *Read carefully through the instructions for the assignment*   How many parts are there to the question or task? What is really being asked? (See pages 242–243.)
- *Consider the purpose of the assignment*   Why this particular topic, and why this particular wording? Is the assignment one that is always set for this class because it covers essential background? If so, what is it that you need to know? Or is it topical, related to recent research or an issue in the news? If so, what is that issue?
- *Consider the completed piece of work*   What should your work look or sound like when it is finished? (See Chapters 12 and 14.)
- *Check the grading criteria*   Display them where you can see them, and use them to guide your work.
- *Scale your research to the time and the page limits*   Consider what is expected, given the scale of the assignment. Be realistic. Do your research and note your findings according to what you can use within the time and page limit available.

What do I need to find out?

For any piece of academic work, you will be required to undertake some research. At the very least this will include:

- background reading to explore the subject and to pick out the key themes and issues
- identifying the leading figures for this topic—the people whose primary research, theories or writings are regarded by academics as essential to know about, even if you do not read their work in detail
- some investigation into the variety of views held on the subject and what has been written on the core issues—do writers agree or disagree, and in what ways and why?
- some specialist reading, such as a recent or important journal article, or perhaps an essential text or set of texts on a given topic.

In other words, start by surveying the area. As an undergraduate, you may not necessarily need to read a great deal on any one topic, but you do need to be aware of the fields you study—what is important, what stands out and why. Develop a feel about which topics are worth focusing on and which are more peripheral.

Managing the peripherals

As you carry out your research, you will come across all kinds of information that will intrigue or fascinate you and that you may want to pursue. You will not have enough time to follow up everything that catches your attention, however, so you must:

- decide what is essential
- decide what else you have time to pursue now
- make a list of topics to follow up later.

Making the most of the library

Library services

The starting place for most research is the library. Visit your college library as soon as possible, and find out about the range of services available. Typically, there will be:

- academic journals
- specialist collections
- photocopiers
- laminators
- binding services
- computers
- CDs, DVDs, films, slides, and video resources
- silent areas and study rooms
- specialist resources for students with disabilities
- facilities for making audiovisual aids for your presentations
- support on how to use library resources.

If the institution is split over more than one campus, ask what is available on each and how you can access different facilities.

Catalogs

Most catalogs are now electronic. There may also be specialist collections for some subjects, as well as indexes for national collections. It is quite usual to need help using these—if you are uncertain, don't be afraid to ask. Online searching is discussed further on pages 130–134.

Make the library your own

To use the library you will usually need your student number and ID card, so make sure you take these with you.

Walk around the library and become familiar with the atmosphere. Sit at different tables—try different rooms. Where would you work best?

You did say to make myself at home in the library

To see how the library works, look up books from your syllabus. Try out the technology. It is designed to be easy to use even if you know nothing about computers—give it a try!

Find out basic information

- How many items can you take out at once?
- How many items can you take home on loan?
- How long does it take for books to come from the stacks (in storage) or from other sites?
- For how long can you have books out?
- Can you reserve books?
- Can you reserve or renew by phone?
- Are there fines?
- How do you make interlibrary loans?
- Are there subject-specialist librarians?

For more information about working electronically, see pages 130–134.

Finding information in the library

Finding books in the library

- Fiction is arranged in alphabetical order by authors' last names.
- Reference books are arranged by subject. Each subject is given a number, which is shown on the spine of the book.
- All the books on a given subject are grouped together on the shelves.
- You can find a book's reference number by looking it up in the library catalog.
- Most catalogs are now electronic. For more about electronic searches, see pages 130–134.

It helps to find books if you already know:

- the author's last name and initials
- the title of the book.

Journals or periodicals

Journals or periodicals usually contain the latest research for your subject, as well as book reviews. Most journal articles have a short "abstract" at the beginning that tells you what the articles are about. Browsing through the abstracts and reviews helps to keep you up to date with the subject. You will be expected to refer to articles in most assignments.

Journals are published at regular intervals during the year. They are collected into numbered volumes, usually one for each year. To find a journal article, you need to know:

- the title of the journal, the year it was published and its volume number
- the name and initials of the article's author
- the title of the article.

Indexes and abstracts

Indexes and abstracts are separate publications that give brief details of journal articles, including who wrote what and where to find it. Sometimes reading the abstracts will be sufficient for your assignment; at other times you will need to read the original article also.

In the indexes, you can search by subject heading and by keywords for all the articles on a given subject. They are updated regularly and are well worth using.

Electronic information

An increasing amount of information is being published electronically. This includes anything from mail-order catalogs to academic journals. A lot of electronic information is located at publicly available sites on the World Wide Web (www), which is accessed via the Internet. Your college may have its own intranet, with websites used only within the institution—you may be asked to write your own "page" on it.

To locate information on the Internet, you type in the address at which it is stored. This will consist of short abbreviations. Spaces, dots, dashes, oblique strokes and letters must be typed in very precisely. This, for example, is the address of the website of Friends of the Earth:

> http://www.foe.org

Having logged on to the Internet, you would simply type this in on the computer screen in the space provided. (You can usually omit "http://".)

On your syllabus, you may be given the names of useful web pages. Type in the address of one and browse the information that comes up on the screen. You can print it out and read or highlight it as printed text.

For more about searching online, see Chapter 6.

Activity

- Check the classification system (or systems) used to group books in your library—Dewey Decimal Classification (DCC), Library of Congress (LC), etc.

- Which number range applies to your subjects for each system?

Identifying and selecting relevant information

Reading selectively

Use the syllabus

- In some classes, your syllabus will list a large number of readings and you will be expected to select from a range. In others, you might get a short list and be expected to read everything on it. If in doubt, ask your instructor what is expected.

Select the latest information

- To keep up-to-date, look under "new titles" in bookstores and look for the latest issues of journals on the library shelves or in the computerized catalog.
- Check if statistics and similar data are up to date. Are more recent figures available? If so, should you use these?

Select the most relevant information

- Look for the information that relates most exactly to your assignment.
- Draw up a draft outline and see what information you will need. Which themes came up in lectures and classes?
- Check the back cover of the book, the contents list and the index to see what the book covers.
- Quickly scan the introduction or conclusion: These may indicate if the book is worth reading. They may even provide all the information you need!
- Browse through the headings to get a feel for the book.

Select by reliability

- Is the source a well-known one in the field, such as a recommended academic journal?
- Is the source likely to be biased? If so, does the bias matter in this case?
- Does the text have a good bibliography? Is it clear where any evidence comes from?
- Is the source from a publisher respected in the subject area? (Information in newspapers or from friends is not usually considered reliable.)
- See also *Critical analytical thinking*, page 149.

Select by amount

- Use your draft outline to work out how much space to devote to each major theme, and then for each topic or example. You will find that you will have very few words to write about any one item.
- Use this plan to guide you on how much to read and note. If you can only write a line or paragraph about something, you probably don't need to read and note very much.
- Consider whether an article goes into too much depth for your purposes: You may only need to read the abstract or one section.
- Keep asking if material is relevant to the essay question or assignment prompt.

What do I actually need to read?

If you usually read books from cover to cover, try the following exercise to see how little you could read and still get what you need.

Activity

- Read any information on the back cover. Browse the contents page, section headings and the last chapter. Take a few quick notes on what seem to be the main points of the book. Record only the gist of what you read.
- Read the introductory and concluding paragraphs of each chapter. When you finish reading, note any extra important information.
- Read the first line of each paragraph. Note any additional important information.
- Now read the whole book. How much really important *additional* information did you gain by reading the whole book? Which parts of the book were essential? How little could you have read to grasp the essentials?

Am I a smart reader?

Do you have strategies for approaching your reading? Which of the following do you do?

Know exactly what you are looking for

☐ Have I considered what questions I'm trying to answer?

☐ Have I considered what information I need?

Use the syllabus selectively

☐ Have I looked at the list of assigned readings?

☐ Do I know what I *need* to read?

RECOMMENDED READING   *need to read*

1 Jones, E. (1952).   *pp. 66-80*

2 Smith, B. (1998).   *Chs 4 - 6*

3 Atkins, J. (1952).   *intro*

Examine sources for suitability

☐ Have I considered each source? Have I considered:
  - if it's on the syllabus?
  - if it's up to date or fairly recent?
  - if it looks readable and manageable?
  - if it has the information I want?

Select relevant parts of the book

☐ Do I browse the book quickly?

☐ Do I use the contents page, the index, the headings and the sub-headings for guidance?

☐ Do I identify which parts of which chapters I need, and put markers in these?

Very relevant book

Activity

Practice finding information quickly

Try using an index (at the back of the book).

- Select an item to look up.
- Note the page numbers given.
- Using these, find the item in the book as quickly as you can.

Index
eggs 6, 19
Elba 114
elk 1, 94
ewes 37

How long did this take you? Could you get faster? Did you notice that when you know what you're looking for, your eyes can pick out information on the page more quickly?

Find information quickly

☐ Have I tried using an index?

☐ Have I gotten faster with practice?

Select relevant parts of the page

☐ Do I read the chapter heading?

☐ Do I read any subheadings?

☐ Do I read the first sentence of each paragraph (which should introduce the topic or idea)?

☐ Do I look at any diagrams, graphs or charts?

☐ Do I read any summaries or conclusions?

Chapter 5

Use photocopies

- ☐ Do I make photocopies of important pages?
- ☐ Do I use marker pens to highlight important words and phrases (only)?
- ☐ Do I jot ideas and thoughts in the margins?
- ☐ Do I take notes about the points I highlighted, to help myself remember them?

Using large photocopies

- ■ For an important diagram or map, make an enlarged photocopy. Attach it to a large poster.
- ■ As you read, photocopy short key passages. Reduce them in size and attach them to the poster.
- ■ Link ideas using color and arrows. Add your own notes.

These posters are very useful when studying for tests.

Chart the main ideas

- ☐ Do I map out ideas so that I can see how everything fits together?

Practice second-guessing

- ☐ Do I keep trying to anticipate what is coming next or what the conclusions will be?

Read interactively

- ☐ Do I think about what I'm reading?
- ☐ Do I question what I'm reading? Do I look for answers to my questions?
- ☐ Do I take notes of the important points and ideas triggered by what I read?
- ☐ Do I challenge the assumptions of the writer, the logic of the arguments and the validity of the conclusions?

Vary reading speed and method

- ☐ Do I keep changing the pace, according to the needs of the text? (See page 102.)
- ☐ Do I scan rapidly for specific information?
- ☐ Do I read quickly to get the general sense of a passage and then read difficult or dense parts slowly?

What is the main point or basic idea I have just read?

Can I sum it up in 10 words?

Do I agree?

Chapter 5

Engage with your reading

Be active in your reading. As you read, always have paper and pen to hand.

There are three major conclusions...

Use markers

☐ Do I label a corner of my own texts with a keyword summary?

☐ Do I insert labeled bookmarks so that I can find details easily, and need fewer notes?

☐ Do I give star ratings to valuable pages, making them easier to find later?

Listen to yourself read

☐ Do I record myself reading important passages?

☐ Do I listen to these as I travel or work around the house?

Using two recorders

■ If you have two recorders, speak your ideas into one as you listen to material on the other.

Maintain your attention

I read that three times and I don't remember a word...

☐ Do I take in what I read?

☐ Do I make sure I'm doing so, by:
  – summing up each section?
  – taking regular breaks?
  – reading interactively?
  – moving on when material isn't relevant?

Create ideal conditions

☐ Do I read with the light from behind, sufficient to light the page but without glare?

☐ Do I sit with a relaxed, upright posture?

Consider time and place

☐ Do I read when I am sufficiently awake and alert?

☐ Does the environment help me focus?

Reading off the computer screen

☐ Do I read best from screen or from paper?

☐ Do I adapt text on my computer to make it easier to read? (See page 142.)

I prefer Arial font 16 blue

Improving reading comprehension

Do I understand what I read?

Do you:

☐ understand most of what you read?
☐ know how much you understand?
☐ understand uninteresting material?
☐ actively monitor your understanding?
☐ know how to improve comprehension?

If you answered "no" to one or more of these questions, experiment with the following active reading strategies to improve your comprehension.

Active reading strategies

Start with something general

Reading is easier if you have a sense of the context and a general overview. Read the most basic text you can find first. Familiarize yourself with the main issues and the vocabulary.

Monitor your comprehension

Read a few sentences, then stop. Without looking back at the text, sum up what you have read in just a few words. Say these words aloud, or jot them down. If you cannot do this, read back over what you have read, using an additional strategy from below.

Guide your reading

Set yourself specific questions to start off your reading. Write them down. Adapt the questions as your reading progresses. The clearer you are about what you are trying to discover, the easier it is to find it in the text.

Reread difficult passages

Academic texts often contain difficult passages. Don't panic! You are bound to need to reread some passages slowly several times.

Highlight keywords and phrases

On your own text or a photocopy, underline in pencil the information you think may be relevant.

Look especially at headings and first and last sentences of paragraphs. Select a few of the keywords you underlined and highlight them in color. Double-underline or star very important points. Make a faint wavy line at the side of fairly important passages. Be selective! If you underline or highlight everything, *nothing* will stand out as important.

Color-code information

Use different colors for different kinds of information—for example, one color for reference names and dates, and one for each of the main schools of thought or major theories for the subject. Later, just seeing that color combination on the page may bring back to you what the page was about.

Ask "depth questions"

Look for the underlying issues:

■ What point is the writer making?
■ Why is this detail relevant?
■ Is the writer trying to answer a particular question?
■ What lessons can be learned from this text?

Apply the C·R·E·A·M learning strategy

Consider how you can apply the C·R·E·A·M strategy (Chapter 4) to your reading.

Relaxed reading

Reading comprehension is improved when the body is relaxed. Use appropriate lighting; have music or silence, as you prefer; and drink plain water. See Chapter 4 on *The C·R·E·A·M strategy for learning* and pages 210–211 on relaxation.

How do I approach reading tasks now?

How could I spend my reading time more effectively?

Improving reading speed

Understanding is the most important aspect of reading, but you will find it helpful if you can also improve your reading *speed*.

How to check your speed

- Find something familiar to read.
- Set the alarm for ten minutes.
- Read for ten minutes at a speed that allows you to understand what you read.
- Count how many words you read.
- Divide this number by ten, to find out how many words you read in one minute.
- Do this using different texts. If you read fewer than 200–250 words per minute, even with material that is clear and interesting, it is worth trying to increase your speed.

Vary your reading strategies

Inspect

Check the title, the contents page, the index, the writing style and the details on the back cover. Flip through to get the feel of the book. Do you *want* to read it? Do you *need* to read it?

Scan rapidly

Scan the page. Which keywords leap out at you? You may sense the "pattern" of the argument or the general subject matter. Is information organized in a way that helps you? What can you pick up from section headings, diagrams, the first lines of paragraphs and conclusions to chapters and the text?

Question

Keep asking questions: What am I trying to find out? What do I need to know? Exactly which parts do I need to read?

Locate specifics quickly

To find a specific piece of information quickly, use

What is slowing down your reading?

Below is a list of some factors that can slow down reading. Do any apply to you? If so, try the relevant strategies for speeding up your reading (page 103).

- ☐ 1 Do you read advanced texts very infrequently?
- ☐ 2 Do you track with your finger along the line?
- ☐ 3 Do you read out loud under your breath, or mouth the words?
- ☐ 4 Do you read books from cover to cover?
- ☐ 5 Do you start reading before you have worked out what you need to know or what you are looking for?
- ☐ 6 Do you read word by word?
- ☐ 7 Do you keep checking back along the line, rereading what you have just read?
- ☐ 8 Do you read difficult sections before you have worked out the general gist?
- ☐ 9 Do you find that the words seem to jump up off the page or that text moves or glares?

---

the index. Go straight to the right page. Move your eye quickly down the page to find what you are looking for.

Read at the right speed

Read at the appropriate speed for the task. This may be fast for case studies, novels and well-developed arguments, and slowly for texts that condense detailed information into short passages or use unfamiliar specialist vocabulary. As you become more familiar with the ideas and vocabulary used, your speed will increase.

Recall and review

Check that you understand what you have read. What is the basic argument or idea? Does the text answer your questions? Are you convinced by the evidence and the arguments offered? How does what you have read relate to what you already knew? Does it confirm or challenge your views? What else do you need to find out?

Strategies for speeding up your reading

For each of the problems noted on page 102, there is something you can do to improve matters.

1 Read more advanced texts

Reading improves with practice. Your brain becomes more used to seeing unusual words and your mind to dealing with complex sentences and ideas. Also, look for subjects that interest you and read more for pleasure.

2 Finger-tracking

Move your finger down the page, directly from top to bottom, to train your eye to move more quickly down the text.

3 Know when to read aloud

Some people read out loud from habit. Reading silently can speed up reading in such cases. However, other people can only understand what they read if they *hear* the words. If you read aloud for this reason, try recording yourself so you can reread "by ear" rather than by eye.

4 & 5 Read selectively and actively

Be choosy in what you read. Use the active reading strategies suggested on pages 98–100, such as working out what you are looking for. You will finish reading more quickly, even though your reading speed may be the same.

6 Read larger chunks

Allow your eyes to take in larger chunks, either by resting them less frequently along a line or by taking in larger sections of text as you browse. Experiment with holding the book further away, so that your eyes can take in more at once. This is also less tiring for the eyes, which allows you to read for longer periods.

7 Build up to difficult texts

Background knowledge of a subject helps to increase reading speed and understanding. If a text looks hard, start with something simpler on the same subject or read the easiest sections first. You can return to complex sections or more difficult books later.

8 Keep your eyes moving forward

Which of these sentences is easier to read?

A Checking back over back over what what you have read makes understanding checking back makes understanding checking back over makes understanding difficult.

B Checking back over what you have read makes understanding more difficult.

Most people find **B** easier to read because they can take in a larger chunk of memorable "sense." Encourage your eyes to keep reading forward to the end of a sentence (to the next period). You will then be reading larger units of sense rather than just words and phrases. You can read the whole sentence again if necessary.

9 Jumping and glaring text

Colored filters (such as see-through plastic folders) placed over the page may reduce "jumping" and "glaring." Experiment with different colors and see if one suits you best. Using tinted paper may help.

Consult an optometrist for advice—you may need glasses with colored lenses or a particular filter.

Enlarged photocopies of text can help.

If the problem is serious and you prefer to "read by ear," speak to the disability adviser at the college. There may be specialist equipment to enable you to scan texts and have them read aloud to you or reading services that record books for you.

Slow reading is sometimes helpful

In some cases slow reading is preferable:

- for texts with condensed information, such as many science and medical texts
- for detailed instructions
- for formulae and equations
- for close analysis of texts, such as for law, literature and history.

Taking notes

Why take notes?

How many reasons can you find for taking notes? After you have noted some, look at the diagram on page 104. Are your reasons the same? Which of these matter most to you?

Activity

Note taking

Select a passage from a book and take notes on the main points of what you read—or find some notes you have already made.

Compare your notes with the suggestions made below. Do you want to make any changes to how you make notes?

How to take notes

There is no one "best method," but it is worth considering the following points.

What do you need to note?

Consider:

- Do you really need this information? If so, which bits?
- Will you really use it? When, and how?
- Have you noted similar information already?
- What questions do you want to answer with this information?

A method for taking notes

- Put your pen down—so you won't be tempted to copy out of the book.
- Read—to answer your own questions.
- Identify and sum up the main ideas. (Hear them in your own words.)
- Jot down one or two words to remind you.
- Note *exactly* where information comes from.
- Note real names and quotations *exactly* as they are written.
- Leave space to add details later.

Organize your notes

- See *Recording and using information* (page 109).
- See *Organizing information: planning your writing* (page 247).
- Use a separate file for each subject area.
- Use file dividers to separate major topics.
- Use a separate page for each minor topic.
- Arrange ideas under headings or questions. (Notice how information is organized in this *Handbook*.)
- Label files and dividers clearly.
- Number and label pages so you can find and refile them easily.
- Keep an updated contents page at the front of each file.

Note-taking styles

Nuclear notes: why take notes?

Is taking notes a useful activity? Why take notes at all?

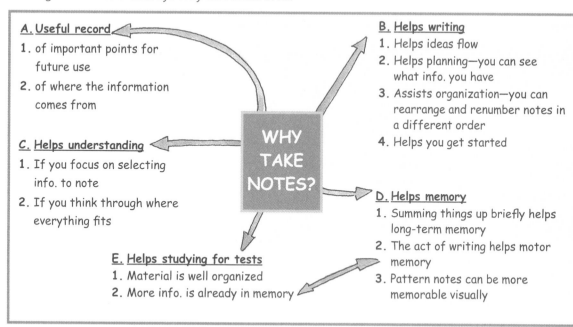

A. Useful record
1. of important points for future use
2. of where the information comes from

C. Helps understanding
1. If you focus on selecting info. to note
2. If you think through where everything fits

E. Helps studying for tests
1. Material is well organized
2. More info. is already in memory

WHY TAKE NOTES?

B. Helps writing
1. Helps ideas flow
2. Helps planning—you can see what info. you have
3. Assists organization—you can rearrange and renumber notes in a different order
4. Helps you get started

D. Helps memory
1. Summing things up briefly helps long-term memory
2. The act of writing helps motor memory
3. Pattern notes can be more memorable visually

Linear notes: strategies for taking notes

① Good note-taking: general
1.1 Think before you write
1.2 Keep notes brief
1.3 Keep notes organized
1.4 Use your own words
1.5 Leave a wide margin and spaces—to add notes later

② Useful strategies
2.1 Note keywords and main ideas
2.2 Write phrases—not sentences
2.3 Use abbreviations
2.4 Use headings
2.5 Number points
2.6 Make the page memorable—with color, illustrations, and so on
2.7 Link up points—using arrows, dotted lines, color, numbers, boxes

2.8 Note sources of info. exactly
2.9 Write quotations in a different color

③ Unhelpful strategies
3.1 Copying chunks and phrases
3.2 Writing more notes than you can use again
3.3 Writing out notes several times to make them neater

④ Tidying messy notes
4.1 Draw a "square" around sections of notes in different colours to make them stand out
4.2 Use a ruler to divide the page up between sections
4.3 Circle floating bits of information
4.4 Link stray information by color-coding it

(See Buzan 1993.)

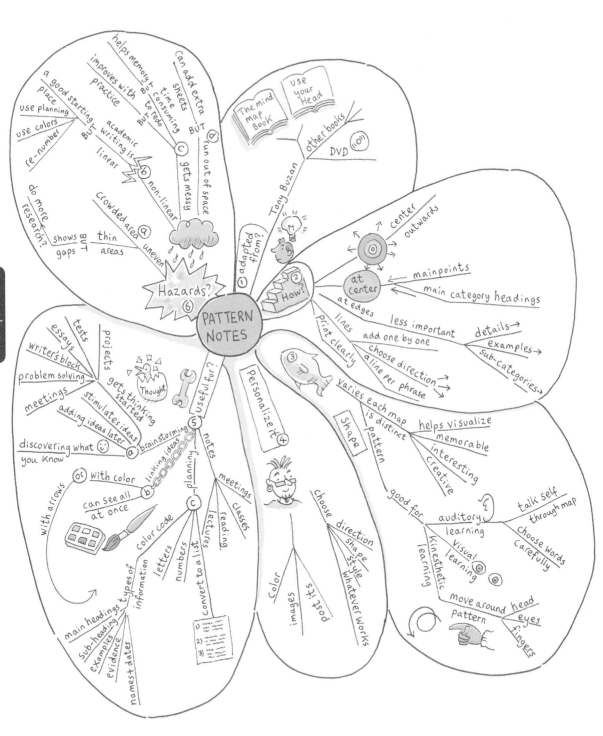

Chapter **5**

Shortcuts in note-taking

Leave space

Leave space in your notes and a wide margin, so that you can add new information and ideas later. (This is much quicker than *rewriting* your notes to incorporate the new information.)

Have just one set of notes

Aim to have just one set of notes. Visual familiarity will make it easier to find information later and to recall information during tests.

Use labels

Carry Post-it® notes with you. When you have an idea, write it on a note and stick this on a blank sheet in a plastic folder. You can move these around as you plan assignments.

Number the pages

Label and number pages. Cross-refer to information already noted elsewhere—for instance, "see red file, page 24, Amphibians."

Use abbreviations

Abbreviations save time. Use them in your notes, but not in assignments.

- Work out a system you'll remember.
- Stick to your system.
- Introduce a few at a time, so that your notes make sense.
- Keep a "key" to your abbreviations near you until you know them.

Useful common symbols

Symbol	Meaning
& (+)	and
+	plus, in addition to
>	greater/more than/better than
<	smaller/less than
=	is the same as/equal to
≠	is not the same as
∴	therefore
∵	because
w/	with
♀	woman/female
♂	man/male
→	this leads to/produces /causes

Useful common abbreviations

Abbrev.	Meaning
e.g.	for example
i.e.	that is, that means
etc.	and the rest
NB	important, notice this
p.	page (pp. = pages)
para.	paragraph
Ch.	chapter (Chs. = chapters)
edn	edition
info.	information
cd	could
wd	would
Govt	Government
Educ.	Education
impt	important
devt	development
C19	nineteenth century

Which abbreviations are used in *your* subject areas?

Taking notes with confidence

Students' solutions

Sonja and James are two students who used to have great difficulties taking notes. Here are their accounts of how they tackled their difficulties, with help from a study skills advisor.

Sonja

There are two things which I find difficult about taking notes.

Firstly, I am not very confident about using my own words—the book always seems to say things better. It is very tempting to use nearly the same words as the book. I imagine that I will rewrite them in my own words later—but then I have the time, or I forget which bits are taken from the book, and end up with the words of the book in my paper without even realizing.

The second thing I find difficult is working out what to take notes about, especially keeping to essentials. I worry in case I leave out information I will need in the future. I can end up with 10 pages of notes from reading only a few pages. It takes ages and there is too much to even look at a second time. When I came to study for my first test, I had too many notes to look at—there were simply too many to read, never mind learn.

Now I spend more time thinking and planning before I even touch a book. I try to work out what information I want. I draw a mind-map with everything I already know, and what I need to find out. Looking at the essay question, I do a rough plan really early, even before I start reading—just to get the shape in my head.

I always start with the easiest book—just to get a picture of what it is all about. With other books, I use the contents page and headings to work out where information is. At this stage I don't write much except something like "gold—producer countries: p. 248 and pp. 265–9."

When I have more idea of what I am looking for and where that information is, I take more detailed notes. Sometimes, I do this by writing a question and putting the information as an answer. When I am not sure if I want some information, I just write a few lines onto an index card, saying where I can find that information later if I really need it.

James

I find it hard to take notes in lectures. I used to record lectures and then type out all my notes—which took up all my time and I got very stressed. These days I go quickly through the books before lectures so I know what is likely to come up in the lecture and then I won't worry about noting it all down. I write out obvious headings on the large index cards that I prefer. Then I only have to add in a few words under each heading—to remind myself of something. When I get home, I listen to the recording and add in other bits onto the cards by hand. It's much quicker than the old way. Sometimes I listen to the recording and then speak my ideas to my computer—it has "speech to text." I don't do this much as it has problems—you have to be careful not to dictate straight from the recording and end up with the lecture in your paper—but sometimes I summarize things this way.

These are just two approaches to dealing with note-taking. Do Sonja's or James's ideas appeal to you? Or have you a better system?

Recording and using information

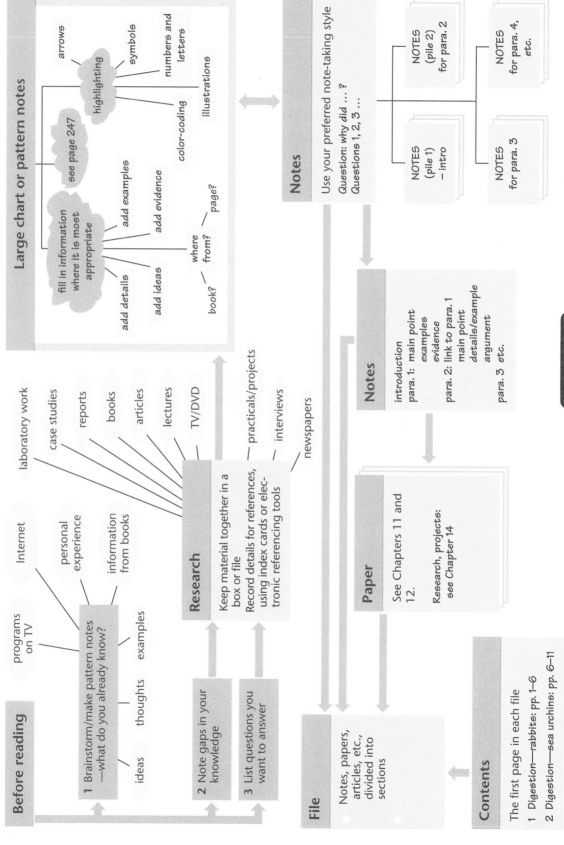

Before reading

1 Brainstorm/make pattern notes —what do you already know?

ideas thoughts examples

programs on TV Internet personal experience information from books

2 Note gaps in your knowledge

3 List questions you want to answer

Research

laboratory work case studies reports books articles lectures TV/DVD practicals/projects interviews newspapers

Keep material together in a box or file

Record details for references, using index cards or electronic referencing tools

Large chart or pattern notes

highlighting arrows symbols numbers and letters illustrations color-coding

see page 247

fill in information where it is most appropriate

add examples add evidence add details add ideas

where from? page? book?

Notes

Use your preferred note-taking style

Question: why did ... ?
Questions 1, 2, 3 ...

NOTES (pile 1) – intro

NOTES (pile 2) for para. 2

NOTES for para. 3

NOTES for para. 4, etc.

Notes

introduction
para. 1: main point
examples
evidence
para. 2: link to para.1
main point
details/example
argument
para. 3 etc.

Paper

See Chapters 11 and 12.

Research, projects: see Chapter 14

File

Notes, papers, articles, etc., divided into sections

Contents

The first page in each file

1 Digestion—rabbits: pp. 1–6
2 Digestion—sea urchins: pp. 6–11

Plagiarism

What is "plagiarism"?

Plagiarism is using the work of others without acknowledging your source of information or inspiration. This includes:

- using words more or less exactly as they have been used in articles, lectures, television programs, books or anywhere else
- using other people's ideas or theories without saying whose ideas they are
- paraphrasing what you read or hear without stating where it comes from.

Even if you change words or sentences you have "borrowed" or put them in a different order, the result is still plagiarism. It is important to familiarize yourself with your college's official policy on plagiarism. Plagiarism is treated very seriously, with potential consequences ranging from failing the assignment to expulsion from the college.

Using quotations

Quotations should be:

- used sparingly—and only if the words really are worth quoting
- brief—a few words or, at most, a few lines.

In writing a quotation, you should:

- copy words and punctuation *exactly*
- use three dots (…) to indicate omitted words
- put "quotation marks" around the words you quote (like this: *"Stunning," wrote the artist.*)
- say exactly where the quotation comes from (see page 113).

Develop confidence in your own words

Use your own words, even if you don't think you write well—they count for more than copied text.

Other people's words make a poor lifeboat

How to avoid plagiarism

- Write all your notes in your own words.
- Note down *exactly* where you read the information you put in your notes.
- In your assignment, write out where ideas and information come from:
  - reference your work (see pages 112–114)
  - make clear when you use direct quotations
  - write a full list of references and, if required, a bibliography (all the books and other materials you used).

If you have a habit of copying:

- Put your pen out of reach.
- Read a passage without taking any notes.
- Stop reading and cover up the page.
- Sum up what you have read. If possible, talk aloud, or record yourself, so you hear your own words and in your own voice. If this remains difficult, look back to *Improving reading comprehension* (page 101).
- Once you can say what the passage is about, note it down in your own words.
- If you want to copy material to use as a quotation, write it in a different color so that you can find it easily. The color will also show you how much you copy.

Detecting plagiarism and copying

Read each of the pieces of text below and decide if the text is an example of plagiarism, and why. The original text, on which the examples are based, can be found on pages 38–44.

Text 1

Research shows that students who do best at problem-solving spend longer than other students at working out exactly what a problem is before they try to solve it. Weaker students look at the surface of the problem and do not see the underlying structure that makes it similar to problems they already know.

Text 2

Many people undervalue their own intelligence because they hold mistaken views about what constitutes "intelligence." This is partly because too much emphasis has been placed upon the idea of "IQ." In addition, early educational experiences can damage self-esteem or be demotivating, undermining a natural interest in learning. There is a body of research that argues that outstanding performance in almost any field of human activity can be fostered if the right conditions are in place. Those conditions include finding the right learning strategy for each person.

Text 3

There is strong evidence to suggest that environment plays a great part in intellectual performance. In Japan, the Suzuki Violin Education Program has trained many children to play the violin to virtuoso level. Being part of a culture that values academic intelligence also helps. Donaldson (1978) argued that the way we reason depends upon the particular context we are in.

Text 4

"There is strong evidence to suggest that environment plays a great part in intellectual performance" (Cottrell, 2012). Cottrell writes: "In Japan, the Suzuki Violin Education Program has trained many children to play the violin to virtuoso level." She also points out: "Being part of a culture that values academic intelligence also helps." Cottrell cites Donaldson (1978), who argued that the way we reason depends upon the particular context we are in.

Text 5

The reasons for appearing "intelligent" or not may depend upon a complex set of factors, all of which interact (Cottrell, 2012). Butterworth (1992) suggests that we can even believe ourselves to be incapable of a task that is well within our capacities. This can occur simply because we do not recognize the similarity of two tasks when the circumstances appear different. This view is supported by research. It has been demonstrated that students who spend more time early on actively looking for similarities between writing tasks and areas of existing expertise are then more successful at the writing task (Bloggs, 2007). This suggests that academic success may be more a question of good strategy and of building upon experience rather than underlying "intelligence."

Text 6

Various psychologists have used experiments on identical twins to suggest that anything up to 80% of our intelligence could be genetically based. Others argue that twins' similar physical appearance and cultural upbringing could account for similarities in their performance. While people who do well on one intelligence test do well on other such tests, there is evidence that such performance is also affected by familiarity with the culture and thinking of those who designed the test.

For discussion of these texts, see page 120

References

Why are references needed?

In academic writing, it is essential to state the sources of ideas and information. Such "references" allow readers to refer back to the sources for themselves.

There are five main reasons for providing references.

1 Acknowledging a source is a courtesy to the person whose idea or words you have used or referred to.
2 By giving the source you make it clear to the reader that you are not trying to pretend somebody else's work is your own. (You are not "plagiarizing" someone else's work.)
3 The source helps your readers to find the original texts or websites to read themselves, should they wish.
4 If you need to check something later, the reference will help you find it again more easily.
5 People will have more confidence in your assertions if they know where your information comes from. Thoroughness in referencing suggests that you will also have been thorough in checking your facts.

When do you need to give a reference?

You must give the reference whenever you draw on a source of information:

- as your inspiration (in general)
- as the source of a particular theory, argument or viewpoint
- for specific information, such as statistics, examples or case studies
- for direct quotations (reproducing the writer's exact words)
- for texts and electronic information that you paraphrase rather than quote.

What information is included in a reference?

Imagine that you wished to read for yourself a source text used by another author. What information would *you* need to locate that source easily? The information usually provided includes:

- the name and initials of the author(s)
- the title, in full
- the year of publication
- for journal articles, the name of the journal and the number of the volume
- the edition, if relevant
- the location of the publisher
- the name of the publisher
- relevant page numbers
- for electronic materials, the webpage address.

You may know that extra information is needed. For example, to find a photograph, print or manuscript, you may need the name of the library, the collection and the catalog number of the item within the collection. The important question to ask is, "Could somebody else *find* this source from the information I have given?"

Where do you put this information?

In the body of the text

Whenever you refer to someone else's work, either directly or indirectly, indicate whose work it is.

Referencing styles vary from subject to subject. Common formats include MLA, APA and Chicago. Make sure you use the format recommended by your instructors. Usually this will be simply the surname of the author(s), the year of publication and possibly the page number(s), using parentheses in one of these ways:

> ... as noted by Cohen and Smith (2008, p. 56), who said ...

> ... two researchers (Cohen and Smith 2008, p. 56) noted ...

At the end of the assignment

Write out full details in a list of "References"—see page 114 for guidance and page 360 for an example of such a list.

Giving references

There are various ways of acknowledging your source materials. **Check if you are expected to use a particular system for your course**. If not, use the author–date system.

The author–date system

When you have used, quoted or paraphrased a source, acknowledge it. Either within the sentence or at the end of the sentence, write in parantheses the author's name, the date of publication and the page numbers. Full details of the source should be written out in the reference section.

Text citations

Here are three different ways of using sources.

Short direct quotation—within the text

> Nonetheless, the film was deliberately inaccurate about the life of José Marti. Jesus Colon (1982, p. 82) pointed this out when he wrote, "José Marti never had a mansion or a hut of his own. Needless to say, he never had slaves."

Paraphrasing

> Nonetheless, the film was deliberately inaccurate about José Marti, who, contrary to the image depicted in American films, spent much of his life in poverty (Colon 1982, pp. 81–2).

Longer direct quotation

A few words, carefully chosen, make the most powerful quotations and demonstrate that you can select appropriately. Avoid long quotations; they are rarely needed. If the exact wording of a long quotation is essential, however, indent it and leave space above and below (as shown on the right). Incorporate the quotation clearly into your writing with linking sentences and by discussing its relevance.

References list

In the "References" at the end of the paper, the reference to Colon would appear in this form (and in alphabetical order):

> Colon, J. (1982). *A Puerto Rican in New York and Other Sketches*, 2nd edn. New York: International Publishers.

Note that for books you don't give page numbers in the "References." For a journal article you give the page numbers for the whole article.

Useful phrases to introduce references

- As *X* points out, …
- According to *X*, …
- To quote from *X*, "…"
- *X* states/suggests that …
- *X* tells/shows us that …
- In an article entitled *Name of Text*, *X* makes the point that …
- Referring to …, *X* says that …
- As *X* stated/wrote/said, …
- In *Name of Text*, *X* wrote that …
- Writing in *Name of Text*, *X* explained that …
- Writing in 1926, *X* argued that …

Angry at Hollywood versions of Latin American history, Jesus Colon wrote:

> After pictures like *Zapata* and *Santiago* we can only hope that these Hollywood vulgarisers and distorters, without the least bit of respect for the history and culture of our Latin American nations, won't lay their bovine eyes upon epic themes like the Aztec struggle against Cortes' conquest of Mexico, or Sandino's fight against American imperialism … (1982, p. 84)

Here we can see that Colon is very critical of versions of Latin American history produced in the United States.

Writing out references

Use index cards

Fill out an index card for each source you use, using paper or cards, or a computer-based equivalent.

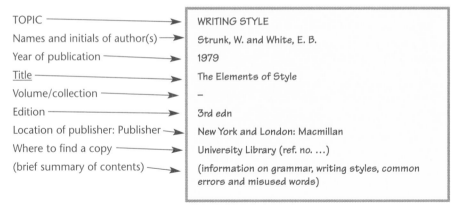

TOPIC — WRITING STYLE

Names and initials of author(s) — Strunk, W. and White, E. B.

Year of publication — 1979

Title — The Elements of Style

Volume/collection — –

Edition — 3rd edn

Location of publisher: Publisher — New York and London: Macmillan

Where to find a copy — University Library (ref. no. …)

(brief summary of contents) — (information on grammar, writing styles, common errors and misused words)

The advantages of this approach are that:

- you will know exactly where to look if you need to double-check some point
- writing the "References" page is much easier
- if you use a computer, you can simply "cut and paste" references when you reuse them.

Conventions in writing references

- Don't number the items.
- Begin each source on a new line.
- List alphabetically, by author's last name.
- If you use more than one work by a given author and published in the same year, label these a, b, c … (2008a, 2008b, 2008c, …) in the text and in the "References."
- Put information in the same order (author, date, title, location of publisher, publisher) as in the examples below or as your instructor recommends.
- Underline the title of the book or journal (or use italics, if available).
- Use quotation marks for the title of an article within a journal.

Include:

- All sources you refer to, including DVDs, CDs, TV, tapes and the like, but not dictionaries or grammar books.
- Don't include in "References" materials you have not used in your assignment.
- List additional sources, which you read but did not use, in a "Bibliography."

Sample references (see also page 360)

A book:

> Zoelle, D. (2000). *Globalizing Concern for Women's Human Rights*. New York: Palgrave Macmillan.

A chapter in a book:

> Humm, M. (1991). "Landscape for a literary feminism: British women writers 1900 to the present." In Forsas-Scott, H. (ed.). *Textual Liberation: European feminist writing in the twentieth century*. London: Routledge.

A journal article:

> Jones, C. (1980). "The welfare of the French footsoldier." *History* **65** (no. 214), 193–213.

Material cited within another text, where you have not quoted the original source:

> O'Connor, J. and McDermott, I. (1996). *Principles of NLP*. London: Thorsons. Cited in Cottrell, S. M. (2012). *The Study Skills Handbook*. Basingstoke: Palgrave Macmillan.

An electronic reference (include the date on which you used it):

> http://www.foe.org. August 18, 2011.

Bibliographies

A bibliography is a list of everything you read for the assignment, whether or not you referred to it in your writing. Your instructor may prefer this to a references list or may even require both. Use the same style as for references.

Chapter 5

Getting the most out of lectures

Lectures are designed to be useful starting points for research, giving a general overview of the subject, its main ideas and theories, and evidence from recent research. Together, these will guide your own reading and reflection.

How to make lectures easier to follow

Before the lecture

- Get a feel for the subject. Read (or just flip through) a book on the subject of the lecture. Look for themes, issues, topics and headings. Look up any technical words you don't understand.
- Write down questions you want answered. Leave space to write the answers under each question either during or after the lecture.
- Jot down your own opinion. Notice if it changes during the lecture.
- Glance through your notes for the previous lecture, and look for links with the next lecture.

During the lecture

Instructors vary about whether they prefer questions during or after the lecture. Instructors usually go quite quickly, and expect you to jot down main themes and references.

- To focus attention, listen for clues as to where the lecture is going. For example: "There are five major categories of ...," "Now I want to look at ..." or "Why did this happen?"
- Good instructors tell you at the beginning which main topics will be covered and in which order or write headings on the board.
- Take notes of headings, questions, sub-points, and references.
- Avoid writing details you can easily get later from a textbook. Keep your attention for your listening. If you are not clear where information comes from, ask.
- In your head, challenge what the instructor says: This will help to focus your attention. Ask, "Is this always the case?," "How representative is this?," "Why is this?" and "Do I agree?"
- Indicate new questions raised by the lecture in a different color.

After the lecture

- Label and file your lecture notes and any handouts.
- Read through your notes. Fill in details from your reading or research.
- Discuss the lecture with others. Compare your notes and fill in any gaps.

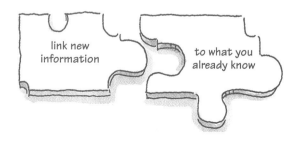

link new information to what you already know

Lecture notes: cover sheet

Subject area/class: Year: Credits:

Subject of lecture: Instructor:

Preparation Questions and ideas prompted by reading or discussion prior to the lecture; what do I want to find out during this lecture?

Opening comments by the instructor Issues, questions, etc., to be addressed during the lecture

Main theme of the lecture

Main points made in the lecture; examples or evidence given (*Use supplementary sheets as necessary*)

Questions raised by the lecture

References to books, etc.

Chapter 5

How helpful are your notes?

Using notes provided by instructors

In advance of a lecture, during it or after it, your instructors may give you printed notes. These may be transcripts of lectures, PowerPoint handouts, outline notes or background text. They may be printed out for you or posted on a website.

Knowing that you have these printed materials, you may be tempted not to make your own notes—or you may feel overwhelmed to receive so much to read all at once.

- If you are given a large set of notes at the beginning of the semester, check how much of these you need to read each week.
- Whenever possible, read lecture notes before the lecture. This will help you to follow the lecture.
- When you are given printed notes, make them your own, for example by highlighting, condensing or annotating them.

Many of the reasons for taking notes outlined on page 105 apply even when you are provided with excellent printed notes. By working on these notes to produce your own set, you will:

- ensure that they make sense to you
- make the content your own
- absorb and remember the information.

How helpful are your notes?

For each of these sets of opposite statements, place a check mark along the line depending on how far it is true of your own notes.

Record your ideas about how to improve your notes. What is the priority?

Easy to read	Hard to read
Brief, to the point	Too detailed
Easy to understand	Hard to understand
Well organized	Poorly organized
Pages numbered/labeled	No system
Easy to learn from	Difficult to learn from
Well abbreviated	No abbreviations
Important ideas stand out clearly	Not easy to see important points
In my own words	Chunks copied from books or lectures
My words clearly separated from quotations	Easy to confuse my words with quoted material
Source material clearly referenced	Hard to see where material comes from

Problem-solving

Why are you given problems to solve?

Exercises in problem-solving are opportunities to learn useful skills with many applications. Such exercises allow you to:

- practice specific procedures
- put theoretical knowledge to practical use
- develop reasoning abilities and creativity in finding answers
- develop your understanding of underlying principles
- research topics in detail.

You can apply a problem-solving approach to any research or study activity.

Stages in problem-solving

1 Define the task

- What exactly is it that you have to solve?
- Is this a particular kind of problem?
- What *sort* of answer is required—a research paper? Formula? A number? Action?
- Is this problem similar in any way to previous problems or tasks you have done? Could solutions from a previous problem apply to this? (See pages 42–43.)

2 Look at it from different angles

- Look for similarities with any other kind of problem you have solved. What has it in common with these? How far will previous solutions work here?
- Reword the problem.
- Sketch the problem as a diagram.
- Identify the parts of the problem that you find most difficult. Is there another way of looking at these?
- Talk it through with others.

3 What information do you need?

- Would any of your notes be useful?
- Which theories or cases apply?
- What other resources would help?
- Who can you ask for information?

4 Consider alternative solutions

- What are the advantages of each solution?
- Would each work?
- What might be the disadvantages of each?
- Which is the best option overall? Why?

5 Write up the problem

- Explain clearly how you tried to solve the problem—your methodology. Explain how you arrived at the solution. (In papers, this stage is generally omitted.)

6 If you didn't succeed, why not?

- Did you link the new problem to similar problems?
- Did you have enough information?
- Did you "play" with ideas enough?
- Did you misunderstand what was required?
- Did you consider alternative solutions?

Organize your approach

It may help if you draw up a chart. For example:

Definition of the problem:		
Similarity to other problems:		
Information needed:		
Resources or people who could help:		
Alternative solutions	Advantages	Disadvantages
1		
2		
3		

(Adapted from Freeman and Mead 1991.)

Practicals and laboratory work

What are practicals and laboratory work for?

These vary a great deal from one subject to another, but some general principles are outlined below.

Practicals

Practicals are designed to help you:

- learn how to use equipment
- practice using equipment and techniques
- see what happens when you put theory into practice
- practice following appropriate procedures
- practice using methods which you may need in professional life.

Health and safety

Make sure you know and understand any health and safety regulations—and follow them carefully.

Laboratory work

Laboratory work is designed to help you:

- develop skills in identifying and clarifying aims
- develop skills in accurate observation
- develop skills in recording data
- practice applying and interpreting data
- practice reporting on your methods, findings and conclusions.

Basic principles

Be assertive

Make sure you get your fair share of time using equipment. Don't be content watching others—give it a try yourself.

Ask

If you are concerned about using equipment with which you are not familiar, ask for help.

Find out

Which theory is the practical supposed to be testing?

Discuss

Discuss your findings with your instructor and with other students.

Read

Read around the subject. How is the theory or the experiment applicable to real life? What kinds of results have other people had?

Record

Record *exactly* what happens. Don't change your results to what you think or know the "right answer" to be.

Many experiments work only in ideal conditions. Your instructors will know this and will be looking to see how you record your method and data, and your discussion of why you think you got the results you did.

Write it up

Write up your method, results and conclusions neatly and clearly. Find out the required format for writing up practicals and experiments in your subject area. Are you expected to include diagrams, tables and graphs? Are you expected to use color?

Review

This chapter has looked at *general* research skills that are common to most subjects, such as identifying and selecting the most relevant information, developing reading strategies and making clear references to your sources. You need some skills, such as being able to focus your listening, take notes, identify key points and acknowledge the sources of your information, whether you are in a class, on a group project, doing case-study observations or on work placement. Although undergraduate research is generally based on reading, other study activities, such as lectures and practical work, are part of the research process. For any new study challenge, you can adopt a problem-solving approach.

Some subjects require you to learn very specific research skills, especially in the final year. These skills will vary according to the subject. Some use sophisticated observation techniques, others use statistics or specialist equipment. Undergraduate work does not usually involve gathering entirely new data or formulating new hypotheses or finding great problems to solve. Whether you are using general or specific research skills, your task at this level is mainly to develop the basic techniques and demonstrate that you understand the principles involved.

The following chapters look at other aspects of research, such as working online, using numbers, and writing up your findings. Chapter 14 focuses on research projects while Chapter 7 looks at the critical thinking skills required as part of research.

Research is not an activity that can be divorced from other areas of study. Chapters 11 and 12 look at ways of writing up your research, and Chapter 7 goes into more depth about how to take critical, analytical approaches to research. It is also worth browsing again through Chapter 4 to see how you can apply C·R·E·A·M strategies specifically to research.

Answers to activity: Detecting plagiarism and copying (page 111)

Text 1 This is plagiarism (pages 43–44). Although a few words have been changed, this is copied out almost entirely word for word, and there are no references. It is not acceptable.

Text 2 This is not an example of plagiarism because it summarizes the original text (pages 38–50) in the writer's own words. The quality of the text could be strengthened by including some references. However, the summary is sufficiently general to mean that references are not essential in order to avoid plagiarism. It is acceptable.

Text 3 This plagiarizes the original text (pages 39–42). It copies, almost word for word, a sentence or bullet point from each of these pages. Instructors refer to this as "cut and paste" or "scissors and paste" writing. It is not acceptable.

Text 4 Text 4 is almost identical to text 3 but is properly referenced. However, instructors would not be pleased to see so little in the student's own words. If this continued throughout the paper, it would receive a very low grade. It would simply be well-referenced copying—which is not acceptable.

Text 5 This text is in the student's own words. The student has made his or her own connections between different parts of the original text in a meaningful way rather than simply "cutting and pasting." The student has read other material on the subject and included this. There is proper referencing both of the source of ideas and of individual pieces of research. This is acceptable work.

Text 6 This student simply paraphrases the source text (page 39). This might be acceptable for writing a summary or a journalistic type of article. However, there are no references and little evidence of any independent thinking or "working" with the material. This may not be deemed to be plagiarism or copying, but for a paper or report it would receive a low grade.

Chapter 6

E-learning, technology, and personalized learning

LEARNING OUTCOMES

This chapter offers you opportunities to:

- identify the skills you want to develop

- understand basic health and safety issues for using a computer

- identify how computers and technology can be used to support study

- learn key terminology

- know how to use the Internet for different kinds of searches

- recognize how to be a successful e-learner

- understand how you could use e-resources and methods for personalized learning

- identify skills and resources for managing an e-group project.

As a student, it is highly likely that you will need a range of computer skills. Electronic media are now essential for the background research for most college assignments. Increasingly, students are required to use a computer in producing papers and other assignments, and often to submit their finished work to the college or individual instructors by email.

Electronic resources are also used in other ways: To supplement class-based teaching; to provide a variety of new learning opportunities; to assist in distance learning; to provide study support; and in communications between students and college administrators.

The level of technological expertise you need depends largely on your program and how it is taught, but also on how you yourself prefer to learn. It is a great help if you have gained some computer skills before arriving in college. However, colleges in the US generally provide classes to develop the relevant skills. These may be offered by the library, by a resource center or skills center, by your department or by a local college. If you need to use specialist software relevant to your program, such as software for statistical analysis, your academic department will probably provide its own training.

This chapter introduces some of the main applications of technology and e-learning that you are likely to encounter as a student in higher education. It supports you in making the most of the enhanced learning opportunities that this technology provides.

Using computers for effective study

Why bother with computers?

Presentation

You can present your work to make a better impression, using headings, tables and other tools (page 262). Computers can also spell-check your work, number pages and count words.

Drafting

You will probably write several drafts of each piece of writing. Computers allow you to edit easily, to move, delete or add text and to correct errors without having to rewrite the whole text for each draft. This saves time and allows you to experiment more when writing.

IT skills

IT skills are now required by instructors and employers. For example, you may be asked to word-process your work, to send your assignments by email, or to find information on the Internet.

Handling data

You can use databases and spreadsheets to sort information quickly, to calculate long lines of figures and to do complex statistics quickly.

Storage and mobility

IT enables you to store large files of information on CD or a flash drive. This makes it easy for you to store information and carry it around.

Almost anybody can use IT

There's no need to be left behind by the IT revolution!

- You don't have to type well.
- You don't need specialist computer knowledge.
- Training and advice is available at most colleges.
- There are computer adaptations to match most disability requirements.

Information technology can help you

To store information   To sort information

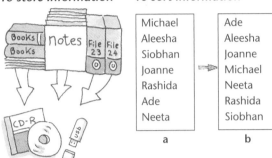

	a		b
Michael		Ade	
Aleesha		Aleesha	
Siobhan		Joanne	
Joanne		Michael	
Rashida		Neeta	
Ade		Rashida	
Neeta		Siobhan	

To do other tasks

This chapter includes further information about using IT for study.

You can also use IT:

- to move text around
- to edit writing
- to prepare statistics
- to create tables
- to count words
- to check spellings
- to store references
- to calculate
- to organize data
- to send and receive email
- to research on the Internet

… *and much more!*

Try it! It's easy. You just follow the instructions on the screen.

Basic health and safety when using a computer

Positioning

Position yourself 13–23 inches away from the screen, with your eyes looking down at 15–20 degrees and your head at a comfortable angle (1). The angle at the elbow should be about 90 degrees (2). Your feet should both be flat on the floor or on a foot rest (3). Remove obstacles that prevent you from stretching your legs.

Seating

Invest in a good computer chair with a stable five-legged base (4). You should be able to adjust the backrest (5) so that your back is supported in an upright position (6). The height should also be adjustable (7), so that your forearms are horizontal. Avoid excess pressure on the underside of the thighs and the backs of the knees (8).

Viewing

Place the computer at rightangles to the light source, so as to avoid glare and reflection on the screen. Avoid bright lights.

Take care of your eyes

Do not stare at the screen for long periods—print out some materials instead. Take frequent breaks. If you study primarily using a computer, be sure to have frequent eye tests.

Contact lens users

The heat from computer monitors may dry out contact lenses. It may help if you wear glasses instead, use tear-substitute drops or consciously blink more often.

Using the keyboard and the mouse

When using the keyboard or mouse, keep your wrists straight (9). Use a light touch. Do not hold

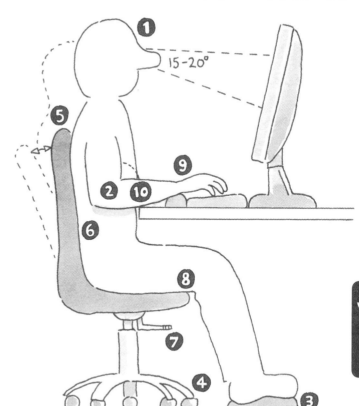

the mouse tightly. Keep it near you so that you do not need to stretch your arm to use it. Leave room to rest your forearm on the desk. Consider using a wrist support (10).

Avoiding problems

Fast typing and repeated use of the mouse or other controls can lead to pain in the upper limbs, especially if you work under pressurized conditions or in the wrong position. Take frequent breaks. Use wrist supports, and avoid fast clicking and keying over long periods.

Some computer users experience headaches. Factors that may contribute to these include poor posture, reading text that is too small, working for long periods without a break, stress, glare from the screen, inadequate seating and poor lighting.

What computer skills do I need?

Below is a list of skills. In the first column, check skills you want to learn; in the second, check those that are priorities. If you have, or acquire, the skill, check the final column.

Skill	To learn	Priority	Can do
Setting up and general skills			
▪ Assembly—connecting computer, keyboard, mouse, and printer			
▪ Switching the computer on and off			
▪ Keyboarding			
▪ Using a mouse or navigation pad			
▪ Understanding toolbars			
File management			
▪ Creating, opening, naming, saving and closing files			
▪ Setting up folders and creating a filing system			
▪ Finding files you have used before			
Word processing			
▪ Moving the cursor around the page and pausing it			
▪ Moving the page—up, down, left and right			
▪ Using the arrow keys to move around a document			
▪ Changing the *font* and size; using **bold**, *italics*, and underlining			
▪ Using bullets and paragraph numbering			
▪ Justifying to the left, justifying to the right or centering text			
▪ Using the *undo* and *redo* functions			
▪ Copying, cutting and pasting text from one place to another			
▪ Deleting text			
▪ Selecting a piece of text and dragging it from one place to another			
▪ Inserting a symbol € © ☎ ✂			
▪ Using headers and footers			
▪ Adding page numbers			
▪ Checking the word count			
▪ Using the spell checker			
▪ Replacing text that recurs throughout a document			
▪ Using drop-down menus			
Tables			
▪ Setting up a table within a document			
▪ Inserting and deleting rows and columns			
▪ Merging and splitting cells			

Chapter 6

Skill	To learn	Priority	Can do
Using the printer			
▪ Specifying the page size and shape			
▪ Selecting a portrait or landscape layout			
▪ Printing a whole document or selected pages only			
Using email			
▪ Sending and receiving emails			
▪ Forwarding emails			
▪ Replying to emails			
▪ Deleting emails			
▪ Ensuring that your mailbox does not overfill			
▪ Setting up email folders			
▪ Sending email attachments (e.g. documents)			
Using the Internet			
▪ Connecting with the Internet			
▪ Navigating around the Internet			
▪ Making the most of the Internet (see page 129)			
▪ Searching on the Internet (see pages 130–134)			
Using software and resources			
▪ Finding, opening and closing required software packages			
▪ Using a calculator			
▪ Using a database			
▪ Using a spreadsheet			
▪ Using PowerPoint			
▪ Installing new software			
Help			
▪ Using electronic help			
▪ Knowing where to go for help			

How you actually carry out each of the activities above will depend on the type of computer and the software you are using.

Other people may be willing to show you how to perform particular operations. Often people find their own shortcuts or have slightly different ways of carrying out the same operations.

We all develop computer skills in varied ways—through training, from software manuals and help systems, with support from friends and colleagues, and by trial and error. Provided that your files are safely stored, don't be afraid to experiment.

- ▪ About which aspects of using a computer do you feel least confident?
- ▪ Of the skills you know you lack, which do you put off learning?
- ▪ How would you best learn new skills?
- ▪ Whether from the list above or in a more specialized context, which skills do you need to develop next?

Organizational skills for studying on the computer

The most challenging aspects of working on a computer are:

- keeping track of where information is filed
- losing information, if something goes wrong
- computer faults of one kind or another, which may eat into your time.

The following suggestions can help to organize your work, avoid frustration and save time in the long term.

Name new files when you open them

It is not unusual for people to save a piece of writing without giving the file a name. They may then think the computer has gone wrong when they cannot find the document.

Choose filenames carefully

- Use names that remind you of the contents of the files.
- Observe the rules for the computer you are using. For example, on many computers you are unwise to put a dot (.) in the filename as the computer may misinterpret letters that follow and make it hard for you to find the file.

Put the filename in the "footer" text

As soon as you have named the file, type its name in the running text at the foot of each page, so that it will appear on the document when you print it out. If you need to find a file several months later, you are unlikely to remember which file relates to the paper document unless you have put the filename in the footer. If you make several drafts of a document, make sure you know which is the latest version.

In the footer, record the name of the file and details of where it is stored, so that you can find it easily in the future. If you have used a CD, you could include the CD's name as well.

Example

Suppose that you are using a personal computer (PC). You have saved the third draft of a paper on Piaget for cognitive psychology in a folder called "cogpsych." The footer might then say:

piaget1c.doc / folder cogpsych / CD cognitive psychology

(On such a computer system, ".doc" indicates that the file uses Word, a word processing package.)

Keep files small

Avoid creating large files, as these slow you down. Divide your material into smaller files. Use filenames that indicate the sequence (for example, "piaget2.doc" and "piaget3.doc").

Use a different file for each draft

Add a number or letter to indicate to yourself that this is the second draft. (For example, you could use "piaget1b.doc" for the second draft of the first part of a long paper on Piaget.)

Save your work every few minutes

If the computer goes wrong for some reason, such as a temporary loss of power, you may lose all the work you have done since the last time you told it to "save." To protect your work, save your work frequently. (You may be able to set the computer to save the file automatically, such as every ten minutes.)

From time to time, copy the file to a CD or flash drive. Losing information and having to start all over again is very frustrating.

Organize your electronic storage

- Copy important files twice, using two CDs or flash drives.
- Label your CDs. Use a case to carry them.
- Keep your flash drives where you can find them easily. Personalize them with paint or accessories so that they are easily identifiable as yours.

Make folders

Most computers have some way of grouping files, so that you can keep files relating to a particular subject together. This is like keeping related papers in files and organizing the files in drawers of a filing cabinet—it keeps related things together and enables you to find what you want more quickly.

Make hard copies

A hard copy is a printout of a document. If there is a problem with the computer or a CD, the hard copy allows you to see what was in the files while you wait for the problem to be fixed. Printed text is easier to proofread than text on the screen.

Keep a list of filenames

Print out a list of the files that are on the CD or flash drive and store this with them. Keep a copy near your computer, if you have one, as this will remind you where to look in an emergency. You may find it helpful to add a few words saying what each file holds, especially if you are limited to a short filename that cannot tell you very much about the file. (Opening files repeatedly to check what they contain wastes time.)

Be aware of compatibility issues

If you are working at home, check if your own software is compatible with that of your college. It is important to install antivirus software and to ensure that this is updated regularly. Many antivirus programs can be set to update automatically when the computer is linked to the Internet.

Manage your time

When planning tasks that will use a computer, leave time for hitches, such as being unable to open large files on the Internet or email, files being sent to you in formats that your computer cannot open or problems with Internet access. Instructors expect you to plan for such hitches—delays of this sort are not usually acceptable as excuses for handing in work late.

Dealing with jams

If your PC stops responding, hold down the three keys ALT, CTRL and DEL. A menu may appear to tell you where the problem lies. You may see a message, such as "Program not responding," and be invited to end the task. Bear in mind that in accepting this invitation you will probably lose any of your work that you have not already saved, so make certain, first, that there is no alternative. Technical staff or a computer helpline may be able to sort out the problem.

Switching off the computer completely and restarting it will clear many problems, but again you may lose material that you have not already saved. Whenever you are using a computer, therefore, be sure to save your files frequently so that you do not lose your work if anything goes wrong.

Use opportunities selectively

The opportunities offered through electronic media are vast. On the Internet, for example, there are social networking forums, chat groups, and distribution lists. Unless you choose carefully what is really valuable for you, however, such facilities will easily eat into your time. Select just one or two such groups at any one time.

ICT and e-learning: key terminology

Asynchronous conferencing Online communication whereby individuals leave messages and make contributions at times that suit them, rather than in live discussion. Compare *Synchronous conferencing*.

Blended learning A combination of e-learning and conventional learning approaches. Increasingly, technology is used to "blend," or personalize, most learning.

Blog (weblog) A web-based log or journal that can be seen by other people. Some students use blogs to keep friends up-to-date with their news. (See page 139.)

Browser A software tool that enables you to look at websites and to save and print web pages.

Cursor A movable line (or other movable character) that indicates where on the screen the next item you type would appear. Click to position the cursor where you want it.

Desktop The main screen displayed when you have finished starting up your computer. Often it will contain one or more *icons* that you can click on to open software packages, to browse the Internet, or to open a saved file.

Drop-down menu A menu of choices that is displayed below the cursor when you click and hold a command word or symbol.

E-learning Learning that makes use of electronic tools and information.

E-portfolio An electronic portfolio or folder in which you gather records of your learning, experience and reflection, including your academic and nonacademic activities. It may be linked to a college portal or LMS. (See page 35 for a list of typical reflective portfolio contents; see page 138 for portals and LMS.)

Flash drive A small "stick" that can be attached to the computer to provide portable memory, allowing you to save and retrieve files and to transfer information between computers.

Hardware The actual "machinery," such as the computer and the printer. Compare *Software*.

Icon A graphic image on the screen that provides a link to a document or program. For example, an icon on a web browser may link to a web page, or a desktop icon may provide a shortcut that opens software or documents.

Logging on, logging off Before using a computer, you will usually need not only to switch it on but also to type in a username and password. This makes your work and your files secure.

Lurking Reading messages in online discussions without yourself contributing.

Menu A list of operations from which you can choose. A menu may appear when you click on an icon or hold the cursor over a command word or symbol. Many such lists are made available from menu bars at the edges of the screen.

RAM (Random Access Memory) The computer's "working memory," where tasks are performed.

Search engine A tool that searches for specified electronic material, typically on the Internet. It will check through millions of web pages for you. (See pages 129–130.)

Software The programs that enable the computer to perform different functions, such as word processing, planning presentations, creating spreadsheets, handling digital photographs or surfing the Internet. Some are automatically loaded when you switch on; others have to be loaded as needed.

Synchronous conferencing Online discussions held in real time—"live." Compare *Asynchronous conferencing*.

URL (Uniform Resource Locator) The unique address for each web page on the Internet.

Wiki A website to which many people can make contributions, adding new material and editing the material already there. The best known is probably Wikipedia, an online encyclopedia. (See pages 129 and 139).

Zip A way of compressing files, typically used to reduce the size of large files. A compressed file can be stored in a smaller space and can be sent more swiftly over the Internet.

Making the most of the Internet

The Internet

The *Internet*, or *net* had its origin in 1969, when the computers of government, scientific and military bodies were linked. Academic and commercial bodies joined later, and eventually people began to produce information for the Internet only, rather than in paper form—now even some books are accessible only via the Internet.

The Internet connects computers from all over the world and enables you to communicate by computer directly with people in other countries. There is no owner or central executive for the Internet: It is just a wide, interconnecting set of computers, with some organizations that try to keep it running smoothly.

Advantages of using the Internet

Range of information

Via the Internet you have access to a great deal of information, including:

- newspapers
- government papers
- government data
- company data
- magazines
- financial data
- library catalogs.

Types of information

Information on the Internet can include:

- sound—voices and music
- film and video clips
- interactive pages
- computer programs
- virtual-reality pages.

The Internet offers you the chance to browse for information across an enormous range of sources without leaving your chair.

Communications

You can send and receive real-time messages from your friends while you study, using email or instant messaging. You can also send your papers and assignments to your instructors in the same way, rather than having to deliver them by hand.

Caution in using the Internet

Is the Internet an authoritative source?

At present there is little editing or censoring of publicly available information. Almost anybody can put information on the Internet. From an academic point of view, much of it is of poor quality, consisting of chat lines, commercial sites and advertising. Before relying on or quoting information found on the Internet, it is important that you check who has provided it, if possible, and try to assess whether or not the source is authoritative.

When were the data entered?

Information can become out of date very quickly. With books we are more aware of this: We can see the date of publication, and even the appearance of the book may suggest that the information may be old and out of date.

People sometimes assume that if data is accessible on the Internet, it must be true and up to date. This is far from being the case. For example, if an archiving project has run out of funding to pay workers to update the information, it may since have become out of date, even though the archive is still accessible.

Can you use Wikipedia as a student?

It is acceptable to use Wikipedia in college. However, at this level of study, you would usually be expected to draw on it only as part of your initial search on a subject. You should then follow up the references it provides to other sources and read some of these for yourself. In your assignments, you would provide a reference directly to those sources you had read, not to Wikipedia itself.

Searching online

Why search online?

Online searching has many advantages, but which of these are valuable to you? Check ☑ those that are.

- [ ] *Excellent resources* Vast amounts of information are stored electronically.
- [ ] *Gaining an overview* The range of resources on offer allow you a general overview of the subject.
- [ ] *Accessibility* Many materials on the Internet are not available elsewhere. Also, if material is available online, you need not travel to the library to view it.
- [ ] *Currency* The latest information may be available, as materials can be updated more quickly online.
- [ ] *Flexibility* You can search using any computer connected to the Internet.
- [ ] *Skill* You can learn to manage large amounts of information.
- [ ] *Checking availability* You may be able to check if paper-based materials are available for loan and when items currently out on loan are due back.
- [ ] *Immediate access* You don't have to wait for books on loan to be returned or for interlibrary transfers to arrive.
- [ ] *Other:*

Disadvantages of online searches

Using the Internet has disadvantages too, however. It can be time-consuming, and you can easily waste a lot of time:

- a lot of the information available is of poor quality
- it isn't always easy to verify the quality, authorship or date of material
- because so much information is available, it can be hard to find exactly what you need.

Don't let these disadvantages put you off! They can all be managed.

Search skills

You can develop skills to help you find relevant information more quickly. If you search online frequently, you will learn methods and shortcuts that will help you work more quickly.

Checklist: online search skills

Check ☑ if you know:

- [ ] how to find your college's electronic catalog
- [ ] how your college's e-catalog is organized
- [ ] how to check online if your college holds a copy of an item you want
- [ ] how to check online how many copies of an item your college holds
- [ ] how to tell if an item is available for use now
- [ ] how to tell if an article can be read on the Internet
- [ ] if test files for your subject are available electronically
- [ ] how to identify articles written by a particular author in recent years
- [ ] which databases are relevant to your subject
- [ ] how to narrow a search of an electronic database if the first search called up too many references
- [ ] how to broaden a search if you can't find what you want
- [ ] when to use truncated and wildcard symbols while searching a database
- [ ] how the operator OR affects a search
- [ ] how the operator AND affects a search
- [ ] how the operator NOT affects a search
- [ ] how to use parentheses to refine a search.

E-learning, technology, and personalized learning

Conducting an online search

Find what you need

There is so much information on the Internet, how do you find what you are looking for?

Web browser First you need software called a web browser that allows your computer to display web pages: This gives you access to the Internet. Some well-known browsers are Internet Explorer, Firefox, Safari, Opera and Netscape. One or more of these is usually provided with the computer.

Search engines A search engine is a program that searches the Internet for specified information and displays a list of web pages which mention that information. It allows you to take advantage of online databases, some of which are cross-referenced to other sites. Popular tools include Google, Yahoo and Bing.

Research tools You can find additional research facilities online, such as those available at http://itools.com/. Using such tools you can access definitions, maps, quotations, language translations, synonyms and much more. Some sites, such as www.onelook.com will quickly check through over 1,000 online dictionaries for you.

Shibboleth Shibboleth is a scheme that manages access to sites of interest to researchers: Registered users (only) gain free access to a broad range of electronic journals and databases. Institutions usually provide student access to Shibboleth.

Starting an online search

- Go online.
- Choose a search tool, such as Google. You may need to type its web address, or your browser may offer a shortcut (such as an icon to click).
- When the search tool is displayed, type your chosen keyword or words into the search field.

- To start the search you will need to click a button that says "Search," "Go" or similar (or perhaps press the ENTER key).
- After a short wait, you will see a list of possible leads, typically summary descriptions or partial quotations from websites, with web addresses.
- Click on entries that look promising: The links will take you automatically to those web pages.

What exactly am I looking for?

If you enter a very general keyword, such as "mouse," you would be offered *millions* of pages—entries that discuss rodents, electronic mice, cartoon mice, pest control, science experiments, mice in children's storybooks, and so forth. To be offered only relevant items, make your search as specific as possible by including more keywords in your "search string." Even "deer mice habitat distribution US" still offers hundreds of pages.

For example, one search gave the following results:

Search string	Number of entries
mouse	733,000,000
deer mouse US	11,900,000
deer mouse habitat US	4,900,000
deer mouse hedgerow US	1,500,000

To save yourself time and effort, choose your search string with care:

- Which keywords best describe what you are looking for? Which are most likely to have been chosen as keywords for making electronic links?
- Consider synonyms—that is, words with the same meaning—such as "city," "town," "urban" and "metropolitan."
- Might unrelated subjects share keywords with your topic? If so, use at least one keyword that applies *only* to your topic.
- Which *specific areas* of your topic do you need to focus on? Which keywords identify these?
- To make your search more precise, use a combination of keywords.
- To find additional material, try different keywords or fewer keywords.
- If a search string proves particularly useful, note it down for future use.

Narrowing or extending your online search

You can vary your search by using OR, AND and NOT (known in this context as "Boolean operators"), and truncation symbols or wildcards. These allow you to broaden or narrow your search in order to find the most relevant pages.

Too many items?

AND

If you type **AND** between two keywords, the seach will produce only those pages that include *both* of the keywords. For example,

> **deer AND mice**

would find only pages that contain both **deer** and **mice**, not those containing only one of these keywords.

Quotation marks (" ")

In many situations you can use quotation marks to specify a phrase rather than a single word. This will narrow down the search and reduce the number of items you find, but must be used with care. For example,

> **"electronic mouse"**

would yield references to computer mice, excluding those that mention rodents, but equally it would only list pages where those two words appeared together in exactly that form.

NOT

Use **NOT** to *exclude* items from your search. For example, to find references to mice but not to pest control, you could enter:

> **mice NOT extermination**

More keywords

The more keywords you use, the fewer pages are listed. For example, a library database search may allow you to specify the author's name, words in the title, the publication date and so on. The more of these you provide, the more precise your search will be.

Too few items?

OR

Use **OR** to search for pages that contain *one* or *more* of two or more words. For example, a search for

> **car OR bicycle**

would list pages that include **car** but not **bicycle**, pages that include **bicycle** but not **car** and pages that include both **car** and **bicycle**. This kind of search is useful when authors may use different terms for the same topic (often synonyms or abbreviations):

> **"vitamin C" OR "ascorbic acid"**

Truncation symbol (*)

The truncation symbol can be used to find variations of a keyword that begin with the same set of letters (the "stem"). For example, **crit*** would find **critic**, **critical**, **critique** and **criticism**.

Wildcards (?)

Wildcards find variations of a keyword, such as alternative words in a phrase or alternative letters in a word. The exact operation of **?** varies between search engines: Check the help system.

- Alternative words: **car ?** would search for **car** plus any other word, and might find **used cars**, **sports cars**, **car insurance**, **car rental**, and so on. Beware: This may yield a long list. In a publications database, for example, **Smith ?** would list publications by *any* author named **Smith**; it would be better to include a specific initial to limit the list (**Smith W**).
- Alternative characters: **wom?n** might find **woman** and **women**; **organi?e** might find **organize** and **organise** (British spelling).

Advanced online searches

Advanced searches

With some databases you can use a more sophisticated search string that uses parentheses ( ) to link operations and to specify their order of precedence. You can continue to use operators, truncations and wildcards (page 132), within and between the groups of keywords.

You need to put some thought into what you are including and excluding. However, experiment and you will soon get a feel for whether your search strategy is finding the kinds of items you need.

Example 1

Suppose you wished to find articles about mice in cities. You might try this search string:

(mice NOT rat) AND (urban OR city OR metropolitan NOT field)

The search engine would list items in the database that:

- include the keyword **mice** but do not include the keyword **rat**

  and also

- include any combination (one or more) of the keywords **urban, city** or **metropolitan**, but *not* the keyword **field**.

However, this search might exclude some useful articles that mentioned "rat" or "field" even once.

Example 2

"global warming" AND (glaciers NOT North)

The search would look for items that:

- include **global warming** as a phrase (excluding items that contain the words **global** and **warming**, but not together)

  and also

- include the word **glaciers** but do *not* include the word **North**.

Again, this would exclude any articles that mentioned the word **North** even once.

Efficient search strategies

An efficient search strategy is one that:

- finds the most relevant items
- does not exclude relevant items
- does exclude irrelevant items
- is successful in the fewest attempts.

Activity

1 If you use AND in a search, you are likely to find additional references. True or false?

2 If you use OR in a search, you are likely to find additional references. True or false?

3 Which search string would find most items?
   A global OR world
   B global AND world
   C global NOT world

4 Which search strategy would find the fewest items?
   A graphic OR design
   B (graphic OR design)
   C "graphic design"

5 How could you enter the keyword "design" to find references to "designs" and "designers" also?

6 For the following topics, how could you search for references to items using alternative versions of the keywords?
   A A compendium of nursing methods
   B Monopoly as a trend in world trade

7 Which search string is likely to be most efficient in finding references to the impact of global design trends on designers?
   A global AND design AND trend
   B global? AND (design* AND trend?)
   C global* OR (design AND trend)

Answers are given on page 148.

Academic resources online

Web sources for academic study

For academic study, you must be very selective about your sources of information, whether these are paper-based or electronic (see page 97). A number of search tools and services are available to help focus your search on reputable resources for academic study: A selection is provided in Appendix 2 (page 362).

The following are some key starting places when making electronic searches for books and articles:

- WorldCat: www.worldcat.org
- Library of Congress e-resources online catalog: http://eresources.loc.gov/
- *education*: www.eric.ed.gov
- *science and social science*: www.webofknowledge.com

Searching for journal articles online

In academic study you are usually expected to know about key journal articles on your subject. Most academic journals now make their articles available online.

Electronic versions of journals, which may be free to you as a student, are usually made available through a "host" service such as:

- ABI Inform
- EBSCO*host*
- IngentaConnect
- Shibboleth

When looking for journal entries, search first for the name of the *journal*, not the name of the article.

You can search journal databases for authors, journal titles, article titles or keywords that interest you, and you can call up short abstracts to check what an article is about.

Thousands of journals are published each year, and this is a very quick and efficient way to look through those that are relevant to your own study.

Research focus

To find research background on the topic that interests you:

- Type in words such as "research" or "journal" as well as the subject.
- Type in names of leading theorists or schools of thought as well as the subject.

If you have a Shibboleth authentication number, conference proceedings and papers are available through the "Web of Knowledge" at: www.webofknowledge.com (select *Advanced Search*).

Saving and ordering web addresses

When you identify sources that are useful to you, save their web addresses so that you can return to them quickly in future. The method of doing this should be easy but will vary depending on your web browser (see the help system). You need to look for the tool in your browser that allows you to save material as a "favorite" or to "bookmark" or "mark" it or similar.

You will soon accumulate many web addresses. The browser will also allow you to set up folders so that you can group your favorite, or most used, addresses. Take care to name these clearly, just as you would with your files.

Be prepared for change

Depending on your computer and your Internet provider, your route through the Internet may vary when you log on next time.

As the Internet is being updated constantly, you may notice that information is presented differently, or has been changed, from one occasion to the next.

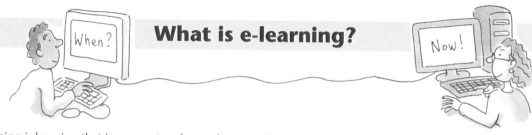

What is e-learning?

E-learning is learning that incorporates electronic technologies into the teaching and learning process. E-technologies are simply tools that, like pen and paper, can be applied in a wide range of situations. Your study program may provide opportunities to use some of the following components.

E-learning resources

These may include:

- a learning management system (see page 138)
- a program website or web pages
- electronic copies of lecture notes and study notes, or podcasts of lectures (page 139)
- electronic links to useful subject websites and journals
- activities to complete before or after taught sessions such as classes and lectures.

Simulations and interactive materials

Interactive materials are expensive to produce and are therefore not suitable for all types of learning. When available, they may include:

- online practice in technical skills
- interactive videos
- learning structured as a game or quiz
- simulated case studies
- wikis to develop as a group (page 139).

Computer-assisted assessment

Part or all of your program may be assessed through multiple-choice questions on a computer. Computerized assessment is demanding—you usually need to study more than for essay-based tests.

Some classes offer computerized assessment for practice. This enables you to check your knowledge as many times as you like, in your own time, until you feel confident about the material.

E-communications

Electronic communications have many uses, such as:

- *writing to people*—emailing and messaging instructors, other students, and contacts at other institutions
- *talking with people*—in chat rooms, using messaging, and holding online conferences
- *getting information*—from electronic bulletins, newsletters, bulletin boards, and weblogs (blogs)
- *submitting work*—sending assignments by email.

For more detail, see pages 140 and 144.

Webcam and video links

Electronic video links are especially useful:

- if your class is split between different sites
- if part of your program is studied overseas
- for links while on field trips
- to link students on your program with students on similar programs elsewhere.

Using cell phones for learning

Some students and instructors use cell phones:

- to discuss assignments with friends
- to text messages about changes to teaching rooms or cancelled classes
- to contribute images to a group project
- to receive text reminders about deadlines for handing in work.

E-surveys and polls

You may be asked to express your views, give feedback or take part in a poll through:

- text polls on your cell phone
- computerized surveys and polls
- "press-button" technology in lectures
- web-based chat rooms.

E-learning: getting started

Ingredients for successful e-learning

Successful e-learning involves a range of conditions, skills and attitudes. These include:

- having the right resources for the activity
- having the confidence and willingness to try new approaches and resources
- willingness to keep updating your knowledge and skills in a rapidly developing area
- developing awareness of when to use electronic resources and tools to provide the best or quickest route, rather than simply because they are there: That is, knowing when an e-resource could add value and when not
- combining e-resources and approaches with traditional approaches in the most effective ways for each activity
- taking an active part in e-learning activities when these are a part of a class or an agreed part of a team project.

- Are you open to using electronic approaches and resources to support study?
- Which of the above do you feel are already areas of strength for you?
- Which do you feel could create barriers to using e-learning?

E-resources: what is available?

At your college you will probably be able to use a range of e-resources, including computers, printers, software and broadband access. Before making purchases for yourself, find out what your college provides and what systems it uses.

What does your college provide?

Check if your college provides:

- ☐ easy-to-use links to electronically available academic sources, on campus and at home
- ☐ assistive technologies to help students with and without known disabilities
- ☐ free use of the Internet from campus
- ☐ free use of broadband Internet from home or housing on campus
- ☐ shared electronic space for your program, such as a student website or intranet
- ☐ chat rooms or forums for your program
- ☐ a Learning Management System (LMS)
- ☐ a student portal
- ☐ e-portfolios
- ☐ workshops on accessing electronic catalogs, searching for information, participating in chat rooms, using LMS, writing blogs, etc.

What do I need to work online?

To work online, you need:

- ☐ A suitable *computer* (a fairly new one).
- ☐ A *phone line* or *cable*.
- ☐ A *broadband connection*. ("Dial-up" connections are relatively slow.) Broadband allows you to download large files, such as lengthy documents, audio files or video files. Mobile broadband is now widely available—this does not require a land-based phone line but download speeds can be slower.

- ☐ A *modem*, to connect the computer to the telephone. (Most computers now have built-in modems.)
- ☐ A *router*, to enable your computer to interpret broadband signals.
- ☐ An *Internet service provider* (ISP), to supply your link to the Internet. ISPs usually charge a fee and vary in the services they offer. Look for one with an inexpensive helpline that is available in the evenings and on weekends.

E-learning and personalized learning

What is "personalized learning"?

The term *personalized learning* refers to approaches to teaching, learning, assessment and study support that recognize people's individual needs and circumstances. Individual students:

- have personal preferences, aptitudes and styles of learning
- have differing motivations for learning
- learn at different paces, such as on a short part-time course or over the course of a lifetime
- learn best in formal or informal settings, alone or with others, independently or with support, through activity or observation, as a discrete activity or integrated into other activities.

Personalized learning and e-learning

Although personalized learning is possible without using technology, e-technologies and resources provide opportunities for far more individualized approaches to learning.

Learning with Web 2.0

The term "Web 2.0" is used to refer to a particular set of approaches that use web-based resources. Generally, these approaches support personalized approaches to learning:

- *Participation*   Web users are encouraged to be active participants in creating and contributing to materials on the web, not just in reading information presented to them.
- *Communication*   Users can use synchronous (real time) and asynchronous (not in real time) communication, through chat rooms, forums, conferencing and messaging services.
- *Active feedback*   Users can provide feedback through voting mechanisms, by rating items or by posting comments.

- *Sharing expertise and resources*   Appropriate resources, tools or platforms can be made available for people to use or distribute, either free or at reduced cost, for their own purposes. This enables new users to build upon what has gone before.
- *Varied resources*   Resources and tools originally developed for social and informational purposes can be adapted to support teaching and study. These include most of the personalized learning resources listed below.
- *User-friendliness*   Resources can be flexible and easy to use, to adapt and update and to distribute.

Whether or not your instructors use Web 2.0 electronic resources, these approaches are likely to inform some aspects of the way they teach and how they expect you to learn.

E-resources for personalized learning

E-technologies and resources that support personalized learning are very varied. They include:

- portals (page 138)
- Learning Management Systems (LMS: page 138)
- e-polls and online surveys (page 135)
- online materials and search tools that help you find them (pages 130–134)
- wikis (pages 128 and 139)
- blogs (pages 128 and 139)
- podcasts (page 139)
- e-portfolios (pages 35 and 128)
- assistive technologies (page 142)
- e-communications, including chat rooms and cell phones (page 140).

Use technology to personalize your learning

Personalized e-learning: portals and LMS

What is a portal?

A portal is an entrance point, or electronic gateway, to a specific set of online resources. Some institutions use portals to organize and present related information.

What you find through the portal depends on how it has been designed. In general, when you log in you are presented with material and links that have been selected because they are relevant to you, your program, its administration and your interests. What is offered depends in part on the information you yourself supply about your own interests.

When would I use a portal?

Depending on how it is designed, a portal might offer some or all of the following.

- *Personal relevance* From when you log on, you may be able to access web pages preselected as relevant only to you or your program.
- *Program administration* You may be able to check if your tuition and fees payments are up-to-date, which classes you are enrolled in, or to find out exam dates or test results.
- *Program resources* There may be links to material related to your program, such as the departmental intranet, online notes or lists of useful websites.
- *Automatic updates* You may be offered the latest information about specific clubs, societies, events and websites you have selected as of interest to you.
- *Messages and bulletins* You can communicate with your instructors, with other students and with societies and groups.
- *Communications* You may be able to participate in a social or learning community with others on your program, through chat rooms, discussion groups or online conferences.

- *Access* You may be able to access the college library and other websites more easily. This is especially helpful when you are off-campus, such as at home or in a workplace: Having logged on at the portal, you may then have access to other college websites without needing to log into each of them individually.
- *E-learning* You may have access to a range of e-learning activities (as discussed below and on page 135).

What is a learning management system (LMS)?

Some colleges use learning management systems (LMS), such as *Web-CT*, *Blackboard* or *Moodle*. These provide additional opportunities for interactive learning. As well as being useful for distance-learning programs, LMS are often used to supplement face-to-face teaching.

What are the advantages of LMS?

LMS may be used to support your study in the following ways.

- *Background information* Providing details of the program, including assignments, syllabi, and test files.
- *Materials* Providing up-to-date online class materials, lecture notes, podcasts, and links to other material relevant to your program.
- *Reminders and guidance* Sending you information about classes, events, and assignment deadlines.
- *Messages and interaction* Allowing group activities, conferencing and online discussions, and tracking who is participating.
- *Assessment* Providing computer-assisted assessment.
- *Additional learning activities* Preparing for classes or lectures, or following them up to consolidate your understanding.
- *Workplace study* Providing links to resources, instructors and other students, for work-based learning.

E-learning: wikis, blogs, podcasts

Wikis

What is a "wiki"?

A wiki is a website containing information that users can edit. You can use software to develop your own wiki in an area that interests you.

Wikis allow users to trace the history of who made what changes to entries and when. In contributing to wikis, you need to be comfortable with the idea that other people will know what you have written. You can add your own contributions to other people's ideas, just as they can add theirs to yours.

When would I use a wiki?

As a student, you might use a wiki:

- because your class has built a wiki for a topic to which all students can contribute
- because it would be a useful resource for new students on your program
- to build knowledge of a topic that many students find challenging
- to build understanding and critiques of a difficult text
- to support a team project or to publish the results of a project
- for a student society or club.

Advantages of wikis

- Wiki is Hawaiian for "quick"—wikis are quick and easy to use.
- The experience of using wikis can develop useful collaborative working and team skills in researching, negotiating and co-writing.
- In learning to evaluate critically information entered into the wiki and in making your own constructive and informative entries, you will develop ancillary skills that are helpful in using other online information.
- The shared creation of a wiki can build a sense of team membership.

> For more information, see:
>
> http://en.wikipedia.org/wiki

Blogs

What is a "blog"?

A blog is a web-based log. In effect, this means it is an electronic journal written by an individual or a group, which other people can read online.

When would I use a blog?

As a student, you might use a blog:

- to keep team members up-to-date about progress in an area of a project for which you have responsibility
- for mutual support, to share experiences with students in similar circumstances
- because your program encourages reflective analysis on your study or your work
- to maintain a research journal
- to explore links between workplace experiences and the theories you are studying on your course
- to provide group feedback on student projects
- to support mentoring.

Podcasts

What is a "podcast"?

A podcast is an audio file or audio-visual file that can be downloaded from a web-based source onto your computer or onto a portable media player such as an MP3 or MP4 player or cell phone.

When would I use a podcast?

- Instructors may make some or all of a lecture available as a podcast.
- Some study resources are available as podcasts. (See http://us.macmillan.com/thestudyskills handbook, for example.)

Advantages of podcasts

You can listen to the material when you like and where you like, and you can listen as many times as you wish in order to fully understand it and remember it.

Using e-communications for study

Benefits of online communication

There are many options for communicating with students and instructors online. These options:

- enable communication in spare moments
- save you having to travel
- can operate in different time zones
- disguise shyness or nervousness
- offer you some time to gather your thoughts and compose a response
- are relatively informal, so that you can express yourself in your own way.

Kinds of online communication

Emails

Emails are one of the simplest means of communicating electronically: You can take your time composing the email and send it when you are ready. You can copy it to as many or as few people as you want.

Instant messaging

Instant messaging allows online communication between a given set of individuals, working in real time. You can tell who else is online and is there to receive messages. Real-time messaging gives more of a feeling of being part of a group than email.

Chat rooms

A chat room enables a group of people to "meet" in a discrete area within a website or LMS and to discuss topics they have in common. For example,

you could set up a chat room for students in your class, year, college or club; or for adult and returning, transfer or work-based students, or for students studying a particular project.

Chat rooms may feel slow or fast-paced, depending on how quickly messages arrive while you are online.

Online conferencing

E-conferencing again uses a discrete area of a website and enables a group to develop an idea or train of thought over several days or weeks. E-conferencing can be useful in canvassing views on a new development or proposal. You can come and go, reading the chain of messages contributed so far and adding your own. You can see who has posted which message and when.

If a lot of people are online simultaneously, you may see a rapid sequence of messages; at other times it may seem more like a slow discussion by email.

Electronic discussions in groups

E-communication can be used in many different activities. Check ☑ those that appeal most to you.

- ☐ Comparing ideas on a set text
- ☐ Sharing views on a "hot topic"
- ☐ Sharing comments on a recent journal article
- ☐ Working out how to solve a problem
- ☐ Discussing whether a theory can be applied appropriately in particular circumstances
- ☐ Discussing how to tackle assignments
- ☐ Comparing results after completing an experiment
- ☐ Group projects
- ☐ Sharing experiences
- ☐ Studying together for tests
- ☐ *Other:*

Personalizing your own study

Find your own e-learning styles

- Make time to learn and keep up to date about new and developing technologies and resources. Ask the college and other students for tips and shortcuts.
- Make technology your friend—use, practice, browse and play with it so that you become familiar with it.
- As you learn, write out the steps for performing different computer operations. Write these in a way that you can follow and remember, such as one step per line. Actively making your own notes will help you learn better than relying on computer manuals.
- Store your step-by-step notes where you will find them easily, on the computer or in a planner or notebook.
- Experiment to find the combination of e-learning and conventional approaches that works best for you. For example, you may prefer to search for materials online but read paper printouts; you may find chat rooms useful for general discussion but prefer to meet face-to-face for particular aspects of project work.

Take part

- Don't be afraid to join in! Make use of the opportunities that are available.
- If there is a chat room set up for your program, take part in it. Chat rooms may seem strange at first, but once students get used to them, they often prefer to exchange ideas in this way.
- Use the links that are built into electronic learning materials. You lose these links when you print out the materials.

> To avoid plagiarism and allegations of cheating, do not share your written work electronically before it is graded.
>
> Do not cut and paste from electronic material—this too can be detected electronically!

Incorporate the computer into study

Use the computer as part of your everyday study strategies.

Stay organized

- Maintain an electronic calendar. Set this to give you advance reminders of appointments.
- Keep an electronic bibliography of all the texts you have read—this will save you rewriting details if you use the same resource for another piece of writing.
- Read about organizational skills for studying on the computer (pages 126–127).

Find information

- Find out about services and events at your college and in the local area.
- Use the library online (see pages 129–134).

Design materials

- Special software is available to help you design questionnaires or surveys for projects.
- You can design forms to gather project information.
- You can design databases to collate and interrogate information that you collect.

Develop your writing

- Using word processing software or specialist software, brainstorm initial ideas for essays and papers before you start to write.
- Develop a piece of writing by editing, cutting and pasting as you formulate your ideas.
- Write up separate sections of reports as you complete distinct supporting tasks.

Use other software

- Use software such as PowerPoint to prepare class or project presentations.
- Use the computer calculator, spreadsheets or statistical packages relevant to your subject to carry out mathematical calculations.

More about personalizing your study

What works for you?

You can usually adapt e-resources and e-learning methods to suit individual requirements. Some ways of doing this are indicated below.

Change how it looks

Many people find it easier to read text on screen if they adapt the color and size of the text or the color of the background. If you have any disability that affects your reading onscreen, such as dyslexia or difficulties with flickering or bright screens, it is worth consulting the college disability service about other adaptations that might help you.

Do you prefer to work:

- using the computer as much as possible?
- using the computer as little as possible?
- with a mixture of methods, for variety?
- in different ways, depending on the activity?

How can you organize your study in line with the methods that you prefer?

Aspect	Your preference
Which color font is easiest to read?	
Which color background is easiest to read?	
Which font style is easiest to read?	
Which font size is easiest to read on screen?	
What zoom size do you prefer?	
What line spacing do you prefer?	
Does the screen seem to flicker as you work? Find out how to change the resolution.	
Which font size do you prefer for printed material?	
Is it easier to read text on screen or on paper?	
Is it easier to do number work on screen or on paper?	
Is number work on screen easier if you tint adjacent rows or columns in different colors?	
Is it easier to write on screen or on paper?	

Listen as you learn

If you find it easier to learn while listening:

- Use any podcasts that are provided.
- Look for information that can be downloaded to a portable device, such as your MP3 player.
- Use assistive technologies, such as screen readers.
- Investigate assistive software (such as Texthelp!) that may allow you to listen to letters, words, sentences, paragraphs or other sections of text either as you type them or when you have highlighted them.
- In some cases you can download computer-voiced text as a podcast.

Updating your e-learning skills

E-technologies that are required:

- Which tools must you use on your program?
- For which of these do you need guidance or more practice in using them?

E-technologies that interest you:

- Which e-tools and resources interest you that you haven't used so far?
- Where will you find out about these?

Managing an e-group project

E-technologies provide excellent resources. Could these help you in any of your own group projects?

Communication

Agree what communication methods will best suit the group. You could use a mixture of face-to-face communications and e-resources, or rely mainly on one method. Check if anyone has a disability or other difficulty that prevents them from making full use of any methods. You may wish to assign someone to manage communications for the group. Check ☑ the methods that suit your group.

☐ Face to face   ☐ By phone

☐ Email   ☐ E-messaging

☐ Blog   ☐ Shared electronic space

☐ Chat room

☐ *Other:*

The project brief

Check the project brief carefully and discuss it.

- What do you have to do?
- What will be assessed, and how?
- What must individuals contribute?
- What must be produced collectively?

Make sure you agree on what is required and when. Record agreements and store them electronically where you can all access them.

Outputs

Check ☑ the outputs from your project.

☐ Report   ☐ Website

☐ Wiki   ☐ Blog

☐ Database   ☐ Newsletter

☐ *Other:*

Resources

As a group, decide which e-resources and paper resources you will use. You might use:

☐ E-journals   ☐ Other journals

☐ Books   ☐ Websites

Ground rules and processes

Discuss how you want to work as a group.

- What are your attitudes to meeting deadlines?
- How will you allocate roles?
- What do you expect from one another?
- What will you do if someone does not deliver what was agreed?
- Have group members any concerns about working together on the project? If so, how can you resolve these?
- What are the group's ground rules on matters such as making contributions and "lurking" in chat rooms?
- What agreements about communications are needed? How often should members log in?

Roles and responsibilities

Decide which roles are needed and who will fill them. Some possibilities are listed below; check ☑ those that apply for your project.

☐ Project leader   ☐ Deadlines manager

☐ Secretary

☐ E-moderator   ☐ Website manager

☐ Research manager   ☐ Blog manager

☐ Data manager   ☐ Wiki manager

☐ Communications manager   ☐ Design aspects

   ☐ Technical aspects

☐ Fund raiser/treasurer

☐ *Other:*   ☐ *Other:*

☐ *Other:*   ☐ *Other:*

Managing e-communications for projects

The downside of online communication

E-communications are a powerful tool that can also be difficult at times. For example:

- It may feel unnatural to start a discussion with people you cannot see.
- There may be no rules, so you may feel uncertain where to start and what is "right."
- Unlike face-to-face conversations, you cannot use body language or facial expression to interpret what people think about your contributions.
- The quality of contributions may vary; some may be boring, hard to understand, rambling or repetitious.
- You may find it annoying if you feel there are people reading but not contributing ("lurkers").
- You may find it tiring if messages pour in quickly.
- Messages may not follow a logical sequence, so it may be hard to follow the thread of an argument.

Ground rules for e-discussions

If you are setting up your own online chat room, forum or discussion group, it is worth spending some time agreeing ground rules for participants.

Which sort of topics would you yourself most want addressed as ground rules? Check ☑ any that apply.

- ☐ The group's staying focused on the core purpose or subjects for the chat room.
- ☐ Use of the space to arrange outside meetings or to discuss other items.
- ☐ "Lurking" (reading messages without making any contribution).
- ☐ "Small talk" and socializing.
- ☐ Making personal comments.
- ☐ Showing respect towards other participants.
- ☐ Managing disagreements.
- ☐ Spelling and grammar.
- ☐ Use of "text-speak" (txt abbreviations).

E-moderated learning

E-moderated learning can include discussion groups using an electronic forum, conference or chat room. The instructor may set up discussion groups and then "moderate" the interactions in order to facilitate the learning that is taking place. Alternatively, they may ask students to take turns at being the moderator.

The role of an e-moderator

If you are asked to moderate a discussion, or if you want to moderate your own chat room, you may need to do the following.

Set up the group

- Set up the forum.
- Let relevant students know that it is there.
- Introduce yourself and invite others to introduce themselves.
- Make the first contributions to get discussion started.
- Invite participants to set ground rules.
- Encourage them to decide what action will be taken if these are not followed.

Help generate discussion

- Stimulate debate by asking key questions or offering useful prompts.
- Summarize the discussion so far.
- Respond to comments.
- Bring out links between contributions.
- Encourage discussions to develop in new directions.

Manage the chat room

- Archive material that is not in use.
- Allocate tasks to group members.
- Contact and support individuals.
- Check that ground rules are being followed.

Managing an e-project

Project name	

Project team

Name	Phone	Email

Instructors

Name	Phone	Email

Project communications

Email address		Chat room address	
Blog address		Wiki address	
E-messenger address		Website	
Other		*Other*	

Roles and responsibilities

Project manager		Project secretary	
Chat room moderator		Blog manager	
Wiki manager		Comm's manager	

Chapter 6

Project brief			

Project output			
(e.g., project website, reports, leaflets, presentations)			

Project resources: e-journals

Name of journal	Web address	Useful for

Project resources: websites

Web address	Useful for	Web address	Useful for

Ground rules for the project team			
1			
2			
3			
4			
5			
6			
7			
Project schedule			
Task	Details	By whom	Deadline
End of project: date			

E-learning, technology, and personalized learning

Review

Students arrive in college with very varied levels of computer skills and knowledge. If you are new to using computers and e-technologies, this chapter has provided an overview of what to expect. It has enabled you to identify the skills and computer knowledge that you might need to develop for success on your program. If you have used personalized e-learning in high school, then you may find that this chapter provides a useful platform for building further research skills and interactive learning online.

In either case, e-learning and e-resources develop rapidly. Being a successful e-learner is less about what you know than about the attitude and openness you bring to the activity. It helps if you are interested in new ideas about how technology can support learning and are open to experimenting. E-learning and personalized learning are used to promote and enable interactive approaches, increased participation and online social learning. This can be demanding if you prefer solo learning or passive approaches to study, but can make study much more interesting, personally challenging and enjoyable.

The new technologies are usually highly adaptable, so check for ways of setting them up and using them in ways that suit you best. For many students with disabilities or who have difficulties studying on campus during open hours, e-technologies provide good opportunities for participating and for accessing a broad range of excellent resources.

Individual students will have their own preferences about how far they want to use technology and about the particular ways they use it. Usually a combination of methods is possible and, for many students, desirable. Find out which combination of e-learning and conventional methods works best for you.

If you are interested in developing your e-learning skills further, you may find the following book helpful: Cottrell, S. and Morris, N. (2012) *Study Skills Connected* (Palgrave Macmillan).

Answers to activity: Advanced online searches (page 133)

1   False. AND excludes references that do not contain both words so there are likely to be fewer references. (Page 132.)

2   True. (Page 132.)

3   *A.* (Page 132.)

4   *C*—the search will find only matches of the exact phrase. (Page 133.)

5   **design*** would find **design**, **designers** and **designs** but would also find irrelevant entries such as **designate**.

6   *A.*   A suitable search string would be: **nurs* AND method*** This would find additional references such as pages that mention **nursing**, **nurses**, **method**, **methodology** or **methodologies**.

   B.   A suitable search string would be: **monopoly? as a trend? in world? trade?**   You might then retrieve an item such as *Monopolies as a developing pattern in the global market.*

7   *B*—this focuses on relevant items but looks for relevant alternatives such **world**, **designers** and **designs**. *A* might narrow your search too far, and C might include many irrelevant items such as **global warming**, **globalization**, or **local design** yet omit reference to **designers**.

Chapter 7

Critical analytical thinking

LEARNING OUTCOMES

This chapter offers you opportunities to:

- understand what is meant by taking a critical or analytical approach

- become more aware of how to use critical and analytical thinking when reading and writing

- develop criteria for evaluating an argument or a line of reasoning in a piece of writing

- develop criteria for evaluating the evidence given in a piece of writing

- learn how to identify and draw valid conclusions.

Critical thinking

Critical thinking means weighing up the arguments and evidence *for* and *against*. Edward Glaser, who developed a test of critical thinking, defined it in this way (1941):

> Critical thinking calls for a persistent effort to examine any belief or supposed form of knowledge in the light of the evidence that supports it and the further conclusions to which it tends.

In other words, Glaser emphasizes the importance of the following:

- *persistence*: considering an issue carefully, and more than once
- *evidence*: evaluating the evidence put forward in support of the belief or viewpoint
- *implications*: considering where the belief or viewpoint leads—what conclusions would follow; are these suitable and rational; and if not, should the belief or viewpoint be reconsidered?

Analytical thinking

Analytical thinking involves additional processes:

- standing back from the information given
- examining it in detail from many angles
- checking closely if it is completely accurate
- checking if each statement follows logically from what went before
- looking for possible flaws in the reasoning, the evidence or the way that conclusions are drawn
- comparing the same issue from the point of view of other theorists or writers
- being able to see and explain why different people arrived at different conclusions
- being able to argue why one set of opinions, results or conclusions is preferable to another
- being on guard for literary or statistical devices that encourage the reader to take questionable statements at face value
- checking for hidden assumptions
- checking for attempts to lure the reader into agreement.

Develop a detective-like mind

To develop critical and analytical thinking ability, you might imagine that you are developing a detective-like mind.

Reading

Critical thinking when *reading* involves the following:

1 identifying the line of reasoning in the text
2 critically evaluating the line of reasoning
3 questioning surface appearances and checking for hidden assumptions or agendas
4 identifying evidence in the text
5 evaluating the evidence according to valid criteria
6 identifying the writer's conclusions
7 deciding if the evidence given supports these conclusions.

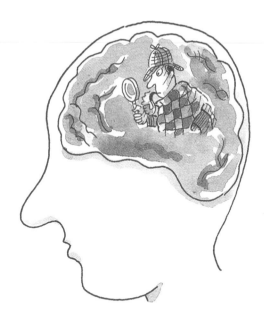

Writing

Critical thinking when *writing* involves comparable processes:

1 being clear what your conclusions are
2 showing a clear line of reasoning—an "argument" or "thesis" leading to your conclusion
3 presenting evidence to support your reasoning
4 reading your own writing critically, as above, as well as your sources
5 viewing your subject from multiple perspectives
6 writing in a critical, analytical style, rather than in a descriptive, personal or journalistic style.

Listening

Critical thinking when *listening* involves the same awareness as when reading, plus:

1 checking for consistency in what the speaker is saying—does the speaker appear to contradict herself or himself; and if so, what is going on beneath that contradiction?
2 checking that body language, eye contact and speed and tone of voice are consistent, or

"congruent", with what is being said—does the speaker look and sound as though he or she believes what he or she is saying?

The following pages explore these issues in more detail and include some basic exercises so that you can try out your critical thinking skills.

Critical questions

In general, when working in a critical way, you will be asking such questions as:

- Why?
- How far?
- How much?
- How often?
- To what extent?
- How do we know this is true?
- How reliable is this source?
- What could be going on below the surface?
- What do we *not* know about this?
- Which is preferable?
- For what reasons?

Chapter **7**

Critical thinking when reading

Critical thinking when reading is essential to academic success as much of the writing you do for assignments will include critical analysis of the work of other people.

1 Identify the line of reasoning

Most of the texts you are required to read as a student will include an argument. In academic writing, an "argument" is:

- a line of reasoning *or*
- an angle or a point of view *or*
- a position that is being defended *or*
- a case that is being made
  - backed up by evidence and examples *and*
  - leading to conclusions.

When reading, you need to keep asking yourself, "What are the main things this writer wants me to accept? What reasons does she or he present to encourage me to accept this?"

Activity 1

Identify the main line of reasoning—that is, the writer's main point of view—in Passage 1, "Rochboro Health" (see page 163 for feedback).

Passage 1: Rochboro Health

Outdoor play has beneficial effects for children in terms of both their health and their levels of social interaction. According to clinical trials carried out by Rochboro County's Health Advisory Council in September this year, children who played outside for over fifty days in the year had a 20% higher lung capacity, and 30% lower incidence of asthma and bronchial conditions than children who played indoors. Children who played outdoors also reported having more friends than those who played indoors. A survey of 30 families by Rochboro Social Amenities Committee found that parents were more likely to let their children play outdoors if they had their own gardens or if there were supervised play areas nearby. Mr. Arkash of Milton Road said his children did not feel safe playing on the Children's Meadow on the outskirts of Rochboro, as his son had been frightened by a fox there in the past. His little son looked quite tearful as his father spoke. "He often cries because he has nowhere to play," said his father. Supervised play areas can be expensive to provide. However, only 18% of homes in Rochboro have gardens. Therefore, to improve the health of all its children, Rochboro needs to provide more supervised outdoor play areas.

Rochboro Playcouncil Newsletter

2 Critically evaluate the line of reasoning

An argument can be critically evaluated in terms of whether it contains:

- relevant, contributing and sufficient propositions (reasons)
- logical progression
- false premises
- flawed reasoning.

Each of these is explored below.

Relevant, contributing and sufficient propositions

The Rochboro Health passage makes a number of statements or *propositions*. For example:

- Outdoor play improves levels of social interaction.
- Only 18% of Rochboro homes have gardens.

These are some of the reasons it gives to support its argument. When examining the line of reasoning, you need to consider if the reasons given are relevant and if they support (that is, contribute to) the overall argument. For example:

- the reference to the isolated incident of a fox is not very relevant to the argument about health
- the reference to the expense of supervised play areas *is* relevant to the argument—however, it weakens or undermines the argument rather than contributing to it, because the piece does not make clear how the expense could be met.

It is important to check that reasons and evidence are both relevant and supportive of the main argument, as this helps you to identify if the writer's conclusion is valid. Even if the writer has given relevant reasons that contribute to the argument, however, she or he may not have given sufficient reasons to prove that this is the *only* conclusion that could be drawn.

> ## Passage 2: Injuries
> There has been a tremendous rise in the rate of industrial injury. This year there were over thirty reports of repetitive strain injury in the factory (Smilex Injury Report 2012). All those injured worked in the fiber department. Ten years ago there were no reported injuries. This shows that our work conditions are taking a more serious toll upon our health than in the past. *Smilex News*

The writer of Passage 2 begins from the premise (starting point) that there has been a great rise in industrial injury. The conclusion is that work conditions are having a more serious effect on health than in the past. The writer gives a relevant and contributory reason: The rise in the number of reported injuries. However, the writer does not consider other reasons why the number of reported injuries might have increased—such as if repetitive strain injury was known about thirty years ago or if people were less likely to report accidents in the past.

In addition, the writer has not looked at figures for any other types of injury or at the health of workers in other departments. He or she makes generalizations based on only one kind of injury

and one part of the factory. The writer may still be *right* about the rise in industrial injury, but has not proved this. He or she has not given sufficient reasons (or evidence) to justify the conclusion.

Logical progression

In everyday conversation, it is common practice when someone is speaking to assume that there is a logical connection between one thing that is said and the next. For written arguments and in academic contexts in general, you need to question if one point does indeed follow logically from another. A line of reasoning will:

- begin from a premise
- follow in logical stages (A leads to B; B leads to C; C leads to D ...)
- lead to a conclusion that follows directly from what has gone before (there are relevant reasons, in a logical order, that build towards the stated conclusion).

The premise in Passage 1 is that outdoor play is good for children's health. The logical progression would be:

- local evidence supports the health argument (that outdoor play is desirable)
- parents' attitudes support this argument
- a lack of facilities prevents outdoor play
- more outdoor play facilities are needed.

False premises

If there were a reason why outdoor play was *not* good for Rochboro children, the writer of Passage 1 would have started from a "false premise." The writer of Passage 2 may indeed have begun from a "false premise"—believing that industrial injury is on the rise in the Smilex factory. No conclusive evidence of this is given, so it may not be true.

It is useful to be on the lookout for false premises: Many arguments are based on weak foundations of this kind.

Flawed reasoning

Here are some examples of "flawed reasoning."

Assuming a causal connection

If two things occur at the same time or place, it is easy to assume either that they must be connected or that one must have caused the other. For example:

> I studied really hard for the test and got a low grade, so next time I won't study and I should get a higher grade.

This assumes a connection between studying and failure, without considering other possible reasons for failure. Similarly:

> The number of cows in the US has gone down, and the amount of cheese consumed is on the increase. Psychologically, people seem to eat more cheese when they feel that it will run out.

This assumes that the increase in cheese consumption is related to the number of American cows, whereas it may have been for other reasons such as increased vegetarianism or a rise in cheese imports. The decrease in the cow population might relate only to herds reared for meat—perhaps the number of milking cows is unaltered.

These examples are chosen to highlight the faulty logic, but flawed reasoning of this sort is not always easy to spot.

Drawing general conclusions based on one or few examples

> The woolen jacket caused a serious skin reaction in the three-year-old, so sale of woolen clothing should be banned.

Here a generalized conclusion is made on the basis of a very small sample of experience—just one example. (The importance of using an adequate sample is explored further below.) There may have been reasons for the reaction unique to that child.

Inappropriate comparisons

In Passage 1, a comparison is drawn between children who play indoors and those who play outdoors. However, it may have been that the children who played outdoors were already healthier, and those who played indoors did so because of poor health that might get worse if they played outdoors. For example, asthma sufferers are often allergic to pollen and might have been discouraged from playing outdoors.

3 Question surface appearances

Critical thinking requires that you examine these factors:

- Is the evidence what it appears to be?
- Might there be other explanations apart from the obvious one?
- Has all necessary information been given, or might other details lead to a different conclusion?
- Are there interested parties who would gain if the conclusions were accepted?
- Are there hidden assumptions or agendas?
- Does the evidence come from a reliable, disinterested source?

Activity 2

Look again at the "Rochboro Health" passage.

- What hidden agendas might there be in this piece?
- What information may be missing that might lead to a different conclusion?

(See page 163 for feedback.)

4 Identify evidence in the text

Identifying evidence in the text is usually fairly straightforward. Look for statistics, examples, case histories, findings from experiments, surveys, questionnaires or case studies. The evidence may be anecdotal—that is, stories told by one or a few people about their experiences.

Activity 3

What evidence is given in the "Rochboro Health" passage? (See page 163 for feedback.)

5 Evaluate the evidence

It is not enough for a student to write in a paper: "There is evidence on both sides." Evidence is not all of equal weight. How can we decide which evidence is better? Some basic steps are outlined next.

Use valid criteria to evaluate evidence

Critical thinking involves identifying valid criteria against which something can be evaluated.

You look healthy to me, as your teeth are not blue

For example, in declaring that somebody is healthy, a doctor takes into account certain criteria, such as body temperature, blood measurements and the absence of known (or common) symptoms of illness. He or she evaluates if signs of potential ill-health are matters for concern and, based on experience and established medical knowledge, comes to a conclusion about whether the evidence points more towards good health than to sickness.

The following sections give some criteria against which you can evaluate evidence in academic texts and for your own work.

Check the date of the research

Data may be out of date or conclusions based upon it may have been revised. How would your attitude to the "Rochboro Health" article change if you found out that it was written in 1300, or 1927, or 2012?

Check the source of your information

Articles in academic or professional journals and in recommended textbooks are usually based on in-depth research and are regarded as more reliable than findings recorded in magazines and newspapers. Newspapers and magazines may be useful primary sources for some subjects, such as cultural studies, but are not generally regarded as "authorities" to quote in papers.

Check for bias in your sources

Bias may not be obvious, and it does not necessarily mean that your source was being "dishonest" or "prejudiced." If somebody has a strong interest in the survival of a particular hospital, for example, the evidence they present may be accurate yet not the whole story. When thinking critically, we need to be continually questioning in our minds if there may be hidden agendas, or reasons why the evidence appears to point one way rather than another.

It is always worth considering what political or economic interests might prevent the whole truth

from emerging. Consider also how easy it would be, or would have been, for alternative views to be printed and circulated. For example, in some societies, such as sixteenth-century Britain, people who spoke, printed or sold certain viewpoints could be punished by death or loss of limb.

Today, it can be difficult for small organizations or individuals to get the funding they need to research and validate an alternative viewpoint. The overall picture may be distorted if not all the evidence has come to light.

While it is not necessary for you to write about issues of economics, politics and media access in every paper, it is important to be aware of who has access to power, resources and information, who does not, and the possible implications.

Beware the allure of numbers and statistics

It is important to check numerical data, and words that *imply* numerical data, as these are often misused and amounts misrepresented in order to sway the reader—see Chapter 13, page 289.

Most/many   Notice words such as "most" and "many":

> Most people said that they preferred oranges to apples.

"Most" is a very vague amount. If it *mattered* whether this statement were true or false, we would need more details. How many people were asked? How many preferred oranges? Under what circumstances?

Percentages Notice when percentages are given. Supposing, instead, the statement above read:

> 60% of people preferred oranges; 40% said they preferred apples.

This looks convincing: Numerical quantities are given. But is the difference between 60% and 40% *significant*? Here we would need to know how many people were asked. If 1000 people were asked, of whom 600 preferred oranges, the number would be persuasive. However, if only 10 people were asked, 60% simply means that 6 people preferred oranges. "60%" sounds convincing in a way that "6 out of 10" does not. As a critical reader, you need to be on the lookout for percentages being used to make insufficient data look impressive.

Sample size Notice also that if just 2 more people arrived who preferred apples, there would be 6 of each. A very small increase in the *sample* (the database of people asked) could easily overturn the original percentage, changing it to 50% for apples and 50% for oranges—no difference at all.

The sample size is the number of people, animals or objects used in the research, whether it's an experiment, a survey or whatever. Small samples give very unreliable information. All other things being equal, the bigger the sample, the more reliable the data. A thousand participants is often taken as a reasonable number for considering statistics to be "significant."

Representativeness The sample should be representative of the overall group being studied. If all those asked about fruit preference came from California and made their living from oranges, we might not consider them to be either typical or reliable as a sample. Similarly, if all those asked about their preferences were women, or age ten, or from New York City, it would not be safe to generalize from them to the rest of the population. To make the sample representative, researchers aim for a good mix of men and women, of different ages, backgrounds and interests.

Conditions of data collection If you found out that those who said they preferred oranges had each been given one free by the person conducting the survey, you might wonder if the participants had had an ulterior motive in giving their answers and if the data were reliable.

Similarly, if the data were collected in face-to-face interviews by personnel wearing the logo of a company known for its orange juice, it is possible that some participants wished to please the interviewers. It is important to find out, where possible, about the conditions in which data were collected, to determine how trustworthy they are. Articles in academic journals usually give full details about the research conditions.

Emotive language and persuader words

Certain words can be very persuasive and can trigger a position of trust in the reader. Which words they are will vary from subject to subject. For example, for some people the word "experiment" summons up notions of scientific accuracy and reliability. However, the fact that an experimental approach was used does not in itself mean that the evidence is sound.

Emotive words The use of words and phrases such as "cruel," "unfair," "abuse," "natural," "normal," "commonsense," "innocent child," "old," "little," "massive," "unique," "extremist," "radical," "youth," "new" and even "final offer" can prompt emotional responses that may lead the reader away from an accurate appraisal of the evidence presented. Emotive images, such as people crying, can be used in a similar way.

Persuader words   These words and phrases draw you in by appealing to what they claim is evident. It may be true that what follows is evident, but you still need to be on the alert when you see such words. They include "surely," "clearly," "obviously," "it is evident that," "it is plain to see that," "naturally" and "of course."

Activity 4

Evaluate the evidence given in the "Rochboro Health" passage, using the criteria outlined above. (See page 163 for feedback.)

6 Identify the writer's conclusions

Conclusions generally come at the end of the piece of writing. However, they may also be found at the beginning of the text or even in the middle. They are then harder to find and tend to be less effective.

Often conclusions are indicated by "trigger words," such as "therefore," "so," "hence" or "thus'; or by the use of imperatives—words indicating that something *has* to be done, such as "must," "should" or "need to."

Activity 5

Identify the conclusion in the "Rochboro Health" passage. (See page 163 for feedback.)

Sometimes the conclusion may not be stated at all—it may only be implied by the arguments and evidence. There may also be more than one conclusion to draw from a text, with some conclusions stated explicitly and others implicit. For implicit conclusions, you need to consider if further conclusions are implied by the reasoning and the context. For example:

In Jonah Smith's new book, the characters are compelling, the story is interesting, it is very atmospheric, and there is a surprising twist to the plot. The book is excellent.

Here the *explicit* conclusion is that "The book is excellent," and the reasons for this judgment have been given—the characters, the story, the atmosphere and the twist to the plot. The *implicit* conclusion is that you too would enjoy this book.

Activity 6

For each of the following short texts:

■ Decide if there is an explicit conclusion and, if so, say what this is.
■ Say what you think the implicit conclusions would be.

 1 You want a plant, you like this one and you can afford it.
 2 The election closed very early, but only Happy Party voters had been told this would happen. Happy Party supporters prevented some opposition party voters from voting. Therefore, the election was unfair.
 3 The tree is dangerous. It is leaning over the children's playground. It is heavy, rotten and could break at any time.

(See page 163 for feedback.)

7 Evaluate if the evidence supports the conclusions

A writer may present evidence that could be considered reliable, being based on good research, but then draw conclusions that are not warranted by the evidence. An exaggerated example illustrates this:

■ Proposition 1 *The karate champion is a woman.* (Verifiable fact.)
■ Proposition 2 *My mother is a woman.* (Verifiable fact.)
■ Conclusion *My mother is a woman, therefore she is a karate champion.* (False conclusion.)

Check for hidden false assumptions

In the above example, the faulty reasoning was based on the false assumption that if *one* woman is a karate champion, then *all* women are karate champions. This false assumption is easy to spot, but it is not always so simple. Researchers may try to be objective, but it is very difficult to stand completely outside of the commonsense views and ideological context of the society in which one is writing.

Example

Take a look at the ideas discussed in the student papers in Chapter 12 about Bowlby's influential studies of the 1950s (pages 283–287). Bowlby's findings (1951, 1969) suggested that infants who were separated from their mothers at an early age had behavioral and emotional difficulties later. This was used to argue the case against mothers working outside the home. The argument for mothers to stay home was no doubt based on genuine concerns for children's well-being, but the conclusion also suited the economic conditions of the time, as there was a shortage of jobs for men who had returned from the Second World War (1939–45).

Later, the conclusion that children were damaged by absent mothers and child care was heavily criticized (Clarke and Clarke 1976; Clarke-Stewart 1988; Tizard 1991). For example, it was argued that Bowlby's data was based on children in very extreme conditions, such as frightened war orphans and sick children in bleak hospitals and institutions of the 1950s. These children were not typical, and needed to be compared with average, healthy children attending friendly, well-run day care centers, who saw their mothers every day. However accurate Bowlby's research may have been, his findings may not have justified the conclusions drawn from them. It is quite likely that Bowlby was affected by the dominant belief system of his day, that a woman's place was at home with the children, and that this influenced his interpretation of the data. It is also likely that his opponents were influenced in their research by changing ideas, such as feminism, or by the rising number of women in part-time work.

It is quite typical for research to progress in this way, with advances being made as later researchers question aspects of earlier research, such as whether the sample was representative or whether the research contained assumptions that were invisible to the researchers at the time.

Passage 3: Children at Play

Children need to play outdoors and yet it is amazing how few children get that opportunity today. Although Smith (2004) argues that 48% of children prefer to play inside, Jones (1964) found that 98% of children in the US prefer to play outdoors. I spoke to some parents in Rochboro who said their children missed out by not being able to play down by the river or roam the countryside in safety. Most children are now television addicts or, worse, are addicted to computer games. Everybody knows that this is damaging children educationally, and yet nothing is done about it. This is certainly true of Rochboro's children, and the main reason is that they do not have anywhere to play. Hardly anybody in Rochboro has a garden. It would be better for their health if they played outdoors, but parents say they won't let them unless supervised play areas are provided. The parents are worried that they cannot see their children when they are playing. What chance is there for the health of citizens in Rochboro if its children do not get to play outdoors and end up as TV addicts?

Critical analytical thinking

Now that you have worked through one passage step by step, try analyzing Passage 3, "Children at Play." This writer covers issues similar to those in Passage 2, so you can compare the passages.

Activity 7

Do you consider that the evidence in the "Rochboro Health" passage supports the conclusion drawn? What assumptions are made in the passage? (See pages 163–164 for feedback.)

Activity 8

- Is the line of reasoning good?
- What is the conclusion?
- How strong is the evidence?
- What are the underlying assumptions?
- How well do the reasoning and the evidence support the conclusion?

(See pages 164–165 for feedback.)

Critical analytical thinking

Use the following checklist to analyze a piece of writing that you need to read for an assignment. You could also use this list to analyze your own writing.

Critical questions	Analysis of the writing
What is the main line of reasoning (the main thesis or argument)?	
Is the line of reasoning clear both in the introduction and in the conclusion?	
What is the key evidence used to support the line of argument? Is the evidence presented in a way that develops the argument and leads clearly to the conclusion?	
When was the evidence produced? Is it up to date? Is it still relevant?	
Is there sufficient evidence to prove the case? Is the evidence relevant? What might be missing?	
What (if any) would have been a better order in which to present the evidence so as to strengthen the line of reasoning?	
Are there any examples of flawed reasoning? Attempts to persuade the reader through an appeal to the emotions? Is evidence interpreted and used correctly?	
Has the writer given sufficient consideration to alternative points of view? Give examples.	

Chapter 7

Critical thinking when writing

Critical thinking when *writing* includes most of the elements of critical thinking when *reading*. It can be more difficult to analyze your own work critically, however, and to recognize and admit to your own opinions and bias.

Students' writing is often weakened because their thinking is not clear before they start to write their final draft. This is partly a question of planning (see Chapter 11) and partly of spending enough time critically evaluating both what they have read and their own ideas and writing. Time spent in critical analysis is equivalent to "elaborating the problem"—a process that, as we saw in Chapter 4, was one way in which those who achieved good grades differed from those with poor grades.

Be clear about your conclusions

It is surprising how often students hand in work which shows that although they have done the necessary reading and even given their work considerable thought, they are not sure of their conclusions. The whole of the piece of writing should lead to its conclusion: If the conclusions are vague or understated, *all* of the writing loses its force.

As soon as you are given a piece of work to do, write down what you think your conclusion will be. Put this where you can see it. Whenever you find out something that requires you to review or fine-tune your conclusion, write out a new one. It may seem paradoxical (or back to front), but your writing will be clearer if you write your conclusions first.

Have a clear line of reasoning

If your conclusions are clear, your argument or line of reasoning is likely to be clear also. The conclusion gives you a target at which to direct your shots.

Keep your writing focused rather than rambling. Bear in mind four key points:

1 Early drafts may be helpful in elaborating and refining your thinking. However, be sure that your final version says what you really think.
2 Work to a writing plan that sets out the reasons, examples and evidence in the most logical order.
3 Consider how best to link ideas and pieces of information, so that your writing is not just a list of facts but a line of reasoning.
4 Keep your argument clear. From the sea of information gathered at the research stage, select the points that best support your thesis and signpost them clearly.

Use evidence to support your reasoning

Use evidence selectively: Too many examples may obscure your line of reasoning. Choose a few items that clearly support your case.

Evaluate your own writing through critical reading

As a student, you also have "readers." Your instructors or examiners will take a critical reading approach when grading your work. Examine your own writing in the same way you would examine someone else's, as outlined above.

Take multiple perspectives

Whether you are reading, listening, observing or writing, you will be expected to be able to analyze your own and others' arguments—and indeed work, designs or proposals—from more than one perspective. This will mean considering *both* their good *and* their bad points, *both* their strengths *and* their weaknesses.

When you think critically and analyze things from several perspectives, the answer is seldom a straightforward one of right or wrong. Usually there are many contradictory pieces of evidence to weigh and evaluate against each other.

Critical analytical writing vs. descriptive writing

Critical writing

In general, students lose more points for lack of critical analysis than for any other single weakness in their work.

Good critical writing generally makes the difference between getting a good GPA and getting a lower GPA. Typical instructor comments on student writing include:

- "More analysis needed."
- "Less description, more critique."
- "Too descriptive."
- "Descriptive rather than analytical."
- "You have told me what the theory is rather than how you evaluate it."

Finding the balance

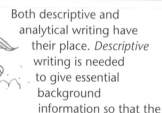

Both descriptive and analytical writing have their place. *Descriptive* writing is needed to give essential background information so that the writing makes sense to the reader. However, this should usually be kept to the bare minimum—if you use up most of your word limit on description, you will have fewer words to use for the *analytical* writing that could bring you high grades.

Skilled writers use descriptive writing in the appropriate sections of their writing (see **Writing the report**, page 330), or weave small amounts of descriptive writing *into* their critical writing.

Some of the main differences between these two types of writing are outlined in the table below.

Descriptive writing	Critical analytical writing
states what happened	identifies the significance
states what something is like	evaluates strengths and weaknesses
gives the story so far	weighs one piece of information against another
states the order in which things happened	makes reasoned judgments
says how to do something	argues a case according to the evidence
outlines what a theory says	shows why something is relevant or suitable
outlines how something works	indicates why something will work (best)
notes the method used	identifies whether something is appropriate or suitable
states when something occurred	identifies why the timing is of importance
states the different components	weighs up the importance of component parts
states options	gives reasons for selecting each option
lists details	evaluates the relative significance of details
lists in any order	structures information in order of importance
states links between items	shows the relevance of links between pieces of information
gives information	draws conclusions

Identifying critical and descriptive writing

Descriptive writing: an example

My name is John. I live at 33 Acacia Drive. I have five sisters and brothers. I am good at team games, and enjoy soccer, basketball, and baseball. Team games were encouraged by both my parents. All of my family took part in sport. Our teachers at Beckfield High School were very interested in sports sciences. We were encouraged to drink lots of water to improve our performance. Our team always did well, so it seems to have worked. I also like to go running. I live in the beautiful Appalachian Mountains, so it is a pleasure to take a healthy run each day.

Almost all of this passage consists of statements and descriptions. There is an evaluative comment ("our team always did well"), and this is linked to possible reasons (drinking lots of water). However, this link is not *analyzed* in depth. The passage overall is descriptive. Compare this to the passage below.

Critical analytical writing: an example

At Beckfield High School, teachers took a scientific approach to high school sports over a three-year period. In particular, students were encouraged to monitor their intake of liquids. All students were required to drink a minimum of eight glasses of tap water a day. The high school did consistently well in sports competitions over this period, and the teachers claimed that this was proof of the importance of liquid intake to good performance. However, it is not clear that the school's sports performance can be attributed to water intake. Beckfield High School's claims were investigated by an independent researcher, Martinez (2008). Martinez argued that although Beckfield's performance was good, its performance in competitions was consistent with what would be expected of a high school of its size. In addition, interviews with students showed that most had not followed the school regulations on drinking water. Most students stated that they drank less than one glass of tap water a day. Although other research does suggest that water intake benefits performance (Fredo, 2005; Mitsuki, 2005), Beckfield High School's claims about the benefits of tap water in its sports success have not been proven.

This is critical analytical writing. There is a clear line of reasoning that takes the reader through what the high school claimed and the basis of its thesis. The writing then weighs the school's claims against other evidence. It draws upon published evidence rather than personal opinion. The writer considers both sides of the argument, taking account of published evidence that does support the importance of drinking water. This research has been weighed against the facts of the case. The writer draws conclusions: The "high school's claims about the benefits of tap water … have not been proved." The conclusion is based upon the evidence.

The passage does contain descriptive writing that gives background detail, such as the first four sentences. Although the passage contains many statements of fact, such as "most students stated that they drank less than one glass of tap water a day," these statements are ordered in such a way that they build up the argument. They are also supported by sentences that introduce the argument, such as "However, it is not clear that the high school's sports performance can be attributed to water intake."

Activity

Identify whether the following passages are examples of descriptive or of critical writing. (Feedback is given on page 165.)

Passage 1

In the West, all life forms are divided into one of two categories: plant or animal. Animals move and take in food. Plants are rooted into the earth in some way and lack locomotion. They photosynthesize their food. Zoologists study animals, and botanists study plants. Bacteria were classified as plants because many kinds of bacteria photosynthesize their food. However, they also have locomotion. Recent research has shown that there is an enormous variety of bacteria. Some are able to survive at extreme temperatures and in the absence of oxygen. Most plants cannot usually survive in those conditions. Therefore, even though bacteria photosynthesize, they are not now regarded as plants.

Passage 2

The difficulty in categorizing bacteria was partly based on the assumption that all life forms were divided into two main categories, plants and animals. Organisms that photosynthesized and lacked mobility were classified as plants; those that had locomotion and ingested food were classified as animals. Bacteria were traditionally categorized as plants because many forms of bacteria photosynthesized their food like plants. However, bacteria also have locomotion, which is associated with animal life. Genetic research has now shown that there are at least eleven major divisions of bacteria, all of which are more genetically distinct than plants are from animals (Fuhrman *et al.*, 1992). In addition, the minute organisms formerly described as "bacteria" are now found to consist of several major kingdoms and domains of unicellular and multicellular life (bacteria, archaea, eucarya) (Woese, 1994). This research is significant as it has shown that the fundamental division of all life forms into "plant" or "animal" was an error, and that plants and animals form only a very small part of a much more diverse range of living organisms.

Passage 3

Scientists do not agree about the extent to which creativity can be linked to activity in the right hemisphere of the brain. It is known that the biochemistry of the two hemispheres of the brain is different. For example, there is more of the neuro-transmitter norepinephrine in the right hemisphere than the left (Oke *et al.*, 1978). Norepinephrine is associated with increased alertness to visual stimuli. It has been suggested by Springer and Deutsch (1981) that this may lead to increased right-hemisphere specialization for visual and spatial perception. However, this link is not yet proven. It is not yet clear whether one hemisphere of the brain can be responsible for any creative task. Moreover, although it might seem reasonable to assume that responsiveness to visual stimulus may be an important factor of creativity, this has also not yet been proved.

Passage 4

The brain contains millions of neurons. These communicate with each other through electro-chemical activity at the synapses found at the end of each neuron. The chemicals that enable this communication to take place are known as neuro-transmitters. Each neurotransmitter is associated with different kinds of message. The different messages to the brain influence the way we respond to events that take place in our internal or external world. Some neurotransmitters are associated with mood swings, with depression, with rapid responses and so forth.

Passage 5

Bowlby's Attachment Theory argues that child development is affected by the closeness of the bond between a mother and her child. Bowlby claimed that even short spells away from the mother during infancy could have a profound effect upon a person later in life. This became known as "maternal deprivation theory." According to this theory, the relationship with the mother during an early "critical period" gives the developing child an "internal working model." This model then forms the foundation of all future relationships.

Feedback on the activities

Critical thinking when reading (pages 151–157)

Passage 1: Rochboro Health

Activity 1: The main line of reasoning

"Outdoor play is good for children's health, so Rochboro needs better facilities for it."

Activity 2: Vested interests

The article was published by the Playcouncil, which is likely to have a vested interest in arguing for more supervised play spaces.

Activity 3: Types of evidence used

The main evidence is of two kinds: surveys and anecdotes. The detail about the Arkash family is anecdotal (it is just one person's experience). There is also a statistic about garden ownership.

Activity 4: Evaluating the evidence

The evidence about health and parental attitudes comes from official sources which could be considered relatively good "authorities" and thus reliable. This evidence is relevant and contributes to the argument.

On the other hand, the writer generalizes from only one set of health factors (those related to the lungs). It is possible that children who play outdoors have *different* health problems—such as skin complaints or broken ankles. Alternatively, it is possible that the children who played indoors did so because they were more prone to sickness already (such as asthma and pollen allergies). Sickness may have been the *cause* of their playing indoors, rather than the *effect*.

We don't know how representative the children in the survey were of all Rochboro children.

The anecdotal details about the Arkash child and the fox are emotive, and not really relevant to the main thesis. The anecdote provides human interest for journalistic writing but would be unacceptable in most academic writing.

No source is given for the figure of 18% garden ownership: We can't judge if it is reliable.

The writer twice mentions the effects of outdoor play on social interaction but gives no evidence or details. She or he could link this in more to the main argument.

Activity 5: Conclusion

The conclusion is that Rochboro should provide more supervised outdoor play areas.

Activity 6: Implicit conclusions

1 There is no explicit conclusion. The implicit conclusion is that you should buy this plant.
2 The explicit conclusion is that the election was unfair. The implicit conclusions are that the election results shouldn't count and that the election should be held again.
3 The explicit conclusions is that the tree is dangerous. The implicit conclusion is that it should be made safe or removed.

Activity 7: Evidence supporting the conclusion

The writer makes a reasonable case and gives supporting evidence. However, there is insufficient evidence to support the conclusion that "in order to improve the health of its children, Rochboro needs to provide more supervised outdoor play areas." We don't know what it is about playing outdoors that led to the health improvements. For example, it may be that children ran about more when they were outdoors and that an indoor running area would have the same effect.

Underlying assumptions

The passage assumes:

1 That playing outdoors is better for all children's health. This may not be the case.
2 That the health of children who play indoors at present would necessarily improve by playing outdoors. This may not be true.

3 That playing outside decreases the incidence of asthma and bronchial conditions.

4 That beneficial effects are available only from outdoor play areas. In fact, it may have been other factors about the outdoor play, such as space to run or things to climb, that led to improved health indicators.

5 That there are not enough supervised play areas already for Rochboro children. No figures are quoted for existing supervised play areas so we do not know if more spaces are needed. The sources the writer quoted don't mention a need for more play spaces. We do not know what percentage of children already play outdoors. All these gaps mean that the writer has not given sufficient evidence to support the conclusion.

Activity 8: Critical analytical thinking

On the right is Passage 3 again, with reference numbers added.

Logical progression: the line of reasoning

This kind of writing is likely to receive a comment such as "What is your point?" It is difficult to identify the thread running through the passage: The line of reasoning is weak. The writer hops backwards and forwards between different types of information, as at (8), having already mentioned these points earlier. The final sentence does not add to what has been stated earlier, at (4).

The conclusion

The conclusion is not clear. The nearest approximation to a conclusion is at (1), "Children need to play outdoors," as this largely sums up the passage. The writing does not draw its information towards a final conclusion, and the final lines of the passage don't lead anywhere. Compare this to the "Rochboro Health" passage, which leads to a clear conclusion.

The evidence

The evidence is weak, with insufficient detail. The places marked (2) all require further evaluation of the evidence: "How many children? How many parents? How representative are they of Rochboro parents as a whole? What other views were expressed? How many exactly have gardens? How do we know this?"

Passage 3: Children at Play

Children need to play outdoors (1) and yet it is amazing how few children (2) get that opportunity today. Although Smith (2004) argues that 48% of children prefer to play inside, Jones (1964) found that 98% of children in the US prefer to play outdoors (2b). I spoke to some parents in Rochboro (2) who said their children missed out by not being able to play down by the river or roam the countryside in safety (3). Most children are now television addicts or, worse, are addicted to computer games (4). Everybody knows that this is damaging children educationally (5), and yet nothing is done about it. This is certainly true of Rochboro's children (4), and the main reason is that they do not have anywhere to play (6). Hardly anybody in Rochboro has a garden (2). It would be better for their health if they played outdoors (7), but parents say they won't let them unless supervised play areas are provided (2). The parents are worried that they cannot see their children when they are playing. What chance is there for the health of citizens in Rochboro if its children do not get to play outdoors and end up as TV addicts? (8)

An instructor might also comment that the writer has not analyzed the sources. At (2b), although the writer uses statistics, these are not recent. She or he offers no possible explanations for why Smith's and Jones' research had different findings—such as that they were looking at two different generations of children. The evidence cited confuses the argument rather than supporting it.

Offering evidence to support reasoning

At (7) and (5) issues about health or education could be developed into interesting points, but no evidence or details are given so the reasoning is weak. Compare (7) to the same point in the "Rochboro Health" passage, which is more convincing.

The evidence: emotive language

At (3) the writer appeals to a "golden age" when childhood was safer or better. Referring to children as "addicts" is also very emotive.

The evidence: sources of information

The assertions at (4) may or may not be true. No reliable sources are quoted, so these may be just speculation.

Underlying assumptions

That "Everybody knows" (5) is an assumption on the part of the writer. How does he or she know what "Everybody knows"? Our own experience might suggest to us that most children are not "addicts."

Does the reasoning support the conclusion?

The main conclusion, that children need to play outdoors, is poorly supported by the reasoning. Although some reasons are given, these are in a jumbled order, without supporting evidence, and are mixed in with irrelevancies, such as computer addiction. It is not clear whether an argument is being made on grounds of children's health.

Identifying critical and descriptive writing (pages 161–162)

Passage 1

This is mainly descriptive writing. The writer describes the way that the living world was divided between animals and plants and gives information about recent research. The passage consists mostly of statements. The statements are not linked and ordered in such a way that they build up clearly towards the conclusion. There is little weighing of the evidence in the build-up to the conclusion. The significance of the conclusion itself is not very clear.

Passage 2

This writing is more critical than the previous writing as it gives a reasoned account for the difficulties in classifying bacteria. It draws on research to show why the difficulties existed and evaluates the significance of the research for the wider question of classifying life forms.

Passage 3

This is critical, analytical writing. The writing evaluates the evidence for the theory that the right brain is associated with creativity. The writer draws out aspects about current findings that may prove to be significant in the long term. The writer questions "reasonable assumptions," making clear what has and has not been proved at the time of writing.

Passage 4

This is descriptive writing. It describes one aspect of how the brain works.

Passage 5

This is descriptive writing. It describes Bowlby's theories but does not critically evaluate them. Compare this with the critical analytical writing on pages 283–285.

Review

Critical analytical thinking is an essential skill for most undergraduate and graduate study, and for many programs it is the most important single aspect of study.

As a student, you need to read, listen, write, speak, think, create and work with increasing critical awareness. You will be expected to bring a critical approach to every aspect of your study. You will be expected to examine arguments, evidence and conclusions closely, as well as the links between these. You will be asked to evaluate other people's reasoning and evidence, using criteria to guide you.

Instructors often use the terms "critical analysis" and "analytical writing" interchangeably. Both terms refer to the "detective-like" approach outlined on page 150 and to your ability to explain how people arrived at different conclusions or results.

The more advanced your level of study, the more sophisticated you will need to become in the way you engage critically with the debates in your subject. As you progress through your program,

you will be introduced to further teaching methods and specialist texts that will refine your critical thinking skills.

In the debates that you encounter as a student, in the media or at work, be *active*. Look for strengths and weaknesses. Take note of how your instructors and peers evaluate evidence and theories, and learn from the way in which they draw on evidence and argue their own case.

This chapter has presented approaches for developing your critical skills that build on what you have learned from earlier chapters. You should now feel confident that you have a mental toolkit that will allow you to approach new material in a critical manner and to incorporate critical analysis into your writing.

If you are interested in developing your critical and analytical thinking skills in greater depth, you may find it helpful to look at a further book: Cottrell, S. (2011) *Critical Thinking Skills: Developing Effective Analysis and Argument*, second edition (Palgrave Macmillan).

Chapter 8

Memory

Remember, remember ...

There are times when we want conscious recall of specific information. This may be for everyday purposes—to have information at our fingertips when we need it, to save time by not needing to check information, or for social occasions such as taking part in a quiz. If as a student you are required to take exams, you may be expected to memorize some details, but knowing that you can remember your material also builds confidence.

People generally underestimate their memory. They focus on what they forget rather than what they remember, and rarely appreciate how sophisticated the memory is.

For example, to read this paragraph requires extraordinarily complex feats of memory. You have to remember the complex workings of a language that took you years to learn; you call upon a memory of thousands of known words; you match the look, sound and meaning of particular written symbols to a memory store of thousands of symbols. You integrate all of this in memory and

make sense of what you read. You do all of this within fractions of seconds.

People worry about memory deteriorating with age. Research by Harris and Sunderland (1981) suggests that older people remember some things better than the young. Older people often expect that their memory will be worse, so they notice more when they do forget—yet greater age means that they also have more to remember. Buzan and Keene (1996) argue that learning *improves* with age—and learning involves memory.

Our brains take in much more information than we need: If we don't make active use of the information, it is as if the path to it becomes lost or overgrown, making it hard to access. The *way* we take in information also affects what we remember.

The more you know about how the brain and memory work, the more you can develop techniques to remember *what* you want to remember, *when* you need it.

Individual memory styles

We each have a combination of memory strategies that work best for us. We each use varied strategies to remember different kinds of information.

Activity: how do you remember things?

Try to recall each of the items 1–6 below. After each one, note down what you did to help you remember.

1 What is your cell phone number?
2 How do you use a pencil sharpener?
3 What was your first day in elementary school like?
4 What did you wear yesterday?
5 Where are your best clothes now?
6 How do you get to the nearest mailbox?

You probably used different strategies to remember the phone number than to recall your first day in elementary school. You may have used some of the following strategies—if not, experiment with them now.

Fact strategies

Many techniques may help in learning a fact such as a telephone number. You might try:

- chanting the rhythm of the number
- using your fingers to map out the pattern of movements needed to dial the number
- seeing the number in your mind
- hearing your voice saying the number
- drawing out the digits with your finger
- writing the number down quickly
- noting any memorable peculiarity of the number, such as a repeated pattern (2727) or a reversible number (1331)
- noting any smaller numbers of personal significance to you, such as the year you were born or a relative's house number, contained within the number.

Event strategies

Trying to recall your first day in elementary school may have called up different types of memory.

- The emotional memory of the event may have come to mind—your excitement at starting elementary school, or your distress at being left by your mother, or your fear of the teacher. You might experience this physically in your body, as a tightening of the stomach muscles, for example, or a change in your breathing.
- You may have a strong visual memory of the journey to the school or of moments during the first day. These may run through your head like a film or a series of snapshots.
- You may be able to hear the noises of your elementary school—the shouts in the play area or the school bell. You may remember certain smells, such as that of dry erase markers on your fingers.

Other strategies

In remembering the six items above, you may have used quite different strategies.

- To remember how to use a pencil sharpener, you may have moved your hands to guide you through the sequence of movements.
- To remember what you wore, you may have recalled the place where you were.
- To remember where your clothes are now, you probably used a mixture: Visual recall of where they usually are, and a check through your memory of recent events to see if there was any reason why they might be somewhere else.
- For the mailbox, you may have visualized the local geography, or remembered a time you mailed a letter, or imagined the walk to the box, or repeated instructions under your breath.

- How good do you think your memory is in general?
- Where do you feel your memory strengths lie?

Check your memory style

What helps *you* remember things? Here's a simple way to find out.

- Color in 10 words on the word chart on the right.
- Read through the chart for 2 minutes, then cover it completely.
- Write down all the words you can remember.
- Read the following section as you check your results.

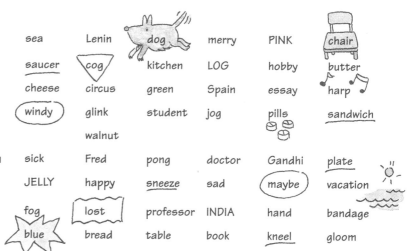

sea	Lenin	dog	merry	PINK	chair
saucer	cog	kitchen	LOG	hobby	butter
cheese	circus	green	Spain	essay	harp
windy	glink	student	jog	pills	sandwich
	walnut				
sick	Fred	pong	doctor	Gandhi	plate
JELLY	happy	sneeze	sad	maybe	vacation
fog	lost	professor	INDIA	hand	bandage
blue	bread	table	book	kneel	gloom

What helps you remember?

Look at the words you recalled. Does the selection of words you remembered suggest that you used any of the strategies below? If so, you have valuable clues about how you can arrange information you *want* to recall.

Your memory may be assisted by any or all of the following.

Recency effect ☐

You may have remembered best the words you learned last.

Primacy effect ☐

You may have remembered best the words you learned first.

Sound ☐

You may have remembered rhyming words, odd-sounding words or words that you heard together in your head.

Locus (place) ☐

You may have associated a word with a place you know.

Real names ☐

You may have a particularly good memory for names.

Visual features ☐

You may have noticed the look of a word (such as the words in capitals or those with shapes around them).

Visual association ☐

You may have linked words with pictures or mental images.

Visual arrangement ☐

You may have remembered where items were on the page. (If so, you may find it easy to recall flowcharts or pattern notes, or be helped by visual spacing or making links with a picture.)

Semantic association ☐

You may have remembered words with meaningful associations, such as bread, butter, sandwich.

Being bizarre and unusual ☐

You may have noticed odd things, such as the words "pong" and "glink" which stand out. (If you did, you may find it helpful to link ordinary things with bizarre images or sounds.)

Stories ☐

You may have linked unrelated items so that they made a story. (This can help with the letters of a difficult spelling. For example, "liaise": Luke Is Always In Such Ecstasy.)

Color and activity ☐

If you remembered several of the words you colored in, you may be sensitive to color; or perhaps you benefit from *doing* things with information you are learning.

Musical association ☐

Did you try singing or chanting information to tunes you know?

Improve your memory

Memory aids

Particular practices can help you remember things. Below are some that are well known, and you may have others of your own.

Self-awareness

Know what tricks and methods you *already* use to remember things.

Repetition or overlearning

This is essential. Go over information at least three times. Check back often, for short lengths of time (rather than once for a long time).

Association

Link what you need to remember with something you already know. See also **Active learning** (pages 83–85).

Mnemonics

Any trick to help you remember is a mnemonic (pronounced *nem-on-ic*). One common mnemonic is to use the first letter of each keyword to make a new "word" that sums up the whole subject—just as "CREAM" sums up Chapter 4. It doesn't matter if the letters don't make a real word.

Active listening

Discuss what you're trying to learn with friends. Listen to your voice saying or reading it. Record yourself. Exaggerate. Use accents. Be dramatic.

Writing things down

In your own words, write things out over and over again.

Personalizing it

Relate what you learn to yourself. (For example, in what way does it *affect* you?

Does it remind you of someone you know or somewhere you have been?)

Play

Play with information. Look for the fun in it. Relax and enjoy the process.

Think about advertisements

Advertising agencies deliberately set out to make us remember their advertisements. The "tricks" and "devices" they employ to prompt our memory can also be used to help us to remember what we study.

Think of three ads (from TV, magazines, billboards, etc.). What makes these three memorable for you?

Devices used by advertisers

Which of these devices are most effective in helping *you* remember?

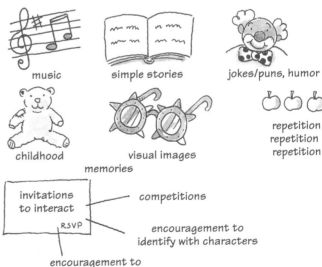

music

simple stories

jokes/puns, humor

childhood memories

visual images

repetition repetition repetition

invitations to interact

RSVP

competitions

encouragement to identify with characters

encouragement to call in

Using the brain

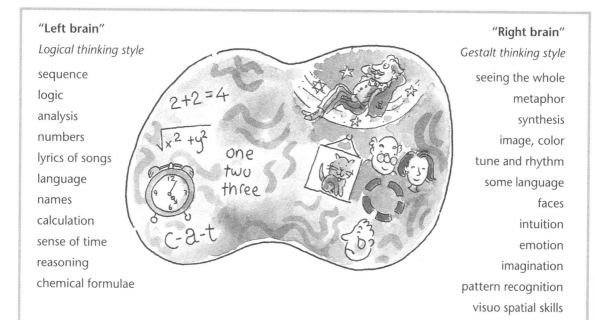

"Left brain"

Logical thinking style

sequence
logic
analysis
numbers
lyrics of songs
language
names
calculation
sense of time
reasoning
chemical formulae

"Right brain"

Gestalt thinking style

seeing the whole
metaphor
synthesis
image, color
tune and rhythm
some language
faces
intuition
emotion
imagination
pattern recognition
visuo spatial skills

Left brain–right brain

The brain is divided into two *hemispheres,* left and right. Research into brain damage shows that different mental functions are affected depending on which hemisphere is damaged. This understanding led to the idea that each hemisphere is generally associated with particular thinking and memory styles.

- The two hemispheres are linked by over 200 million nerve fibers (known as the *corpus callosum*).
- There is a crossover effect: Each hemisphere controls the opposite side of the body.
- The body is designed to help the two hemispheres to work together.
- Each hemisphere is also skilled in the mental capacities of the other hemisphere.

The hemispheres work together

Most activities involve using both hemispheres. For example, to remember a song, you need to bring together both the lyrics (left hemisphere) and the tune (right hemisphere). To remember a person, you need to link the face (right hemisphere) and the name (left hemisphere).

If something in one part of the brain makes learning difficult, the brain has a tremendous capacity for finding a different route to learning. This suggests that if something proves difficult to learn or memorize in one way, there is likely to be a different way your brain could learn it.

Many people identify more with either the logical or the Gestalt thinking style. Do you think you are more "left brain" or "right brain" dominant? You can use your preferred style to link information across the hemispheres. This encourages the parts of the brain to work better together and makes learning easier.

Using left and right brain to improve memory

Although the brain uses both hemispheres for almost any activity, you can encourage this process, giving greater brain integration and making use of more of your brain.

If you have a "right brain" preference

- Draw a diagram or picture to show how varied information links up.
- Personalize information—find a way to make it relevant to your own life or experience.
- Use shape and color to highlight and organize information.
- Use different colors for different topics.
- Sing the information you have to learn.
- Move around as you learn—try to recall what you have just learned as you do the housework or walk to the bus stop.

If you have a "left brain" preference

- Write out the information by hand.
- Turn the information into lists.
- Number items of information so that the sequence is clear.
- Use headings to break up the information into different categories.
- Turn information into flow diagrams so you can see progression.
- Build up from details until you get the whole picture.

Locate the information in the brain

Make an experiment. While trying to visualize or recall information, first look up and to the left; then do the same but looking up and to the right. Also try looking left, then right, and then down to each side.

Which direction worked best? Does this hold true for different kinds of information? When you need to recall something, look first in the direction that is appropriate for you for that specific kind of information.

For optimum memory, combine different methods

Whatever your left- or right-brain preference, find a way of linking those skills to the skills associated with the other side. For example, if you are a picture thinker, number and sequence your pictures. If you use lists, then sing or color them. "Left brain" thinkers need to ensure they have the whole picture and can see how everything fits together. "Right brain" thinkers need to ensure they appreciate the sequence, order, and hierarchy of importance.

When learning something, combine a mixture of memory strategies—

look at it	say it aloud
repeat it with rhythm	sing it
write it	draw it
number it	color it
give it a shape	act it out
turn it into a diagram	make it bizarre

—and use any other device you find useful from this chapter.

The triune brain

The brain is also divided "top-down" into three main areas of activity: *reptile brain*, *limbic system* and *neocortex*. McLean (1973, cited in Rose 1985) referred to this as the "triune brain."

The neocortex

The neocortex is what people generally think of when they speak of "grey matter" or imagine a brain. It controls intellectual processes such as language, thinking and handling numbers.

However, the neocortex is only part of the story: Other parts of the triune brain also affect what can be learned and remembered.

The mammalian brain (or limbic system)

The mammalian brain is located above the brain stem, roughly in the middle of the brain, and consists of a number of organs that control functions such as emotions, pleasure, moods, romance and immunity to disease.

The reptile brain also affects study

In evolutionary terms the reptile brain is the oldest part of the brain. It is situated in the brain stem at the base of the head and manages our basic instinctual and survival responses.

The reptile brain interprets stress or anxiety as a danger to our survival. It tries to help us "escape" by drawing the main resources of the body to the large muscles and producing extra adrenalin, so that we are in a heightened, alert state, ready to run away. Resources are taken away from the areas of the brain that we use for academic study: Logical argument is not needed for basic survival. Being in "survival mode" is not very helpful to study—if we don't use up the adrenaline by moving the big muscles, we may feel tense, overalert, easily distracted and unable to concentrate.

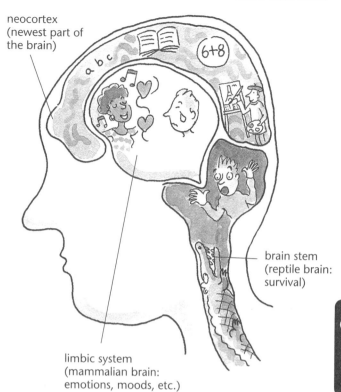

neocortex (newest part of the brain)

brain stem (reptile brain: survival)

limbic system (mammalian brain: emotions, moods, etc.)

Learning

Learning involves interaction among these three aspects of the brain, which are linked through the limbic system.

Some psychologists believe that emotions are the main link among the three areas. Emotions are a great stimulus to memory. The Accelerated Learning Movement uses music, images, color and associations to create unconscious emotional arousal, facilitating faster learning.

A state of "relaxed alertness" helps the imagination, and increases suggestibility and openness to new information. It can also stimulate left–right brain interaction (Rose 1985).

Optimizing study with the triune brain

The following strategies will help you study as effectively as possible.

- Stay relaxed, so that you avoid "survival mode." If you feel tense, go for a walk, stamp your feet, exercise or move around as you learn: This will use up excess adrenaline.
- Once you are relaxed, give yourself a positive emotional outlook on the task in hand: That it is

easy, enjoyable, exciting, fun, interesting, full of surprises.

- Use your imagination to "reframe" difficult or boring subjects as challenges. Set yourself targets, such as "I'll learn three pages in the next half hour" or "This will be the most creative set of pattern notes I have made so far," so that your interest and emotions are involved.
- When studying, listen to music that has an expressive and recognizable melody played on string instruments and has a steady bass rhythm of about 60 beats per minute. Possibilities include classical baroque music (such as Bach or Vivaldi), classical Indian, and New Age healing music.
- Use your imagination to make strong visual links between ideas.
- Make your notes visually striking, pleasant and appealing to the eye.

Stages of the memory process

Another way of using the brain to improve memory is to work with the different stages in the memory process (see page 175).

(see page 175)

> **Four stages in the memory process**
>
> 1 *Taking in information*—noticing or attending to information, and absorbing it.
>
> 2 *Retaining it*—in short-term memory.
>
> 3 *Encoding it*—interacting with the information in working memory so that the brain can store it in long-term memory.
>
> 4 *Recalling it*—retrieving or remembering information, whether on purpose, by accident or in dreams. Recall can seem accurate even when it is not.

Stage 1: Taking information in

What we already know and have a name for affects how we direct our attention, what we notice and therefore what goes into memory. We need to maintain our attention in order to remember.

If you study on "automatic pilot," little attention is involved so you will remember less. You will remember more if you:

- direct your attention consciously and purposefully
- focus in a relaxed way—not with hard concentration
- take breaks and make changes in what you are doing, so as to maintain relaxed attention—a few minutes moving around or doing something different is sufficient
- link information to what you know
- give names and labels to information
- deliberately arrange or adapt information so that it is structured and yet stands out as odd, distinct, different or more interesting—so that it grabs your attention.

Stage 2: Retaining information long enough to remember it

Rehearsing new information in short-term memory helps the working memory hold onto it. Repeating it gives the brain time to call up stored memories to help you make sense of the information and encode it for storage.

Rehearsal must start within a few seconds, as information fades quickly. Rehearsal is a useful strategy for holding onto names, dates, numbers, formulae and instructions for long enough to write them down. You can then employ other memory strategies to remember the information long-term.

Stage 3: Encoding information—the key to memory?

The brain encodes new information so that it can be represented in the memory. Codes may be oral, auditory, kinesthetic (using touch and feelings), verbal, semantic (related to meaning), visual, emotional or motor (using a muscle sequence).

For example, when you tell a story, the brain encodes the pattern of fine-muscle movements you used to speak and stores them. It can also encode and store the sound of your speech on your own ear; the images and emotions that the story brought to mind; the look of the text; and details such as who was in the room or the buzzing of a neon light. The brain links information it has encoded—so any one aspect could trigger the whole memory later. The more facets of an experience the brain has encoded, the more triggers there are to memory.

It follows that you can assist your memory by *choosing* to encode information in several ways. Some are suggested below, but create your own too.

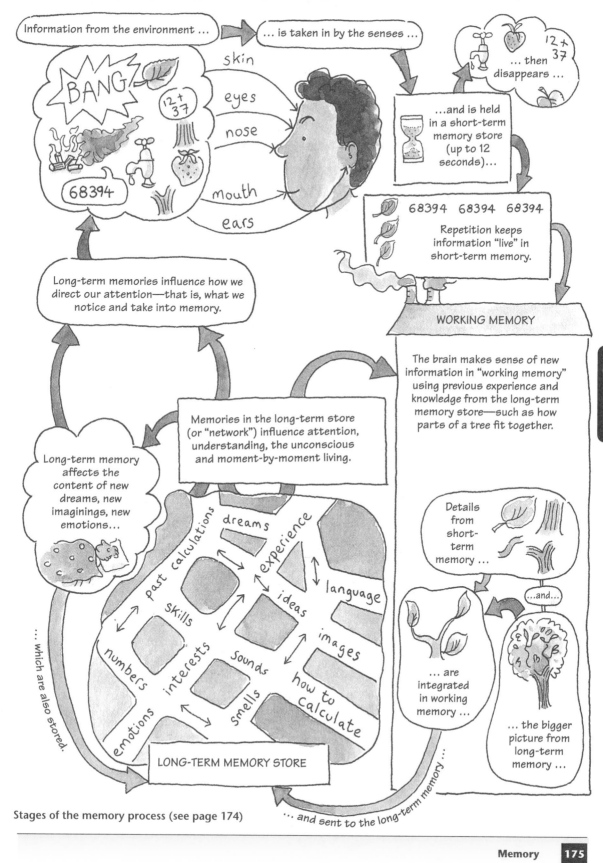

Stages of the memory process (see page 174)

Suggestions for multiple encoding

Use your environment

- Use a different room to study for each subject.
- Notice aspects of the environment such as the light or feel of the room—how do you feel in that place?
- Attach your notes to the furniture. Notice their location.
- Associate a different location with each subject. Associate furniture, windows, plants and ornaments with particular topics.

Use your clothes

- Associate items of clothing with topics in your learning—a shoe could represent one aspect of foreign policy; each button on a shirt could represent a quotation. Clothes with patterns, pockets and buttons are especially useful.
- Wear these clothes when taking the test as a memory trigger.

Use the parts of your body

Parts of your body are especially helpful as triggers to memory, as your body will be there with you during the test!

For example, each hand could represent an essay plan—each finger one major topic; each segment of each finger a principal reference you would use. The fingernails could represent counterarguments; the knuckles could be associated with relevant quotations.

Use motor memory

- Study on the move. If you exercise, associate each movement with something you wish to remember. To refresh the memory, go through the exercise in your mind.
- Writing, drawing and speaking also use motor memory: The fine-muscle sequence is recorded by the brain.

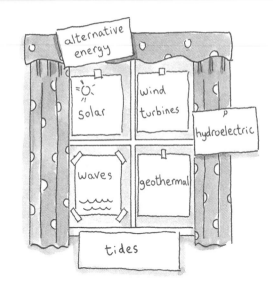

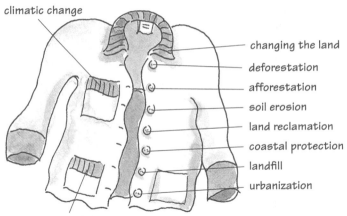

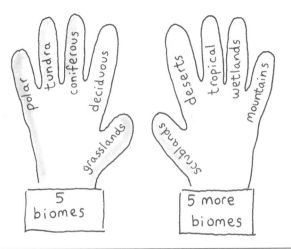

Use auditory memory

- Using a digital recorder, record yourself and then play this recording back.
- Sing an outline for a possible essay question to a well-known tune. Make a list of which tunes go with each subject.
- Go over a topic with a real or imaginary friend, or your cat.
- Read notes aloud in peculiar voices. Overdramatize to make the notes memorable.

Use visual memory

- Make page layouts clear and attractive.
- Turn your material into a film sequence that you can watch in your mind's eye.

- Assign to a topic an object such as a car, and label different bits of the object with the things you need to remember: the steering wheel with your main point; the four wheels with four main theorists; the doors with examples of practical applications of the theory; items in the trunk could remind you of background information or historical development; and parts of the engine or objects on the front seat could indicate future developments.
- To remember complex lists and formulae, such as accountancy balance sheets, use a sequence of images, linked by a story.
- Use scale (size) and visually distinct images to separate out similar or confusing material, such as information about similar theories. Arrange these in a visual hierarchy.

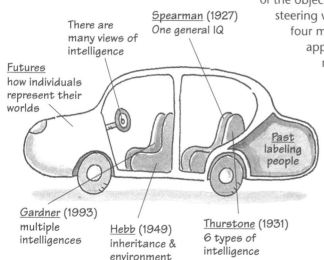

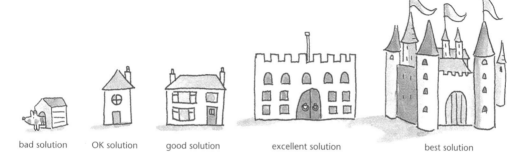

bad solution   OK solution   good solution   excellent solution   best solution

Use color

- Assign each subject area a different combination of colors.
- You may find it useful to use a given color for references or for formulae throughout your notes, so that you can spot them easily.
- Give each theme a different color. As each theme appears, highlight it in the color you allocated to it. You can then see at a glance which pages cover what and which combinations of themes come up together. This makes reading more interactive and finding information faster.
- Use color on pattern notes (page 106) or in concept pyramids (page 251) to indicate information of similar types or levels. Organizing your information clearly in this way can aid recall (see page 180). You may also find that you remember different color combinations easily.
- To help you recall sequences of information, use color combinations that are familiar to you, such as the rainbow, traffic lights or the order of stripes on national flags.

Use verbal memory

- Reduce information to keywords.
- Organize information into hierarchies under headings (see concept pyramids, page 251).
- Write out your information in the fewest words possible—this process encourages interaction with the material.

Use semantic memory

- Spend time considering the *implications* of what you have found out. For example, who is affected? What would it mean for the future? What changes might arise? What theories could this information overturn? What are the moral, legal or ethical consequences?
- Think of a different way of saying what you have already written.
- Decide which are the three most important aspects of the subject, or the most important theories or ideas. Then decide which one is the *most* important.
- Consider all the ways in which one area of a subject is similar to another.

Stage 4: Recall

Good recall is linked to how much attention and awareness you bring to the process of taking in the information and encoding it.

Overlearning to aid recall

If you want to recall information at will, such as for tests or for complicated sequences that you use regularly, you may need to "overlearn." Overlearning is a combination of:

- active learning (see Chapter 4)
- using the techniques from this chapter
- checking back over and over again what you have learned, without looking at prompts.

Strategy for overlearning

1 Make a set of pattern notes or an outline for an essay plan on a large index card or on paper, so that you have an overview.
2 Write names, dates and keywords for the references for each topic on index cards. Check that you can recite or reproduce the information on the card from memory.
3 If you can't, put the prompt card into a plastic folder (so it won't get smudged) and carry it around with you. Glance at it briefly in spare moments, such as at the bus stop or while doing the dishes.
4 Do this several times over a few days. Just looking at the prompt from time to time, or running the information through your head, will keep the memory fresh. Little and often is more effective than simply repeating the information over and over on one occasion.

If the information is hard to remember, there is probably a way of encoding it that suits you better, so experiment with something different.

Memory thrives on organization

Activity

1 Read List A for 15 seconds, then cover it.
2 Recite a nursery rhyme (to prevent rehearsal).
3 Write down the words you remember.
4 Check List A and jot down your score.

Now do the same with List B, including the underlined words. Even if you did not do well with the first list, give it a try.

List A

plum	elbow	giraffe	trailer
puppy	banana	foot	apple
pony	cherry	barge	bungalow

List B

Fruit	Animal	Home	Body
plum	giraffe	house	foot
banana	puppy	apartment	knee
apple	donkey	bungalow	elbow
cherry	pony	trailer	hand

You probably remembered many more items from List B. List B is more memorable because:

- grouping similar items together helps recall
- using group headings helps recall
- being able to see that there are only four types of information gives the task manageable boundaries
- many of the items on List B were also in List A—and going over information again helps recall.

Organizing information into pyramids

Concept pyramids (see page 251) organize associated information into hierarchies. They are excellent memory aids.

In an experiment in 1969, Bower and other psychologists asked a group of people to learn 112 words. The words were grouped and linked meaningfully, as in List B above, and organized into four pyramids. People remembered 100% of the words by the third attempt.

By contrast, a second group of people were given the same words, also arranged into pyramid shapes, but this time with the words randomly assigned to each pyramid—they were not meaningfully (or semantically) linked. The second group remembered only 47% of the words by the third attempt.

This suggests the importance of both:

- linking information meaningfully, *and*
- organizing ideas into hierarchies or concept pyramids.

Pyramids, pattern notes and pictures

Some people prefer to organize information as pattern notes or other images. Combining pattern notes, concept pyramids and pictures can give a great boost to your powers of recall.

Pattern notes and pyramids

Pattern notes work best when generating ideas and for recalling information from memory. Well-organized pattern notes are easier to remember.

- Let your imagination wander when you make the initial pattern. Let the ideas flow (page 106).
- If the initial pattern shows no clear hierarchy of ideas, reorganize the words to fit into a concept pyramid. This may take some time, but it clarifies your thinking (see Chapter 11).
- Color-code the different levels of the hierarchy. For example:
  - red for main headings
  - pink for less important headings
  - yellow and orange for intermediate-level information
  - dark green for key evidence, and light green for details about evidence
  - dark blue for specific examples, and light blue for details about examples
  - violet for references (names and dates).
- Draw circles, boxes or other shapes around crucial information, so that it stands out.

You may find it helpful to build up pattern notes as a series of concept pyramids, or to work back and forth between a pattern and pyramids. You may wish to rework only some parts of the pattern into concept pyramids, and then to stick these pyramids back onto the original pattern with glue or poster tack. There is scope for all kinds of imaginative adaptations.

Pattern notes can be as big as you want—just keep adding and linking information.

Pictures and pattern notes

- You can select any image to anchor your memory—like the car suggested on page 177.
- Associate each part of the picture with one aspect of the topic you wish to remember.
- You can incorporate images into patterns and pyramids. Draw them, or cut images out of magazines and stick them on.
- Add small pictures to increase your interaction with the material and to make it more visually memorable. The better, brighter, odder, and more exaggerated the pictures, the more memorable the pattern.

The example below develops one section of the pattern notes on page 106. The initial ideas have been reorganized into a concept pyramid. Reworking your ideas in this way clarifies the relationship between different ideas, and sorts them into groups and sequences. It can also highlight gaps in your thinking, and suggest new ideas.

Personalize it

Choose what suits you · Use a variety of tools

Shapes · directions → · style · Whatever works · Color · post-its · different papers

that emerge as you note · relevant to the subject · leads the eye to key information · easy to read · experiment

that jogs the memory

to organize information by hierachy · T cells · bell curves

"Chunking" information

Short-term memory is the aspect of memory that allows us to store away some information for a few seconds while we focus on a different aspect of the problem, such as keeping a phone number in our head while we find a pen to write it down, or remembering to carry and add a digit to the next column when we add up numbers larger than 10.

Nobel-Prize winner Herbert Simon found that we can generally hold five "chunks" of information in short-term memory (1974). However, the "chunk" can vary enormously in size: It could be a single word or number, or a phrase, or a whole story, or how to count up to a million. Try this out for yourself.

- Read the list under "Small chunks."
- Cover the list, then try to remember each phrase exactly.
- Do the same for the "Bigger chunks" list.

You should be able to remember roughly the same number of chunks, irrespective of their size—for example, five sets of two words and five sets of longer sentences.

"Chunking" helps long-term memory

The same principle can be used to help organize information in your long-term memory. This is especially useful when studying for tests. For example, if for one topic you have ten references to remember, arrange the names in the order in which you are likely to use them and then make up a story to link them together into one chunk. Give the story a simple name. The crazier the story, the easier to remember. Good English does not matter for this purpose. In the example, the names are printed in bold.

This is a useful tactic to use whenever you have to remember information that does not link up easily. Most of your course material links up more naturally, and understanding how it fits together as a whole reduces it to a single chunk or fewer chunks.

Small chunks (2 words)

Happy Birthday	No Smoking
No way	Niagara Falls
Mouthwatering	Photo album
Small change	New Year

Bigger chunks (7–10-word sentences)

The rain in Spain falls mainly on the plain.

There is no business like show business.

Once upon a time there were three little pigs.

There is no escaping from your conscience.

Somewhere over the rainbow, way up high.

I hope you know what you are doing.

To be or not to be, that is the question.

The pen is mightier than the sword.

Example

Names to memorize

Gordon	Pilkington	Snodgrass
Collins	Rockford	Rider
Manchu	Frankle	Webster

Linking story

Bike story

Mr. **Gordon**, drinking gin, shouted at glassy Mr. **Pilkington**, that the **Snodgrass** needed cutting before the colicky **Collins** children slipped off their bikes onto the **Rock**ford. The first bike **Rider** was **Manchu**-ing [chewing] candy and fell off because his Fr-**Ankle** got caught in the spokes. He fell into a spider's **Web**ster.

What do we remember?

Flanagan (1997) argues that we remember:

- 20% of what we read
- 30% of what we hear
- 40% of what we see
- 50% of what we say
- 60% of what we do
  and
- 90% of what we read, hear, see, say *and* do.

These are clearly not scientific figures, but they suggest the importance of interaction with the material and of using all your senses. This chapter has aimed to give you ideas on how to work towards that 90%—or better. Participants in Bower's research (see page 179) were able to gain 100% recall, and that was without multi-sensory involvement. By combining all of these strategies, you can greatly enhance your memory potential.

Review

Memory is an active process. There are innumerable ways of enhancing it: If one doesn't work, try another approach that might suit you better.

Work with your own learning style and memory preferences to try out new ways of remembering things. Creativity and imagination are essential ingredients. To remember well, it helps if you are relaxed, if you have fun with the memory process and if you play with information until you find a helpful mnemonic. Be aware that what works for one kind of information might not work for another—some trial and error is involved.

You can enhance your memory by using your brain fully. Be aware of your "left brain"/"right brain" preference, the action of the three parts of your triune brain and the different stages of the memory process. The way you encode and organize information is particularly important.

Take charge of your conscious memories. You may achieve remarkable improvements!

Chapter 9

Test-taking

LEARNING OUTCOMES

This chapter offers you opportunities to:

- find out more about different types of tests and how you can best prepare for each

- develop ideas for approaching studying in the long term and in the buildup to tests

- consider other preparation needed apart from study

- develop strategies and techniques to help during the test

- learn ways of managing stress in order to facilitate your learning

- feel you have some control over the test-taking experience.

The prospect of tests and exams can be extremely stressful, whether you have performed well or badly in the past. You may even feel resentful—that it is a waste of your time, or that you know the material but cannot show your knowledge under test conditions. Understanding the reasons for tests, and knowing you have some control over the process, can help to create the positive mind-set needed for a successful test-taking experience.

The purpose of tests

The main purpose of tests is for instructors to check that you have understood the work covered in the class and that the work which demonstrates this is entirely your own.

Preparing for tests involves a high release of energy and an unusual degree of focus, which produces a very intense kind of learning. That focus and intensity are not easy to reproduce under any other conditions.

Different types of tests

The tests you will be asked to take are likely to vary. Possible formats include short-answer questions,

multiple-choice questions (MCQs), true or false questions, fill-in-the-blank questions or essay-based exams. Often tests may require you to answer questions based on several of these formats.

Each type of test calls for a different set of preparation and test-taking strategies. You need to think through, and in some detail, exactly what is being examined in each kind of test and how you can best prepare for each.

For each type of test, you need to consider:

- What is specific about this kind of test?
- How appropriate to this kind of test are the strategies and approaches that I used for other types of test?
- How should I adapt my current strategies, or develop completely new ones, for this kind of test?

Fortunately there is no need to reinvent the wheel for every kind of test. Many of the skills covered in this book will help you to study for different kinds of tests.

What does studying for tests involve?

The pressure of tests stimulates you to draw together the strands of your study and to acknowledge areas that need more work. You can view this pressure negatively, as stress and the likelihood of failure, or positively—as a challenge encouraging you to heighten your own expertise.

As a test approaches, it is useful to make adequate preparations.

- Organize your notes. The process of sorting out what is essential from what is interesting in a general way reminds you of what you have covered.
- Reduce your notes to key headings, points and references (name and date only).
- Make master cards with key memory triggers for whole topics. These can be in the form of pattern notes or concept pyramids.
- Check your own learning. Work interactively with materials, then write out or record what you have learned. Check back to your notes and find the areas you omitted. Write and check three times to build up your memory.

Use test files

Some instructors make previous tests available to students as a form of study guide. Ask your instructor if they agree to share previous tests with the class. This allows you to become familiar with the wording of tests, which can sometimes be off-putting: Questions may seem vague as they cannot "give away the answer." It is important to get used to this style well in advance of the test.

- Remember that each question links to an area of the class. You need to find that link and consider which issues the question is directing you towards.
- Look for patterns of recurring questions.
- Depending on the type of test, work out if there is a minimum number of topics you need to study for to answer the required number of questions.

Select what to study

Selection is crucial when studying for tests.

- Multiple-choice tests usually cover a breadth of material, and you will probably have to study everything. (See pages 192 for ideas on how to manage this.)
- For other types of tests or essay-based exams, select which topics you are going to study. For example, if you will need to answer three essay questions, study at least five topics.
- Work out answers to a range of possible questions for each topic, so that you feel able to deal with almost any question that might be set on the topics you have chosen.
- Select the most important theories, references and evidence for each topic. It is much easier to do this before the test than during it.
- Organize the selected information so that it is easier to remember (see Chapter 8).

Draw up a schedule

Work out exactly how much time you have to study, given potential "emergencies," and time to relax.

- If they carry equal points, divide the time equally between the subjects you are studying, and then between the selected topics.
- Set aside time for doing practice tests.
- Read about time management (pages 66–79).

New reading just before the test

Opinion varies on whether you should read new material just before tests. It can keep your thinking fresh and bring your work into perspective. If reading new material confuses you, however, just focus on the notes you have already.

Effective studying

Ten common pitfalls ...	... and how to avoid them
1 Leaving study until the last minute.	Studying is a way of pulling your understanding together in preparation for the test or exam. You can include and plan for study time from the *beginning* of the course. Here are some examples. ■ When planning and reading for a part of the class, write possible test questions on separate pages. Jot brief notes, or page references to material, under each question. ■ Make your notes readable, attractive and visually compelling as you go through the course—this builds the memory. ■ If possible, start to overlearn names, dates and key details from index cards at odd moments early in the semester (see page 178). Even if you forget them, they will be easier to learn a second time around. ■ Begin intense studying about four weeks before each test or exam. ■ Read the sections on "Tests" (pages 190–191 and 204–205) well before the test.
2 Reading through notes over and over again.	■ Use creative and interactive strategies (see Chapters 4 and 8). This keeps your mind alert and helps to integrate information. ■ Instead of just reading, read in order to *find out*. The best way to do this is to look for material related to possible test questions. Ask your instructor if there are test files for your course or invent your own questions. ■ Discussing previous test questions with friends makes this process more interesting. ■ Time yourself taking practice tests without your notes. This will show you areas that you know well and build your confidence for these, as well as showing you which topics need more study.
3 Writing notes out over and over again.	■ This can be a good strategy if you learn through "motor memory." Working to *different* essay plans keeps the information fresh and develops your thinking about the subject. ■ Some people find that rewriting notes interferes with visual recall of their original set of notes. For them, it is preferable to develop one good complete set of notes, plus a series of index cards. ■ Reduce information to a series of memory triggers. Reduce a set of triggers to one keyword or image.
4 Writing out essays and learning them by heart.	This is time-consuming and counterproductive—it is unlikely that the identical question will come up on your test. It is better to spend time reflecting on, and practicing, a range of answers, so that you overlearn the material (see page 178). You will then be able to work with it flexibly during the test, selecting exactly what you need for the exact question given.

Ten common pitfalls ...	... and how to avoid them
5 Finding ways of putting off studying for tests (such as "urgent" things that need to be done, watching TV or chatting with friends or family).	■ Make a study schedule that leaves empty spaces to cater for real emergencies. Do a spell of studying before each "urgent task." ■ Use watching television or other distractions as a reward—put them in your schedule. ■ See *Tricks for getting started* (page 237). ■ You may be missing company. Try studying with other students, or involve others in your learning. Explain a subject to them: Can they understand your explanation? Could they test you on your memory triggers, or ask you questions from your notes?
6 "I can't force myself back to study."	■ Go back over Chapter 4. Check your motivation. ■ Rather than "forcing" yourself, *encourage* and *entice* yourself to study through short-term goals, challenges, creativity, and company. ■ Check that your schedule has sufficient breaks for rest.
7 "I start to panic. I feel I'm never going to get through it all or remember it."	■ Work with positive-minded people. ■ Read about *Dealing with stress* (pages 206–211) and *Memory* (Chapter 8). ■ Work steadily to small goals (page 72). ■ Speak to a professional learning advisor or counselor at your college.
8 "I can't cope with the boredom of it. I start to daydream or wonder why I'm bothering."	■ Work in a lot of shorter spells. ■ Boredom suggests that you are not using a variety of interactive learning techniques, nor your creativity (Chapters 4 and 8). ■ Look for ways of introducing variety into your study sessions. ■ Look for unusual angles on the material you have or images that sum up the material. Think of ways in which seemingly unrelated material could be linked. Invent an essay question or a test for yourself. ■ To stretch your mind and increase your interest, set yourself greater challenges. For example, read a more advanced article on the subject and consider how you could weave any relevant material into your answers.
9 "I have too many responsibilities to make revision practical."	■ Make use of short spells of time, on buses, coffee breaks and the like. ■ Break the work into small pieces. Always carry some work with you. ■ Carry an exam question in your head and scribble down ideas in odd moments.
10 Stopping before the process of overlearning is complete.	■ It is important to keep checking back what you have learned and to reduce your material to shorter, key memory triggers. ■ Keep asking yourself: "How can I use what I have learned to answer other questions that might come up?" ■ Overlearning takes time—use free moments well.

Study strategies

A good study mentality requires creativity, interactive study techniques, a high degree of motivation, time management, working well with others, writing skills and being able to use your powers of selectivity, critical thinking and memory.

As you can see, if you have used the strategies suggested in earlier chapters, you have already advanced towards doing well in your assessments. Check the boxes beside specific learning activities listed below if you think that they would help you. Work these into an *Action plan* (page 189).

Have a study mentality for the whole semester or year

- ☐ Make your notes clear, visual, colorful, dynamic and memorable. Leave lots of space to add new information later in the semester.
- ☐ Make up index cards of key information as you go along.
- ☐ Go over your work at regular intervals so that you have less to do at the last minute.
- ☐ See "Studying pitfalls" (1) on page 185.

Use time carefully

- ☐ Start as early in the year as possible.
- ☐ Draw up a study schedule.
- ☐ Draw up a *Priority organizer* (page 78).
- ☐ Make a study *Time circle* (page 73).
- ☐ Use stray moments to study.

Keep a positive mind-set

- ☐ Work on your motivation (Chapter 4) and your attitude towards tests. Regard difficulties as challenges for which you can devise new strategies.

Work with others

- ☐ Arrange study sessions with friends.

Ask for help

- ☐ Check the syllabus for your class or ask your instructor for details on what will be tested, when, how and why.
- ☐ Find out from instructors how test answers differ from papers written for class.

Use memory triggers

- ☐ Devise memory triggers (Chapter 8).
- ☐ Distill your notes to key points, keywords and memory triggers.
- ☐ Learn by heart essential information only, such as dates, names and formulae.

Study by ear

- ☐ Record yourself answering questions— listening to your own voice can help memory.

Stay healthy

- ☐ Sleep, relax and take plenty of breaks.

Use test files (if you may!)

- ☐ Check which questions come up regularly.
- ☐ Brainstorm answers to past questions.

© Stella Cottrell 1999, 2003, 2008, 2012
The Study Skills Handbook, Palgrave Macmillan

Chapter **9**

Studying and test preparation

- [ ] I can find something positive for me in taking these tests
- [ ] I can develop the right frame of mind for these tests
- [ ] I know exactly when the tests are
- [ ] I am aware how many questions will be on each test
- [ ] I have read the course details carefully to check what I am expected to know about the subject
- [ ] I have organized my notes so that the material is easy to learn
- [ ] I can work out how many topics I need to study for each test
- [ ] I am aware of the range of questions that can come up for each topic
- [ ] I have made a realistic study schedule, with clear priorities
- [ ] I know how to work on test answers using test files
- [ ] I have started to practice writing out answers at speed
- [ ] I am aware of the memory strategies I need to study for the test
- [ ] I know how the points are weighted for each question
- [ ] I am aware of how to use time most effectively during the test
- [ ] I am aware of how to avoid common pitfalls
- [ ] I am aware of the differences between test answers and class assignments
- [ ] I know how to manage stress and use it effectively

In what ways have your past study strategies and your approach to tests helped or hindered your test-taking success? What can you change or improve for your next tests?

Studying: seven-point action plan

1 ▶ **Positive state of mind** e.g., checking my motivation; giving myself positive messages; working on stress; accepting the challenge. *Things I will do to stay positive:*

2 ▶ **Time** e.g., going over my work from early in the year in different ways; organizing a schedule, *Priority organizer* (page 78) or study *Time circle* (page 73); dealing with my excuses for not studying; using free moments. *I will:*

3 ▶ **Variety** e.g., working in many short spells; using varied and interesting ways of going over my material. *I will:*

4 ▶ **Overlearning** e.g., rewriting notes, index cards, new draft outlines, memory triggers. *I will:*

5 ▶ **Practice** e.g., doing past questions; working under test conditions; having a trial run. *I will:*

6 ▶ **People** e.g., sharing study with other people where possible. *I will:*

7 ▶ **Selection** What topics will I study for? What level of detail can I really use under test conditions? *I will:*

Advance preparation for the test

Find out basic information

- How many tests will you have?
- When are they likely to take place?
- What form will they take?
- How will you be assessed?
- Are there going to be practice tests beforehand?
- Are you allowed to access previous tests?

Keep a record of this information—see the *Tests* checklist on page 191.

Find out the "test instructions"

Familiarize yourself with the instructions given on tests: These can be difficult to understand if you read them for the first time under the stress of the test itself. They usually tell you about where to write your name and ID number and how many questions you have to answer. (The instructor may read the instructions aloud at the start of the test.)

Plan out your time in advance

For each test, work out the time that you will start and finish each question—this is one less thing to do during the test. At the start of the test, write down your timings and keep sight of them.

Practice

Like most things, test performance improves with practice. Take any practice tests that are provided, even if you feel you are not at all ready—the experience is important. If there are none, arrange your own with friends or by yourself.

- Pick out an old test or make up your own questions.
- Arrange the seating so that you cannot see each other's papers.
- Write the answers within a set time limit—work alone, in silence.

- Afterwards, discuss your answers with each other.

The week before

- Drink plenty of water in the week before the test so that you are not dehydrated.
- Build in movement and exercise so that you work off excess adrenaline.
- Work daily on relaxation, so that your thinking remains clear and focused. You will still feel some nervous energy, which is useful for tests.
- Learn the information on your "master cards." Check your understanding and memory. Find ways of keeping up interest and motivation.
- Organize cover for any domestic or work responsibilities. Plan for emergencies. If possible, arrange for child care or other support from the day *before* the test, so that you are free for a final study session.
- Avoid people who may make you feel unsure of yourself—those who are super-confident and those who panic!

The night before

- Check over any test details you have.
- Prepare what you will need—pens, ruler, water, a snack, your ID card, a sweater and so on.
  - Avoid people who panic.
  - Have a snack and a hot, relaxing bath before bed. Leave plenty of time to sleep.

The day of the test

- Eat well before the test, to keep up your stamina. Slow-releasing carbohydrates, such as bread and cereals, are best.
- Leave lots of time for the journey in case of delays.
- Arrive in good time so you have time to get settled.

Tests

Subject:	Topic:	
Date:	Day:	Time:
Campus:	Building:	Room:
Length of test:		

Number of questions I have to answer (in each section, where applicable):

Preparation: Time needed for reading through questions; choosing questions; planning answers.

Final check: Time needed to check for sense, for errors, that questions are correctly numbered, neatening the script, and so on.

Total preparation and final check time needed:

Time left for writing answers (total time *minus* preparation and final check time):

Total marks available for each question	Length of time to spend on each question	Time to start each new answer
1		
2		
3		
4		
5		

Any unusual features of the test or test conditions?

Which aids—dictionaries, calculators, etc.—are permissible for this test?

What must I take to the test? ID card? Pens? Colored pencils? Any special equipment? A sweater? Water? Snacks, to be eaten quietly? Glucose tablets?

Multiple-choice questions (MCQs)

Typically, multiple-choice tests (MCQs) use closed questions and provide a choice of 4-6 answers. MCQs create their own kinds of challenge calling for different kinds of strategies.

Multiple-choice: An easy option?

Students sometimes underprepare for MCQ tests, thinking that they require less preparation or that they will be able to guess the answers. However, note that:

- Questions are often set in such a way that they are easy to answer only if you have studied all the material; this can make them more demanding than essay-based exams.
- Many of the options may be partially correct—and so, therefore, not the right choice. You need to know your subject well in order to recognize correct options.
- Penalties may be imposed for wrong answers; depending on the size of these, guessing may be a risky strategy.

Studying for MCQ tests

Consider which of the strategies below you can use more effectively when studying for tests; check the boxes to remind yourself which items to come back to and use.

Plan to manage "breadth"

For MCQs you generally need to cover everything. To help manage this:

- ☐ Keep up with coursework week by week.
- ☐ Review it regularly, even if only to browse your notes to refresh what you covered.
- ☐ Summarize factual information onto cards. Carry these around, checking them frequently.

Focus your reading to sharpen recall

MCQs test knowledge in precise ways. Rather than simply rereading or browsing through your class notes, use more focused approaches.

- ☐ Read notes and texts in shorter bursts.
- ☐ Pause frequently to check if the material would lend itself to a MCQ.
- ☐ Jot down onto cards any MCQs that occur to you, using one card for each Q and A.

Test understanding

- ☐ Check that you understand the significance of theories, concepts, theorems, case studies and research studies relevant to your subject.
- ☐ Consider how you would test someone else's understanding of these through multiple-choice or "true/false" questions.

Design your own MCQs

Designing your own MCQs in the style of previous tests helps you to work in an active way with course material and to remember it. It also helps you to enter the mind-set of the instructors and to anticipate the kinds of questions that you can prepare for.

- ☐ Identify how each part of your program could be tested through MCQs.
- ☐ Check how past test questions were designed and worded.
- ☐ Devise sets of closed questions and answers; write these on cards as above. Use as "flash cards."
- ☐ Study with other students; test each other.
- ☐ Think about what you would consider as "trick" questions—and prepare for these.

"The answer is in the question"

Read carefully and clarify the task

In MCQ exams, the most common reason for losing points is misreading the question. If there seem to be too many correct choices, it is likely that you need to read the question with more precision.

- Note the exact wording used.
- Use the stem separately for each choice (see below).

Choosing an answer

- Before looking at the possible answers given on the test, answer the question in your head. Then look to see if your answer is one of the available choices.
- Eliminate any answers you think are definitely incorrect.
- Work quickly and steadily to ensure you do not run out of time.

Find the "stem"

Each question generally contains words that can be turned into a "stem statement." If you can isolate the stem, this will make it easier to identify what you are being asked.

For the question "Which of the following is not a capital city?," the stem would be:

… is not a capital city:

Apply the stem to each of the choices, so you can test out which sounds correct. For example:

London … is not a capital city.
Tunis … is not a capital city.
Montreal … is not a capital city.
Paris … is not a capital city.

This can help you to recognize correct and incorrect answers. If you are still not certain of the answer, at least you may be able to eliminate some incorrect answers, reducing the options.

Rephrase questions

Rephrase complicated questions so that it is clearer what is being asked.

- Put them into your own words so they make sense—retain the sense of the original.
- Rephrase into "true/false" choices (page 194).

Convert negatives

"Negatives" (*not, never, neither this nor that,* etc.) are easy to overlook and more difficult to interpret.

- Rephrase negatives so they read as positives.

Example: **Which of these cities is not in Canada?**

(a) Pittsburgh   (b) Toronto   (c) Ottawa   (d) Vancouver.

Rephrase as positive statement(s):

Which of the following *are* Canadian cities? Which one(s) then remain? (Toronto, Ottawa, and Vancouver).

Qualifiers

Qualifiers are words that narrow or define your choices. Common types of qualifiers are:

- **words defining time:** Never, always, during, prior to (X date) …
- **superlatives:** the most, the least, the highest…
- **specific circumstances:** whenever X occurs, if X is the case, assuming X, unless…

An answer that appears correct at first may cease to do so once you check the qualifiers. For example, the two questions below would call for different answers from the choices (a)-(d).

Example: Large or largest?

Q: "Which of the following is a large number?"
Choices: (a) 4 (b) 12898087 (c) 6256798 (d) 7
A: Choices (b) and (c) would apply.

Q: "Which of the following is the largest?"
Choices: (a) 4 (b) 12898087 (c) 6256798 (d) 7
A: (b) only one answer can be the largest.

True or false statements

Typically, *true/false* tests provide you with a statement, or series of statements, each of which you must identify as true or false.

Example

It is always windy in Chicago.

☐ True   ☐ False

Check for false statements

- Where part of a potential answer is "false," then the whole statement must be false—even if some aspects are true.
- The opposite is not true: If part of an answer is true, that doesn't necessarily apply to the rest of the statement. Continue to check each part of the statement in case any information is false.

Qualifiers in true/false questions

Absolutes: Where the qualifiers are words such as "always," "the only," "the best," "never," this sets up conditions that are harder to meet. It is less likely that something always or never occurs, so the answer is more likely to be false. Check this possibility first—though don't rely on it as a rule.

Generalities: Qualifiers such as "sometimes," "might," "rarely," "in general," leave greater possibilities that something could occur. Such qualifiers tend to lead to "true answers." Check this possibility—though don't rely on it as a rule.

Rephrase MCQs as true/false options

If you are unsure of an answer in an MCQ test, it may be easier to identify the answer if you convert the question into a set of true/false options.

- Identify the stem (see page 193).
- Rephrase into "positives" (see page 193).
- Apply the stem to each choice of answer, asking yourself if the statement is true or false.
- If more than one choice appears to be true and you are allowed more than one answer, then select all that you consider to be true.

Avoid risky strategies

Be wary of advice that suggests that you can second-guess the answer based on the structure or content of one or more of the choices. Instructors will be aware of strategies used by students who don't know the material, and so may design questions in a way that prevents such strategies from succeeding.

Decide if each of the following is a sound strategy.

Put a check mark ✓ beside those you consider to be a sound strategy.

☐ (a) I haven't used option (D) yet so I'd better use it for one of the next few answers.

☐ (b) I have used the third choice for several answers in a row, so it must be time for a different choice.

☐ (c) The instructor has provided much more information in this choice than for all the other choices. It is more likely that this is the right answer or they wouldn't have bothered—I'll choose this one.

☐ (d) One of my choices is "all of the above." I can see that two of the three statements above are correct so it is likely that "all of the above" is the right choice. I'll go for that.

☐ (e) One of my choices is "none of the above." I know one of the choices is correct. This means that the answers can't be "none of the above."

☐ (f) Instructors are more likely to set questions where the answer is a positive statement than a negative. I am not sure of the answer so I'll choose the positive statement.

See page 212 for feedback.

Strategies for answering questions

For each of the strategies below, check box 1 (✓) if this is a strategy you already apply well and systematically. If not, check box 2 if you think this is a strategy you want to apply in future.

	Do now	Will do
1 **Read instructions** Familiarize yourself with the instructions for the test—follow these carefully.	☐	☐
2 **Note how many choices you can make** Can you select just ONE or more choices?	☐	☐
3 **Provide your own answer** Before looking at the choices, see if you know the answer. Then check if that is provided as a choice.	☐	☐
4 **Find the stem** Read each question carefully, identifying the stem (see page 193).	☐	☐
5 **Rephrase a negative stem as a positive** Negative words,,, such as *no, not, never, none, neither this nor that*, etc., make questions more complicated. Rephrase the stem so that it reads as a positive.	☐	☐
6 **Use the stem** Apply the stem to each of the choices, to double-check your answer and to see if any other choices could also apply. If you don't know the answer, using the stem may help you spot the right choice.	☐	☐
7 **Check for qualifiers** If you are unsure of the answer, check for qualifiers such as *all, always, the most, sometimes* and also *when, if, whenever, both this and that*, etc. Make sure that the qualifier is included in your stem, and apply this to each choice. This may eliminate some choices.	☐	☐
8 **True/False** Rephrasing the stem and each answer as true/false statements can help you spot correct answers or eliminate incorrect ones.	☐	☐
9 **Eliminate unlikely answers** If you can't spot the correct answer, use your subject knowledge and logical reasoning to reduce your number of choices. Work out which of the remaining choices is the most likely.	☐	☐
10 **Best guess?** If there is no penalty for a guess, then guess rather than leaving a blank. If there is a penalty for an incorrect answer, weigh the probability of whether your guess is right or wrong.	☐	☐

Chapter **9**

Taking multiple-choice tests

Read the instructions

- Read all initial instructions carefully.
- Check each question's instructions and wording carefully in case these vary.

Browse the whole test

Gain a sense of:

- how many questions you need to answer—so that you can pace yourself well
- the topics covered—so your brain can start to search for information on those topics
- the focus of questions and the wording used—so you can think through anything unexpected
- which questions will take you the most time.

Use the time effectively

- Work quickly but steadily.
- Don't rush your reading and checking of answers: This leads to mistakes.
- Use any leftover time to check carefully through the questions and your answers—you may have misread something earlier.

Apply your strategies

- Remain calm. Apply any strategies you may have practiced for managing stress (see page 209).
- Apply the test-taking strategies that you have practiced in this chapter.

Use your knowledge and reasoning

- Apply reasoning and logic in order to make a sensible guess if you don't immediately recognize the correct answer.
- Avoid making false assumptions (see page 193).

Self-evaluation of study strategy For each of the strategies below, consider if you already use this strategy effectively.	Already do this	Could do in future
1 **Apply all the strategies on the strategies checklist:** page 196.		
2 **Best order** Work steadily through all the questions to which you know the answer or can work out the answer easily. This ensures that, if any difficult questions take up more time than others, you won't miss out on points for questions you could have answered later in the test.		
3 **Keep track of completed answers** Circle lightly but clearly any questions to which you will return later. Erase each circle when you complete the answer.		
4 **Troubleshoot** Mark any questions likely to consume your time. Decide how you will deal with them, depending on the proportion of points they carry. If they carry few points, leave them until last.		
5 **Plan and track your time** Once you complete the questions that were easiest, count how many questions remain. Divide your remaining time between these. Keep track of how you are using time.		
6 **Highlight keywords in the questions** such as negatives (*no, not, never, un-*) and words or qualifiers that help circumscribe the issue, (*ever, always, whenever, if*, dates, names, timescales, specific circumstances).		
7 **Devise personal strategies** Use your experience of doing practice tests to identify personal strategies that suit you and fit the style of the MCQ tests used for the class.		

Short-answer tests

- Short-answer tests require answers shorter than those typical of essay-based papers.
- Answers are usually factually based—unlike papers for essay-based exams, which tend to be more analytical and creative.

Why are short-answer tests set?

- To check the depth of your knowledge base in the subject: The questions tend to require detailed factual knowledge of a particular area.
- To check the breadth of your knowledge: Several short-answer questions mean that more areas of the course can be tested.

Types of short-answer questions

Typically, short-answer questions are used when the answer required involves:

- listable items, such as the key functions of parts of the body or key aspects of a piece of equipment
- the main aspects of a particular theory, and reasons for its significance
- stating where a quote comes from in a set text and providing reasons for its significance
- details of a simple experiment, which wouldn't be sufficient to form the basis of a long-answer question
- details of specific procedures, such as how to manipulate a limb, produce a chemical under certain conditions, or deal with a specific problem
- the main similarities or differences between two groups that are often contrasted.

Getting organized for short-answer tests

Unlike essay-based exams, where you can usually choose to study for a smaller number of topics and leave out some without too great a risk, for short-answer tests, you need to know all of your class material well.

Organize your material

Summarize class material into questions followed by lists of key points.

Make a checklist of key definitions, specialist terms, controversial issues, and significant dates and facts—study the list systematically.

Write out and learn succinct and precise definitions of key terms.

Look for ways of further condensing your summary answers.

Identify good examples

Identify examples that best illustrate key concepts and themes, so that you can draw upon these quickly during the test.

Consider how you would word examples in a concise way during the test—sometimes the name, date and a few keywords that indicate a piece of research or theory will suffice.

If relevant to the subject, write out short quotes (of a few words only) to exemplify points that you might wish to make.

And the 9 main functions of the liver are . . .

Preparing for short-answer tests

Use "flash cards"

- Write out your questions and answers onto index cards, use one card per question.
- Make a numbered list of the key issues for each question.
- Write out formulae, definitions or quotations.
- Write a few succinct sentences that sum up—and join up—the information.
- Carry cards around with you so that you can refer to them in a "little and often" approach.
- Make good use of free moments to study.

Count out the points

There is usually a specific, and countable, number of points to make for short answers. For example, if you are asked to outline the role of a certain vitamin in the body, or list the properties of halogens or describe the working of an engine, there will be a set number of commonly acknowledged or prescribed items that the instructor looks for. When studying:

- Identify what such countable items would be for each question you are studying.
- Write that number next to the question, as a reminder of how many items you need to recall.
- Set out your material so that each item is visibly distinct.
- Number each item.
- Enumerate each item, either in your head or aloud, as you study it.

Practice

- Invent as many realistic questions as you can, if possible using test files to see the kind of questions that have appeared on previous tests. This will increase your chances of having practiced the kind of questions that will be set for your test.
- Answer these under test conditions.
- If you do not know the answer, use logic and common sense to identify potential answers or sensible guesses.
- Note if you are tempted to include irrelevant material or to write in an excessively wordy way, just so that you have something down on the page.
- Check your answers against your notes to see how well you remembered the information.
- Develop memory-joggers to help recall under test conditions. (See Chapter 8.)

Edit your practice answers

- Read through your answers, checking each point against the question set.
- Put a line through any material that is irrelevant to that question. Be strict with yourself.
- Note how much material you crossed out—this represents time that could have been spent on another question.
- Note if the relevant material is written as succinctly as it might be. If not, practice rewriting your answers so that they are brief, condensed and to the point.

Taking short-answer tests

Use time strategically

- Check the points given for each answer. Divide your time according to the points carried by each.
- Work quickly: Short answers are to the point and don't usually require planning out.
- If the test includes other kinds of questions, such as longer essays, leave sufficient time to answer those.

Identify exactly what is being asked

- Note how many parts there are to the question. Work systematically through each part, crossing it off as you complete it, so that unanswered sections remain visible.
- Note the process words such as "analyze," "define," "explain." Follow directions exactly, doing what is asked and no more.
- Note the key terms: Which specific areas of the topic are included in the question?
- Remain focused on what is asked: Avoid adding unnecessary material.

Be concise

If you can convey the required information in one paragraph, there is no need to use five. Avoid padding answers with irrelevant material just to make it look as though you know more about the subject. This could lose you points—and wastes time that could gain you points on another question.

Structure your answers

If you are expected to write answers of more than a few short sentences, then structure these as you would a paper, using:

- an introductory sentence to define the terms or issue
- a sentence or paragraph on each point
- a concluding sentence.

Make each point stand out

- Ensure that you cover all your "countable items" for each question.
- State each point so that it stands out distinctly. If necessary, start a different sentence for each, rather than combining two or more points within a single sentence. This makes it more likely that the instructor will identify each point and allocate points accordingly.
- Read your answer to check that good points are not lost in complex or overcondensed sentences.

Preparing for essay-based exams

You have less time in an exam to cover a subject than you have for class assignments. This doesn't mean you have to write at superhuman speeds in order to cover the same ground. Your instructor will expect shorter answers, and wants to see that you can recognize the most significant information and be selective.

Select what to study

Decide which topics you are going to study. If possible, look at previous tests. If you are required to answer three essay questions, study at least five topics.

Identify the essentials

For each topic you decide to study, find out:

- how the subject breaks down into key themes or topics
- the main points of view, or schools of thought, on each topic
- key debates in the subject over time
- recent important debates
- the *major* pieces of research for each topic, who conducted these and when, and the significance of the research
- the *most recent* significant research on the subject and its relevance
- which point of view you find most convincing and why.

Organize the information so that it is easier to remember (see Chapter 8).

Map it out

Draw a chart to draw together, for each theme:

- Key schools of thought on the theme.
- Themes covered by each key school of thought.

- What is convincing about their arguments?
- What are the weak points in their arguments?
- Do those weak points really matter?
- Who were the main opponents of this approach?
- Names of key contributors and the decade (or year) when their contributions were made.
- Very brief details (a few lines at most) of the major pieces of research on this subject and why these are important.

Summarize

Summarize the essential information:

- as headings and key points, to structure the information
- in several paragraphs, as the basis of an essay
- in one paragraph, as a theme within an essay
- in one sentence, in case you need to make only a brief reference to it, and for use in conclusions.

Active selection

Learning too much information can mean that you have to spend time during the test deciding what not to include. It is more effective to work that out before the test. Take time to consider what detail you do not need to include for specific questions.

Practice

- For each topic, make draft outlines for a range of possible questions.
- Discuss questions with others. Work out outlines together.
- Time yourself writing answers using *some* of your draft outlines without looking at your notes. This shows you which areas need more work and helps to increase your handwriting speed and your ability to think and write under pressure.

Taking essay-based exams

Writing exam essays

Follow a similar procedure to that used when writing any other essay or paper. Use structure, organization, evidence and a clear line of reasoning—without these, you will get very few points for content.

Exam essays can be *easier* to write because:

- you need less evidence and fewer examples
- you can write less about each point
- you can miss out some background detail
- you don't need to give a bibliography or supply detailed references
- minor grammatical and spelling errors, and rushed handwriting (provided it's readable), are generally less important.

Selecting which question(s) to answer

- Read each question through at least twice.
- Work out what is expected, in general, for each question. Which part of the class does it refer to? Towards which issues is the question directing you?
- If a question sounds like one you have done before, check the wording very carefully before you select it. A slight difference in wording might require a very different answer.
- Check all questions you could attempt. Check twice the ones you could answer best. Don't rush this—it's vital that you choose the questions

that will do you justice.

- For the questions you select, highlight keywords in the title. Notice how many parts there are to the question. Read questions through again very slowly to make sure you have not misread any keywords. At this stage you may realize that a question is not what you thought, and may need to select a different one.

At any time, note down ideas you have about any of your selected questions on a separate sheet. Note the relevant question number beside each idea.

Use pyramid questions to guide you

Learn the pyramid questions (page 254) as a song, a list or a chant. Use them to guide your essay outline during the test. This is especially useful if you experience great difficulty in organizing and structuring information quickly or if you go blank during tests.

Doing well in essay-based exams

Common pitfalls ...	and how to avoid them
1 Doing silly things Silly things can fail students or lose points or the instructor's goodwill.	Well before the test, find out what is required. Be sure to write your name or test number on the answer paper and on additional sheets. Read the questions. Check the back of the test. Answer the right number of questions. During the test itself, schedule time to check such details carefully.
2 Mystifying the test The instructor won't pore over your script for hours or see through your answer to what you don't know. There is no "magic ingredient" you have to deliver.	Instructors have a large pile of exams. They want to get through these as quickly as they can, with just a few minutes for each. They may check your introduction and conclusion for the gist of your thesis, skim the answer to evaluate your line of reasoning, check that you are using material from the class to support your answers and evaluate roughly what grade the work is worth. They are unlikely to grade it as closely as they would grade class assignments. Sometimes a second instructor goes through the same process. Only excessively bad grammar, spelling errors or handwriting are likely to stand out.
3 Using time poorly and answering too few questions	Give equal time to questions that carry equal points—and more time to any that carry extra points. The law of diminishing returns applies to the amount of time spent on any one question: If you spend twice as long on one question, you are very unlikely to get twice as many points. You are more likely to pass if you give reasonable answers to the set number of questions than if you spend all your time writing outstanding answers but miss out one question completely. If you run out of the time you have allocated to one answer, leave a space—there may be time to go back to it at the end.
4 Writing everything you know about a topic There is no value in simply writing down all you know to prove you've learned it.	The instructor is not interested in how much you know—indeed, you may get no points at all for simply listing a lot of information. Just as for other assignments, points are given for showing you can make sense of the question, relate it to course issues, develop a line of reasoning, evaluate opposing viewpoints and offer supporting evidence.
5 Abandoning structure and the usual essay-writing techniques	Because of the speed at which instructors work, they appreciate answers with clear, well-organized structures, good introductions and conclusions, correctly numbered questions and clearly labeled scripts that are easy to read. You lose goodwill if your script is messy, illegible or confusing to read.

CHECKLIST

Test-taking strategy

Do I ...	Yes	No	Things to do, or to watch out for
For all types of test:			
read the whole test carefully?	☐	☐	
follow all instructions?	☐	☐	
answer the correct number of questions in full?	☐	☐	
plan time well, so that I can check through my answers?	☐	☐	
know exactly how long I have for each question?	☐	☐	
allocate time according to the points available?	☐	☐	
use all of the available time?	☐	☐	
spend time working out what the questions mean?	☐	☐	
ask myself what the instructor is looking for?	☐	☐	
feel confident about what I am expected to do?	☐	☐	
find I have studied for enough topics?	☐	☐	
use examples from class materials?	☐	☐	
keep strictly to answering the question set?	☐	☐	
avoid irrelevant detail and going off on tangents?	☐	☐	
get to the point quickly?	☐	☐	
avoid flowery language and vague introductions?	☐	☐	
keep focused on the test during the test?	☐	☐	
check my answers for mistakes?	☐	☐	
check my answers to see if they make sense?	☐	☐	
For essay-based questions, do I also:			
read each question at least twice?	☐	☐	
spend enough time considering the best questions for me?	☐	☐	
find questions that are similar to ones I have practiced?	☐	☐	
know what a "good" answer looks like?	☐	☐	
know which writing style is appropriate?	☐	☐	
know the correct format or layout?	☐	☐	
plan my answers (on paper or in my head)?	☐	☐	
develop a clear argument (where appropriate)?	☐	☐	
include an introduction and a conclusion?	☐	☐	

If you answered "yes" to most of these questions, then your chance of success is high. If not, look again through the relevant sections of this *Handbook* and work out what you need to practice. If you are still uncertain about any aspects, consult with your instructor.

Chapter 9

The day of the test

Basic considerations

- Leave plenty of time to get there.
- Make sure you have your watch or clock.
- Remember to take your pens, water and any equipment you need.
- Eat breakfast slowly—and enjoy it.
- Avoid sugars, as these can lead to a drop in sugar levels during the test. If you have a sweet tooth, taking glucose tablets during the test will help maintain your energy.
- Focus on positive thinking, such as how much you know for this subject and what is good in your life, so that demotivating thoughts can't gain a foothold. Let negative thoughts float away.

At the venue

- Consider whether you would benefit more from talking to others or spending time on your own.
- Make sure you leave ALL study notes, written material and any other forbidden items out of sight, either in your bag or outside of the room, as required.
- Organize your space.
- Check you can see the time easily.
- Breathe out slowly and deeply, or use any breathing exercises you may have practiced (see pages 210–211).
- Find a positive, calm, focused state of mind.

Getting ready

- Read the instructions slowly, at least twice.
- Fill out personal details as required.
- Read through the whole test. Always check both sides, even if you think one side is blank.
- Divide your time equally among sections that carry the same points. Jot down the times you will begin each question.

"What if I go blank?"

- Don't try too hard to remember. Leave a space—it may come back later.
- You may be too tense—use a relaxation exercise you have used before (pages 210–211).
- Use a "getting started" trick: see page 237.
- Keep writing. On spare paper, jot down any words that have anything to do with the question. These should eventually start to prompt your memory into action.
- Ask yourself questions, starting with the most basic—who? when? what? how?—until you become more focused.

Dealing with stress

A *mild* degree of stress can be helpful, providing a challenge with stimulation, excitement and focus. Some people deliberately search out stress to make life more exciting.

Studying towards deadlines and tests involves different amounts of stress for each student. Added life pressures, such as shortage of money, difficult relationships, bereavement or changes in your work, family or housing situation, can all add to your stress level. If stress is maintained at high levels, then our health as well as our intellectual functioning will be affected. It can then become increasingly hard to cope with any aspect of life, and not just study. Such stress can build up over time, without us realizing that we are coping less well with its effects.

Know your own triggers

When do you start getting worked up?

☐ When things are not going your way?

☐ When work mounts up?

☐ When you are trying to please too many people apart from yourself?

☐ When other people seem to be doing things badly, or better than you?

☐ When you set yourself unrealistic goals?

☐ In traffic jams, or using public transport?

☐ When you feel pressurized by too little time?

☐ If you start to compare yourself to others?

☐ Just before a test?

☐ Other triggers?

Spot the signs

Do you ...

☐ lie awake worrying?

☐ feel guilty when you aren't working?

☐ get frustrated easily?

☐ get a dry mouth, heavy pounding or a "butterfly" feeling in the heart, sweaty hands, nausea or twitching muscles?

☐ grit or grind your teeth?

☐ flare up easily at other people?

☐ regularly eat in a hurry, or go on binges?

☐ smoke or drink "to unwind"?

☐ drop or break things frequently?

☐ notice signs of increased irritability, tearfulness or moodiness?

Unhelpful levels of stress

Although some stress is useful, by providing the energy that enables you to do the extra work needed, too much stress undermines our performance and over time can have very serious effects. "Too much" stress includes:

(1) **Too much at once** There are just too many things to cope with at once. To reduce the stress, you have to reduce the number of things you are working on at present or devote effort to managing the stress.

(2) **Too long** The short-term response suitable for a "state of emergency" can become a way of life. If it continues for a long time, our systems start to become overwhelmed, and our functioning starts to deteriorate or even stops.

Impaired academic performance

If stress levels are too high, it is hard to maintain concentration, our attention wanders, we find it hard to settle down to study. Memory can be affected, and at times we may not be able to recall even information we know really well. It becomes harder to plan and to find solutions to problems.

Impaired physical health

Over time, high levels of the chemicals associated with stress can damage body tissues and organs. At a basic level, just grinding our teeth can wear them away and give us jaw pain or extreme headaches that make it hard to sleep or study. Our immune systems can be affected, making us prone to illness.

Impaired mental health

If stress levels are maintained for long periods, we can start to lose our ability to function in everyday life. Sleep is affected, which impairs performance and also our ability to perceive the world around us accurately. Our perspective can become distorted, and we can experience panic attacks, depression or helplessness.

Social impact

Stress can make it difficult for us to be around other people: They can seem very irritating or deliberately obstructive. It can be hard to feel affection for those we are close to, and we can become irritable or emotional quickly, so that it is hard for other people to be with us.

If you suffer from excess stress, you need to take steps to reduce it. The signs can be extremely varied.

In your journal, list the times when you get most stressed—or what makes you feel tense. Describe what happens. What do you do to handle the situation? What else *could* you do?

Look at the suggestions on pages 208–209. Check things you could try out. Which *one* will you try first, or next?

Managing stress

Stay relaxed

Sleep properly

☐ Aim to sleep for 7 hours each day. More or less than this can tire you.

Take breaks

☐ Give yourself regular breaks in whatever you are doing.

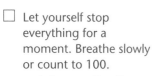

Use the STOP! exercise

☐ Let yourself stop everything for a moment. Breathe slowly or count to 100.

- Let yourself smile—even if this is difficult.
- Spread out your hands and relax your fingers. Let your hands and feet be still.
- Repeat "Stop" to yourself until you feel calm.

Monitor your state of mind

One aspect of stress is the attitude we take towards challenges. The situation and feelings that panic one person may excite and interest another.

Listen to the voice in your head

☐ If you tend to think "I can't …," "Other people can …" or "I'm useless at …," you need to change the record!

- Turn the message around: "I can …," "I have already …," "I am able to …," "I am going to …"

Question your way of thinking

Ask yourself questions such as:

☐ Is there another way of thinking about this?
☐ Am I being a perfectionist?
☐ Am I expecting too much of myself (or others) in the current circumstances?
☐ Am I getting things out of proportion?
☐ What is the effect on me of having this attitude?
☐ Am I blaming myself for things that can't be helped?
☐ What can I do to improve matters?

Manage your time

Be organized

☐ Organize yourself to avoid stress. Make schedules and action plans to avoid predictable crises and panics. Take control of your time.

Set priorities

☐ Work out your priorities and when you will do each of the tasks. Work out which things can wait—and let them (see page 78).

Take care of your body

Get exercise

☐ Do something energetic—walk, swim, run, play a game, clean the room, do some gardening. Get rid of pent-up energy and excess adrenaline (see pages 172–173).

Chapter 9

Have a healthy diet

☐ Check what you are putting into your body. Could you fill it with less coffee, less smoke, less alcohol and fewer chemicals? Does your body need bigger helpings of substances that help it renew itself—such as food and water?

Relax

Treat yourself

☐ Take a relaxing bath. Don't rush it. Light a candle, or treat yourself to aromatherapy oils.

☐ Put some time aside every day just to enjoy yourself or to do nothing. Try to get at least 20 minutes on your own in quiet.

Celebrate success

☐ Reflect on your achievements over the day or week—and reward yourself.

Daydream

☐ Imagine that the floor is a cloud or a big ball of cotton, and that you are sinking down into it and floating away.

☐ Imagine that you are on a magic carpet. Look down at the landscape moving beneath you. Where would you like to visit?

☐ Imagine that you are on a mountaintop, enjoying the view.

Use a relaxation exercise

☐ Take time to relax, consciously.
1. Lie on the floor or sit in a comfortable chair.
2. Close your eyes and breathe out slowly several times. Don't force the breathing.
3. If your mind is racing, do the "Stop!" exercise (page 209).
4. Notice where your body feels tense.

Then do each of the following several times.

5. Clench your toes tightly, count to three, then "let go." Repeat this several times.
6. Repeat this with all the muscles you can, working from your toes up to your neck.
7. Pull your shoulders right up to your ears— and let them drop. Repeat several times.
8. Screw up all the face muscles. Then relax. Open your mouth into a big yawn.
9. Imagine yourself in a peaceful, beautiful, safe place. Listen for sounds and look at the colors there. It can be any place, real or imaginary. This can be a safe "retreat" in the mind for you to go when stressed.

Breathe calmly

☐ After relaxation, sit or lie comfortably. Close your eyes. Put on relaxing music if you wish.
1. Imagine that you are breathing in calm and tranquility with each in-breath and letting go of stress with each out-breath.
2. Think of one word you find soothing, and repeat this in your mind.
3. Do this for about ten minutes—or longer if you like.

☐ If you find that difficult, just stay still and be quiet. Listen to the sounds around you.

You can also try the calming and relaxation exercises on the next page.

Chapter **9**

Calming exercises

The voice of reason

Talk yourself through your worries. Ask yourself "Questions of Reason," such as those below.

Questions of Reason

- Most people pass tests, so if I work steadily and keep my head, isn't it likely I will too?
- What can I do, practically, to reduce my worry and resolve problems?
- Who can I speak to who will make me feel good about myself and about life? Why not arrange now to meet them soon?
- Who can I speak to who will give me good advice? Why not arrange this right now?
- If the worst-case scenario occurs, what practical options will be open to me? There are always other options.

Affirmations

If you tend to be self-critical, or to feel negative about your own performance, then consider one or two sets of words that would make you feel more positive and motivated. A line from a song, or a quotation from a celebrity, may help. Make a point of looking at these, and taking them in, at least twice a day.

Write it large

Write your affirmation in large letters and put it where you can see it when you are studying at home and where you brush your teeth.

Write it small

Write the affirmations so you can carry them in your purse or wallet, or use them as a bookmark.

Slow renditions

The aim of this activity is to stop your mind (and pulse) from racing by taking time to find a more reasonable pace.

- Choose a poem, song or chant that you like and know well. Choose a few lines from it.
- Repeat these lines slowly, preferably aloud, and look for pleasure in the sound of the words and the beat.
- If you find you are rushing just to get through it or that you have repeated the words without taking notice of them, then start again, going more slowly.
- Give yourself permission to take this time to give the words justice.

Note the sounds

Put aside 10–30 minutes so that you have a definite break.

- Lie on the floor, with your head supported, and close your eyes.
- Take notice of your own body. How does it feel? Are there any aches and pains you weren't aware of?
- Working upwards from your toes, ask yourself if each part of your body, in turn, is feeling tense. If so, think about that part of the body relaxing into the floor and releasing its tension into the air.
- When your body is as relaxed as possible, turn your attention to the sounds around you.
- Don't aim to label the noises, just note them and let them pass.
- Listen for moments of quiet: How do these make you feel? Note any moments of tranquility.
- When you have finished, don't rush straight back into frenetic activity: Give yourself time to absorb the experience.

Take action to manage stress

Identify the causes

If you have identified signs of stress and acknowledged that you are feeling unwanted levels of stress, then the next stage is to identify the causes and do something to change these.

For example, you may feel that "tests" in general are to blame, whereas it is more likely to be something specific in the way you think about tests and approach them that generates unnecessary stress.

Unrealistic goals?

Unrealistic goals are a frequent cause of stress. For example, you may be so determined to achieve a certain grade that you are neglecting other things that you value. You are more likely to achieve your own peak performance if you set yourself a goal that is challenging but realistic for your circumstances.

Consider if you are setting yourself realistic aims, given:

- the time you have at your disposal
- what you have achieved in the past
- what other people could realistically achieve in the same time
- the skills and knowledge you have already gained in this subject compared with those you have still to acquire.

Take action

- If you notice a change in your health, talk to a doctor about this.
- Use exercises and activities such as those on the following pages to manage your stress levels.
- If you worry about time pressures, speak to an academic advisor or learning center staff: They may be able to offer further study strategies.

Students' experiences

I get very nervous several weeks before tests. What do I do? Apart from biting my nails, mostly talking to my mom on the phone. She always helps me get my feet on the ground.

I do have mega test anxiety. I spend hours worrying, and then I worry that I'm worrying, and then I blame myself for wasting time worrying. None of it gets me anywhere, but it fills the hours so I feel I have done something. Well, I'm not so bad since I started yoga. The class is very calming and the regular break does me good. It's calming being away from student life for a while.

Music. I put on my headphones, choose something really wild and turn it up loud. I might even dance along if noone else is in

I went to the Student Services office about money but ended up talking about everything else. They recommended 3 sessions with a counselor. I wouldn't go at first as I thought it meant admitting failure. I only went because I found out my friend had gone. It was the best thing I could have done. They helped me work out for myself what I needed to do, so I felt I had more space to think.

Running: I run a mile a day and that clears my system of worry and leaves me clear-headed.

I have a really good friend that I talk to. He always puts things into perspective and helps me stand back and take a longer term view. There's always more than one way to look at things!

Review

Tests are a culmination of your learning—not just of the class content but also of strategies you have developed since starting your program. Many of the strategies that help you to do well on tests are similar to those needed for any assignment: organization, selection, developing your point of view and line of reasoning, and structured writing skills.

This means that studying and preparation for tests are not separate events, completely divorced from the other learning activities you undertake in the year. If you have worked steadily all year, taking tests will be more manageable.

Don't build tests out of proportion. If you don't pass, you may be able to submit a make-up assignment to help improve your grade. If not, it's not the end of the world—there's life beyond tests and success without a degree. Your health, family and friends are not worth sacrificing for the sake of a degree.

Regard heightened nervous energy and some stress as useful friends. However, take care to relax and keep stress to a manageable level. Remember that the instructors generally *want* you to do well. They will be looking for ways to give you points and help you pass.

If you wish to hone your studying and test-taking skills, you may find it helpful to read further: Stella Cottrell, *The Exam Skills Handbook: Achieving Peak Performance*, second edition (Palgrave Macmillan, 2012).

Taking tests can be exciting. By the time a test is over you will probably feel that you really know your subject! Immediately after the test you may feel a little deflated—be prepared for that. Arrange something enjoyable and relaxing as a reward.

Celebrate your achievements.

Answer to activity: Sound strategies (page 195)

(e) is a sound strategy as it must lead to a correct answer. All of the others are not sound as they are guessing at particular ways of thinking on the part of the examiner. Although these approaches are sometimes recommended, they are not good strategies as they could very easily lead to incorrect answers.

Chapter 10

Group work and presentations

Academic work in college generally focuses on the achievements of individuals. In part, of course, this is to ensure that each person is awarded a degree for their own work. In recent years, however, more attention has been paid to the importance of training students in the skills of working with others. These skills are referred to as "people skills" or "interpersonal skills."

There are a number of reasons for this change, including:

- recognition that people learn in different ways— some people learn much better through group work and discussion

- recognition that, if they are to succeed, students often need more support than they received in the past—mutual support groups are one way of achieving this

- more attention being given to the skills needed by graduates once they enter employment— good interpersonal skills are now an essential part of most jobs that graduates would expect to enter

- the growing ability to provide much more varied programs, whether face-to-face or online, with increased emphasis on combining independent study with group and team work.

For these reasons, both the college curriculum and training by employers are increasingly dedicated to improving people skills.

While e-communications and e-projects are covered in Chapter 6, this chapter focuses on *face-to-face* interactions among people in groups. Most of the general principles it discusses, such as taking care to be constructive, supportive and nondiscriminatory, apply equally to *all* interpersonal communication.

Chapter **10**

Studying with others

Most courses schedule group work of one kind or another because they value the additional learning that takes place.

Contexts

Some of the contexts in which you may be required to work with others include:

- classes
- group projects
- mentor schemes
- work placements
- discussion groups
- support groups
- lab groups
- art "criticism" groups.

The format of these will vary, but there are basic principles and skills common to many different group contexts. These are addressed in this chapter.

Identify one occasion when you were in a group that worked particularly well.

What made the group successful? How did that group differ from other groups you have taken part in?

Working cooperatively

Working cooperatively creates opportunities to:

- share ideas—so each of you has more ideas
- gain other perspectives and points of view, which otherwise you might not have considered
- tap into a wider pool of experience, background knowledge and styles of work
- stimulate each other's thinking
- clarify your own thinking through talking and through answering questions
- gain others' assistance in remaining focused on the main point—freeing you up to explore a thought with the group
- learn to deal with challenge and criticism
- realize there are more dimensions and answers to a question than you can discover on your own.

Interpersonal skills

This chapter introduces some basic interpersonal skills that are useful for academic study. These are building blocks for people skills that are used in other contexts, such as employment.

Self-evaluation: studying with other people

Rate yourself on the following aspects of studying with others.

Aspect	1 very weak	2 weak	3 OK	4 good	5 excellent
Appreciating what other people have to offer					
Listening to what other people say					
Making a point effectively in groups					
Understanding how to plan for successful group work					
Knowing how to be an effective group member					
Knowing how to deal with difficulties in a group					
Understanding how to deal with unfairness in groups					
Contributing effectively to classes					
Knowing how to share work without cheating					
Making an effective oral presentation					

Ways of working with others

Supportive working

Talk through your difficulties and concerns—others may feel the same way. Help each other to find solutions.

Encourage

Let others know what they do well. Ask their opinions. If you appreciated a particular contribution, tell them!

Collaborate

Give each other suggestions about the best things to read for an assignment. Talk about what you have read. Share strategies for coping with work, children, money, projects.

Divide different aspects of your study among you: For example, you could each check a different library or organization for information, or you could be guinea pigs for each other's project questionnaires.

Cooperate

Go through your lecture notes together and see if you picked out different points. Photocopy assignments once they have been graded and read each other's. What differences do you notice?

Offer constructive criticism

If you disagree with another person's ideas and if the issue needs to be addressed, then phrase your suggestions in a positive way. Suggest ways forward for improvement, rather than criticizing what is wrong or was wrong in the past.

- Offer criticism only if invited to do so.
- Point out what is good, as well as what could be improved.
- Comment on behavior or products, not on people.
- Be realistic—only suggest changes that can be achieved.
- Be selective—choose one or two items that would make a real difference.

> ### Hazards to watch out for
>
> #### Beware of copying
> All completed pieces of written work must be in your own words—so be careful that you don't appear to be copying other people—nor they copying you.
>
> #### Share work fairly
> If you share tasks out, make sure it is on a fair basis. Consider what is fair in the circumstances and what to do if someone really cannot do what they agreed to do.
>
> #### Encourage others, but look after yourself
> Encourage other people if they are feeling demotivated—but avoid being drawn into anybody else's depression or negativity.

- Be precise—give a clear example.
- Be sympathetic—use a voice and a manner that help others accept your criticism.

Receive criticism

- Listen attentively.
- Take time to think about what has been said. Look for the truth in it.
- Thank others for constructive comments.
- Ask questions to clarify anything you do not understand.

Planning to prevent difficulties

If you are going to work with somebody else over a period of time, think through what you hope to gain from working together and what hazards may arise. You could each write down your reflections under three headings:

- "Advantages"
- "Potential difficulties"
- "Ways we could deal with these difficulties."

Go through all the advantages together to encourage you to proceed. Consider each potential difficulty and brainstorm ideas for ways of dealing with it. Be creative in looking for strategies. If you are truly stuck, speak to another friend or your instructor.

Talking and listening skills

Good communication is a two-way process. It requires both good listening skills and participation in the discussion.

Do you talk *to* people, or *at* people, or *with* people?

- People who talk *at* you are listening to themselves. They leave no space for a response.
- People who talk *with* you are keen for you to join in.
- People who talk *to* you consider you, and your response, carefully.

How well do you listen?

- Ask someone to watch you while you are listening in a group.
- Ask for comments about your nonverbal signals to various group members.
- Are you surprised at this feedback?
- Do you come across to others in the way you imagined?
- If not, what would you like to change?

In your journal, consider how well you listen to others. Do you:

- take in what other people say?
- give other people room to speak?
- let other people finish before you start?
- use encouraging nonverbal signals?
- "switch off" when bored or if you dislike the person?

Could you do anything differently to put others more at ease when they are speaking?

Which nonverbal communication are you sensitive to? What do *you* find encouraging? What do you find *discouraging*?

Nonverbal communication

We indicate to other people how well we are listening through our verbal responses and also through nonverbal communication, such as:

smiling

eye contact

expression

reassuring nods and gestures

position—who has to "look up to" someone to listen?

sniffing, snorting or fidgeting

the way we stand

the way we sit

silences

  ### Better listening

Try to tune in to speakers. Some of these techniques may help:

- Consider the speakers' feelings.
- Find ways of encouraging them.
- Focus on the content—think of some way this could be of value to you.
- Listen for keywords and jot them down.
- Think of a question you could ask (when they have finished speaking).
- Link what they are saying to something you already know.
- Find one positive comment you could contribute.

Making your point

Speaking in a group

If you are anxious at the idea of speaking out in a group or class, the following may help.

Before the group

- Make a decision to speak at least once during the group—even if it is only to hear yourself say "yes" out loud. Build up from a small base.
- Get to know other group members, if possible, so that you feel more at ease.

During the group

- Sit next to somebody you find reassuring.
- Write down what you want to say—if necessary, read it out.
- Think of an example, or evidence, or an illustration to support your point.
- If you are nervous, breathe out slightly more slowly than usual.
- Take your time when speaking—aim to speak more slowly than you would usually.
- Make eye contact with at least one person in your audience.
- Be brief. When you have made your point—*stop*. Avoid going back over what you have already said.
- Be clear. If something sounds confused, say "I'll make that clearer" or check people have understood.
- Speak up so everyone can hear. If people have to strain to hear you, they will be less sympathetic to what you are saying—and you may have to say it all over again.
- Act as though confident, even if you don't feel it.
- Don't apologize—smile!

After the group

- Congratulate yourself on any progress.
- Keep any mistakes or stumbling in proportion—it is not the end of the world.
- Decide what you will do next time.

Being judged by your voice

Many people feel self-conscious about the way they speak or about their accent. If you feel anxious about your voice, remember:

- your voice is an important part of you—everybody has an accent, and no accent is better than any other
- your voice, or accent, is less important than your ideas and opinions
- other people may be just as self-conscious about the way they speak
- concentrate on getting your message across and making sense, rather than on pronunciation
- there are many successful people with all kinds of accents.

Group sabotage

It is quite easy to sabotage a group. Often this happens unintentionally, because people are nervous or worry about being judged by others.

How might you sabotage a group unintentionally—for example, by being late, not preparing, whispering or chatting? What could you do differently?

Although there are many benefits to working in groups, being part of a group is not necessarily easy. Dealing with the challenge of the group develops a range of skills.

The following steps are helpful for classes and group work.

Create a supportive group atmosphere

Remember that people have feelings

Be aware that people are often anxious that they will be criticized or found wanting. Be constructive in your comments and aim to be kind, rather than scoring points.

Address anxieties directly

In the first session, brainstorm how everybody in the group feels about being in it. What were their concerns before arriving? Did other people feel the same way? It helps to know that you are not the only person who has concerns.

Discuss how the group could turn worries into opportunities.

Make ground rules

This is especially important if you are forming your own support or project group. Ground rules should address the anxieties raised above. Include:

- the time you will meet
- what to do if someone dominates or does not pull their weight

- what kinds of behavior or comments are unacceptable.

Investigate group strengths

Brainstorm the range of skills and experience in the group. Who prefers to do artwork, run meetings, write? Be clear and speak out about what *you* would like to do. If several people want to do the same thing, rotate roles or share tasks out. Include all group members.

Create an effective group environment

Set clear agendas and boundaries

Be clear about the purpose of the group and each meeting.

- Set an agenda for group meetings and decide how long to spend on each item.
- Be clear which meetings are for work and which for socializing—and stick to this.
- Arrange meeting times and venues well in advance, so that everyone can attend them.

Check progress

If the group does not seem to be working well, address this directly. Each person in turn should say what they feel could be done to improve things, including assessing what they personally could do differently.

- Does the group need to bond more through a social activity or by meeting earlier to socialize?
- Are tasks shared fairly?

- Is somebody dominating the group?
- Are you considerate enough about each other's feelings and ideas?

Try to avoid negative criticism or allocating blame.

Task allocation

- Be clear about who is doing what.
- Ensure that tasks are allocated fairly.
- Set clear deadlines for completion.

Group roles

For each session, decide who will take which role.

Chairperson

Although these are everybody's responsibilities, the chair helps the group to form an agenda and keep to it, ensures that everyone gets to speak and that their views are heard, sums up main points, and keeps the group focused on the task.

Timekeeper

The timekeeper ensures that the group keeps to the agenda and the time schedule. Sometimes he or she will time spoken contributions.

Recordkeeper

The recordkeeper notes who is going to do what and when, and any other decisions made.

Task manager

The task manager checks, between meetings, that everyone is doing what was agreed.

Being an effective group member

Sharing responsibility

The responsibility for the group lies with each member. If a problem arises, even if it seems to be the fault of one person, every member shares responsibility for sorting out the problem so that the group can work.

Getting the most out of discussion

Before

- Ensure you have done any tasks agreed for the group.
- Read up on the subject. Think about it.
- What questions do you want answered?

During

- Check that everyone can see and hear everyone else.
- Be open to hearing something new.
- Jot down useful information.
- Jot down questions to ask.

- If you don't understand something, ask.
- Link what you hear to what you already know.
- Make contributions—for example, raise points that interest you.

After

- Go over your notes and summarize them. Add any new details and thoughts.
- Check that you know exactly when you will do activities arising out of the group. Are they in your planner?

Helping the group to succeed

Be encouraging
Encourage others. For instance, you might say, "I found it interesting that …"

Include everyone
Speak to everyone in the group, not just particular individuals. Make sure that everybody has a chance to speak.

Use "body language"
As you listen, show your attention by smiling, by nodding agreement and so on. If you want to speak, make clear signals.

Listen to other students
Your fellow students deserve your respectful attention as much as your instructor does—just as you deserve theirs.

Indicate when you agree
Express your agreement: "So do I …;" "Yes, that's true …"

If you disagree
Instead of just rejecting the other person's ideas, explore them: "What makes you think that?;" "Have you thought about …?"

Help the flow
- Contribute to the discussion—but don't dominate it.
- Ask questions—but not too many.
- Take responsibility: Don't leave everything to one person.
- Encourage the group to keep to the subject.

Admit mistakes
Acknowledge your errors, and apologize: "Sorry, my mistake;" "Oh, I see! I misunderstood …"

Make suggestions
Share your ideas: "Why don't we …?"

Build on other people's ideas
"That's an important point you made, for several reasons …"

Offer information
Share your knowledge: "There's some useful information on that in …"

Sum up for the group
"Well, have we agreed on these two points so far? First, … ? And second, …?"

Dealing with difficult moments in the group

Strong emotions in a group

When strong emotions are expressed, people may feel nervous—yet these emotions are often honest expressions of what someone is feeling.

Emotions arising from strong opinions

A strong attack on somebody's views can be distressing; people often identify themselves with their own opinions. If you reject the *opinion*, the *person* may feel rejected. The group may need a ground rule that *opinions* can be challenged, but not the person who holds them.

Emotions arising from group problems

If the emotion arises out of the group not working properly, then address how the working of the group could be improved.

For example, it might be that some people feel their views are ignored. What would make them feel they were being heard? Would that be realistic? Can a compromise be found?

Emotions arising from outside the group

People bring into any group events or emotions from everyday life. This can be disrupting, as it is not clear where sudden strong emotions are coming from.

It may help to take a minute or two at the start of each session to say what has been going on for group members. You may also need ground rules about strong emotions—such as "If one person is aggressive towards another, the rest of the group will intervene."

Tears

If people are distressed, for whatever reason, let them have a few minutes' quiet or some space to express their emotions. Don't worry about tears—crying can release pent-up stress. Distressed people may need to be alone or to speak with just one other person quietly for a few minutes. Show kindness. Ask the person what he or she needs.

Silences

Silences often seem longer than they really are. This is because we so rarely experience silence.

Silence can be very productive, however. Sit with it and value it, especially if the group needs to discuss something of weight. Don't feel obliged to fill silences with questions or jokes.

Deadends

If silences suggest stagnation or stalemate, try a new approach.

- Think of several different ways to break the task into smaller parts.
- Is there a way of turning the problem on its head?
- Brainstorm ideas—might one work?

Imbalances in group interaction

Group discussions can easily become unbalanced if:

- one or two people dominate
- two people are locked into an exchange
- there are no spaces in which quieter people can get into the discussion.

The chairperson or group members can address these imbalances directly:

- by thanking dominant members for what they have contributed and reminding them that others may wish to speak
- by asking if anybody who has not spoken would like to
- by pointing out any imbalance so that the group can discuss it and deal with it.

Some contributions—such as updating the group at the start of a session about your day or week—are important but can drift on too long. Set time limits in such cases.

Group problems can also arise through more serious issues, including discrimination, prejudice and unfairness. These are addressed next.

Prejudice, unfairness, and discrimination

Prejudice and unfairness can create stress and ill-health, such that people cannot perform to the best of their abilities. They can also produce tensions and anger, which affect the study of everybody in a group or class.

Unfair discrimination, of any kind, should be the concern of *everybody*.

Your experiences of unfair treatment

Most of us have experienced prejudice in some way during our lives. It may have been name-calling, being left out of activities or bullying. Some such incidents hurt but are soon forgotten. Others cut so deeply that they affect us for many years.

Other people's attitudes, especially if combined with restricted opportunities, can make it difficult for a student to achieve his or her full potential. This may have been true, in the past, for many students at your college. Their difficulties may have been due to others' racism or sexism, or their attitudes to disability, lesbian and gay people, single parenthood or other factors.

Challenge 1

Think about an occasion when *you* were treated unfairly, because of somebody else's attitudes. For example, can you recall an occasion when you were blamed for something you did not do, or when people tried to embarrass you for no good reason?

What were your feelings and attitudes then?

Did the incident have any long-term effects—such as on your confidence?

Avoiding unintentional discrimination

Some people set out to hurt others deliberately, but a great deal of discrimination is unintentional, caused by thoughtlessness or awkwardness. Most of us are upset if we realize that we have unintentionally caused distress to somebody else.

Challenge 2

This exercise aims to help you to avoid those moments when you say or do something you know you will regret.

- Think of a group you are in or have been in, or may be in when the semester begins.
- There are dozens of ways in which members of that group could discriminate against each other, perhaps without anybody realizing. What situations can you think of?
- What questions could you ask yourself to monitor if everybody is being included, or if prejudice is leading to someone being left out?

When you have completed this exercise, compare your ideas with those on page 222.

The atmosphere may become very tense

Chapter 10

Dealing with unfair discrimination

Taking responsibility

Sooner or later you may notice that unfair discrimination is taking place, whether against yourself or against other people.

- Find out who has responsibility for equal opportunities or could give you advice, such as a Student Counseling Service.
- Ask the people you think are being discriminated against how they feel. Which course of action would *they* prefer to take—what would *they* wish to happen?
- Make clear what behavior you find unacceptable.
- Find some support for yourself—other students who agree with you, or a relevant support group or society.

If you witness or are involved in either a serious incident or discrimination over a long period, keep detailed records. Include:

- the time, date and place of each incident
- names and contact details for witnesses and any other people who were present
- exactly what was said and done.

Be willing to get involved.

- Come forward as a witness.
- Let the people who are being discriminated against know that they have your support.
- Speak out—let other people know you are aware of the harassment or discrimination and that you don't support it.
- If an issue arises during a class, ask that it be addressed.
- Make a formal complaint, for example, through the student union or using the college's grievance procedure.

Monitoring what's happening

Ideas from Challenge 2

- Does everybody get a chance to contribute, or do some people (or groups) dominate?
- Is everybody's experience and background included in the way subjects are discussed? Are there assumptions that everybody is heterosexual? or Caucasian? or able to get about easily?
- If people have accents, or dialects, or stutters, are they treated with the same respect when they speak?
- When people make comments or ask questions, are they sensitive to the feelings of others—or aware of issues that might cause distress?
- Where does the group meet? Can everybody get there, even in a wheelchair or using a cane?
- Do you know when somebody is trying to lip-read? What could group members do to make this easier? Examples include keeping hands and writing materials away from their faces and not sitting in silhouette against the source of light.
- What might cause interference or pain for someone using a hearing aid?
- What words or behavior might other people find offensive?
- Are there people who look left out, or uncomfortable, or angry? Why is this happening?

Coping with unfair discrimination

Facing discrimination

Some of us know from experience that we are quite likely to encounter some form of discrimination when we meet new people or enter a new situation.

It can be helpful to think through some of the things we fear might happen—and make plans for coping with those situations in case they *do* occur. You may not have the chance to study in higher education again: It is important that you have a strategy, where possible, to minimize the effects of other people's prejudices so you can focus on your studies.

Things you can do

If you feel best when you *do* something:

- See the suggestions under *Dealing with unfair discrimination* (page 222).
- Make sure you have a strategy for *Dealing with stress* (see pages 206–207).
- Try not to think about the stressful episode just before sleeping. Instead, do something that relaxes you—read, have a relaxing bath, listen to music, etc.
- Don't blame yourself.
- Talk to someone you can trust, and who will be able to discuss your options.
- Write down how you feel—acknowledging your feelings may help you to work through them.
- Keep a written record of what has happened, in case you need it as evidence. This gives you something which demonstrates that the discrimination is real. It might also help you to put the episode out of your mind until you can do something constructive about it.

Looking after yourself

Remember: You are right to feel that you should not have to put up with discrimination.

Most colleges have an equal opportunity policy, a harassment policy and a grievance procedure, together with staff who have responsibility for enforcing these. The students' union may also be able to help if you feel uncomfortable about speaking to college staff directly.

When you experience unfairness or discrimination, what do you usually do?

What kind of personal reaction is most likely to help you as a student, so that you still feel positive about yourself?

Has discrimination prevented you from doing something you wanted to do?

How are you going to prevent that from happening again?

How can you prepare yourself to deal with discriminatory situations?

How well do I contribute to classes and groups?

Class:

Aim of this evaluation	*Strategy*
■ To make classes and groups work more effectively, both for me and for others.	■ To evaluate my contributions using this chart, discussion and reflection.
■ To ensure that everybody feels included and safe in contributing.	■ To compare my self-evaluation with a colleague's evaluation of me.
■ To ensure that, as a group, we cover the material we need to cover.	■ To use our evaluations to develop a joint strategy for better classes.

Self-evaluation chart

1: considerable room for improvement   5: excellent

1 Had I done the necessary preparation for the group or class?	1	2	3	4	5
2 Did I make contributions during the session?	1	2	3	4	5
3 Did I speak for more than my fair share of the time?	1	2	3	4	5
4 Were my questions and comments relevant to the discussion?	1	2	3	4	5
5 Did I listen to, and consider, points raised by other people?	1	2	3	4	5
6 Was I encouraging to the main presenter or other speakers?	1	2	3	4	5
7 Was I as encouraging as I could have been to the less confident people in the group?	1	2	3	4	5
8 Did I take a full part, or was I shy or withdrawn?	1	2	3	4	5
9 Did I take relevant notes and references?	1	2	3	4	5
10 Did I keep my attention on the session, or did I get distracted?	1	2	3	4	5
11 Did I make all my contributions to the group, or were some to my neighbor only?	1	2	3	4	5
12 Am I clear what I have to do for the next class/group session?	1	2	3	4	5

Chapter 10

Other people's evaluation of my contribution to classes

Discuss your performance with a friend or other group member. Ask this person to tell you three things you do well and three things you could improve.

Use the questionnaire (page 224) to stimulate your thinking. How well *do* you contribute? What changes would you like to make? When will you make them?

The functioning of the group

Consider the overall working of the class or discussion group.

Identify three things the group needs to work on as priorities. How will you raise these issues with the group?

Study support networks

Types of support network

Some classes organize a study support group or network. This may be led by a "mentor"—a student from the year above. If no such group exists, you may like to set one up yourself. You could get together by phone or email, or meet after class or in somebody's home.

Many of the principles discussed in relation to other groups also apply to study support groups.

What a support group can do

The work of the support group is limited only by your imagination, but the following activities are generally helpful to most students.

Encourage each other

Arrange to call each other to encourage work on a particular activity.

Look for a constructive comment you could make about each group member's progress. Write these out on separate pieces of paper and give them to each other to take home. At home, put your list where you can see it, to encourage yourself.

Review lectures

Review a lecture, clarifying the main points. Fill the gaps in your own notes. Each person records different things, so by sharing information you each end up with a fuller set of lecture notes.

Solve study problems

- Give one person, *A*, five or ten minutes to describe a current study problem, while the rest of the group listen without interrupting.
- As a group, spend ten minutes clarifying the problem. Brainstorm as many ideas as you can for dealing with the problem. Now *A* listens without interrupting.
- Finally, Person *A* has ten minutes to choose an option, decide how and when it will be done, and negotiate support from the group.

Repeat the process for other members of the group. Then, at the next meeting, check that each of you carried out your intentions.

Share background reading

Read different texts around the subject, and summarize the main points for each other. Discuss your ideas about what you read.

Befriend each other

Simply listening to each other can be very helpful—don't underestimate its value.

Sharing work without cheating

Some kinds of work can be shared with other people, whereas sharing other activities would be considered to be cheating. Below are some key points. If you are in any doubt, however, always check with your instructors.

All in your own words ...

In general, any writing you submit should either be in your own words or referenced as described on pages 112–114.

- When you discuss ideas in a group, write them down as notes with bullet points. Avoid writing sentences you have heard—others might write down the same sentences and copy them into their assignments, and this would be seen as cheating.
- If you record discussions, do not type out what is recorded. If you do, you may accidentally copy someone else's words into an assignment—this too would be cheating.
- You may be asked to work as a group to design a project and collect data together. In such cases, always take your own notes about the design, methods, data collection, results, discussion and conclusions. Write the final account from your own notes—not from anyone else's.
- Don't share out writing tasks between group members. It is usually a requirement that the whole of an assignment is written entirely in your own words.
- If text is sent to you by other group members, never copy and paste it into an assignment—this would be cheating. The person who sent it might also use the text in their own assignment, and this would be noticed.
- Don't let anybody see your writing before the instructor has graded and returned the whole group's assignments. If someone copies your work and hands it in as their own, you may also be held responsible.

- Always write your own references. Mistakes easily creep into references, and instructors are usually good at detecting copied errors.

Accidental cheating?

Instructors are usually adept at finding identical and near-identical sections in students' work. Software is available that can help them to find work copied from the Internet or from other students.

If your instructors find the same wording in more than one assignment, they will suspect that cheating has occurred. This could mean that you would have to retake the whole class. You might even be asked to leave the institution. Cheating is a very serious academic offense.

Tasks that can be shared

There are many tasks that *can* be shared out among friends, support groups or project group members. These include:

- deciding on the group project title
- clarifying each other's understanding of class material by discussing lectures, notes, texts, cases, experiences, ideas
- discussing new ideas and publications
- sharing administrative tasks, such as booking rooms, keeping agendas of meetings or writing for permission to interview people
- undertaking a literature search and then identifying key texts and sections that everyone should read
- discussing and deciding on a methodology
- checking out useful websites
- collecting data
- discussing data and what it means
- helping one another to learn software packages
- encouraging each other to succeed.

Making a presentation or giving a talk

What is the purpose of a presentation?

Students are often asked to give presentations. This process is useful because:

- presentations get class discussion going
- they produce a variety of perspectives
- some people present themselves better verbally than on paper
- the ability to give presentations is a skill required in many occupations.

How are presentations assessed?

In some classes, presentations may form part of your assessment. There are many ways of assessing presentations. Find out from your instructors what criteria will be used. In general, the important feature of a presentation is that you have an *audience*—and you need to communicate information to them. This means that the talk should be very focused.

- Make a few main points. Don't swamp the audience with everything you know.
- Select a few concrete examples that are easy for the audience to visualize.
- Structure the talk very clearly, using just a few headings. Know the order in which you are going to make your points.
- Repeat main points, and summarize what you have said. When people take things in by ear, they need to be reminded of the direction your talk is taking and how the major points link up.
- Use a handout or PowerPoint slide, numbering three or four main areas you are going to address.

Preparing your talk

It always takes longer to *say* something than it does to read through it in preparation. Also, you need to speak slowly in a presentation so that people can take in what you say.

- Prepare only what you can deliver at a reasonably slow pace.

- Divide your material into the *essential* points that you definitely want to make and *extra* material you can use if there is time.
- Prepare a strong closing summary.

The postcard technique

- Break your talk into sections.
- Give each section a heading.
- Write one heading, and a few easily read prompt words, onto each postcard.
- Number the cards in the order that you want to introduce those points.
- These will give you confidence that you have something to say and give structure to what you say.

Using electronic aids

Software such as PowerPoint is useful for preparing your talk and handouts. If you use PowerPoint:

- use large text: at least 32-point
- introduce new pages from the same direction
- use only one PowerPoint slide for every 2–3 minutes of the talk
- avoid animations, sound effects and flashy graphics, unless these are really essential.

Using other audio-visual aids

If you are not very confident with IT, you could prepare a large poster or diagram to illustrate your talk. Use other aids such as music or video sparingly, and only where they make a specific point—not just to provide variety.

Practicing

Practice your talk several times, going slowly and timing yourself. If it is too long, edit it down.

Overcoming nerves

Many people spend so much time worrying about giving a talk that they leave no time to prepare what to say. You can reduce nervousness in the following ways.

- Prepare carefully—be confident about what you are going to say, and how you are going to say it.
- Make a conscious effort to relax (see page 210), especially 2–3 hours before the talk.
- Arrive early so that you do not need to worry unnecessarily about the journey.
- Be in the room before everybody else. Instead of suddenly being confronted by a sea of faces, it's your space. Smile at your audience as they arrive.
- Have water to drink.

- Don't apologize for anything you feel could be better. Act as though you are quietly confident that your talk is excellent, and you will be halfway to convincing your listeners.
- Look up. Make eye contact with at least two people in your audience.
- At the beginning, summarize what you are going to say—and in which order.
- Go through your cards or slides in turn. Make each point clearly.
- Pause and take a breath after each point. This gives your audience time to absorb the point. It also makes you look more professional.
- At the end, briefly sum up what you have said.
- Prepare a good line to end with. If you're not sure how to end, simply smile and say "Thank you."

Giving the talk

- Read the section *Making your point* (page 217).
- Use a clock to time yourself.
- Wait until everybody is settled and quiet before you start speaking.
- Tell the audience whether you would prefer questions at the end or during the talk.
- If possible, speak from your postcards, from a poster or from memory, rather than reading. The talk will flow better and will be easier to listen to. However, if you are unable to give the talk in any other way, write it out in full and read it.
- Remind yourself to speak more slowly and loudly than you would usually.

How effective am I in giving a talk?

Aspects of giving a talk	Rating		How could I improve this aspect?
	low	high	
1 Was my main argument clear?	1 2 3 4 5		
2 Did I begin with a brief outline?	1 2 3 4 5		
3 Did I stick to my outline?	1 2 3 4 5		
4 Did I sum up at the end?	1 2 3 4 5		
5 How good was my opening?	1 2 3 4 5		
6 How well did I finish?	1 2 3 4 5		
7 How appropriate were my handouts or audio-visual aids?	1 2 3 4 5		
8 Did I move logically from one point to the next?	1 2 3 4 5		
9 Did I give good examples to support my points?	1 2 3 4 5		
10 Did I answer questions well?	1 2 3 4 5		
11 Did I make eye contact with most of those present?	1 2 3 4 5		
12 Did everybody feel included?	1 2 3 4 5		
13 Did I respect the different viewpoints of those present?	1 2 3 4 5		

What feedback did the audience give me?

Being aware of your audience

The more talks you give, the more you will gain confidence in adapting the talk to suit the audience.

Here are some useful things to remember:

- Your audience's attention will tend to drift: Key points may be missed. State essential points more than once, using slightly different words.
- Your audience's attention span may be short. Break up your talk into a few clear sections. Make planned brief pauses between sections.
- Focus on the key points. Avoid unnecessary details, and don't go off on tangents—you may confuse your audience.
- It is harder to follow a complex argument or a sequence of points when listening rather than looking. A clear chart or handout will help your listeners follow you.

- If you run short of time, don't rush to fit in more material or more overheads. Instead, edit the talk to fit the available time. (You can plan such reductions when you practice your talk.)
- Audiences usually like "stories." Use relevant examples, images and case studies to engage their attention.

- How confident am I about speaking in groups and making presentations?
- What techniques suggested in this chapter would help me?
- Which three things would be most useful to try out first?

Review

It is likely that you will be expected to work with others during your time as a student, whether in classes, support groups or project groups, and in any case you will find yourself in groups just by being around other students on campus.

If the groups you are in work well, you will gain. You will benefit from different perspectives and views, your own thinking will be stretched and your ideas refined, and you will have a source of support. Whatever groups you are in, it's in your interest to help them function at their best.

Nevertheless, it is quite natural for groups to have problems. For example, they can bring out people's anxieties, some of which may appear as aggression

or failure to contribute. In dealing with such difficulties you will develop a wider range of interpersonal and problem-solving skills, which will be useful in work and in life generally.

As in other areas of study, there are strategies that can be applied to specific areas—such as listening to others, getting your point across, working together and making a presentation. Reflection on, and self-evaluation of, your own contribution is especially important for this area of study.

Overall, it is easier to work with others if it is clear what the boundaries are, what is expected, who is doing what and when, and if everyone acts with everyday consideration for the feelings of others.

Chapter 11

College-level writing

LEARNING OUTCOMES

This chapter offers you opportunities to:

- become more aware of any writing skills that you need to improve

- develop the writing habit if you have been away from formal education

- learn how to get started on a piece of writing and overcome writer's block

- learn how to examine assignment prompts

- develop a procedure for writing research papers and reports

- understand what is meant by "concepts" and "concept pyramids"

- develop strategies for organizing your ideas, planning your writing and structuring research papers and reports

- learn how to complete the basic steps of writing an assignment, such as writing drafts, editing and presenting your work by hand or using a computer.

Academic writing

Writing a good assignment is both a challenge and one of the most rewarding aspects of study. Almost all students find their writing skills develop significantly in college. This is due partly to the additional practice and partly to an increase in critical awareness developed by analyzing issues from many perspectives.

Writing cannot be separated from other processes, such as reflection, goal-setting, organization and research. Although this *Handbook*, of necessity, addresses these skills in separate chapters, in practice you will find that they are interrelated. You will make best use of this chapter if you are already confident about the material in Chapters 4 and 5. Before you complete your first or second piece of

writing, you may find it helpful to browse through Chapters 7, 12 and 14 too.

This chapter looks at skills and stages common to many types of academic writing assignment. It takes you step by step through the different processes involved in writing a piece of coursework, such as a research paper or report.

As your writing skills develop and you become more aware of what is required, you can be more flexible and creative in your approach to writing. However, be wary of instructors who say they value "individuality": This often means "be individual within the conventions of our subject area." Make sure you know what is acceptable and what is not in each subject.

How good am I at managing writing tasks?

On the chart below, check the appropriate box and rate how you well you perform the skill now (9 = excellent, 1 = weak/needs a lot of work).

Do I know ...	Yes	Rating	I just need practice	Not sure	No	Pages
■ how to get into the habit of writing?						233–234
■ how to get started on a piece of writing (or overcome "writer's block")?						236–238
■ what a research paper is?						239, 283–288
■ a procedure for writing research papers?						240
■ how to analyze assignment questions?						242–243
■ how to organize information?						246–247
■ how to use and organize concepts?						251–254
■ how to structure a research paper?						248
■ how to structure a report?						328
■ how to write good paragraphs?						256–259
■ how to write a persuasive argument?						158, 275–276
■ about different academic writing styles?						159–161, 245, 273–280
■ how to use personal experience in writing?						280
■ how to draft, edit and proofread?						255, 260–261
■ how to present my writing?						262–263
■ what gets good grades?						281
■ how to use feedback to improve my grades?						282

What are the two main priorities for improvement in your next piece of writing? Highlight these two in color.

Repeat this self-evaluation when your next piece of writing is returned, using the instructor's feedback.

Writing for the fearful

Make any mark rather than worry about a blank page

If your writing skills are *very* rusty, try some of the following short exercises. If you are more confident, skip forward to the next section that you find useful.

Get the writing habit

- Write one word ten times, in different handwriting styles. Which is most comfortable?
- Write out a story you enjoyed as a child.
- Write to a friend saying what you hope to get out of being a student.
- Jot down ten words you like the sound of. Write a short piece that includes all those words. Be as crazy as you like.
- "Just a minute": Give yourself one minute to write about one of the following:
  - (a) The worst thing I ever ate …
  - (b) The most embarrassing thing that ever happened …
  - (c) I'm lucky because …
  - (d) What gets on my nerves is …
  - (e) Anything you like.

Write for five minutes

1 Choose any subject.
2 Don't stop to think. The idea is to get used to writing continuously, whatever the content. Just write as much as you can.
3 When you can write for five minutes, extend the time to ten minutes and build up your limit.

Write from prompts

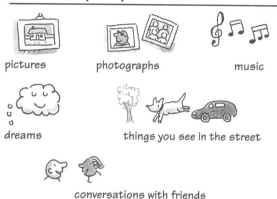

pictures   photographs   music

dreams   things you see in the street

conversations with friends

Let yourself be inspired by what you see, hear, think or dream.

Make a life chart

- Include important events in your childhood, family, education, interests, work, and so on.
- Write a few lines about each item.
- Choose one item and write about this in more detail. Describe what happened, how you felt about the episode at the time, how it affected you in the long term, whether what happened was unusual and so on.

LIFE CHART

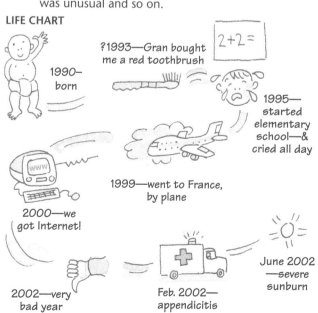

Developing your writing

Most experienced writers rewrite their work over and over, refining their thoughts, finding a better way of saying something, making a long-winded section a bit briefer or adding more details to develop an idea.

Rewrite 1
Filling out the writing

- Take one piece of writing you have done.
- Jot down a list of five extra details you could add to give a fuller picture.
- Add something you know about someone else's ideas: from television, radio or reading.
- Add a personal opinion about some aspect of what you wrote.
- Rewrite the piece, adding the new detail.

Rewrite 2
Playing with your ideas

Play around with what you have written. For example, you could:

- change the order of the sentences around
- change some of the words
- add more details
- change the order of the paragraphs
- ask a question and turn what you have written into the answer
- write from the opposite point of view.

Rewrite 3
Organizing your material

- Select one of your pieces of writing.
- Read through it, underlining each major idea in a different color. For each change of subject, change the color. If a subject comes up again, use the color you used before.
- When you have finished, check how often the color *changes*.
- Rewrite the passage so that all the parts underlined in a given color are grouped together.

Anxieties about writing

Typical comments from students

Anxiety about writing is very common in college.

"I start a sentence, cross it out, start it again, cross it out, throw the paper in the trash, start a sentence, cross it out …"

"I just see the assignment prompt and panic. I think, 'I don't know anything about that!'"

"I can't get down to it—I keep putting it off and then I'm in a huge rush to finish it."

"Some people just write out a report in a night—I have to write it over and over again."

Maybe some of these comments strike a chord with you? What do you find difficult about getting started on a piece of writing? The next list may clarify your thinking.

What stops me from writing?

- ☐ The blank page is very offputting.
- ☐ My mind goes empty.
- ☐ I don't know where to begin.
- ☐ I just can't get down to it.
- ☐ I am not as good as other people.
- ☐ The ideas go round and round in my head.
- ☐ I am embarrassed about my handwriting.
- ☐ I am embarrassed about my spelling.
- ☐ I worry about grammar and punctuation.
- ☐ Other reasons.

 In your journal, note down your thoughts and observations about any difficulties *you* have in getting started.

Similarities between academic writing and other activities

Every day you are involved in situations that require you to plan and to make decisions. Think of one activity you completed recently, such as planning a vacation, choosing this college or organizing a party. On a separate sheet, describe exactly what you did, from start to finish.

The activity probably involved six stages. Check the stages you went through to complete your activity.

☐ 1 Deciding in general what to do.

☐ 2 Collecting relevant information or materials to complete the task.

☐ 3 Planning the order to do things.

☐ 4 Carrying out the plan.

☐ 5 Checking that you were going about the task in the right way.

☐ 6 Reflecting on how you would do it better next time.

Academic writing follows a similar pattern of planning and decision-making. Suppose you were asked to write about "The influence of theories on cloning animals." You may know very little about the subject, and you may have no clear opinion. But you can approach the writing task much as the activity you analyzed above.

Activity

Approaching a writing task

To plan a piece of writing you would probably take the steps shown in the table, but not in the order given.

- Rearrange the steps in the order you would be likely to carry them out.
- Consider a second order you could use.
- Then look below and compare your responses.
- Would your own suggested order suit you better?

Possible sequences

10 11 12 9 6 1
6 2 13 7 8 4 5

12 11 9 10 1
6 2 13 8 7 4 5

	Steps taken	Order
1	Decide how you would do better next time	
2	Make a draft outline	
3	Put the ideas in order	
4	Research the subject (reading, interviews, experiments, etc.)	
5	Examine the assignment prompt and decide what is required	
6	Write a rough draft	
7	Take notes from your reading (or interviews, experiments, etc.)	
8	Select the relevant information to include	
9	Write the final draft	
10	Write out the references (books and other sources of information)	
11	Read through the writing, checking for sense and small errors; make corrections	
12	Check if your text is within the word or page limit	
13	Separate main ideas from supporting detail and examples	

Overcoming writer's block

The following activities can help to overcome writing blocks. Which would be most useful for you?

☐ **Scribble**

Scribble ideas fast, in any order—whatever comes into your mind—then rearrange what you have written and rewrite it.

☐ **"It's only a draft"**

Think of each piece of writing as something you will develop through several drafts. As it's just a draft, it doesn't have to be good—it's just something to work on.

☐ **Write in pencil**

This will remind you that your draft is a rough one—mistakes are allowed!

☐ **Write on loose paper—not in a book**

If you don't like what you have written, you can throw it away. Alternatively, you can cut it up and rearrange it.

☐ **Ignore mistakes in early drafts**

Don't worry about minor corrections, such as spellings—you can sort those out in the final draft.

☐ **"For your eyes only"**

Remind yourself that nobody but you needs to see early drafts. Handwriting, untidiness and mistakes don't matter at this stage. Could a trusted friend or relative help you to proofread, later, for mistakes?

☐ **Experiment**

Try different starting methods—see *Tricks for getting started* (page 237). Which ones work best for you?

☐ **Start anywhere**

Write things in any order that suits you—you can rearrange them later. For example, it may be easier to write the introduction last.

☐ **Mark the paper**

If blank paper puts you off, make any mark or doodle on it so that it's *not* blank. The paper is only a tool—it can't judge you.

☐ **Write by talking**

If you find it hard to express yourself in writing, say it out loud and record yourself. Then copy this out and redraft it.

☐ **Take one step at a time**

Break the task into manageable steps. Look back to the C·R·E·A·M strategies (Chapter 4), such as setting mini-goals.

☐ **Use the computer**

If you use a computer it is easy to change what you have written. You can use a spell checker, and nobody sees your handwriting!

☐ **Brainstorming on the computer**

Brainstorm headings and ideas, typing them quickly on the computer screen. Print them and cut them out. Rearrange them on a large piece of paper (perhaps using poster putty or sticky tack), until you have the order you want. Use this plan to "cut and paste" the headings on the computer. Then write the text to go with the headings.

☐ **Use specialist software**

Use a computer package (such as Inspiration) that allows you to brainstorm and organize ideas both as patterns and as linear notes. You can color-code ideas on screen; if you have a color printer, you can get a color printout. This can be very useful if you have difficulties organizing your writing.

☐ **Rest and relax**

If your mind goes blank, you may be tired or stressed. See *Managing stress* (page 209).

Chapter 11

Tricks for getting started

Here are some ideas for getting started on a piece of writing.

- You can combine several of these.
- Which ones do you want to try?
- In your journal, keep a record of which work best for you.

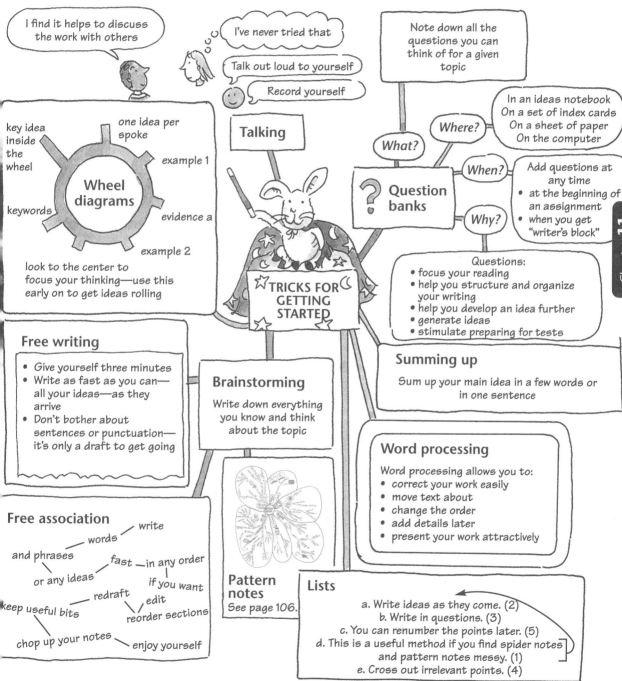

I find it helps to discuss the work with others

I've never tried that

Talk out loud to yourself

Record yourself

Note down all the questions you can think of for a given topic

Talking

In an ideas notebook
On a set of index cards
On a sheet of paper
On the computer

What? Where? When? Why?

Wheel diagrams

key idea inside the wheel

one idea per spoke

example 1

keywords

evidence a

example 2

look to the center to focus your thinking—use this early on to get ideas rolling

Question banks

Add questions at any time
- at the beginning of an assignment
- when you get "writer's block"

Questions:
- focus your reading
- help you structure and organize your writing
- help you develop an idea further
- generate ideas
- stimulate preparing for tests

⭐ TRICKS FOR GETTING STARTED

Summing up

Sum up your main idea in a few words or in one sentence

Free writing

- Give yourself three minutes
- Write as fast as you can—all your ideas—as they arrive
- Don't bother about sentences or punctuation—it's only a draft to get going

Brainstorming

Write down everything you know and think about the topic

Word processing

Word processing allows you to:
- correct your work easily
- move text about
- change the order
- add details later
- present your work attractively

Free association

write

words

and phrases

fast — in any order

or any ideas

if you want

redraft

edit

reorder sections

keep useful bits

chop up your notes

enjoy yourself

Pattern notes

See page 106.

Lists

a. Write ideas as they come. (2)
b. Write in questions. (3)
c. You can renumber the points later. (5)
d. This is a useful method if you find spider notes and pattern notes messy. (1)
e. Cross out irrelevant points. (4)

Students' solutions to writing blocks

Here two students describe how they incorporate some of the ideas mentioned in this chapter into their own way of working. How would you adapt their methods to suit you?

Marco

WHAT I USED TO DO

I used to find myself staring at the blank page, not knowing where to begin. I had done the reading. I knew in my head what I wanted to say. Nonetheless, getting started on a piece of writing seemed harder than climbing Everest. The page was too empty. Whatever I wrote seemed wrong. I used to write the first line and cross it out twenty or thirty times—maybe more—get a fresh piece of paper, and do the same thing again.

WHAT I DO NOW

I realize now that I used to aim at writing my good draft long before I was ready. My plans were too skimpy to be useful. I was actually trying to develop my ideas, organize information, write a final draft and compose good academic English all at the same time. No wonder I found it hard.

The first thing I do now is draw a face smiling up at me. It reminds me that this is only a draft—not my best copy, so it does not matter if I make mistakes. Next, I look away from the page, and maybe put my pen down. I think of a few things I want to include in my writing and jot them down in a list. When the list is getting long, I turn it into a mind map—I think other people do it the other way around but it seems to work OK for me like this. I push each part of the map as far as I can take it by asking questions (*who? why? how often? always? everywhere? example? how do I know this?* etc.) As I read or go through my class notes, I add bits to the map.

When I have all the information I need on my mind-map, I look at the main themes and number them in the order they should be in my writing. I do the same with the topics I will cover under each theme, and any other material—so I know exactly where everything fits. I draw a different-colored circle around each theme on the mind map so it stands out. Sometimes I turn the mind map back into a list to be clear what I am doing.

I then start with whatever topic looks easiest and just write the basics—not being too fussy at this stage about whether it sounds good—it's just a starting place. I remind myself that I am free to write any sentence or parts of sentences in any order that I find easiest to do. I can always correct and edit and move things around later. When I come to rewrite it, lots of ideas and obvious corrections come quite easily, because I have something to look at.

By the time I write my best version, I am already nearly there. By working in stages, there is not that awful moment when writing actually "begins"—it has developed bit by bit.

Ayeesha

I have revolutionized my writing. I am a "headings and points" (1, 2, 3) person. I type these straight onto the computer. This organizes everything easily. Then it's like joining up the dots. I write a sentence or two about each point. Everything under one heading is a paragraph. Then I write my conclusion and the introduction. I keep correcting tiny bits as I go along—I am a perfectionist, I suppose. At the end, I print it out, erase the headings and find a hundred things to correct—mostly quite small. Then I print it out again, and find twenty corrections and so on. I feel like an artist fine-tuning until I am happy with it. Well, I am never a 100% happy. No piece of writing is perfect. You just have to make a decision that "that's it," the best you can do in the circumstances, and hand it in.

Research papers and other academic writing

Academic writing

The following pages look at the basics of:

- what a research paper is
- a seven-point procedure for approaching writing tasks
- analyzing the assignment prompt
- structuring your writing
- drafting, editing, and proofreading.

The next chapter looks at more advanced features of academic writing: Aim to read the two quite close together.

What is a research paper?

A research paper is a piece of writing which is written to a set of writing conventions. The diagram below gives some brief answers to questions many new students ask.

- A research paper is a piece of writing with a particular structure and layout (see page 248).
- Usually it is written in a formal, academic style: The language is different from the way you speak or the way you would write to a friend—it is not conversational (see page 273).
- You are expected to keep very strictly to the task set. You are usually given an assignment prompt: Often this is referred to as "the question," even if it isn't actually worded as a question.

In each paper you can:

- explore a topic in detail
- develop and organize your own ideas through writing
- develop your writing skills
- express your views about a topic
- engage with critical debates in the subject.

Papers also help instructors to assess your progress and to assess and grade your work.

Ask your instructors why they give you papers to write—they may have additional reasons.

What?

Why?

Writing research papers

How often? *Where?* *For whom?*

- Typically, you may write between two and eight papers each semester, but this varies from class to class.

Write wherever suits you, or as required:

- at home
- in the library
- in the classroom.

You write papers for:

- your instructors
- yourself
- (sometimes) other students.

A seven-point procedure for writing assignments

Until you develop your own method of writing papers and other assignments, you may find this seven-point procedure helpful.

1 Clarify the task

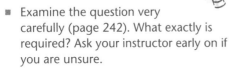

Before you start research, make sure you know what you are looking for.

- Examine the question very carefully (page 242). What exactly is required? Ask your instructor early on if you are unsure.
- Write one line to sum up your basic opinion or argument. Adapt it as you proceed.
- Brainstorm or make pattern notes to record what you know already.
- What do you need to read or find out?

2 Collect and record information

Get the information you need, but be focused.

- Be selective—you can't use everything.
- Write a set of questions to guide your research—and look for the answers.
- Check the page or word limit to see how much information you can use for each point.
- Keep a notebook nearby to jot down ideas.

Types of material

You can use any relevant material:

- factual information
- ideas, theories, opinions
- experience.

Sources

Many sources of information are available to you, including:

- books, articles, official reports, surveys
- class and lecture notes, data from laboratory work and projects, the Internet, interviews
- television, radio, newspapers, videos.

Method

Keep asking yourself:

- "Do I need the information?"
- "How will I use this information?"

Recording

Record information as you go along (see page 109):

- where you found information and ideas—for your references list (see page 114)
- notes of themes, theories, dates, names, data, explanations, examples, details, evidence, page numbers (see page 104).

3 Organize and plan

Organize your work as you go along (see page 247).

- Make a big chart to link ideas and details.
- Make a rough outline plan early on—you can refine it as you go along.

Planning

Keep checking what you are doing. Careful planning:

- helps to prevent repetition
- clarifies your thinking
- helps you organize your material.

4 Engage, reflect, evaluate

When you have gathered the information, think about where you have got to.

- What have you discovered?
- Has your viewpoint changed?
- Have you clarified your thesis?
- Have you enough evidence/examples?
- What arguments or evidence oppose your point of view? Are they valid?
- Is it clearer to you why this task was set?

6 Work on your first draft

Develop your first draft. You may need to do this several times, improving the assignment with each version. Leave time between drafts for your ideas to simmer.

- Rewrite your early draft (see page 255). Adapt the structure (pages 248, 328) and organize the writing into paragraphs.
- Make sure your argument is clear to readers.
- Check that you have included evidence and examples to support your points.
- Write out your references (or bibliography).

5 Write a draft outline plan and first draft

Now structure your writing.

- Refine your plan. Work out the order to introduce your ideas, using pattern notes or headings and points.
- Work out how much space you have for each point. What must you leave out?
- Write a first draft. Write quickly: It is only a draft. You may find it easier to type headings onto the computer first.
- Start with whatever seems easiest.
- Keep going: Don't worry about style.
- To begin with, state things clearly and simply in short sentences.

> 1 Title
> 2 Introduction
> 3 Main argument—notes Q (red)
>   evidence for—notes Q, p. 3–4
>   evidence against: Q, p. 5 (orange)
>   evaluation of evidence
> 4 Alternative theory: notes R (yellow)
>   example of application
>   evidence for
>   evidence against (lemon)
>   why not convincing
> 5 Alternative theory 2: notes S (green)
>   evaluation of evidence
>   why not convincing
> 6 Underlying issues—notes T (blue)
> 7 Conclusions
>   a
>   b
>   c

7 Final draft

Edit and check your final draft (see page 261).

- Enjoy "fine-tuning" your writing.
- Read it aloud to check that it is clearly written.
- Keep redrafting until you are happy with the text.

Analyzing the assignment prompt

Pick the assignment prompt to bits

However they are worded, all assignment prompts contain a central question that has to be answered. Your main task is to apply what you know to a particular problem. It is *not* to show how much you know—however brilliant your piece of writing, if it does not "answer the question," you may get no points at all.

You are graded partly on how well you select and organize information to meet the requirements of the question or problem—even in exams. Use the prompt or question to guide you in selecting what to read and note.

Focus on the assignment prompt

It's essential to take time making sure you understand what is required.

- Read the assignment prompt aloud slowly three times.
- Underline or highlight words that tell you the *approach* to take (see page 243).
- Underline words that guide you on how to select the *subject matter* of the assignment.
- Write out the central question to help you take it in.
- How many sections are there to it?
- Write it out more fully, putting it in your own words. What is the assignment really looking for? What are the underlying questions?
- What topical issues does it refer to?
- Discuss the question with someone else.
- How does it link to what you have read or heard in class? What else does it ask that you need to find out?

Take notes

Write down in your own words exactly what the question requires. It may form a useful part of your introduction later.

- Note obvious questions arising from the assignment prompt, such as "Why did this happen?," "How often ...?" or "How typical ...?"

Pick the assignment prompt to bits

- Ask yourself why this question was assigned. Is there some public or academic controversy you should know about? Are there important issues to include?
- Note down your reflections on the question and your opinions.
- What do you already know? Do you have evidence to back up your opinions?
- What do you not know yet? Where or how can you find out more?

Use the question

Keep focused on the question

Put the question where you can see it easily.

Keep checking the exact wording

As you research and write, remind yourself of the *exact wording* of the question. It is easy to forget the focus of the task and drift off on a tangent.

Introductions

In your "Introduction" (the first paragraph of your writing), refer directly to the question in order to focus your reader. Say how you interpret it. You can do this by rephrasing the question in your own words. (If you misunderstood the question, at least the reader will be aware of what has happened.)

Conclusions

In your conclusion, refer back to the question to demonstrate to your reader that you are still answering the assigned question. Link your final sentence to the question contained in the assignment prompt.

Academic keywords used in assignment prompts

These words indicate the approach or style expected for the piece of writing.

Account for   Give reasons for; explain why something happens.

Analyze   Examine in very close detail; identify important points and chief features.

Comment on   Identify and write about the main issues, giving your reactions based upon what you have read or heard in lectures or classes. Avoid purely personal opinion.

Compare   Show how two or more things are similar. Indicate the relevance or consequences of these similarities.

Contrast   Set two or more items or arguments in opposition so as to draw out differences. Indicate whether the differences are significant. If appropriate, give reasons why one item or argument may be preferable (see Chapter 12).

Critically evaluate   Weigh arguments for and against something, assessing the strength of the evidence on both sides. Use criteria to guide your assessment of which opinions, theories, models or items are preferable.

Define   Give the exact meaning of. Where relevant, show that you understand why the definition may be problematic.

Describe   Give the main characteristics or features of something or outline the main events.

Discuss   Write about the most important aspects of (probably including criticism); give arguments for and against; consider the implications of.

Distinguish   Bring out the differences between two (possibly confusable) items.

Evaluate   Assess the worth, importance or usefulness of something, using evidence. There will probably be cases to be made both *for* and *against*.

Examine   Put the subject "under the microscope," looking at it in detail. If appropriate, "Critically evaluate" it as well.

Explain   Make clear why something happens or why something is the way it is.

Illustrate   Make something clear and explicit, giving examples or evidence.

Interpret   Give the meaning and relevance of data or other material presented.

Justify   Give evidence which supports an argument or idea; show why decisions or conclusions were made, considering objections that others might make.

Narrate   Concentrate on saying *what* happened, telling it as a story.

Outline   Give only the main points, showing the main structure.

Relate   Show similarities and connections between two or more things.

State   Give the main features, in very clear English (almost like a simple list but written in full sentences).

Summarize   Draw out the main points only (see "Outline"), omitting details or examples.

To what extent   Consider how far something is true or contributes to a final outcome. Consider also ways in which the proposition is not true. (The answer is usually somewhere between "completely" and "not at all.")

Trace   Follow the order of different stages in an event or process.

Chapter 11

Devising your own assignment question

Some classes may require you to devise your own assignment questions. There is an art to devising these, as a good question can help you to produce a forceful piece of work. In choosing your question, consider each of the following elements.

Core questions

Good assignment prompts usually contain one or two key questions that the assignment should answer. It may contain a question, such as:

> To what extent are interest rates affected by consumer spending?

However, the question is not always obvious. For example:

> Compare and contrast the effects of consumer spending and stock market variations on changes in interest rates.

Although the wording is different, the core questions in both cases are "What affects interest rates the most? What else affects interest rates to some extent?"

In addressing each prompt, you would be expected to compare and contrast the effects of different factors on changes in interest rates and to include similar material in each paper.

Factors to contrast

Choose a question that allows you the opportunity to analyze, to compare, to contrast and to evaluate different options. This will make the paper more interesting to read, will allow you to consider various perspectives and will let you develop a stronger structure.

Keeping it simple

- Avoid long, complex questions.
- Avoid using several questions at once.
- If you use a quotation, keep this short and follow it with a typical assignment question.
- To check if your question is clear, ask a nonexpert if she or he understands it.

Research evidence

Ensure that you can:

- find published research to support the topic easily access this material
- easily collect any new data you need.

Scale: choose a specific area

Ensure that the question:

- is narrowly defined—it should be very clear exactly what you will cover
- is manageable—refer to specific groups or places or categories, rather than "the whole area" of a subject
- can be discussed in reasonable detail within the page or word limit.

Issues for debate

Select an area in which you can debate issues relevant to your subject. Devise a question that allows you to discuss these issues and differences of opinion about them. This will help you to develop a good line of reasoning (see Chapter 7).

Activity

Read the following assignment prompts. What do you think are the weaknesses in each?

1 Reptiles.

2 "The world is a safer place today than it has ever been." J. K. Moody (2008). Is this really true?

3 What were the main changes in the use of technology within the American home during the twentieth century? What was the incentive behind innovation? Who promoted change? Did these affect women differently from men? What forces have hindered change?

4 The negative effects of violence on TV.

5 Describe how placebos work.

For a discussion of these assignment prompts, see page 264. For guidance on devising topics for projects and dissertations, see page 320.

Common features of all academic writing

Although the wording of assignment prompts may differ, almost all academic writing requires you to do certain things.

Use source materials

Do not simply state your personal opinion or say what is in your head. Instead, use material from reading, class and lecture notes and other sources to give reasons, evidence, examples and case studies.

Compare and contrast

Most assignments require some element of comparing and contrasting, especially of theories, models or research findings. You will probably have to read different opinions and weigh them against each other.

Use criteria to evaluate

State which criteria you use to evaluate evidence: For example, that you are using the most up-to-date figures, or figures drawn from the largest survey, or a well-known expert's opinion for a particular reason (such as that he uses evidence from twenty well-conducted experiments). See Chapter 7, *Critical analytical thinking*.

Show awareness of complexities

Demonstrate that you are aware that answers are not always clear-cut. For example, although the expert you quote seems to have the best argument, his twenty experiments may all have used small children whereas the question set refers to teenagers. Acknowledge weaknesses in your own argument and strengths in opposing arguments. State clearly why there are difficulties coming to a firm conclusion one way or another.

Follow an argument

In your writing, show a line of reasoning that gives direction to the writing, so that one point follows logically from another. (See Chapters 7 and 12.)

Make a decision

Show which side of the argument, or which model or theory, is best in the final analysis. Even though the case may be fairly evenly weighted, show that you are able to make a decision on the basis of the evidence.

Follow a set structure

There is likely to be a set structure for the type of writing and a particular style for each subject area. (Different styles are considered in the next chapter.) *All* academic writing requires that you group similar points together in one paragraph or section, rather than scattering them through the text.

Be "discursive"

Link your points so that they feed into sentences and paragraphs, and so that each paragraph follows naturally from the previous one. All should contribute to a central guiding line of reasoning. (This is different from presenting a random set of points, for example, or headings with bullet points under them.)

Be emotionally neutral

Most academic writing requires you to stand back and analyze dispassionately, as an objective onlooker.

Structuring your writing

The structure and organization of your work is just as important as the content. What matters is not just what you know but the way that you organize it.

How do you structure academic writing?

Like a building, a piece of academic writing gains its structure and shape from several elements.

Design: your argument

What you are trying to say (your argument) should provide the structure for the whole piece of writing. Your reader should be able to follow your line of reasoning easily: How it moves from *a* to *b* to *c*. (See page 275 and Chapter 7.)

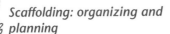

Scaffolding: organizing and planning

Organize and plan your work before you start.

- Group ideas together, in files or on paper.
- Devise a working plan to guide your research.
- Make a draft outline for your writing.

(See pages 247 and 249.)

Central framework: formal structure

Different formal structures are required for different kinds of writing, such as research papers or reports (see pages 248 and 328).

Bricks: paragraphs

Writing is organized into paragraphs, and each paragraph itself has a structure. Clear paragraphing assists the reader. (See pages 256–258.)

Cement: wording

You can use language, such as linking words and emphasis, to highlight your point and show the direction of your argument. (See page 259.)

Organizing information: grouping things together

First try this ...

For each box, work out:

- How many circles are there?
- How many triangles?
- How many *types* of triangle?

Box A

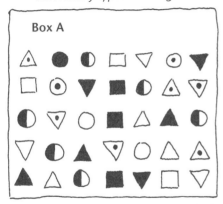

Box B

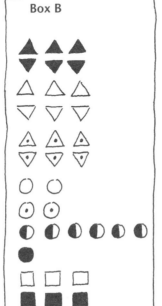

Comment

You probably found it quicker and easier to find the answers for Box B. If so, why was this the case?

Why group information?

Grouping ideas and points has several advantages.

- You will be able to find things more easily.
- You will find it easier to draw up your writing plan and follow it.
- Your thinking will be clearer.
- Your readers will be able to follow your argument more easily.
- You will get in a mess if you don't.

(See pages 109 and 247.)

Organizing information: planning your writing

Below are four steps you will need to take in organizing information for an assignment. Each step makes the next one easier. (See also *Recording and using information*, page 109.)

1 Divide the work into topics

When taking notes, it may be easier to use a separate sheet for each main point or topic. Or you may like to use a large sheet of paper, writing out points so you can see them all clearly.

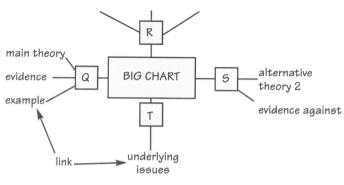

2 Rearrange your notes

- Spread your notes out so that you can see them.
- Look at what you have.
- Group related information.
- Arrange the material in the best order.

notes about Q (red)	notes about R (yellow)
notes about S (green)	notes about T (blue)

3 Write a draft outline

Write your first outline before you have done any research. Often you will find that you know more than you thought. The outline helps to shape your ideas and focus your reading. You can adapt it as you go along.

1 Title

2 Introduction

3 Main argument—notes Q (red)
   evidence for—notes Q, p. 3–4
   evidence against: Q, p. 5 (orange)
   evaluation of evidence

4 Alternative theory: notes R (yellow)
   example of application
   evidence for
   evidence against (lemon)
   why not convincing

5 Alternative theory 2: notes S (green)
   evaluation of evidence
   why not convincing

6 Underlying issues—notes T (blue)

7 Conclusions
   a
   b
   c

4 Organize information into paragraphs

Color-code each pile of notes. The plan shown uses the sequence of colors of the rainbow, to assist memory. Divide your notes with colored dividers. Give each paragraph a color: Underline main points in this color. Maintain this color-coding onto pattern notes, outline plans and rough drafts.

Having grouped the information and formed the plan, you can start writing. Each paragraph should have one main idea—with supporting detail or evidence. Each paragraph should relate to one set (or page) of notes. (See page 256.)

Chapter 11

Structuring a paper

1 ▶ Title/question

As stated earlier (page 242), every assignment prompt contains an actual or implied question. The whole of your paper must focus on the assignment prompt and address that question.

2 ▶ Introduction

In your introduction, explain what the paper is going to do.

- Explain how you interpret the question, and summarize your conclusion.
- Identify issues that you are going to explore.
- Give a brief outline of how you will deal with each issue, and in which order.

Length: about one-tenth of the paper.

3 ▶ Develop your argument or line of reasoning

Paragraph 1

- This paragraph covers the first thing your introduction said you would address.
- The first sentence introduces the main idea of the paragraph.
- Other sentences develop the topic of the paragraph. Include relevant examples, details, evidence, quotations, references.
- Lead up to the next paragraph.

Paragraph 2 and other paragraphs

- The first sentence, or opening sentences, link the paragraph to the previous paragraphs, then introduce the main idea of the paragraph.
- Other sentences develop the paragraph's topic. (For more about paragraphs, see pages 256–258.)

4 ▶ Conclusion

The conclusion contains no *new* material.

- Summarize your argument and the main themes.
- State your general conclusions.
- Make it clear why those conclusions are important or significant.
- In your last sentence, sum up your argument very briefly, linking it to the central question.

Length: about one-tenth of the paper.

5 ▶ References and/or bibliography

References and bibliography

List all the books, articles and other materials you have referred to within the paper. (See page 114.) If a bibliography is required, list relevant texts, including those you read but did not refer to in the paper.

The structure given here is the most basic. It underlies not just research papers but many other types of writing. The structuring of different types of academic writing is discussed in Chapter 12.

Planning your writing assignment

As you become more aware of different writing formats, you can use the appropriate structure to guide your planning.

Plan spatially: draw out your pages

Before beginning any research:

- Carefully check the page or word limit for the assignment.
- For assignments with word rather than page limits, work out roughly how many words you write or type on one page. (This may be about 250 words.) Calculate how many pages your paper will occupy. (For instance, 1000 words at 250 words per page will occupy 4 pages.)
- Take that many pieces of paper. Draw out in pencil how much space you will give to each section, item or topic, as in the sample paper

below. How much space or how many words can you allocate to each section? Or to each topic or example?

- It may take a few attempts to get the balance right. Note how little or how much you can write for each topic or example.
- If you wish, continue to plan out your paper, point by point, on these sheets. Notice how much space each item can take.

With this spatial plan, can you now see:

- how many pages of your writing your assignment will take?
- where sections or topics will be on the page?
- how your word or page limit divides up?
- how little or how much you need to read and note for each item?

A draft outline for the paper on pages 283–285 (1000 words)

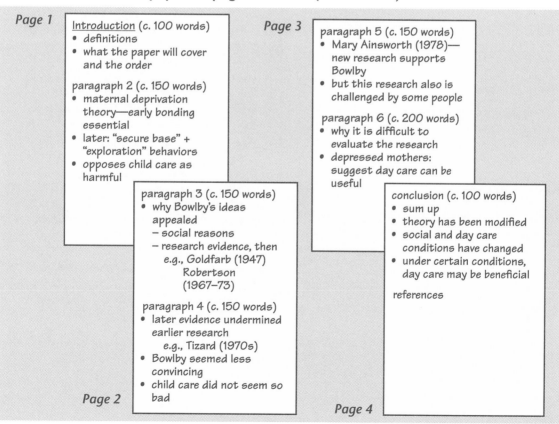

Page 1

Introduction (c. 100 words)
- definitions
- what the paper will cover and the order

paragraph 2 (c. 150 words)
- maternal deprivation theory—early bonding essential
- later: "secure base" + "exploration" behaviors
- opposes child care as harmful

paragraph 3 (c. 150 words)
- why Bowlby's ideas appealed
  - social reasons
  - research evidence, then e.g., Goldfarb (1947) Robertson (1967–73)

paragraph 4 (c. 150 words)
- later evidence undermined earlier research e.g., Tizard (1970s)
- Bowlby seemed less convincing
- child care did not seem so bad

Page 2

Page 3

paragraph 5 (c. 150 words)
- Mary Ainsworth (1978)— new research supports Bowlby
- but this research also is challenged by some people

paragraph 6 (c. 200 words)
- why it is difficult to evaluate the research
- depressed mothers: suggest day care can be useful

conclusion (c. 100 words)
- sum up
- theory has been modified
- social and day care conditions have changed
- under certain conditions, day care may be beneficial

references

Page 4

Planning stages

Develop your draft outline

Make a first draft outline

Make pattern notes or a structure plan showing what you know, what at this stage you think are the main issues, your questions and things to find out.

Action plan

Convert your list of things to find out into an action plan with priorities (page 78).

Plan your time

Use the **Working backwards from deadlines** sheet (page 79) and your planner to map out when and where to complete each stage of the writing process. (This becomes easier after the first assignment, when you have a feel for your own pace of working.)

What is the *minimum* you can do? What additional research would you *like* to do, if you have time? Depending on how well you proceed, you can adapt your reading and note-taking to suit.

Rework your plan

If necessary, rework your draft outline as you proceed. You may rework this several times as your thinking becomes more sophisticated. This is part of the process of understanding a subject.

Make a clear final outline

Clarify your final outline. If necessary, use correction fluid to remove unwanted text, use color to highlight certain areas, or rewrite untidy parts afresh and stick them over the area to be clarified.

Notice if you use "neatening the plan" as an excuse to put off writing the first draft.

From pattern notes to linear plan

It's essential to be really clear about the structure of your paper before you start writing your final drafts. If you're not, your writing and thinking may appear confused.

Pattern notes are very effective at the planning stage, but you may find it difficult to write assignments directly from them. They illustrate connections and resemble the way the mind organizes information in networks, whereas writing is linear and sequential—one point follows another. Pattern notes are also mainly descriptive. On notes of this sort, it is harder to analyze, evaluate and contrast, yet these are what a paper requires.

The following approach can help in translating pattern notes into writing.

- Use the pattern notes to brainstorm what you know and to generate ideas. Encourage your creativity rather than worrying about organizing information at this stage.
- Use color, numbers and connecting lines to link related information on the pattern.
- Redraw the pattern notes, placing together all connected information.
- As a halfway stage between pattern notes and sequential writing, you may like to draw up pyramids (see page 251). On a separate sheet, make a pyramid for each major section of the pattern. With practice, pyramids will clarify how your information is structured.
- From the notes or pyramids, write out your main headings, with main points and items listed under each. Use the color-code from the pattern notes to guide you. Position these lists on your spatial plan (page 249).

Concept pyramids organize ideas

What is a concept?

A *concept* is a mental representation of a group of items that are similar in some way. For example, the concept "cutlery" includes objects as different as a four-pronged fork, a hollowed, round-ended spoon, and a sharp-edged knife. Conceptually, these all share the characteristic of being tools used in eating food. Sometimes the phrase *conceptual category* is used instead of "concept."

Why concepts are useful

When we come across a new object, the brain matches the main features of the new experience against those of previous experiences. It can then make a good guess at what kind of thing the new object is—its concept category:

"branches, trunk, leaves, bird's nest: must be a tree"

Once it has identified the category, the brain can second-guess, or infer, other information:

"If it's a tree, it must have roots and sap. It won't leave the area. I don't need to take it for walks. Sorted!"

This ability to identify and share conceptual categories enables us to communicate more easily with other people: We don't need to describe everything in minute detail whenever we speak. In academic writing, if ideas are well organized, the reader can second-guess meaning and other information more easily.

Concept pyramids organize ideas

We can organize concepts into hierarchies—shaped like a triangle or pyramid, as in the simple one for "tree" below. You don't *have* to use concept pyramids—but they give you an extra analytical tool.

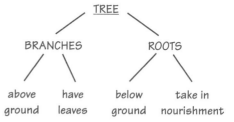

The most general information, or the most inclusive heading, is placed at the top of the pyramid. Aspects of the tree are placed below. Details of those aspects are placed below again and so on.

Each level of the pyramid shows information of a different category. There are technical names for different category levels, but everyday terms work just as well.

Technical term	Everyday term
Superordinate category	Upper level (*tree*)
Intermediate or basic category	Intermediate level (*oak tree*)
Subordinate category	Lower level (*red oak tree*)
Exemplar	Example (*this red oak tree*)

On another pyramid, *plant* might be the upper-level concept, and *tree* would then be at the intermediate level.

Example: concept pyramid for contrasting birds and mammals

The example below shows a more detailed concept pyramid, showing how different levels of information about animals can be arranged.

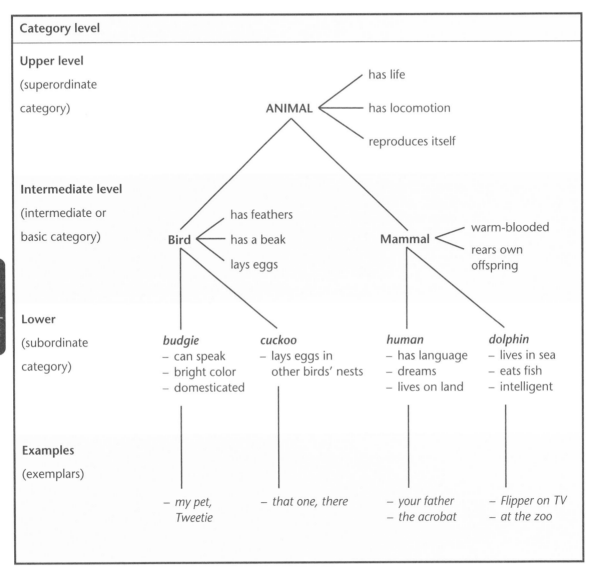

Category level

Upper level

(superordinate category)

ANIMAL
- has life
- has locomotion
- reproduces itself

Intermediate level

(intermediate or basic category)

Bird
- has feathers
- has a beak
- lays eggs

Mammal
- warm-blooded
- rears own offspring

Lower

(subordinate category)

budgie
– can speak
– bright color
– domesticated

cuckoo
– lays eggs in other birds' nests

human
– has language
– dreams
– lives on land

dolphin
– lives in sea
– eats fish
– intelligent

Examples

(exemplars)

– *my pet, Tweetie*

– *that one, there*

– *your father*
– *the acrobat*

– *Flipper on TV*
– *at the zoo*

Examples at different levels

If the upper level were *painting*, an intermediate level could be the style, *Impressionism*. A lower level would be painters, such as *Monet*, and examples could be Monet's paintings *Water Lilies*, *Wisteria* and *Poplars*. You might have separate hierarchies of details of the paintings—with *size*, *color*, *design* or *brushwork* as category headings.

If the upper level were *instrument*, an intermediate level could be *drum*, and a lower level might be a *timpani drum* or *African drum*. Specific examples would be *that drum on the table* or *Connor's new drumkit*.

Draft outlines as pyramids

Paper structures consist of several concept pyramids combined into one piece of continuous writing. A halfway step between pattern notes and linear writing, the concept pyramid incorporates more structure and linear development. Unlike pattern notes, it enables you to evaluate the weight (or level) of one kind of information against another—and to see this visually.

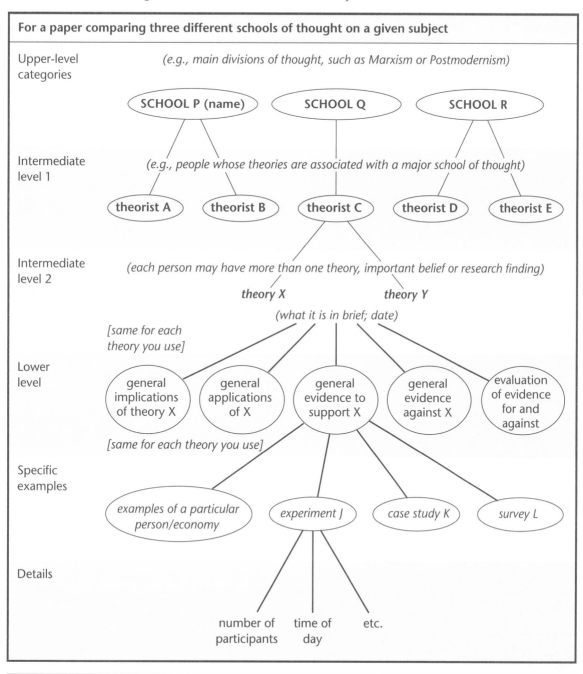

For a paper comparing three different schools of thought on a given subject

Upper-level categories

(e.g., main divisions of thought, such as Marxism or Postmodernism)

SCHOOL P (name)   SCHOOL Q   SCHOOL R

Intermediate level 1

(e.g., people whose theories are associated with a major school of thought)

theorist A   theorist B   theorist C   theorist D   theorist E

Intermediate level 2

(each person may have more than one theory, important belief or research finding)

theory X   *theory Y*

(what it is in brief; date)

[same for each theory you use]

Lower level

general implications of theory X   general applications of X   general evidence to support X   general evidence against X   evaluation of evidence for and against

[same for each theory you use]

Specific examples

examples of a particular person/economy   *experiment J*   *case study K*   *survey L*

Details

number of participants   time of day   etc.

Use pyramid questions to help in planning

Ask yourself key questions to search for or organize the information at each level.

Upper level

- How many major schools of thought are there on this question?
- Which ones are the most relevant and need to be included? (If unsure, go down to the intermediate level and check who said or wrote what.)

Intermediate level

- Which theorist (or judge, writer or similar) said what, when?
- How can you sum that up briefly?

Lower level

- Overall, how good is the general evidence to support this position or theory?
- What are the general implications of the position or theory?
- What are the general applications of the position or theory?
- What is the general evidence against the position or theory?
- Overall, how good is the evidence for or against?

Exemplar level

- Do you need to include specific examples of applications, implications or evidence? Which are the best examples?
- Given the word limit and the time available, how much detail should you give? For instance, have you space only to mention the name and date and one line about this research? Or are you short of words, in which case you could give more details?

Use pyramids to help with word limits

Having mapped out your information as a pyramid, do you have the right amount of words for your page or word limit?

Too much information

If you have too much information, you will need to leave something out.

- If you have several examples at any one level, select just one or two examples of them. Do the same with the other levels.
- If you have already used most of your available space, you may be able to refer to specific examples by name without going into detail. (This depends to some extent on the subject.)

Too little information

If you have too little information, you can build up to the page or word limit.

- Add more examples at the middle or lower levels.
- Write more about your specific examples. Evaluate the significance of the examples for the overall assignment.

Balancing the pyramid

In general, it is more important to explore ideas at the middle and lower levels than to give a lot of detail for specific examples. (See page 180.)

Writing drafts

The art of writing is in the craft of redrafting

Professional writers redraft many times before they are happy: Writing rarely flows out "all at once" in its final version.

Writing is easier if the research, planning and organizing have already been done and if you focus on different processes in each draft.

Draft 1: a quick draft to get ideas down

Use your outline. Don't worry about style or good English.

- Focus on the assignment prompt: Write out your interpretation of the question.
- What is your core idea? Write out your central idea or the main line of your reasoning.
- Write headings and subheadings from your outline (the pyramid, or whatever), but leave these out of the final draft of a paper.
- Add in details below each heading. Link headings and points into sentences.
- Use your outline: Keep looking back to it after writing each paragraph.

Draft 2: fine-tune the structure

Check that information is grouped and ordered—especially into paragraphs (page 256). If not, cut up your text with scissors and rearrange it, or color-code and number paragraphs in the order in which you will rewrite them.

Check that the line of argument is clear from one paragraph to the next—if necessary, add in sentences to link ideas. You may need to do this more than once.

Draft 3: fine-tune the style

Read what you have written aloud. How does it sound? Can you improve the flow or style? Add sentences or details where needed.

Draft 4: finishing touches

Aim to leave at least a day between drafts. Your mind will go on working on your ideas. After a break, you will find it easier to spot passages that need rephrasing. See *Editing your draft*, page 260.

Drafting on the computer

People vary in what they prefer to do on paper, what they do on the computer and how often they move between the two. Experiment to find out what suits you.

Drafting on the computer is a more continual process—you will probably find you make many small corrections and move text about as you go along. Leave spell checking until the final draft.

File management

If you intend to make major changes to a draft, save a copy of the document with a number at the end of the name ("Filename2"). Then edit the copy. If you change your mind, you can revert to the earlier draft or use information from it.

Divide large documents (such as those which include a lot of graphics) into separate files, adding "a," "b," "c," and so on at the end of the filename. You will be able to move around the file and find information more quickly. Later you can paste the parts together into one long document, or start the page numbers for each part to follow on from the previous file.

Keep track of changes by renaming the "version" of the file when you finish for the day—e.g., *Paper 6 Respiration v3.doc*. Copy the name and version into the document footer before printing it out, so that you can tell easily which is your latest version. In case of loss, print out drafts as hard copies, and keep copies of files on a CD or a flash drive.

Listen to your essay

If you have a screen-reader that turns text into speech, listen to the computer reading your text aloud. Otherwise, read it aloud yourself. Listen for meaning and for punctuation pauses.

Print your essay

It is easier to read and edit your work on paper printouts rather than working on screen. The shimmering of the screen may tire your eyes, and you may not always be able to use a computer when you wish.

Paragraphs

Paragraphs are made up of sentences. Usually they are several sentences long.

Each paragraph is organized around a central idea or theme, which is usually made clear in the first sentence of each paragraph. It groups similar ideas and material together. All sentences relate to the main idea of the paragraph.

Successive paragraphs follow each other in a logical order, taking the reader from *a* to *b* to *c*. Words or phrases within paragraphs link them to earlier or later paragraphs.

Paragraphs help the reader

Paragraphs break up the text into manageable portions. A page is easier to look at when divided into three, four or five sections.

Paragraphs also organize meaning. They help your readers to think clearly about what you have written.

First sentence

The first sentence of each paragraph:

- is usually the "topic sentence" that introduces the subject of the paragraph
- starts on a new line
- is preceded by a gap—either an indent on the same line, or a blank line before.

Later sentences

Other sentences of each paragraph:

- develop the theme of the paragraph's "topic sentence"
- follow each other in a logical order—one sentence leading to the next.

Last sentence

The last sentence:

- sums up the paragraph or leads into the next paragraph.

Activity 1

Choose two or three pages from one book.

- Read the topic sentences—the ones that sum up the main theme of each paragraph. These are often, but not always, the opening sentences.
- How well do the topic sentences sum up the main ideas of those paragraphs?
- How are the paragraphs linked?
- If paragraphs lacked a clear topic sentence, were they more difficult to read?

Activity 2

How good are *you* at paragraphing? Separate the following passage into sentences and paragraphs.

A Life of Adventure

mary seacole was born in 1805 in kingston jamaica her mother practiced as a "doctress" using medical knowledge that women had brought from africa and developed in the tropics from her mother mary inherited her medical skills as well as her ability to run a boarding house from her father a scottish military man she inherited her fascination with army life marys own medical reputation was established during a series of cholera and yellow fever epidemics she made her own medicines and emphasized high standards of hygiene as well as enforcing strict quarantine on victims by these methods she saved many lives at the outbreak of the crimean war mary volunteered her services to the british army although she had worked for the army before at its own request this time she was turned down undaunted mary made her own way to the war zone once in the crimea she not only nursed the soldiers but also ran a hotel and sold food wine and medicines after the war mary was treated as a celebrity she was decorated by the governments of four countries in england a poem in her honor was published in Punch magazine and even the royal family requested her company and medical expertise.

Activity 3

- Reread the paragraphs for Activity 2.
- Decide the main theme of each paragraph and sum it up in 1–4 words.
- Check your version with that on the next page.

Activity 2

A Life of Adventure

Mary Seacole was born in 1805 in Kingston, Jamaica. Her mother practiced as a "doctress," using medical knowledge that women had brought from Africa and developed in the tropics. From her mother, Mary inherited her medical skills as well as her ability to run a boarding house. From her father, a Scottish military man, she inherited her fascination with army life.

Mary's own medical reputation was established during a series of cholera and yellow fever epidemics. She made her own medicines and emphasized high standards of hygiene as well as enforcing strict quarantine on victims. By these methods she saved many lives.

At the outbreak of the Crimean War, Mary volunteered her services to the British Army. Although she had worked for the army before, at its own request, this time she was turned down. Undaunted, Mary made her own way to the war zone. Once in the Crimea, she not only nursed the soldiers but also ran a hotel and sold food, wine and medicines.

After the war, Mary was treated as a celebrity. She was decorated by the governments of four countries. In England, a poem in her honor was published in *Punch* magazine, and even the royal family requested her company and medical expertise.

Activity 3

The main themes of the paragraphs are:

1 general information: birth and background
2 early medical reputation
3 the Crimean War
4 after the war.

Did you find it easier to read the text for Activity 2? If so, did this increase your appreciation of the value of good paragraphing and punctuation?

Did you have difficulty adding in the punctuation? If so, you could ask your instructors if any additional support is available.

Chapter **11**

Make time for relaxation and exercise—you can go on thinking about your assignment!

Writing paragraphs

If you have difficulties with paragraphing, divide your page into three columns:

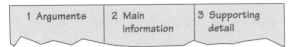

- In column 1, jot down the ideas, theories, opinions and line of reasoning that you want to include in your writing.
- In column 2, jot down the main examples and types of evidence that support your line of reasoning.
- In column 3, write down lesser details, facts, names, statistics, dates and examples that support your main argument.
- Each paragraph should have:
    – one item from column 1
    – one, two or three items from column 2
    – several items from column 3.
- Items selected for each paragraph should all help to make the same point.

Alternatively, using a concept pyramid:

- Each paragraph is likely to need one item at the intermediate level, one at the lower level, examples and a few details.

Checking your paragraphs

When you have finished your early drafts, you can check how well you have paragraphed your writing by doing the following exercise.

1 Read each paragraph

Read each of your paragraphs in turn. Decide what is the main topic of each.

2 Sum up the topic

Sum up that topic in about 1–4 words.

3 Give the topic a name and color

Write the topic in the margin. Give it a color.

4 Which is the topic sentence?

Which sentence is your topic sentence—the one that sums up the topic? Highlight it. Is it at the beginning of the paragraph? If not, would it be more powerful there?

5 Is everything relevant?

Check whether everything in each paragraph relates to the topic sentence. If you're unsure, circle it and check whether it would be better in a different paragraph. Is anything superfluous? If so, cross it out.

6 Is everything in the right place?

Once you have color-coded the topic for each paragraph, check each topic in turn: Have bits of it wandered into other paragraphs? Highlight with the topic color any bits that have gone astray. For example, if you wrote in paragraph 2 about bird habitats and have written more about bird habitats some paragraphs later, highlight both in the same color. Then cut out separated items of the same color and paste them together. Rewrite the paragraph, integrating the bits you have moved.

7 Are sentences in the best order?

In each paragraph, are the sentences in the best order? Is it clear how each sentence leads on to the next?

8 Is the line of argument clear?

Is it clear to the reader how each paragraph relates to the others? Is it clear how each paragraph leads on to the next?

9 Is every paragraph relevant?

Is every paragraph relevant to the assignment prompt?

Linking ideas together

Certain words are used to link ideas and to signpost to the reader the direction your line of reasoning is about to take, such as adding more emphasis or introducing an alternative viewpoint.

Below is a selection of words used to link ideas, depending on the direction of your argument.

Adding more to a point already made

- also; moreover; furthermore; again; further; what is more; then; in addition
- besides; above all; too; as well (as)
- either; neither ... nor; not only ... but also; similarly; correspondingly; in the same way; indeed
- in fact; really; in reality, it is found that ...
- as for; as to; with respect to; regarding

Writing in lists

- first; second; third
- another; yet another; in addition; finally
- to begin with; in the second place
- moreover; additionally; also
- next; then; and to conclude; last; finally

Putting the same idea in a different way

- in other words; rather; or; better; in that case
- to put it (more) simply
- in view of this; with this in mind
- to look at this another way

Introducing examples

- that is to say; in other words
- for example; for instance; namely; an example of this is
- and; as follows; as in the following examples; such as; including
- especially; particularly; in particular; notably; chiefly; mainly; mostly

Introducing an alternative viewpoint

- by contrast; another way of viewing this is; alternatively; again; rather; one alternative is; another possibility is
- on one hand ... on the other hand
- conversely; in comparison; on the contrary; in fact; though; although

Returning to emphasize your earlier viewpoint

- however; nonetheless; in the final analysis; despite x; notwithstanding x; in spite of x
- while x may be true, nonetheless
- although; though; after all; at the same time; on the other hand; all the same; even if x is true; although x may have a good point

Showing the results of something

- therefore; accordingly; as a result
- so, (then,) it can be seen that
- the result is; the consequence is
- resulting from this; consequently; now
- we can see, then, that; it is evident that
- because of this; thus; hence; for this reason; owing to x; this suggests that; it follows that
- in other words; otherwise; in that case; that implies

Summing up or concluding

- therefore; so, my conclusion is
- in short; in conclusion; to conclude; in all; on the whole
- to summarize; to sum up briefly; in brief; altogether; overall; thus; thus we can see that

> **Activity**
>
> How are these words used in the sample essays on pages 283–288?

Editing your draft

Editing is working on your draft in order to improve it. When you edit, you can …

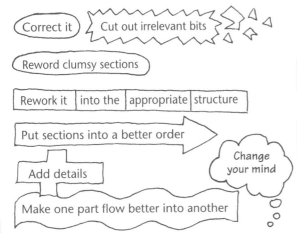

Correct it
Cut out irrelevant bits
Reword clumsy sections
Rework it into the appropriate structure
Put sections into a better order
Add details
Make one part flow better into another
Change your mind

Different kinds of editing

You may need to go through your work several times, checking for different things.

1 Meaning

- Does it make sense? Read it aloud slowly.

2 Organization and structure

- Have you used the appropriate structure?
- Is connected information grouped together?
- Is information presented in the best order?
- Is the work well paragraphed? (See page 256.)

3 Evidence

- Have you backed your argument with evidence, examples, details and/or research?

4 References

- Is the source of your information clear?
- Are your quotations accurate?
- Are references written correctly? (See pages 113–114.)

5 Style

- Is the text easy to read?
- Is it too chatty? Or too stuffy?
- Are any sections confused?
- Is it precise enough? (See page 268.)
- Is the style appropriate? (See Chapter 12.)

6 Punctuation, spelling and grammar

- Have you written in sentences? (See "Proofreading" below.)

7 Presentation

- Is the text legible?
- Does it look neat and well presented?
- Does it follow any presentation guidelines you were given?

 Which aspects of editing do you need to spend most time on?

Proofreading

Edit your draft until you are happy that it is written as well as it can be. Then do some final proofreading.

- Read it once again aloud—does it make sense?
- Look for mistakes such as typing and spelling errors. Look up doubtful spellings or ask someone.
  - If you used the computer's spell checker, check especially for words that may have been correctly spelled but that were the wrong words—such as "there" instead of "their."
  - When checking spellings, you may find it helpful to work backwards through your writing, word by word, to avoid drifting into skim-reading.
- Everyone has their own pattern of errors. If there are certain mistakes you make repeatedly, note these down and be particularly careful in checking for them.

Chapter **11**

Editing final drafts

Check ☑ each box below when you have finished checking that point.

Content and argument

☐ The text answers the central question(s) posed by the assignment prompt (page 242).

☐ Sufficient space has (or words have) been given to the most important points.

☐ All the information included is relevant to the set question.

☐ The main line of argument is clear, not lost in a sea of detail.

Research material

☐ There are sufficient examples and evidence to prove or illustrate my points.

☐ My own ideas and opinions are clear to the reader.

Structure and grouping

☐ The text is in the appropriate structure or format.

☐ Ideas are suitably linked.

☐ Each paragraph is well structured.

☐ Ideas are presented in the right order.

☐ It is clear how each paragraph links to the others (page 259).

Style

☐ The style is appropriate for the class (Chapter 12).

☐ The text is not too chatty or glib.

☐ It is free of slang and colloquialisms.

☐ Technical vocabulary is used correctly.

☐ The words used are my own. (There is no plagiarism.)

☐ The text is not repetitive.

☐ The text can be read aloud easily.

Clarity

☐ There is nothing the reader will find confusing.

☐ The language is clear and straightforward.

☐ The reader will easily follow the line of reasoning (Chapter 7).

☐ It is clear which sentence in my introduction summarizes my viewpoint or thesis.

☐ Sentences are of reasonable length and are uncomplicated.

General

☐ The introduction is suitable.

☐ The conclusion is suitable.

☐ Spelling, grammar and punctuation are correct.

☐ References are correct.

☐ The bibliography (if needed) is accurate.

☐ I have taken on board feedback I received for earlier work (page 282).

Presenting your writing

The fine details of presentation may vary from one instructor to another. Use the checklist on page 263 to guide you. In general:

- For research papers, write the title at the top of the first page; for reports and projects, write the title on a cover page.
- Write on one side of the page only.
- Make sure your name is on every page.
- Number every page.
- Leave space to one side or between lines so that your instructor can add comments.
- Your final text should be neat and legible. Occasional minor corrections made neatly by hand are acceptable, but if there are a lot of corrections, or sections of text need to be reordered, print the paper out afresh.
- If you are given instructions about binding projects, follow them carefully. Normally, though, most work doesn't need special binding or folders—on the contrary, folders often make more work for your instructors.

Word-processing your assignment

It may suit you to use one font or size while working and another for the final printout to hand in. For example, you might use very large type on the screen, making it is easier to read, and then reduce the size before printing it out.

For your final draft:

- use only one font throughout
- use only one type size for your main text
- use a clear, simple font for your final draft—not script designed to look like handwriting
- you may like to vary type size for headings, depending on how important they are—if so, be consistent in the way you use them.

Font style and size

Presentation

Presentation

Presentation

Presentation

Presentation

Presentation

Presentation

Presentation

Presentation

Presentation

Presentation

Organize text on the page

Use tabs and other facilities to indent the text or lay it out in particular ways.

You can center headings

| You can have the text aligned at the left. | You can have the text centered. | You can have the text justified, with straight edges on both sides. |

Make text stand out

Highlight headings or keywords using

bold   *italics*   <u>underlining</u>

Present work clearly

- Number pages.
- Print your name and the title of the assignment in the footer on each page.
- Produce neat bullet or number points, with indented text.
- Produce graphics for your statistical information.

Instructors' preferences

Your instructors may have preferences about the technical aspects of presentation listed below. You can use a photocopy of this chart to clarify details with instructors and remind yourself of the appropriate presentation for a given subject or instructor.

Instructor/Subject	Requirements
▪ Typed, handwritten or word-processed?	
▪ Paper size?	
▪ Use one side or both?	
▪ Begin each section of a report on a fresh page?	
▪ Use headings?	
▪ Number paragraphs?	
▪ Leave a wide left-hand/right-hand margin?	
▪ Write my name on each page?	
▪ Write the title on each page?	
▪ Use double spacing (leave every second line blank)?	
▪ Write as "one," "I" or "we"? (Address the reader as "you")?	
▪ Use passive or active voice? (Passive: "The essay was written." Active: "I wrote the essay.")	
▪ Which method is to be used for references? Any special layout for references?	
▪ Bibliography needed? Any special layout?	
▪ Anything else? (E.g., use of diagrams, charts, graphs? Standard keys on maps? Use color in diagrams? Is annotation needed?)	

Chapter **11**

Review

This chapter has looked at how to develop your writing from small beginnings, so as to build your confidence and familiarity with writing. Although academic writing is a distinct kind of writing, you will profit from making *any* kind of writing a daily activity. You will build up speed, become more able to think and write simultaneously, become more aware of how you can improve your writing and grow in confidence.

The chapter also looked at how to approach a piece of academic writing as a set of manageable steps. This links with the work in Chapter 4, on setting mini-goals. Many of these subskills will soon become second nature. With practice, you will find that you combine separate stages quite easily and find quicker ways of doing things.

Check your learning outcomes

- Look carefully at feedback from your instructor. If it is not clear where you have lost points, ask for an appointment to discuss this. Take with you a copy of the self-evaluation questionnaires on pages 232 and 261.
- Using your instructor's feedback and advice, complete the self-evaluation questionnaire on page 232 again. Notice which areas you now feel confident about and which you would still like to improve.

You may also find it helpful to browse through Chapters 7 and 12-14 before your next assignment.

Basic English skills

It is difficult to get the highest grades in college if your basic English skills, such as grammar and punctuation, are weak. It is worth investigating any language workshops at your college or at a local community college.

Answers to activity on page 244

1 The assignment prompt is far too general. Compare this with a stronger question, such as: "To what extent have reptiles been more successful than amphibians in adapting to environmental challenges?"

2 The assignment prompt is too general. You could give more focus by adding: "Discuss with reference to …" and add a specific region, time scale and field of inquiry. For example: "Discuss with reference to the control of nuclear waste in Europe and the Pacific rim" or "Discuss with reference to the impact of cell phones on personal safety."

3 This assignment prompt is too long and contains too many questions. An alternative question for this topic could be: "Domestic technology since 1970: labor-saving or labor-creating?"

4 The assignment prompt is biased towards one (negative) point of view and contains no obvious question.

5 Descriptive papers are unlikely to give opportunities for the critical, analytical reasoning that gains good grades. Contrast this with: "How effective have placebos been in testing medical interventions for children?"

Chapter 12

Developing your writing

LEARNING OUTCOMES

This chapter offers you opportunities to:

- become aware of some of the conventions of academic writing, including
  - basic stylistic conventions
  - being precise
  - distinguishing fact, opinion and argument

- become aware of different approaches to research and academic writing

- understand the influences of the scientific model on most areas of academic writing, including nonscience subjects

- understand better what is meant by terms such as "subjectivity" and "objectivity," "quantitative" and "qualitative"

- learn to use the four main writing styles used in higher education:
  - descriptive
  - argumentative
  - evaluative/analytical
  - personal/experiential

- know what gets good grades on an assignment and how to use instructor feedback constructively

- know what a good research paper looks like, and gain practice in grading papers yourself.

Writing improves through practice and informed reflection. As you progress through higher education, your instructors will expect your writing style to continue to improve. In particular, your writing should demonstrate that you are aware of academic conventions and when to use them.

You will also be required to move flexibly between different writing styles, moving from precise description to critical analysis to evaluative summary, depending on the task.

This chapter helps you to build your awareness of what is expected in academic writing. Browse through it before doing your first assignment. Return to look at it in more detail, along with Chapters 7 and 14, before writing your assignments.

Stylistic conventions for academic writing

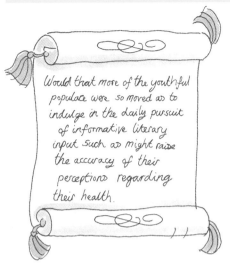

Would that more of the youthful populace were so moved as to indulge in the daily pursuit of informative literary input such as might raise the accuracy of their perceptions regarding their health.

Studies by World Youth (2009) reveal that young people benefit from reading about their health.

So basically, you need to go read more, man!

There is no single style that can be used in all academic writing. Each discipline has developed its own particular styles or follows a system, such as MLA or APA. In some subject areas you may find that even various branches of the discipline use quite distinct writing styles.

The following conventions apply to *most* academic writing. Nevertheless, if your instructors offer specific guidance, follow their directions.

Use formal English

Academic English is more formal than the language used in everyday conversation, emails, letters, magazines and most newspapers. It shouldn't sound "chatty." It also avoids slang and colloquialisms such as these:

- "The writer is *out of order* when he suggests …"
- "The new plans were *just the stuff.*"
- "These findings need to be *taken with a grain of salt.*"
- "The argument was *a bit over the top.*"

Aim for clarity

Write so that your reader can easily follow what you are trying to say. Do not use long words and technical jargon simply in order to sound impressive. Check if your sentences are so long and complicated that they are hard to follow. Avoid

antiquated language, convoluted sentences or mannerisms—as well as using up your page limit and obscuring your argument, these could be offputting to your readers.

Learn how to use specialist vocabulary

It is important to learn the specialist styles and technical terms used in your subjects, and also to extend your vocabulary.

- If you are not familiar with specialist terms, look for explanations of these terms in introductory textbooks or glossaries.
- Pay attention to how such terms are introduced in books and articles—note the different forms used, such as noun and verb forms, and past tenses.
- Do not litter your writing with terms that you yourself do not understand—it is better to write in your own words than to sound as though you do not understand the words you are using.

Browse through several articles for one of your subjects, looking just at the writing style.

- What features do each of the pieces share?
- Are these features of your own writing?

Avoid abbreviations and contractions

Write words out in full:

- "dept." as "department"
- "e.g." as "for example"
- "didn't" as "did not"
- "they're" as "they are"
- "isn't" as "is not"

Be impersonal

Most classes prefer you to avoid personal pronouns such as "I"/"we" and "you." Instead, sentences begin in impersonal ways such as:

- It can be seen that …
- There are a number of …
- It has been found that …

Be cautious

Academic writing generally sounds cautious. Writers indicate that they are aware that nothing is completely certain. They use words that express this lack of certainty, such as:

- appears to; seems to; tends to; may; might; possibly; probably; apparently; generally; seemingly.

They may use phrases such as:

- in some cases, this …
- the evidence suggests that …

Avoid misplaced conjunctions

The following words are not used at the start of sentences: *or, and, but, yet*.

Numbers

Numbers below a hundred are often written out in full, such as:

- thirty-one percent
- nineteen members.

However, figures are retained in statistical and scientific work:

- 31 percent
- 15°F
- 7.3 newtons.

Be objective

Academic writing avoids personal, subjective words such as "nice," "wonderful," "worthwhile," "usual" or "natural" because the reader's understanding of these words may be very different from your own.

Avoid apologies

Don't apologize to the reader for any weaknesses you think there may be in your research or writing, such as that you found the subject difficult or that you had no time to write a conclusion. Write as if you are confident of what you are saying—even if you don't feel it!

Addressing the reader

Avoid asking readers questions or telling them what to think.

Be concise

Edit out unnecessary words:

A man called Jay Singh invented …

In a book called *Scottish Pathways*, …

Use continuous prose

Write in full sentences, grouped together into paragraphs (see page 256). For research papers and research projects, avoid lists of points: Incorporate the points into sentences. Lists and headings may be acceptable in reports.

Being precise

Example of a vague sentence

Some people did not like the idea at the time and made the politicians stop it but then he attacked him publicly.

Why is it vague?

- "some people"—who exactly?
- "the idea"—which idea?
- "at the time"—when? date?
- "the politicians"—all politicians? or a certain group? or a political party?
- "made the politicians"—how did they "make" them?
- "stop it"—stop what? how was it stopped?
- "people did not like the idea"—why not?

It can be confusing to have more than one pronoun (such as "he," "she," "it," "this" or "that") in a sentence.

Activity: Which of the following is most precise?

1 A man governed the United States.
2 George W. Bush served as President of the United States of America between 2001 and 2009.
3 A man governed the United States during 2001–2009.
4 George W. Bush governed the United States for several years and introduced many policies that affected various aspects of people's lives.

Answer

Response 2—the others all contain vague information.

... rather than sort of not saying quite what you mean, if you know what I mean ...

Using facts, opinions or arguments

I think there should be fewer ads on TV.

Opinions

Opinions are personal beliefs. These are not always based on good evidence and may even run *contrary* to the evidence.

What is considered "natural" or "normal," for example, is generally a matter of opinion. Even if most people agree with you, it is still opinion, unless you can give *evidence* that what you think is likely to be true.

There were an average of 35 ads an hour on channel X, on July 25 2011.

Facts

Facts can usually be checked against evidence. Facts used in academic writing are generally those

gathered and recorded in some formal way, such as in journals or official records.

Ads for toys should not be shown on TV because research by Dr. Meehan (2010) suggests that they ...

Arguments

Arguments are *reasons* (which can include facts) given to support a point of view.

As you write, question what you write

As you write, keep checking for precision. Ask yourself questions, such as "when exactly?," "why exactly?" or "who?" Check that you have given your readers enough detail for them to know exactly what you are talking about.

Writing for different subjects

Different approaches

Each academic subject has a slightly different approach regarding:

- *research methodology*—how to conduct research
- *evidence*—what is regarded as appropriate and sufficient
- *writing genre*—the preferred writing styles and conventions
- *objectivity*—how far your approach should be objective or subjective, quantitative or qualitative, scientific or personal.

As a student, you will need to identify the approaches taken by your subjects and produce work appropriate to each subject. Be aware that even *within* a subject, approaches can vary depending on the area of study.

The influence of the "scientific" model

Academic writing has been heavily influenced by the notion of being "scientific"—even when the subject is not obviously about science. Although this view is changing, the approach you are expected to take is likely to be affected by some of the principles of the scientific model, so it is helpful to know what it involves.

The main features of the scientific model are:

- objectivity
- a testable hypothesis
- replicated results
- controlling for variables
- quantitative analysis
- accurate description
- qualitative analysis.

Objectivity

The scientific model values objectivity. This means that instead of relying on personal opinion or common sense, scientists test possible explanations against the available evidence. If data is objective, two people undertaking the same research in the same way should arrive at the same results and conclusions.

A testable hypothesis

A hypothesis is a possible explanation of why or how something occurs, consistent with available evidence. The hypothesis is formulated in a way that can be tested.

A hypothesis cannot be proved true, but it can be proved *wrong*. If a hypothesis survives many attempts to prove it wrong, increasingly it may be considered reliable and trusted as a "theory."

Replicated results

For a piece of scientific research to be taken seriously, another researcher needs to have repeated the research with similar results. This

"replication" indicates that the first results were reliable and not just a "one-off" or due to individual opinion or bias. (However, it is still important to think hard about whether bias may be built into the research method itself.)

Controlling for variables

Scientists need to know that what they *think* they are testing is what they are *actually* testing. They need to make sure that "variables"—all the things that can change, such as the weather, or the time of day, the people involved or the materials used—have not influenced the results unexpectedly.

Usually research experiments are run many times to check the effects of different variables. The researcher tries to change only one variable at a time, keeping everything else constant. This is known as "controlling for variables."

For example, researchers comparing the effect of blue light or red light on plant growth would check that everything *apart* from the color of the light was identical. For each light color they would use the same type and size of plant, the same amount of water, the same levels of nutrients, the same temperature and the same air source.

Quantitative analysis

Scientific research relies heavily on quantitative data. This means it focuses on changes or differences that can be *measured*. Standardized measurements are used—such as number, time, weight and length—so that results are easy to compare objectively. Thus experiments might investigate:

- whether the height (measurable) to which a particular kind of plant grows depends on the temperature of the environment (measurable)
- whether fruit yield (measurable) depends on the amount of light (measurable)
- whether how many words somebody can read in a given amount of time (measurable) depends on the size of print (measurable) or the age of the person (measurable).

The approach is: "If *this* changes while everything else stays the same, does it have an effect on *that*?" This could also be stated as: "If *X* changes while *A*, *B* and *C* stay the same, does it have an effect on *Y*?" Quantitative analysis involves analyzing the relationship between changes in one variable and changes in another.

When changes in *X* exactly match changes in *Y*, the changes are said to be "correlated." It is important to understand, however, that correlation does not prove that changes in *X* *cause* changes in *Y*, or vice versa. Correlation may be due to chance, or both *X* and *Y* may be affected by a third variable, *Z*.

Accurate description

When writing up research, scientists describe their methodology, research conditions and results exactly, so that anyone who wishes to replicate their research can set up near-identical conditions. You will be expected to write accurate descriptions in the same way, such that someone else could replicate your research.

Descriptive writing for reports is very precise: No unnecessary words are used. (See pages 159–161 and 274.)

Qualitative analysis

In qualitative research, the data used are not easily measurable. The experiment is not completely objective: Some judgment and interpretation are involved. It is acknowledged also that the researcher is in some way part of the experiment itself and may unintentionally influence its results—for example, by having a role in making sense of the research.

Scientists use qualitative analysis in the "Discussion" part of a report, where they make sense of their results and offer possible reasons for why things did not go as expected. Here they evaluate strengths and weaknesses, such as in the way they designed the experiment or worded the experimental hypothesis.

Nevertheless, science generally regards subjectivity as a "problem," and often uses language that makes it sound as if no scientists were involved—as if the experiment just happened on its own:

> The experimental design could have been improved by …

rather than:

> I could have improved the design by …

Alternatives to the scientific model

Most academic disciplines are influenced by the scientific model. However, subjects vary in how far they value the different aspects of the model. The main differences are in varying attitudes to subjectivity and to qualitative data.

Subjectivity and objectivity

Subjectivity simply means bringing yourself, your own views, opinions, experiences or value judgments into your research or writing. In counseling or fine art, a high value is placed upon subjectivity—that is, upon personal emotions, feelings, intuitions and experiences. It is the opposite of *objectivity*, the aim of the traditional scientific model.

In many subjects, however, you need to combine the two: To analyze both objective criteria, such as the results of independent surveys, market research or case studies, and your subjective response—your feelings, tastes, interests or intuitions.

(See also *Using personal experience*, page 280.)

Quantitative approaches in nonscience subjects

Science subjects tend to avoid research where it is difficult to control for variables or to quantify results. For example, issues such as gender, romance or childhood change over time, but as these changes are not easily measurable they would not usually be studied by scientists.

Nonscience subjects often find ingenious ways of categorizing such information, however, so that it can be roughly standardized according to set criteria. This enables a wider range of issues to be studied in relatively objective ways.

Example: attitudes to children

A researcher interested in how attitudes to children changed over time would aim at finding an objective way of analyzing data rather than simply relying on her opinion. She might choose to focus on how often popular magazines referred to themes of "childhood innocence" and "goodness" compared to themes on "disciplining bad children." One approach could then be to count how often a popular magazine included each theme, and compare data over ten-year intervals to see if the number of references changed significantly over time. This would give quantitative data.

The researcher here would also have to classify her information carefully to be clear what type of material should be included under her chosen themes ("innocence" and "discipline"). Classification of words and themes involves some subjectivity, as people mean different things by the same words. For example, someone quoted in one of the magazines as saying "A good child does as his mother says" might have meant that he obeyed because he was well disciplined or that he obeyed because he was naturally virtuous—or something else entirely.

Qualitative analysis

It is not always easy to draw a line between what is quantitative and what is qualitative—as you can see from the example above of attitudes to children. In that instance, the researcher needed to make subjective judgments about what was *meant* by innocence or discipline. Usually social science researchers acknowledge their subjective role in the experiment as interpreters of the evidence. Social science and arts subjects may aim at objectivity and quantification where this is possible but are also interested in the subjective—how decisions and interpretations are arrived at. They are more accepting of overlaps between objectivity and subjectivity.

As a student you may be asked to make qualitative evaluations about project evidence, about decisions made during field trips or about art or literature. Your instructors will look for:

- the relevance of the detail you select
- the criteria you use in making decisions
- the aptness of your interpretations.

PLANNER

Polar opposites in academic approaches

For each of the aspects numbered below, find out whether it is the convention in your subject areas to be nearer the North or the South Pole. This may vary both depending on your class and the type of assignment.

Consider how far each dimension is important for your assignment. You could indicate this by placing a check mark on the dotted line.

North Pole

1 Every attempt is made to control the conditions under which the research takes place, so that the researcher can decide which variables to manipulate and measure

2 Results can be generalized—that is, they would hold true if the research were repeated

3 Numbers and standardized measurements make it easier to generalize results

4 Objective views are formed, based on evidence and facts rather than personal opinion

5 The role of the scientist in the research is minimized and rarely discussed

6 Individual differences are not important— generalized findings are valued

7 Personal experience is regarded as individual and irrelevant: it is not referred to

8 The language is clinical, neutral, impersonal and dispassionate, even if the researcher is passionate about the subject

South Pole

1 Every attempt is made to keep the research true to real life—that is, to give it "ecological validity"

2 The unique is considered worthy of study— results may be impossible to repeat exactly

3 Creative interpretation is highly valued

4 Subjective responses, feelings, intuition and creativity are regarded as valuable resources

5 The role of the researcher is made explicit—it is considered useful to discuss how the researcher's presence influenced the results

6 Individual instances, and opportunities for detailed interpretation, are valued

7 Personal experience is highly valued as giving insight and a deeper understanding

8 The language used allows the personality and feelings of the writer to shine through

Different styles

Compare the following two styles of writing. The first is conversational:

> Mount Pepé is going up—it's going to take everything with it when it goes. And I mean everything—villages, farms, trees, the lot. It's frightening to think of how powerful a volcano can be. Think of the damage they cause! Remember Pompeii and Mount St. Helens!

The second is in a general academic style:

> In order to assess whether it is necessary to evacuate the villages on Mount Pepé, three main factors need to be taken into consideration. The first, and most important, of these is the element of safety. According to seismic experts currently working on the volcano, there is likely to be a major eruption within the next ten years (Achebe 2011). According to Achebe, the eruption is likely to destroy villages over a radius of 120 miles (Achebe 2012, p. 7).

Notice the differences between the two examples. For each piece, consider questions such as these.

- Does it use full sentences?
- How formal does it sound? (What is the writer's "voice"?)
- How is emotion expressed?
- Is personal opinion expressed? If so, how?
- How are other people's views included?
- Is the sequence logical?
- Does the piece observe the conventions listed on pages 245 and 265–271.

Styles of academic writing

Although academic writing is distinct from other kinds of writing, it isn't all the same. There are different styles *within* academic writing, including:

- descriptive
- argumentative/analytical
- evaluative/analytical
- personal, drawing on the writer's own experience.

These are explored in more detail below.

Finding the appropriate style

When writing an assignment, it is important to choose the appropriate writing style.

Look at the two examples below, of draft introductions to a paper in response to the questions, "What problems faced King Henri IV on his accession to the throne? How successfully did he solve them?" The first follows the guidance for introductions given on page 248 and analyzes the problem set. The second uses descriptive writing, giving background details not relevant to the question.

The first example is of a good introduction:

> In 1598, Henri IV was anointed king of a war-torn France, the country having been split by religious and political wars since the death of Henri II almost half a century earlier. The problems Henri IV faced were essentially threefold. He needed to resolve Catholic–Protestant divisions within the country; to curb the power of the Guise, Montmorenci and Bourbon factions that threatened to subvert royal power; and he needed to restore the French economy. This paper will look at the three areas in turn, but will also show how they were interrelated. It will demonstrate how Henri IV tackled each, and argue that ultimately he was extremely successful in solving what had seemed intractable problems.

The second is an example of interesting but irrelevant description (for a *history* paper):

> Henri was brought up by his grandfather in the mountains of Navarre. His grandfather was a very religious man and brought his grandson up as a Protestant. Because of his religion, he wanted Henri to appreciate the simple things in life—the fields, the flowers, good wholesome food such as bread and local cheese, and the beauty of the natural surroundings. Henri was allowed a great deal of freedom and was allowed to roam barefoot in the mountains and to play with animals ...

Compare each example to the conventions listed on page 245.

Which writer might find it easier to write a good observation case study (page 274)?

Descriptive writing

You are likely to include descriptive writing in most assignments. In some ways it is the easiest style, as we are used to describing things in everyday life. On the other hand, it is easy to give too much detail and forget the underlying purpose of the description. At a higher education level, you are unlikely to be asked to describe anything just for the sake of describing. There will usually be another purpose, such as:

- being precise about methods used in an experiment
- giving essential background information so that you can analyze significant features in more detail later.

You may be required to:

- *describe what happened*—for example, outlining the main events in a history paper, or your methods and results in a project report
- *describe main features or functions*— for example, of different bodily organs in a biology paper
- *summarize the main points of a theory or an article you have read*—for example, in reviewing a book or in introducing the ideas of another author within an assignment.

What gets points

You will gain points for:

- identifying relevant themes to include
- identifying the *most* relevant facts in what you include
- clarity, precision and accuracy
- presenting items in the best order
- keeping to the point
- indicating the significance of what you describe.

Examples of descriptive writing

Note the differences between the two following types of descriptive writing. The first is from a cognitive psychology report.

> **METHODOLOGY**
>
> **Participants**
>
> There were twenty English first-language speakers in each condition, forty subjects in all. These were matched for age and gender across conditions.
>
> **Procedure**
>
> (See Appendix 1 for instructions.) Each participant was tested separately. They were asked to indicate whether each string of five letters (such as *yongt*) presented on the computer screen was a real word. For real words they pressed the "y" key on the keyboard; otherwise they pressed the "n" key …

The second example is from an observation case study from the social sciences.

> The man did not appear to be interacting with the child. The train entered Fairview station, and he looked to the stroller, perhaps to see if it was obstructing the exit. He looked out of the window. The child pointed to the door and leaned towards him; he instantly leaned towards her to listen.
>
> She said, "Get off soon?"
>
> He replied, "Not now. In five minutes we're getting off." The child still leaned towards him, but he didn't say anything else and looked away. The child turned away and put the teddy on the seat. The man leaned across her, picked up the teddy and returned it to her lap, saying "Hold it." They looked at each other for a moment. The child half-smiled, and they both looked away, so they were looking in opposite directions.

From this you will see how descriptive writing can vary depending on the subject. Look carefully at journal articles and other examples from your subject area to find the appropriate style for your subject. (See also pages 159–161 and 330.)

Argumentative/analytical writing

Most instructors want papers to be analytical, examining "What exactly?" and "Why exactly?" in detail. Chapter 7 looks in more detail at argument as part of critical analytical thinking.

They also want papers to be "discursive"—to discuss ideas and opinions, and to show reasoning. In a persuasively argued paper, the writer—that is, you—tries to influence the opinion or thoughts or actions of the reader.

> Find the "Editorial" section in two quality newspapers. How do the writers try to persuade you to their points of view?

What makes good argumentative writing?

To argue a point of view effectively, you need to do the following.

- State a point of view or opinion and a clear line of reasoning to support it.
- Offer evidence or examples to support your argument.
- Show where the evidence comes from and that it is reliable. (For example, it should not *all* be personal experience or what you have heard somebody else say.)
- Show that you have considered any possible arguments that might *contradict* your case or opinions.
- Be able to demonstrate convincingly why your argument or thesis is the best (that is, why you think you are right).

Your case will not look very convincing if you merely argue, "Well, that's my opinion" or "That's my experience" and fail to consider any alternatives seriously.

Writing the argument

1 State your position

Sum up your argument in one brief, clear sentence.

Don't be tempted to sit on the fence. You can sound cautious and show that there are strong arguments on more than one side, but indicate which side *you* find most convincing.

2 Support your argument

- Show why your point of view is a good one.
- For each main point, give evidence (dates, names, statistics, examples, opinions from other sources).

  > Here is the evidence, your Honor ...

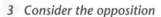

- Consider: "Would the evidence stand up in court?" Is it really convincing?

3 Consider the opposition

Assume that your reader disagrees with you: You have to convince the reader with good evidence and examples.

- What could your opponents argue?
- What evidence might they have?
- How could you persuade a neutral party that your case and your evidence are better?

>
> Develop an argument.
> - Choose a subject about which you feel strongly.
> - What is the debate? Engage in it.
> - What is your own case or position?
> - List your reasons for taking that position.
> - List possible arguments *against* it.
> - How could you reply to each of them?
> - Use the planner on page 276 to write out your argument.

Framework for an argumentative paper

Main proposal/hypothesis/argument:

Reasons or arguments in favor	Evidence and examples
1 _____	1 _____
2 _____	2 _____
3 _____	3 _____
4 _____	4 _____

Opposing arguments	Reasons and evidence
1 _____	1 _____
2 _____	2 _____
3 _____	3 _____
4 _____	4 _____

Reasons why my arguments are stronger; weaknesses in the reasoning or evidence for the opposing arguments

1 _____

2 _____

3 _____

Conclusions

Evaluative/analytical writing

Most academic writing will also include an element of evaluation, even if this is not obvious from the essay question or assignment prompt. You may be required to evaluate:

- two or more schools of thought
- two or more theories or theorists
- which of several items, models or ideas is best for a purpose
- how well another writer has analyzed a subject.

Features of evaluative writing

Nearly all evaluative writing involves the following processes.

Comparing

Find the points of similarity, and show that you are aware of any minor points of difference within areas of overall similarity.

Contrasting

Set items in opposition, in order to bring out the points of difference.

Evaluating significance

Evaluate the *significance* of any similarities or differences. Do they matter? Do they have important implications for which model should be used? Or for probable outcomes (which animal is likely to survive, which treatment should be offered, etc.)?

Making a judgment

Indicate which theory or side is preferable. Give the reasons for your opinion, based on an analysis of the evidence.

Showing your criteria

Show the criteria you used in arriving at your opinion, such as that you used data or research evidence as the basis of your decision.

Get the balance right

In evaluative papers—such as "compare and contrast" papers—it is important to be balanced in the kind of information you use to make a comparison. You need to compare like with like.

"Compare and contrast" at the same category level

Suppose you are asked to compare and contrast two animals in terms of their habitat. First you need to compare them at the basic category level, making it clear you are comparing, for example, birds with mammals (see diagram, page 252). You could then compare cuckoos with dolphins, as these are at the same category level (on this diagram, the lower level). You should not compare cuckoos to mammals, as these are not equivalent concepts—they are at different levels on the pyramid.

Balance

If you use a specific case study about cuckoos, it should be balanced, if possible, by a specific case study of dolphins.

Check your content for balance

When you have completed a draft, make a plan of what you have actually written, using a concept pyramid. You may find that you have spent a disproportionate amount of time on one area, such as one middle-level subject (birds), and included too many examples from a lower level (cuckoos, mockingbirds, flamingos). By contrast, you may have said very little about mammals as a basic category but referred to ten pieces of specific research on dolphins.

This paper would show imbalance: It would not balance like with like. Use your pattern notes or pyramid to plan your piece of work, selecting a similar number of examples at each level.

Organizing information for "compare and contrast" papers

One easy way of organizing information for "compare and contrast" papers is by making a grid and writing information in the appropriate columns.

- Use one column for the information about one theory or item.
- Group similarities together.
- Group differences together.
- At the end, jot the main points in the boxes for the introduction and conclusion.

Introduction: Main themes:		
Areas to be compared and contrasted	A Birds	B Fish
Similarities 1 group behaviors 2 3 4 5	flocks	shoals
Differences 1 respiration 2 locomotion 3 4 5	flies (wings)	swims (fins)
Significance of similarities or differences. (How did I decide if something was significant?)		
Conclusion. (Draw the reader's attention to the main points.)		

An empty grid for use is printed on page 279.

Three ways of writing the paper are given below. Whichever one you use, be consistent with it for that paper. Before you begin writing from the grid, it is a good idea to map out your points spatially (see page 249).

Method 1

This method is straightforward but tends to use more words than the others.

Work down the chart.

- Write out all your points for column A.
  - Write your points for column B, in the same order as for column A. Highlight the point of similarity or contrast.
- Do the same for any other columns.
- Draw together the significance of the similarities and differences.

Method 2

- Work across the chart.
- Select one item from column A and "compare and contrast" it with column B (and any other columns).
- Go onto the next item in column A and compare that to column B (and any others). Continue until all points are covered.
- Draw together the significance of the similarities and differences.

Method 3

If the similarities are so strong as to make the items almost identical, state in the introduction that you will look at similarities together and then at points of contrast separately.

- Describe one way in which A and B are similar.
- Continue until all points of similarity are covered.
- Continue with points of contrast as for either method 1 or method 2 above (depending on which is clearest to read).
- Draw together the significance of the similarities and differences.

Framework for a "compare and contrast" paper

Introduction: Main themes:		
Areas to be compared and contrasted	A	B
Similarities 1 2 3 4 5		
Differences 1 2 3 4 5		
Significance of similarities or differences. (How did I decide if something was significant?)		
Conclusion. (Draw the reader's attention to the main points.)		

Chapter 12

Using personal experience

It is often useful to call upon personal experience in order to make your learning concrete. Reflection on what happened to you, or how you dealt with a similar situation, can help your thinking—even if you don't make a direct reference to it in your writing.

Find out whether a class expects you to write about personal experience. Some subjects expect this, whereas in others it will be inappropriate.

And then I thought that as I had been living at the same address for two years it was time for a change. So, in 1987 I moved down to Missouri. I lived in Barr Road, but I soon moved to Small Street ...

Writing from experience

Use your personal experience as a starting point. Consider what lessons can be drawn from your experience, then start your research. Personal experience should not be your main evidence—unless your instructors specifically ask for this.

- If you include personal experience in your writing, consider how typical it is. Has any research been done—do you know of relevant reports or articles?—which shows that *your* experience is true more generally?
- Compare your experience with other people's. If theirs is different, why is that?
- Keep your description short. Avoid long lists and detailed accounts of events.
- Be careful what you say about anyone you mention (by name, or if it is obvious to whom you are referring). Check that they do not mind being included—especially if they are known to those who will read your paper.

Analyze your experience

- How is it relevant to your class?
- How does it link to theories you have studied?
- How does your experience support or contradict the views of a writer or theorist you are covering in class?
- Can any lessons be drawn from it?
- Can generalizations be drawn from it?
- What evidence is there to show that your experiences are typical or unusual?

> ### Example
>
> Suppose you wrote about your own experience, saying:
>
> > Working this way, I found that I was less stressed and my work improved.
>
> You could provisionally generalize this:
>
> > It would appear that the absence of stress can produce more effective results.
>
> You would then need to ask questions such as:
>
> - How valid is this generalization?
> - Do other people feel the same way as you?
> - Are there circumstances where stress can produce *better* work?

Personal writing and academic writing

There are some general differences between personal writing and academic writing.

Personal writing	Academic writing
emotional	logical
can be intuitive	uses reasoning
active voice: "I find that ..."	passive voice: "It was found that ..."
anecdotal	uses evidence
data from one person	wider database
subjective	objective
tangents may be important	keeps to a logical sequence

What gets good grades?

To get good grades, you do not necessarily have to work longer hours. You *do* need:

- to identify the task or problem correctly
- to discover the underlying issues
- to find out exactly what is expected of you.

Although all subject areas have their own assessment criteria, the following general requirements provide a good guideline as to how points are allocated.

Level descriptors

- Does your college provide details of the characteristics of each level of study?
- If so, what do these mean for your current assignment?
- What is expected at the next level up—are you working towards that level yet?

Grading criteria

- If your college or instructor provides grading criteria, check these before you start your assignment and again at the end.

Lowest grades

The lowest grades are awarded for work that:

- has weak structure
- shows little research, thought or reflection
- is mostly descriptive, with little analysis or argument
- considers only one point of view.

Instructors' comments may resemble these:

"You have just written out my lecture notes and paraphrased a few lines out of books, without considering why this is such an important issue."

"The student seems to have written out everything he knows about the subject, in any order, with lots of mistakes, and has not answered the question he was asked."

Better grades

Better grades are awarded for work that:

- shows evidence of background learning
- shows some understanding of the underlying issues
- meets the set criteria
- answers the question that was put
- develops an argument or a point of view
- draws conclusions
- shows the relationship between different issues or concepts within the subject area
- reveals some thought and reflection
- organizes information into a structure
- gives evidence and examples to support arguments and main points.

Highest grades

Highest grades are awarded for work that includes all of the features necessary for "better grades" and in addition:

- reveals a good understanding of why the topic is significant, including underlying issues and concerns, and where and why there is controversy
- engages actively with subject-related debates in a thought-provoking way
- reveals understanding of how the topic relates to broader issues, beyond the subject area.

Using feedback from instructors

"What if I get bad grades for my work …?"

Although "grades" such as "B" or "84%" can be an indicator of how well you are doing, the *comments* you receive are more important. You may feel discouraged and feel inclined to throw your work in the trash if it is returned covered with your instructor's handwriting, but do read the comments—they are likely to be your passport to better grades.

No, no, no!

This is <u>gobbledygook</u>!

It can be distressing if instructors seem insensitive in their comments. Sometimes this is due to bad teaching on their part, but try not to be oversensitive to their remarks. It is best not to take any harsh comments personally. Focus instead on the issues behind the words.

It is also quite usual to have strong feelings about your grades—especially if the amount of effort you put in does not seem to be reflected in the grade. You may feel angry or disappointed, or want to give up altogether.

Don't give up. Wait a day or two, then start an action plan.

Action plan for using instructor feedback

Read through your work and the instructor's comments. Be constructive. Keep asking yourself, "How can this help me to improve my work?"

1 After each comment, check if you understand what it was that made the instructor write it. Highlight any comments that you feel are useful to you for your next piece of work.
2 Divide a piece of paper into:
   – major issues: areas which lose a lot of points, such as not answering the question, lack of evidence, poor argument, weak structure
   – minor errors: spelling, punctuation, grammar.
3 Go through your instructors' comments, listing them under "Major issues" or "Minor errors."

4 Compare this with lists you completed for any previous work. Which comments appear more than once?
5 Number the items in order of priority (with "1" for the most urgent matter to work on), or use the *Priority organizer* (page 78).

Action plan	
Major issues	Minor errors
2 paragraphing	① spelling authors' names
3 referencing	3 commas
① structure	2 "-ed" endings for past tense

Making improvements

1 Select one, two or three priority issues from each list to work on in your next piece of work. Set yourself realistic targets.
2 Consider how you will deal with each item on your list. Don't panic! Think constructively.
3 Make sure you understand *why* you received that feedback.
4 Reread any relevant sections in this guide.
5 Discuss your work with other students.
6 If there are comments you do not understand, or if you are not clear why you received the grade you did, ask your instructor to explain.
7 If you do not know how to improve your "priority areas," ask your instructor for advice.
8 Find out what gets good grades—*ask*!
9 Ask your instructor for examples of the kind of work she or he would *like* you to produce.

- How well do you use your instructors' feedback?
- How could you make better use of feedback from instructors and from other students?

What is a research paper like?

Paper 1

Below is a sample first-year paper for an assignment of 1000 words.

1 Read through it. Research papers should be addressed to an "intelligent reader" who does not know much about the subject, so it should not matter if this is not your area.

2 Once you know what the paper is about, put yourself in the role of an instructor grading it. This will give you a better sense of what your instructors are looking for.

3 Even though you may not know the subject, you can still evaluate it according to the criteria set out on the *Editing your draft* checklist (page 260) or the *What gets good grades?* list (page 281). Add your comments down the side of the paper or in your journal.

4 Compare your own comments with those on page 285.

5 Has reading these comments changed your view about how *you* graded the paper?

The question set

How has Bowlby's Attachment Theory been modified by the findings of later research? How have theories about attachment affected ideas about child care?

The paper

Page 1

Attachment theory originated in the work of Bowlby (1907–90). The theory was that an infant's ability to form emotional attachments to its mother was essential to its survival and later development. This raises important questions about what circumstances could affect the mother–child bond and the effects on the child of different kinds of separation. This paper looks in particular at Bowlby's work on maternal deprivation and at how early research and the later work of Mary Ainsworth seem to support Bowlby's Attachment Theory. It also looks at later challenges to that evidence, which suggest that short spells of separation may not have bad effects upon attachment nor on the child's development. The relative effects of these theories on attitudes towards day care will be explored throughout the paper and brought together towards the conclusion.

Bowlby's Attachment Theory originally claimed that if bonding was to occur between a child and its care giver, there must be continuous loving care from the same care giver (the mother or "permanent mother substitute"). Without this, he argued, chances of bonding were lost forever, and the child was likely to become delinquent. Originally this was formulated as a theory of "maternal deprivation." Later Bowlby focused more specifically on the first year of life, which he called the "critical period." During this time, he believed, the child organizes its behaviors to balance two complementary predispositions. These predispositions are first "proximity-promoting behaviors," which establish the mother as a secure base, and second "exploration," away from the mother. Bowlby argued that the infant develops "internal working models" of its relationship with the mother that becomes the basis of later relationships. He argued that the mother should be at home with the child for these behaviors to develop, and that day care was harmful.

Bowlby's ideas were popular with governments at the time, as there was a shortage of jobs for men returning from the Second World War: Day care during the war had enabled many women to work outside the home. There was also other evidence that appeared to support Bowlby. Goldfarb (1947) compared children who had experienced continuous foster care from nine months onwards to those reared in institutions. He found that the foster children were less likely to suffer intellectual, social and emotional difficulties. Similarly, children who stayed in hospitals showed distress and little affection to parents when reunited with them (Robertson 1967–73). Bowlby's own research into adolescent delinquency indicated childhood maternal deprivation as a recurring factor.

Much of this research evidence has since been revised. Bowlby's adolescent research was based on evacuees in the postwar years, a time of unusual trauma and disruption. With respect to Goldfarb's research, the Tizards (1970s) found that although children's homes could have a negative effect on development, this could be because of unstimulating environments and the high turnover of care givers. Some four-year-olds in children's homes had more than fifty care givers. Similarly, the hospital conditions of Robertson's research were stark environments where parents were discouraged from visiting and the children were very ill. This is a different situation from pleasant nurseries with healthy children who go home to their parents each evening.

Although Bowlby's theory of maternal deprivation has been largely discredited,

Mary Ainsworth (1978) built on Bowlby's ideas about exploratory bases and separation anxiety in her now widely used "Strange Situation" experiment. Findings based on the Strange Situation would appear to support Bowlby and the idea that child care is undesirable. However, there are criticisms of the conclusions drawn from the Strange Situation. Clarke-Stewart argues that the Strange Situation does not take into account how far the mother and child were used to being separated. Cultures such as Japan and the USA vary in how much they value independence in children and so each would interpret the results of the Strange Situation very differently (Super and Harkness 1981). Japanese children tend to get very distressed during the Strange Situation, whereas American children tend to cope better. This could suggest that Japanese children have insecure attachments to their mothers and American children have secure attachments. However, it could be a reflection of different child-rearing patterns—Japanese mothers are less likely to work than their American counterparts.

One of the difficulties in evaluating research based upon Bowlby's theories has been in finding valid comparisons. Most research tends to be based on US mothers and families under economic and social stress, who are not representative of all mothers (Burman 1994). One useful comparison group for day-care children would be children whose temperaments prevented their mothers from going to work and mothers who then became depressed.

It has been found that mothers at home with two children under five are more likely to become depressed. Depression in mothers has also been linked with delinquency in children. Research has found that three-year-old children of depressed mothers were more likely to have behavior problems than children of mothers without depression. This suggests that day care might benefit both mother and child.

Bowlby's original Attachment Theory has been modified; there is now less emphasis on the "critical period," on the irreversibility of early weak bonding and on the necessity of exclusive, continuous maternal care. Separation and reunion behaviors are still regarded as useful indicators of later difficulties, although it is now recognized that many other factors such as marital discord have to be taken into consideration. In general, there has been greater recognition that it is the quality of care, rather than the quantity, that is important. Subsequent modifications in the theory have accompanied changes in child-care, hospital and nursery school environments. Although there is still popular belief in maternal deprivation, many professionals now agree that day care can be of some benefit, if both home and day-care environments are of good quality.

References

Burman, E. (1994). *Deconstructing Developmental Psychology.* London: Routledge.

Oates, J. (1995). *The Foundations of Child Development.* Milton Keynes: Open University Press.

Prior, V. and Glaser, D. (2006). *Understanding Attachment and Attachment Disorders: Theory, Evidence and Practice (Child & Adolescent Mental Health).* London: Jessica Kingsley Publishing

Smith, P. K., and Cowie, H. (1988). *Understanding Children's Development.* Oxford: Blackwell.

Chapter 12

Comments

Overall this is a reasonable paper. Good points include:

- the introduction and conclusion (see page 248)
- the clear line of reasoning—on the whole, the paper follows the introduction
- ideas are well ordered and paragraphed
- the style is very clear and precise
- the research evidence has been evaluated in terms of its good points and bad points
- the writer's point of view (her general disagreement with Bowlby) is clear, as are her reasons.

The paper could be improved, however, to get a higher grade. For example:

Fulfilling undertakings made in the introduction In the introduction, the writer says she will bring together ideas on day care at the end of the paper, but she has not done so. The area of day care has been rather neglected in comparison with her discussion of the theories.

Answering the question Because the writer has neglected the day-care side, she has not really answered the second part of the question in full. Look again at the questions set.

References in the text Although the paper is quite well referenced, paragraph 6 makes several statements without saying where the evidence comes from.

References at the end The references given in the text are written out well, but only a few of them have been given fully at the end. All references must be written out in full.

Now compare Essay 1 with a second essay on the same subject.

How has Bowlby's Attachment Theory been modified by the findings of later research? How have theories about attachment affected ideas about child care?

1   The world of psychology contains many theories about children, some more useful than others, although all add something to our overall knowledge about children, so none should be dismissed as unhelpful. One such theory is that of "attachment," which was the idea of a psychologist called Bowlby. What are the main elements of Bowlby's theory? Well, first there

5   is his early work about attachment. Second, there are his adaptations of his theory into his later ideas about maternal deprivation. There was a lot of research to support Bowlby at the time, and his ideas were very useful to society so it is not surprising that he had a big following in his day. Later, some of his ideas were discredited but some of his ideas were picked up by Mary Ainsworth. She developed something called the "Strange Situation,"

10   which has been used by many people interested in the welfare of children.

Bowlby actually believed that it was a tragedy for the child if the mother was not with him throughout his early childhood. He was very opposed to the idea of mothers going out to work. During the war, a lot of mothers had left their children in special nurseries set up by the government. These nurseries enabled women to work in factories making armaments or

15   to go out to grow food and any other jobs formerly filled by men. Many women enjoyed this newfound freedom and learning new skills like building bridges, driving buses and being radar operators. Bowlby argued that the women's gains were at the expense of the child. He used examples of children that had been abandoned in the war to show that a lack of good mothering had led these children into delinquency and other serious life-long problems.

20   Later Bowlby argued that it might be acceptable for the mother to be absent if there was a suitable kind of care giver who was always present so that the child got continuity. He felt that it was from this care giver or the mother that the baby was able to learn how to form any relationships. So basically, if the baby did not have its mother, it did not have a sense of how to form a relationship, so then it was not able to have the building blocks of any

25   relationship which made relationships in general always difficult. He was actually influenced by the ideas of Lorenz who found that ducklings who lacked their mother at a critical age adopted other objects such as toys to be their mother instead. Bowlby said that human babies also had a critical period for bonding with their mothers—actually up to nine months old. Harlow found that monkeys were also disturbed and when they grew up were not able

30   to look after their babies.

Mary Ainsworth found that if babies were put in a situation with a stranger, they behaved differently depending on whether they had a good relationship with their mother. She said that how babies behaved with a stranger and then afterwards with their mother for leaving them alone with the stranger let you predict whether the baby would be a delinquent later.

35   She said her experiments using the Strange Situation showed that babies who were in day care were more likely to grow up delinquent. But is this really the case? Not every psychologist thinks so and it is important to consider other views. Many feminists are upset with Bowlby and think that he is just trying to make women feel guilty for wanting to reach

their full potential. Germaine Greer thinks that it is not just a mother's responsibility to raise
40 a child and that the whole community should be involved so that if the child were lost and
wandering around, someone would recognize him and could look after him.

Some people think day care may actually be good for children. Studies have shown that
day care can, in fact, make children more intelligent and better able to get on with other
children. Not all mothers feel fulfilled staying at home with their children and some might
45 end up developing mental illnesses like depression, where they feel very low and may even
be suicidal. Drug treatments and counseling can help women recover and depression is a
very treatable condition. It is surely better for a child to be in good day care, rather than
staying at home with a mother who is depressed?

So, there are some strong arguments for and against attachment theory. Bowlby makes
50 some very interesting points about the importance of mothers and the need children have
for good care. His research does seem to indicate that poor care leads to children becoming
delinquents. On the other hand, there are times when mothers would do better for their
children by being out of the home so you cannot assume that it is always best for the child
to be with its mother. Looking at society today, we are seeing more and more children with
55 problems. The rise of delinquency in children today requires greater consideration by
researchers to work out what the causes are.

References
Psychology by Richard Gross, published in paperback by Hodder Arnold in 2005
John Bowlby—*Attachment Theory*

Grading Paper 2

Using the checklists on either page 261 or 281:

1 Underline sections that you think could be improved.
2 Write comments in the margin as if you were an instructor giving the student advice.
3 Are you able to identify why Paper 1 would receive a better grade than Paper 2?

When you have finished, compare your comments with those below.

Feedback on the exercise

Focus   The first sentence is too general and adds nothing to the paper.

Length and conciseness   This paper is 862 words long, which is rather short. It should be 950–1050 words for a 1000-word paper (Paper 1 is 954 words). Overall, too many words are used to say too little. This means that the writer will not cover

as much relevant information in the paper as someone who writes in a more concise style, and will therefore lose points. (See especially lines 3–4, 22–25 and 45–48.)

Line of argument   t is not clear from the introduction what the writer's line of reasoning or main argument will be. This is also the case in the conclusion, which does not identify a clear point of view.

Addressing the question   The first half of the paper does not address how Bowlby's theories were modified by research findings. The second half does not consider the impact of attachment theory on day care.

Structure   The early comments about the usefulness of Bowlby's ideas could be omitted as the paper looks at this later (lines 6–8).

Detail   The writer goes into too much unnecessary detail at various points of the paper, for example, about women's work during the war and about treatment for depression. Neither is strictly relevant to this paper, and such details waste valuable space.

Paragraphing   Paragraph 2 is far too long, and its central point is not clear.

Referencing   No dates are given for the references cited, for example, for the work of Lorenz (line 26), Harlow (line 29) or Greer (line 39). Few of the references cited within the text are listed at the end of the paper. The two texts listed at the end are not referenced correctly.

Precision   Some of the research evidence cited is rather vague. Paper 1 makes it clear that there were two stages to Bowlby's research, but this is not clear in Paper 2.

Vocabulary   Words such as "actually" and "basically" are not generally used in academic writing (lines 11, 23, 25, 28 and 42).

Clarity   Some sections (such as lines 29–30 and 32–34) could be written more clearly.

Review

Academic writing has certain formal writing conventions, such as not using slang or abbreviations. It is precise—it's difficult to gain points if your writing is vague.

It is important to be clear in academic writing when you are giving your personal opinion. Academic writing generally values opinion when it is used to support a line of reasoning and is backed up by evidence ("facts").

Most academic writing is influenced by the scientific model, which values objectivity and quantitative data. Different academic subjects vary in how much they value subjectivity (your personal response) and qualitative analysis (your awareness of your role in the process of evaluating evidence).

There are four main styles of writing used within academic writing. Some pieces of work will require you to use several styles within a single assignment.

Almost all writing involves an element of argument and evaluation. Descriptive writing and personal writing need to be used with care.

Good grades are allocated for specific reasons—not for general smartness. It is important to be aware of how grades are allocated in your subjects. Use your instructor's feedback constructively, and don't be put off by what seems to be criticism. Instructors want as many students to succeed as possible—and their comments are intended to help you improve your grades.

If you grade papers yourself, using checklists to give you criteria against which to assess them, you will start to see writing through the eyes of your instructor. This will help you to evaluate your own writing: You will become less dependent on getting feedback from someone else before you know if your writing is good or bad.

Chapter 13

Confidence with numbers

Most subjects in college involve using numbers—it isn't only science and math subjects that require you to analyze and present data and to perform numerical operations. In addition, you may also be required to take a math placement test or math classes as part of your program.

Many students feel uncertain about their abilities in working with numbers. They may struggle to remember what they learned at high school about "percentages" and "averages," or feel perplexed about terms such as "mode," "median" or "quartile." If you don't feel confident with numbers, it may be tempting to skim quickly over texts that contain figures, data or mathematical terms, hoping that you can avoid thinking about them.

Gaps in basic numerical skills can make study seem unnecessarily daunting. If numbers worry you, then it may be reassuring to know:

- You are not alone!

- For most subjects, even a little knowledge about using numbers goes a long way.

- Often colleges recognize that students may have difficulties with number skills and provide additional support.

- The topics in this chapter cover the basic number skills required for most study programs.

I'll leap through fire, walk on burning coals, clean dishes for a year— but _please_ don't make me do fractions!

But surely everyone _loves_ fractions?

What do I need to know?

What kind of number work is necessary?

The amount, level and type of numerical work all vary with the study program or course. Simply through practice during your program you will probably become used to working with numbers as required.

How do numbers add value?

When you are making an argument, you can generally make a better case if you can present numerical data that support what you are saying. A numerical table, for example, may sum up a great deal of information concisely and clearly, saving you thousands of words. The numbers you present must be *accurate* and *well selected*, and it should be clear why you have included them.

For example, "Many students have jobs" is vague—it could be interpreted in different ways. Compare this vague statement with two precise numerical statements: "75% of students from the University of Aremia are employed part-time"; "Almost 40% of students at Exford College work part-time in hospitality or sales."

Note here that the accompanying words help to define the context and the meaning of the numbers. Your presentation needs to show this combination—the right numbers and the right words to explain them.

Subjects that require specialist skills

Some subjects require specific statistical methods or other specialist knowledge: If so, these are usually taught as part of the program. If you find that you are struggling, ask your instructors for additional support or set up a student group to practice the numerical work together.

Build your confidence with numbers

The first obstacle many students face is anxiety. If you feel you "can't do math":

- Stay calm.
- Work through the steps systematically.
- Don't rush.
- Recognize your weak spots.
- Practice—then practice some more.

Overcoming your barriers

If you lack confidence in using numbers:

- Look at the barriers outlined below and on page 292. Check any that apply to you.
- Think about how you could overcome each barrier.

1   I don't understand numbers at all ☐

A lot of basic number work is actually quite easy if you just follow a set of steps in sequence. Easy-to-use tools can also help. Math may seem mysterious, but if you learn the steps and follow them exactly, you will get the right answer. The more you understand what you are doing, however, the more confident you will feel and the likelier you will be to spot an answer that doesn't look right.

Don't overcomplicate your thinking. Most math that you will need will build on a few simple basics, such as adding, taking something away, multiplying or dividing. It is highly likely that you can do such calculations, even if you do occasionally make mistakes.

2   I make too many little mistakes ☐

It is easy to make minor errors—don't let this discourage you.

- Many mistakes happen simply by missing a step from the correct sequence, or in basic adding, subtracting, multiplying or dividing. The secret is to check back carefully over your math, just as you proofread written work.
- The more you practice, the more you will notice the kinds of mistakes you are most likely to make. You can then check for those in particular.
- If you are better with words than numbers, write out instructions in a way that makes sense to you.
- Set out the sequence of "how to do it" for each operation. Using a layout that you can easily follow:
  - write only one step per line
  - leave space between steps
  - highlight key points in color.

3 ▶ I can't track numbers ☐

- If you find it hard to track down columns of figures, check if it is easier if you work on graph paper.
- If you still switch columns, color adjoining columns or rows differently—this will help lead your eye down each column.
- Using a calculator or "speaking calculator" may help.

4 ▶ I quickly forget how to do math ☐

- As stress makes memory worse, focus on what you *can* do.
- Write down formulae for the mathematical operations you need, such as calculating a percentage (see page 299).
- Put these formulae where you can find them easily when you need them—maybe in your planner or in a labeled file on your computer.
- Use the formulae from time to time: This will jog your memory.
- To help you recall the operations you need most often, devise personal memory joggers (see pages 176–181).

5 ▶ I'm no good at basics such as multiplication and division ☐

- Multiplication just means adding the same number over and over. "17 x 20" means adding 17 repeatedly: 17 + 17 + 17 + 17 … .
- Often there are several different ways to get the right answer: Find out which way works best for you. In the example above, you could just write the number 17 twenty times in a long list, and then add up the list.
- Simple calculators make multiplication and division easy, and your computer will usually provide a calculator in its accessories.
  - *Multiplication* Enter the first number, then a multiplication sign (x) or an asterisk (*), then the second number, and press "Enter" or the "equals" sign (=).
  - *Division* Enter the amount you want to divide up, then the diagonal line (/), then the number you want to divide by, and "Enter" or the "equals" sign (=).

- You could refer to a visual table (such as that on page 361) or learn multiplication tables for speed.

6 ▶ I can't do things you're supposed to know, like calculating averages and percentages ☐

If you don't often use these, it is easy to forget how to do them. This chapter explains the common operations that many students need.

7 ▶ I don't know the technical terms ☐

Don't be daunted by technical terms in math. The basic processes are not complicated—you can pick them up through instruction and practice. (See page 311.)

8 ▶ I don't trust numbers and statistics, so I don't want to work with them ☐

Knowing how to interpret data helps you know when to trust numbers. It also enables you to identify flaws in other people's arguments and to detect occasions when figures are being cleverly manipulated. (See pages 153–155 and 293–294.)

9 ▶ I don't know how to interpret information in graphs and charts ☐

Graphs and charts are important not only in presenting your own work but also in understanding what you read. Practice will help. (See pages 153–155 and 307–310.)

10 I need to collect and present numerical data, but I don't know where to start ☐

The key to collecting and presenting data is to focus on the purpose of your research. What are you trying to find out? What data do you need to find the answer? (See pages 321–326.)

- What do you think are your main barriers in working with numbers?
- What would help you overcome these?
- What will you do to overcome these?

Can you trust numbers?

How useful are numbers?

Many people have strong opinions about numbers, especially statistics. It is easy to assume either that numbers "prove" a case or that all statistics are "lies." In reality, numbers simply provide information, and the *value* of that information depends on what else you know about it and whether it suits your purpose.

What are "statistics"?

"Statistics" has two meanings:

- the methods and techniques for measuring, organizing, interpreting and describing numerical information (data)
- specific sets of data produced to measure a given subject.

Populations and samples

The total number of instances of something—all the plants in a meadow, for example—is the *population*. It is seldom possible to measure every individual in the population, so instead you can measure just some of the individuals—a *sample*.

If the sample is typical of the population, statements that are true for the sample are also true for the population as a whole: Such a sample is said to be *representative*. If the sample is untypical of the population as a whole, however, it is said to be unrepresentative or *biased*. If the samples are representative, you can use them to draw inferences about the whole population—these are known as *inferential statistics*.

Good measurements must be accurate: They should measure in full what they say they measure and should not be measuring anything else. Measurements gathered for one purpose cannot necessarily be applied in other situations—you must judge whether or not data tell you what you need to know.

The relevance of the numbers

Whether or not data are relevant depends on what is being asked of them. When considering a specific set of data, ask yourself:

- Does it provide useful insights? Does it indicate oddities I need to investigate further?
- Does it help me spot any trends?
- Does it affect how I should think about a subject?

Know the context

To interpret data, you need to know about the context in which they were collected. Suppose someone won a TV songwriting competition by gaining 56% of the phoned-in votes. Would a music producer be wise to invest in this artiste? The producer would need to know more. How many people watched the show? What proportion of them phoned in? Were they representative? Perhaps:

- the winner was supported by people who phoned in more than once
- the winner was popular with phone voters but not with people who buy recorded music
- the phone lines were not working properly.

Questioning numbers and statistics

Do numbers provide proof?

Numbers may appear to be convincing, but they may not be as reliable as they seem. When using any set of data, be objective and critical. Consider:

- Do these data measure what they purport to measure?
- Are they likely to be accurate?
- Could they contain errors or misprints?
- How were they collected? Might this have led to mistakes or inaccuracies?
- Who wanted them collected? Why?
- When were they collected? Are they up to date? If not, does that matter?
- Are they representative? Or do they refer only to particular sets of people or particular circumstances?
- Do they cover exactly what you are looking for? Do they throw useful light on the issue you are investigating?

Are the data based on estimates?

Some data are based not on actual counting but on *estimates*. For example, a newspaper report of the size of a crowd at a public demonstration may be no more than an "informed" guess. The estimates made by the organizers and by the police may differ—and neither may be correct.

Are the data likely to change?

Estimates may change rapidly or over time. For example, the first estimate of casualties immediately following a disaster may differ from estimates made later as more accurate information becomes available. Data about the overall impact of the disaster may change as long-term consequences, such as environmental effects, gradually become apparent.

Are the data still up to date?

Check if there is a later or an earlier set of data that are more accurate or with which you can compare the current data. For example, if a shop claims that it won a "Customer Satisfaction" survey ten years ago, you would probably wonder if current customers are satisfied. Remember, too, that it takes time to collect, analyze and publish data: Some are out of date even before they are published.

What was actually measured?

Historical data need to be treated with caution. During some historical periods, whole sections of populations were simply ignored when making counts. For example, the number of casualties typically cited for the Great Earthquake of San Francisco in 1906 omits the Chinese casualties, even though the Chinese population at the time was significant. For much of history, only the views of people regarded as "important" were counted: We cannot know what "most people" thought if they were not allowed to vote or to register their opinions.

What kind of "sample" was used?

We are often presented with claims about the average number of televisions in each home, how the average voter will vote in the next election or what proportion of pets prefer a particular food. Such figures do not measure every home, every voter or every pet—that would take too long and be too expensive. Instead, a sample is taken, much smaller than the whole population, and is treated as if it were representative of the whole. For the result to be reliable, the sample must be big enough to be a fair representation of the population—if not, claims about proportions or rising or falling trends will be unreliable.

What kind of "averaging" was used?

Different kinds of average may throw a different light on an issue. Which sort is being used? Is it appropriate? (See pages 301–304.)

For more about examining data critically, see *Critical analytical thinking*, pages 153–155.

Fractions

A fraction is part of a whole. We acknowledge this in everyday speech:

- "Buy this at a fraction of the cost …"
- "If you had the right tools, you'd get that done in a fraction of the time."

In math, a *fraction* represents one of a number of equal parts of a complete unit. Thus a fraction could be a part of a price, a time, a width, a group ("set") or any other unit.

The language of fractions

The language of fractions is straightforward. For example, if you cut a cake into 8 equal slices, each slice would be one *eighth*. If instead you divided it into 6 equal parts, each part would be a *sixth*. If you shared it out in 20 equal slices, then each piece would be a *twentieth* of the whole cake. If you then ate 3 of those 20 equal pieces, you would have eaten *three-twentieths*. If you gave a friend 2 of 5 equal slices of the cake, you would have given *two-fifths*.

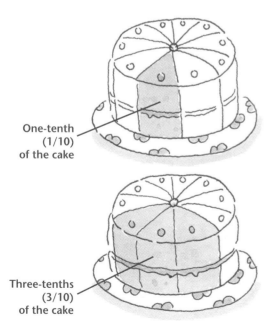

One-tenth
(1/10)
of the cake

Three-tenths
(3/10)
of the cake

Written fractions

The lower number, or *denominator*, such as the 4 in $^3/_4$, represents the total number of equal parts into which the whole unit is divided.

The top number, or *numerator*, such as the 3 in $^3/_4$, represents the proportion of the equal parts into which the whole is divided.

Fractions of a set

The set of stars below consists of 28 items. They are divided into 7 equal parts, or fractions: Each line represents $^1/_7$ of the total. The shaded area covers 3 of those 7 parts, or $^3/_7$.

Example: fractions of 28

A set of 28 items divided into 7 equal parts consists of 7 groups, each of 4 items. With the items laid out as below, you can see the relationship between the total set and the set divided into sevenths.

1 ★★★★
2 ★★★★
3 ★★★★
4 ★★★★
5 ★★★★
6 ★★★★
7 ★★★★

- As you can see, $^1/_7$ of 28 items is 4 items.
- $^3/_7$ of 28 items is 3 × 4 items = 12 items. To check this, count the items.

Proper and improper fractions

In a *proper fraction*, the top number is smaller than the bottom number (e.g., $^3/_4$). In an *improper fraction*, the top number is bigger than the bottom number (e.g., $^4/_3$): the fraction is greater than 1. A *mixed number* combines a whole number and a proper fraction (e.g., $1^1/_3$).

More about fractions

1	1/2	1/3	1/4	1/6	1/8	1/12
1 ★★★★ ★★★★ ★★★★ ★★★★ ★★★★ ★★★★	1/2 ★★★★ ★★★★ ★★★★	1/3 ★★★★ ★★★★	1/4 ★★★ ★★★	1/6 ★★★★	1/8 ★★★	1/12 ★★
						1/12 ★★
				1/6 ★★★★	1/8 ★★★	1/12 ★★
			1/4 ★★★ ★★★		1/8 ★★★	1/12 ★★
		1/3 ★★★★ ★★★★		1/6 ★★★★	1/8 ★★★	1/12 ★★
			1/4 ★★★ ★★★	1/6 ★★★★	1/8 ★★★	1/12 ★★
(whole set: 24 items)	1/2 ★★★★ ★★★★ ★★★★			1/6 ★★★★	1/8 ★★★	1/12 ★★
		1/3 ★★★★ ★★★★	1/4 ★★★ ★★★		1/8 ★★★	1/12 ★★
				1/6 ★★★★	1/8 ★★★	1/12 ★★
1 × 24	**2 × 12**	**3 × 8**	**4 × 6**	**6 × 4**	**8 × 3**	**12 × 2**

Comparing equivalent fractions

The chart above shows equivalent fractions. By tracking across you can count, for example, how many one-twelfths are equivalent to two-thirds.

- The height of each column is divided so that you can compare fractions visually.
- The items in each column add up to the same total number (24), so you can also count out the relative proportions.

Comparing fractions

When fractions have the same bottom number denominator), it is easy to compare them. For example, with $3/12$ and $5/12$, you can tell that 5 portions are more than 3 portions of the same size.

When the bottom numbers differ, however, comparison is more difficult. Which is bigger, $1/4$ or $2/9$? You need a new denominator that can be divided both by 4 and by 9. The easiest way is to multiply these two different denominators together to find a *common denominator*. In the case of $1/4$ or $2/9$, a common denominator is found from $4 \times 9 = 36$. Each of the two fractions can then be expressed as a number of $1/36$ths.

You then need to work out the equivalent number of $1/36$ths for each fraction. To maintain the proportion, multiply the top number (the numerator) by the same number as the bottom number (the denominator) in that fraction:

- For $1/4$: To get 36 at the bottom, you multiply 4 by 9, so multiply the top,1, by 9 also. The result is $9/36$ (that is: $1/4 = 9/36$).
- For 2/9: To get 36 at the bottom, you multiply 9 by 4, so multiply the top, 2, by 4 also. The result is $8/36$ (that is: $2/9 = 8/36$).

The question, "Which is bigger, $1/4$ or $2/9$?," can now be answered by substituting the converted fractions. "Which is bigger, $1/4$ ($9/36$) or $2/9$ ($8/36$)?" It is now clear that $1/4$ ($9/36$) is bigger.

Adding and subtracting fractions

Once you have converted numbers so that they have a common denominator, you can also add and subtract fractions easily. You simply add or subtract the top numbers:

$$9/36 + 8/36 = 17/36$$
$$5/36 + 11/36 = 16/36$$
$$9/36 - 8/36 = 1/36$$
$$30/36 - 10/36 = 20/36$$

Using fractions

Uses of fractions

We use fractions in everyday life:

- to share any item in equal parts
- to share out profit in proportion to the level of investment
- to work out a sale price when items are reduced by a fraction, such as "$1/3$ off."

Calculating the fraction of a quantity

We can also calculate actual numbers and total amounts when we are given fractions. For example, if we know that in a survey of 800 people, three-quarters were women, we can work out how many women were questioned.

In 800 participants, $3/4$ were women.

1 Divide the total number (800) by the bottom number (the denominator) in the fraction (the 4 in $3/4$): 800/4 = 200.
   (That is: $800 = 4/4$, so $1/4 = 200$.)
2 Multiply the result by the top number (the numerator in the fraction (the 3 in $3/4$): 200 x 3 = 600.
   (That is: $200 = 1/4$, so $3/4 = 600$.)

Example 1

To calculate $3/4$ of a sample of 200:

1 Divide 200 (the total) by 4: 200/4 = 50.
2 Multiply the 50 by 3: 50   3 = 150.

Example 2

A shop is offering an item for $1/3$ off its usual price of $120. This means that the item would cost you $2/3$ of $120. To calculate this:

1 Divide $120 by 3 (bottom number): $120/3 = $40.
2 Multiply $40 by 2 (top number): $40 x 2 = $80.

The reduction ($1/3$) is $40; and the cost ($2/3$) is $80.

Multiplying fractions

When you multiply fractions of a whole number, you are multiplying a *part* by a *part*, so the result is even smaller. For example:

- a half of a half ($1/2 \times 1/2$) is a quarter ($1/4$)
- a half of an eighth ($1/2 \times 1/8$) is a sixteenth ($1/16$).

Improper fractions

Sometimes you see a fraction in which the top number is bigger than the bottom number. This simply means that the fraction amounts to more than one whole item or set. For example, $7/6$ is the same as $6/6 + 1/6$ or $11/6$.

Activity

1 In each case, which fraction is larger?
   a $1/5$ or $1/6$ c $4/7$ or $5/9$
   b $2/3$ or $7/11$ d $4/5$ or $5/6$

2 Add each of the following fractions:
   a $1/3$ and $1/2$ d $1/4$ and $2/3$
   b $1/6$ and $1/8$ e $2/7$ and $3/5$
   c $1/2$ and $5/6$ f $1/9$ and $3/4$

3 Calculate each of the following:
   a $2/3$ of $750   d $2/9$ of 81
   b $3/4$ of 160   e $3/5$ of 620
   c $5/6$ of 72   f $2/7$ of 91

4 Calculate the total given that:
   a $1/2 = 100$ e $3/4 = 120$
   b $1/4 = 100$ f $1/7 = 10$
   c $1/3 = 50$ g $2/7 = 10$
   d $2/3 = 50$ h $4/5 = 20$

5 Multiply:
   a $1/2 \times 1/2$ d $1/3 \times 1/3$
   b $1/2 \times 1/4$ e $1/3 \times 1/2$
   c $1/4 \times 1/4$ f $2/3 \times 1/2$

Answers are given on pages 312–313.

Chapter **13**

Understanding percentages

What is a percentage?

A percentage (%) is a way of stating any fraction as a proportion of 100.

$^1/_{100}$ = 1% (1 percent)

$^{23}/_{100}$ = 23% (23 percent)

$^{59}/_{100}$ = 59% (59 percent)

A proportion of the "whole"

The whole of anything—the full amount of an item or a group of items—is 100%.

If you divide this total amount, 100%, into smaller parts, each part will be a proportion of the whole 100%. All the pieces together add up to 100%.

Example

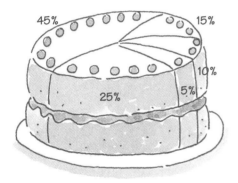

Consider this cake, which has slices of different sizes. The five slices of the cake add up to 100%.

If some of the cake is eaten, the remainder can be expressed as a percentage of the original whole cake.

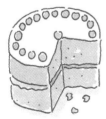 

75% remaining	25% gone

Percentages written as fractions

Percentages can be written as fractions, in which the bottom number is always 100:

Why use percentages?

If proportions are stated relative to a standard number, 100, it becomes easy to make direct comparisons. For example, suppose you want to compare how effective two sports clubs are in attracting student members. If there are 17 students in a total of 34 members in Club A and 13 out of 52 in Club B, it is hard to make direct comparisons between the clubs. If the figures are both converted into percentages, however, they can be compared easily on this single scale: 17/34 = 50%; 13/52 = 25%.

Reliability

The reliability of percentages depends on the sample size: see page 155.

Percentages: "more than one cake"

Imagine two cakes of equal size. The "whole amount" of cake, 100%, is *two* cakes. Now suppose that 75% of one cake and 25% of the other cake are eaten. Although the amount eaten is equivalent to 100% of *one* cake, it is only 50% of the "whole amount" of cake—*two* cakes.

 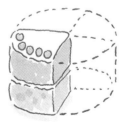

25% of Cake 1 eaten = 12.5% of the whole amount (two cakes)	75% of Cake 2 eaten = 37.5% of the whole amount (two cakes)

Total amount eaten = 12.5% + 37.5% = 50% of the whole amount (two cakes)

Calculating percentages from fractions

A fraction is a part of a whole, such as a half or third. When it isn't easy to see how fractions or proportions of different items compare, it is worth converting fractions into percentages.

Easy conversions from fractions and percentages

On page 298, the proportion of students in the membership of one club was shown to be 17/34 or 50%. This fraction is easy to convert to a percentage if you recognize that 17 is half of 34—"half" is always 50%. Other useful conversions are listed below.

One-half =	$^1/_2$		=	50%
One-quarter =	$^1/_4$		=	25%
Three-quarters =	$^3/_4$		=	75%
One-third =	$^1/_3$		=	33%
Two-thirds =	$^2/_3$ =	2 × 33% =		66%
One-fifth =	$^1/_5$		=	20%
Two-fifths =	$^2/_5$ =	2 × 20% =		40%
Three-fifths =	$^3/_5$ =	3 × 20% =		60%
Four-fifths =	$^4/_5$ =	4 × 20% =		80%
One-sixth =	$^1/_6$ =		=	16.7%
Two-sixths =	$^2/_6$ =		$^1/_3$ =	33.3%
One-eighth =	$^1/_8$		=	12.5%
Two-eighths =	$^2/_8$ =		$^1/_4$ =	25%
Three-eighths =	$^3/_8$ =	3 × 12.5% =		37.5%
Four-eighths =	$^4/_8$ =		$^1/_2$ =	50%
One-tenth =	$^1/_{10}$		=	10%
One-twentieth =	$^1/_{20}$		=	5%
One-fiftieth =	$^1/_{50}$		=	2%
One-hundredth =	$^1/_{100}$		=	1%

It is worth playing with these basic fractions and percentages, and looking for relationships between them. For example, to find three-fiftieths, multiply one-fiftieth (2%) by 3 to give 6%.

Look for proportions that help you calculate a percentage quickly in your head. For example, "24 out of 96" is the same proportion as "1 in 4" (4 × 24 = 96) or 25%. If you know your "tables," you will find it easier to recognize proportions.

Converting fractions to percentages

1 Divide the part by the whole.
2 Multiply the result by a 100.

Activity

Converting fractions to percentages

Turn the following fractions into percentages. For this activity, ignore any numbers that follow the decimal point on your calculator. Example: 27/134 × 100 = 20.149. Just write 20.

a $^4/_8$	**e** $^9/_{11}$	**i** $^{117}/_{327}$	**m** $^{667}/_{713}$
b $^{44}/_{88}$	**f** $^{196}/_{567}$	**j** $^{67}/_{84}$	**n** $^{19}/_{38}$
c $^{19}/_{56}$	**g** $^{11}/_{91}$	**k** $^{87}/_{181}$	**o** $^{765}/_{999}$
d $^{76}/_{145}$	**h** $^{128}/_{256}$	**l** $^{12}/_{96}$	**p** $^{65}/_{230}$

Calculating percentages

a In a sample, 6 of 11 plants are deciduous. What percentage is deciduous, and what percentage is not?

b In one school, 41 out of 230 children have reading difficulties. What percentage have reading difficulties? What proportion do not?

c Out of a population of 234,560 people, 23,456 people went to see a movie. What percentage of the population saw the movie? What percentage did not?

d 873 of 9,786 participants took part in the competition online, 2,314 by texting and the rest by phone-in. What percentage participated by each method?

Answers are given on page 313.

Example: 17/34 = 0.5 (17 = "the part"; 34 = "the whole")
0.5 × 100% = 50%

If you didn't recognize 17/34 as 50%, don't worry—you can use the formula above to convert any fraction into a percentage. Using a calculator, key in the operation, in order, as in this example:

$\boxed{1}\boxed{7}\boxed{/}\boxed{3}\boxed{4}\boxed{\times}\boxed{1}\boxed{0}\boxed{0}\boxed{=}$

Rounding up and down

Strings of digits can be hard to read and to work with. "Rounding" makes them easier to manage.

Whole numbers

A whole number is one with no fractions or decimal points attached to it, such as 75 or 921.

Numbers followed by decimal points

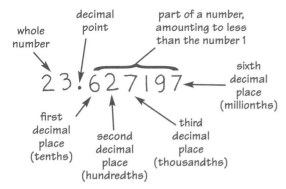

The digits that follow a decimal point represent only a *part* of a whole number. However many digits follow the decimal point, they represent less than the number 1.

When you convert a fraction into a decimal, there may be more digits after the decimal point than are useful. This is where "rounding" helps.

Rounding money

You may be used to "rounding up" or "rounding down" when using money, rounding to the nearest dollar or other unit of currency. For example, if you owed a friend 4 dollars and 75 cents, you might "round up" and repay 5 dollars, telling your friend to keep the change. Similarly, if you owed 4 dollars and 10 cents, your friend might "round down" and accept just 4 dollars.

Rounding numbers

Example: rounding down 986.748

Rounding numbers follows the same principle as rounding money. To round 986.748 to just its first decimal place:

- The digit in the first decimal place is 7.
- If the digit immediately to the right of the 7 (in the first decimal place) is *4 or less, round down*—remove everything following that decimal place. Here the digit in the next decimal place is a 4, so round *down*, removing the 4 and the 8, and leaving 986.7.

Example: rounding up 986.752

- The digit in the first decimal place is again 7.
- If the digit in the next decimal place is *5 or more, round up*—increase by 1 the number in the decimal place you want. Here the digit in the next decimal place is 5, so you round *up*, removing the 5 and the 2, changing the 7 to 8, and leaving 986.8.

You can round up or down to whole numbers, or to one or more decimal places.

More examples

To round 756.483921 to the nearest whole number Everything before the decimal point is the whole number: 756.

To round 756.483921 to two decimal places The digit immediately to the right of the second decimal place is 3. For "4 or less, round down." As 3 is less than 4, round down: 756.48.

To round 756.486111 to 2 decimal places The digit immediately to the right of the second decimal place is 6. For "5 or more, round up." As 6 is more than 5, round up: the 8 in the second decimal place increases to 9, giving 756.49.

> ### Activity
>
> Round these numbers to one decimal place.
>
> | | | |
> |---|---|---|
> | **a** 41.34675 | **d** 99.88 | **g** 66.55 |
> | **b** 912.172 | **e** 1.714 | **h** 6.10987 |
> | **c** 22.222 | **f** 10.08 | |
>
> *Answers are given on page 313.*

What are "averages"?

Discussing a set of numbers

Many kinds of research involve collecting data by counting. For example, you might want to know:

- how many people take vacations abroad, and where they go
- how many plants and animals there are on a piece of seashore
- how many children are immunized in different communities, and against which diseases
- how much students earn.

For instance, suppose you were investigating road safety and you were measuring the traffic through a suburb. You might count how many people there are in each vehicle that passes through the suburb in a given period of the day. You might collect a set of numbers such as this:

3, 2, 5, 41, 1, 76, 1, 97, 3, 1

It would be hard to discuss this list in your report because the number of people per vehicle varies between 1 and 97. It would be even harder to make comparisons, for example with the figures at a different time of day or in another suburb.

Averages

One way to deal with this is to use a single number that in some way *summarizes* or *represents* the set of numbers. It needs in some way to be typical of the set. It needs to be an *average* number.

- An average would help us work more efficiently with large sets of numbers.
- It would help us spot patterns and trends.
- It would help us compare numbers more easily.

Choosing the average number

In choosing one number to represent a set, we need to decide which would be the best number to use. The lowest one? The highest? The one in the middle? The one that appears most often? In discussing students' income, for example, we might choose as an average:

- the *median*—the amount that falls midway between $0.00 and the income of the highest earner *or*
- the *mean*—the amount that each student would receive if their total earnings were equally divided between all of them (as if sharing out a pool of money equally between members) *or*
- the *mode*—the amount that students earn most frequently.

Calculating averages

The three averages are not all the same. For instance, for the list of numbers already given—3, 2, 5, 41, 1, 76, 1, 97, 3, 1—the mean is 23, the median is 3, and the mode is 1. All three averages might be useful in different contexts.

The following pages look at how to calculate these three commonly used representative averages.

Calculating averages: the mean ("equal share")

What is the mean?

Most people, when they refer to an "average number," are talking about the "mean" number. This is the method you would use to find out how to distribute money, objects, time or other items into equal shares or amounts.

> ### Calculating the mean
>
> Calculating a mean is relatively simple, especially with a calculator. You just:
>
> 1 Add up all the numbers in the set in order to find the grand total, or "sum," of the numbers.
> 2 Divide the sum by the number of items in the set: That gives you the mean average.

Example 1

Consider the set of numbers given on page 301:

> 3, 2, 5, 41, 1, 76, 1, 97, 3, 1

To find the mean for this set:

1 Add the 10 numbers together:

   $3 + 2 + 5 + 41 + 1 + 76 + 1 + 97 + 3 + 1 = 230$

2 Divide the total passengers (230) by the number of vehicles (10):

   Mean = 230/10 = 23

"23" might seem a strange number to consider as "representative"—most vehicles carried far fewer passengers, and 7 of the 10 vehicles each carried only 1–5 passengers. Nevertheless, this figure could still provide a point of reference when comparing overall information about volume of movement from one place to another, or at different times.

Example 2

This set of numbers records the number of US dollars held by each of 6 tourists:

> $34, $31, $200, $11, $19, $88

To find the mean for this set:

1 Add the 6 numbers together to get the total number of US dollars held by the 6 tourists altogether:

   $34 + $31 + $200 + $11 + $19 + $88 = $383

2 Divide the total dollars ($383) by the number of tourists (6):

   Mean = $383/6 = $63.8

If the tourists shared their money equally between them, they would each have $63.8.

> ### Activity
>
> Calculate the mean number, or average, for each of the following sets of numbers.
>
> a 1, 2, 3, 5, 6, 7, 8, 9, 11, 15, 17
> b 234, 19, 1, 66, 2002, 7
> c 7, 7, 6, 8, 9, 8, 11, 7, 6, 11, 2, 14, 5
> d 11, 22, 33, 44, 55, 66, 77, 88, 99, 111
> e 7, 14, 19, 8, 6, 11, 21, 32, 8, 19, 21, 5
> f 23, 36, 42, 56, 57, 58, 59, 59, 59, 69, 69
>
> *Answers are given on page 313.*

Calculating averages: the median ("middle number")

What is the median?

The *median* is the midway point in a set of numbers that have been put in order of increasing size.

Calculating the median

1 Lay out the numbers in the set in order, from smallest to largest.
2 The median is the middle value. The way of calculating this place depends on whether there is an odd or an even number of items in the set.

   Odd number of items Find the middle item in the ordered list: This value is the median.

   Even number of items Find the middle two items in the ordered list. Add them together and divide by 2: this value is the median.

We represent the median height

Example 1: odd number of items

Here is a set of test scores:

23, 36, 42, 56, 57, 58, 59, 59, 59, 69, 99

There are 11 scores in the set, and they have been laid out in order from lowest to highest. The median is the number that falls in the middle. For 11 numbers, the middle is the 6th place. The 6th value, the median, is 58.

Example 2: even number of items

Here is another set of test scores:

36, 42, 56, 57, 58, 60, 61, 69, 69, 70

Here there are 10 scores in the set, and again they have been laid out in order from lowest to highest. For 10 numbers, there is no single middle value.

- The two middle numbers (5th and 6th places) are 58 and 60.
- 58 + 60 = 118.
- The median is 118/2 = 59 (59 is the mean of the two middle values).

Activity

Calculate the median for each of the following sets of numbers.

a 1, 2, 3, 5, 6, 7, 8, 9, 11, 15, 17
b 234, 19, 1, 66, 2002, 7
c 7, 7, 6, 8, 9, 8, 11, 7, 6, 11, 2, 14, 5
d 11, 22, 33, 44, 55, 66, 77, 88, 99, 111
e 7, 14, 19, 8, 6, 11, 21, 32, 8, 19, 21, 5
f 23, 36, 42, 56, 57, 58, 59, 59, 59, 69, 69

Answers are given on pages 313–314.

When is the median useful?

The median is especially useful for small sets of numbers, as in the examples above. Other averages are often affected by extreme differences between the numbers, known as "extreme values," such as the 99 in example 1. The median is less affected by extreme values, so it may be more representative of the set of numbers as a whole.

Calculating averages: the mode ("most frequent")

What is the mode?

The *mode* is the number in a set that appears the most frequently.

Example

Look again at this list of test scores, sorted into ascending order:

23, 36, 42, 56, 57, 58, 59, 59, 59, 69, 99

The number that appears most frequently in this set is 59: This is the mode. In this set, 59 is the test score that occurs most often.

When is the mode useful?

The mode is especially useful when you have a large set of data in which there is only a small range of values. For example, national data on family size would be a large data set, with perhaps millions of numbers, yet the *range* of values would be quite narrow—the number of children per family is likely to be between 0 and around 12 at most. If, in practice, most families had 3 children, it might well make better sense to use this value—the most frequently occurring number of children in a family—rather than to use a mean or a median, which would probably be a decimal, such as "2.12" children. The mode can be valuable when making comparisons within large populations, as when carrying out research regionally or nationally into the effects of family size on health or income.

However, using the mode can make it harder to see trends. For example, if there were a new trend in which increasing numbers of families had 3 or more children, this trend would not be apparent if one knew only that 3 children was the most common number in a family. In contrast, the mean, a more precise decimal number, might show a rise in average family size, such as from 2.8 to 3.3.

Comparing means, medians, and modes

23, 36, 42, 56, 57, 58, 59, 59, 59, 69, 99

- In this set, the mode—the number that occurs most frequently—is 59.
- The median—the number that falls in the middle place—is 58 (calculated on page 303).
- The mean—calculated by adding all of the items in the set (617) and dividing the sum by the number of items in the set (11)—is 56.

These are all accurate statistics, but they do not match. This is one reason why "statistics" sometimes seem to "lie." As arguments are often based on comparisons of averages, it is important to know:

- What was included in the data set? (For example, were all the test scores included, or were any omitted?)
- Which method of calculating the average was used? Is this kind of average suitable?
- Would a different method of calculating the average give a different outcome? (It might, depending on the numbers involved.)
- When averages are compared in an article or report, were these averages calculated using the same method, whether mean, mode or median? (Each average might be higher or lower, depending on the method used.)

Activity

Find the mean, median and mode for the following numbers. Consider how extreme values (unusually small or large numbers) affect each average.

a 1, 1, 1, 3, 3, 4, 7, 7, 10

b 28, 14, 21, 28, 26, 62

c 19, 170, 17, 19, 19, 16, 20

Answers are given on page 314.

Five-number summaries and quartiles

What is a five-number summary?

The numbers in a set may be similar and closely related, or they may be varied with features such as very high or low scores—*extreme values*—which are quite unlike the other numbers in the set. The variety of numbers and the way in which they are clustered or spread in a set is called the *distribution*.

If you know just an average number for a set and nothing else, you cannot tell anything about the distribution of numbers in the set and if it is in any way unusual. Are the data reliable, or might they be distorted or unrepresentative in some way? Can they be used as they are or do they need further investigation?

The effect of extreme values

Suppose, for instance, that in a group of 12 students (a small sample), 11 students received a test score of 72% and 1 student received just 3%. You might expect the average score for the whole group to be 72%—after all, that is what all but one of the students received. If the average used was the *mode*, it would be 72%. If the average used was the *mean*, however, it would be around 66%.

The single score of 3% in this set is an "extreme value": It skews the results for the set as a whole. When data sets are small, or when means are used, extreme values can be quite misleading. In larger samples, extreme values have less impact.

The five numbers

Extreme values are just one of the possible sources of distortion when one chooses a particular number to represent the whole group. To address such problems, statisticians have found that in describing a set it is helpful to state not just one number but five numbers.

First the numbers in the set are put in sequence, from the smallest to largest. Then five numbers can be recorded:

1 *Minimum number* The first in the sequence.
2 *Maximum number* The last in the sequence.
3 *Median* The mid-point of the sequence.
4 *Lower quartile (LQ)* The value one-quarter of the way along the sequence.
5 *Upper quartile (HQ)* The value three-quarters of the way along the sequence.

Summaries and averages

The table below shows a five-number summary. Consider this information compared to that provided by averages. It may help to note that:

- The mean for the scores, by calculation, is 64.67%. The mode is 79%.
- The mean is brought down by the 2 extreme values, 2% and 3%. It would otherwise have been 70.32% (1547/22).
- Without the 2 lowest and 2 highest scores, the mean is 68.25% (1365/20).

Example: a five-number summary

Below is a set of class exam scores for 24 students. These are placed in order, from lowest to highest, and the number of their place in the sequence is written below for ease of reference. The positions of the lower and upper quartiles must be calculated (as for medians: page 303).

Score (%)	2	3	40	47	56	58	60	61	64	65	66	67	67	68	76	78	79	79	79	82	86	87	90	92
Place	1	2	3	4	5	6	7	8	9	10	11	12	13	14	15	16	17	18	19	20	21	22	23	24

Minimum	Lower quartile (LQ)	Median	Upper quartile (UQ)	Maximum
1st place	The value midway between the 5th and 6th places	The average of the 12th and 13th places	The value mid-way between the 18th and 19th places	24th place
= 2	= 57	= 67.5	= 79.5	= 92

Using five-number summaries

Examples of five-number summaries

Class A

For Class A, a set of 11 test scores is:

23, 36, 42, 56, 57, 58, 59, 59, 59, 69, 99

The five-number summary for this set would be:

1 Minimum number   23
2 Lower quartile: LQ (3rd score)   42
3 Median number   58
4 Upper quartile: UQ (9th score)   59
5 Maximum number   99

Class B

For Class B, a set of 16 test scores is:

7, 27, 27, 27, 55, 55, 64, 65,
66, 66, 67, 68, 69, 70, 71, 78

The five-number summary for the set would be:

1 Minimum number   7
2 Lower quartile: LQ (4th score)   27
3 Median number (mean of 65 and 66)   65.5
4 Upper quartile: UQ (12th score)   68
5 Maximum number   78

Using the five-number summary

Consider Class B. If the only fact you knew about the scores for this class was that the *mode* (the most common score) was 27, you would gain a quite mistaken impression of the group's performance.

Even without a list of all the class scores, however, the five-number summary would give you a much more accurate picture. Looking at these five numbers only, you could see that the scores in the class were widely distributed, from 7 to 78, and that at least half the group must have scored 65.5% or higher.

Similarly, if you knew only that the mean was 55%, you would be unable to appreciate how well some students had done while others had struggled. The five-number summary makes the distribution clear.

The five-number summary thus gives a better "feel" for the whole set of numbers. When you have large sets of numbers, such a summary can be very useful.

Presenting five-number summaries

Five-number summaries can be used to compare two or more sets of data. The numbers can be presented in table form so that the equivalent numbers can be compared easily. For example, the two test scores for Classes A and B would be presented as below.

Table to compare test scores for Class A and Class B, using a five-number summary

Scores	Class A	Class B
Minimum number	23	7
Lower quartile (LQ)	42	27
Median number	58	65.5
Upper quartile (UQ)	59	68
Maximum number	99	78

Activity

Draw up five-number summaries for the following sets of numbers, as in the examples above.

a Set of class scores: 10, 31, 39, 45, 46, 47, 48, 55, 56, 57, 58, 59, 61, 63, 64, 65, 66, 67, 68, 69, 71

b Number of pets per household: 0, 0, 0, 0, 0, 0, 0, 0, 1, 1, 1, 1, 1, 1, 1, 2, 2, 2, 2, 2, 2, 2, 3, 3, 4, 4, 5, 17

c Life expectancy for males in sample families (in years): 32, 39, 41, 56, 58, 64, 65, 67, 69, 70, 71, 71, 73, 73, 73, 73, 74, 77, 77, 78, 81, 84, 89, 92

Answers are given on page 314.

Using tables, charts, and graphs

Tables, charts and graphs provide a kind of visual shorthand—they condense complex information and present it clearly.

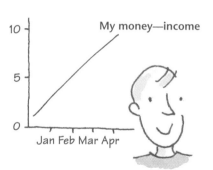

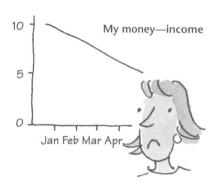

Why use tables, graphs and charts?

- Good tables and charts present information in clear, orderly, systematic ways.
- You can "see" key information more quickly than when you read it as text.
- You can see relationships, detect patterns and trends and draw comparisons easily.
- You may find visual information easier to interpret.
- You may see aspects to tables and charts that their authors did not see—that is, you may bring an additional interpretation.

Read the labels

Headings and labels help you to interpret the data appropriately.

- *Headings* Read the main headings carefully. Note each word or phrase, and be sure you know exactly what the graph or table is meant to represent.
- *Labels* Read the labels on rows and columns, axes and lines. These should tell you precisely what each represents.
- *Key* If color, shading or symbols are used,

look for the key that explains how to interpret these. This is usually a box above, below or to the side of the table, and tells you the meaning of each color, shading type or symbol.

Take time; be systematic

Each table presents information differently, so take time to understand what the table is showing you.

- Familiarize yourself with the style, symbols and measurements.
- Note dates and the source of information.
- Work your way systematically along each row, column, line and so on.
- Keep checking back to the key and the measurements.
- Work out amounts. Look at any "totals" that are presented—what do these tell you?

Just one word can change the meaning of the graph

Interpreting graphs

Why use graphs?

Graphs are useful in indicating trends, including how one aspect, or *variable*, changes in relation to another. For example, a graph might show:

- how income rises or falls over time, or in relation to a factor such as world oil prices
- how sales vary relative to cost
- how an insect population increases or decreases with seasonal temperature or rainfall.

Drawing graphs

A graph has two axes, horizontal and vertical. Each axis is divided into equal measures and labeled to specify the scale and unit of measurement being used, such as "Weight in ounces," "Volume in gallons," "Income in $1000s", or "Temperature in degrees Fahrenheit."

Reading graphs

Read all the textual information, such as headings, labels and units of measurement.

Follow one line on the graph. Track it in relation to measurements on the horizontal and vertical axes. From these measurements, note the changes as you move along a line.

Are there any sharp rises or falls? What do these suggest?

Heading
This should state exactly what the graph is meant to show, including dates.

Axis label
Each axis should be labeled to state exactly what it represents.

Vertical axis
This is divided into equal measures. (Here the axis scale marks intervals of $5000.)

Horizontal axis
This is divided into equal measures. (Here the axis scale marks intervals of 3 months.)

Source and date
The date and source of the information should be stated.

Labels or key
Lines are labeled or a key is used to indicate what each line represents.

Average earnings in Aremia, Jan.–Dec. 2011

Average income ($1000s)

Key:
- —— Women
- – – – Men
- ······· Whole

Source: Aremia Official Statistics, 2012

Horizontal axis: Jan, Apr, Jul, Oct, Dec
Vertical axis: 0, 5, 10, 15, 20, 25, 30, 35, 40, 45, 50

This graph

This graph indicates that in Aremia in 2011, women's average income was lower than men's average income, but that women's income was rising more quickly.

Activity

a What was the average salary for Aremian men in October?

b In which quarter did Aremian women's earnings rise above $20,000?

Answers are given on page 314.

Interpreting tables

The table below provides raw data for two student groups, A and B, with names, courses and test scores for 24 students. Examine the data to see what it tells you. For example, at first view, which course seems most popular? Which group does best in the test? Are these interpretations reliable?

Data set: 24 students' test scores, by subject and group (Aremia University, 2012)

Test scores for Group A

Student	Course	Test score	M/F
Belinda	Geology	67	F
Darren	Oriental Studies	41	M
Dilshad	History	54	F
Elizabeth	Math	64	F
Femi	English	61	M
Francis	Oriental Studies	60	M
Geraint	Psychology	65	M
Omar	Geology	67	M
Patrick	Geology	72	M
Rosa	Geology	71	F
Sunjit	Geology	54	M
Thandi	Geology	58	F

Test scores for Group B

Student	Course	Test score	M/F
Assunta	Politics	60	F
Chiara	Social Work	57	F
Diane	Math	55	F
Horace	Psychology	68	M
Joachim	Film	23	M
Joseph	Nursing	69	M
Kiran	Arabic	53	M
Natasha	Film	49	F
Niall	French	44	M
Otto	Physics	62	M
Soraya	Film	57	F
Zoe	Fine Art	31	F

A set of only 24 students is unlikely to be representative of a large college population. You probably noticed that the most popular course overall is Geology, selected by 6 of the 24 students (25%, or 1/4 of students). Unless this is a specialist college, it is unlikely that a quarter of the students all study one subject.

If we looked only at the data for Group B, it would seem that Film was the most popular course and as if nobody studied Geology. Each group shows considerable variation in subject choice. With only one or two students taking each subject, in most cases, the sample size is too small for us to make generalizations about subject popularity.

These data on program choices are unstable—if we were to add data about additional groups, it is likely that the proportions who had chosen each subject would change.

The mean test score overall for each group would allow one comparison between the groups. The total score for Group A is 734 and there are 12 students, so the mean score is 734/12 = 61. The total score for Group B is 628: The mean score is 628/12 = 52.

This is a big difference between the two groups. To interpret these data, you would need to know more. For example:

- How were these two groups selected?
- How do scores for these groups compare with those for the university overall?
- Does the high number of geologists in Group A distort the data?
- Are there other particular differences between the two groups, such as the proportions of men and women or the proportion working part-time? Do these differences affect group scores?

You would also want to know what was being tested. For example, if the test was in geology, we would expect the geologists' scores to be higher!

Interpreting charts

Showing relationships

Tables, graphs and charts can be used to present two or more sets of information in a way that makes it easier to see how one set of information relates to the other, to find patterns and trends and to draw comparisons.

Bar charts

Bar charts contain less detail than tables, but summarize data in a way that makes it easier to read.

For example, the chart below presents the average score for two student groups, A and B (page 309), and for their university as a whole. It breaks the data down to show the mean figures for whole sets and also separately for men and women. Note that the scores are shown from 50 upwards.

Mean test scores by group 2011–12

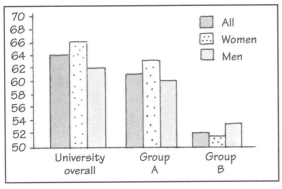

Source: Aremia Assessment Report, July 2012

Pie charts

Pie charts are useful in indicating the *relative proportions* of the various components that make up a whole. They cannot provide statistical precision, however.

Consider the information about the courses taken by two groups of students (page 309). The pie charts below compare the data for the 24 students with data for the college as a whole.

Distribution of students by subject, 2011–12

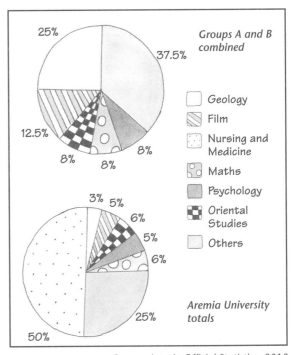

Source: Aremia Official Statistics, 2012

Activity

From the bar chart above, is Group A or Group B more representative of the university as a whole?

How do mean average scores for these groups compare with those for the university overall?

Answers are given on page 314.

Activity

Examine the two pie charts. In what ways were the 24 students representative or unrepresentative of the whole university?

Answers are given on page 314.

Technical terms

Average A number that is in some way "typical" of a group of numbers and that can be used to "represent" them. What is meant by "typical" depends on the context, and three kinds of average are commonly used: *mean, mode* and *median.* (See below and pages 301–304.)

Data "Data" is the plural of the Latin word *datum* (meaning "something given"). Data are facts, observations and measurements; collectively data provide information. Numerical data are collected by sorting, measuring and counting. For example, measurements of people's heights and weights, or of sales or industrial production, or even of conditions on Mars, all provide numerical data.

Data set A complete collection of information on a particular topic. For example, all the data collected in a survey of transport in Baltimore, Pittsburgh or Detroit would together provide the data set for that survey.

Denominator The bottom number in a fraction (see pages 295–296).

Elements The basic categories of data used for collection, counting and analysis, such as "Income," "Pieces of broken pottery," "Respondents to the survey about font styles."

Extreme values Numbers that are much lower or much higher than the rest of the set. For instance, in the set 16, 55, 56, 56, 56, 57, 59, 61, 61, 63, 64, 68, 88, the numbers 16 and 88 would be "extreme values."

Mean The middle point of a sequence. This is the usual meaning of the word "average" in everyday conversation. (Calculation of the mean is explained on page 302.)

Median The middle number in a sequence: One way of expressing an average. (Calculation of the median is explained on page 303.)

Mode The number in a set that occurs most often: one way of expressing an average. (Calculation of the mode is explained on page 304.)

Numerator The top number in a fraction (see pages 295–296).

Percentage The number of occurrences in each 100 instances. For example, suppose 25 out of every 50 people are able to swim. The same proportion can be given as 50 people in each group of 100 people: "50 percent" or "50%." (Calculation of percentages is explained on page 299.)

Prime numbers Numbers that, without resulting in a fraction, can be divided *only* by themselves or by the number 1. For example, the number 7 can be divided only by 1 or by 7—division by any other number gives a fraction. The same is true of 3, 5, 11, 13, 17, etc.

Qualitative data Information that comprises subjective descriptions rather than objective measurements. For example, a survey of pets might record owners' reasons for choosing a particular animal and how they feel about their pet. (See page 270.)

Quantitative data Information that comprises objective measurements rather than subjective descriptions. For example, a survey of pets might count the number of each kind of animal, and the annual cost of keeping it. (See page 270.)

Raw data The basic information as collected, with no interpretation. (See page 309.)

Rounding "up" or "down" Replacing a number with a simpler number that is no longer as accurate but is easier to work with. (See page 300.)

Statistics Sets of data, and techniques for working with them. (See page 293.)

Variables The aspects of the elements (or countable items) that may differ from one item or group to another. For example, a shopping survey might consider the kinds of product bought, the quantity of each, the number of shopping trips each week, the amount spent, the age and gender of the shopper and so on.

Vulgar fraction Another name for a fraction (see page 295).

Review

This chapter has provided information about, and practice in, several aspects of working with numbers. The areas covered—such as working with fractions, calculating averages, and interpreting graphs and charts—challenge many students at times, even when they are good at other aspects of number work. Although the necessary mathematical operations are not particularly difficult to learn, they are easy to forget if you do not use them regularly.

Here are some key messages from the chapter:

- You can overcome obstacles and barriers to using numbers, even if you have found these difficult in the past.
- Numbers must be *interpreted*—in themselves, they provide no authority.
- In using numbers to find answers or make interpretations, you can be much more confident if you:

  – don't rush at the task
  – take time to absorb what is required
  – work systematically through a sequence of steps or rules for working out the right answer
  – check your answers repeatedly
  – practice often the numerical operations and tasks that are relevant to your program.

- Words can be just as important as the numbers themselves. Make sure you read the instructions, labels, headings, explanations and any other verbal information carefully.

If specialist techniques or statistical software packages are required for your course, your college is likely to provide sessions that explain how to use these. To cope with these more specialist areas of your program, however, you will probably need first to be able to understand and perform the basic numerical functions outlined in this chapter.

Answers for Chapter 13

Using fractions (page 297)

1 a $^1/_5$
   b $^2/_3$ ($^{22}/_{33}$) is bigger than $^7/_{11}$ ($^{21}/_{33}$)
   c $^4/_7$ ($^{36}/_{63}$) is bigger than $^5/_9$ ($^{35}/_{63}$)
   d $^4/_5$ ($^{24}/_{30}$) is smaller than $^5/_6$ ($^{25}/_{30}$)

2 a $^1/_3$ and $^1/_2 = ^2/_6 + ^3/_6 = ^5/_6$
   b $^1/_6$ and $^1/_8 = ^4/_{24} + ^3/_{24}$
      $= ^7/_{24}$
   c $^1/_2$ and $^5/_6 = ^3/_6 + ^5/_6 = ^8/_6$
      $= 1^2/_6 = 1^1/_3$
   d $^1/_4$ and $^2/_3 = ^3/_{12} + ^8/_{12}$
      $= ^{11}/_{12}$
   e $^2/_7$ and $^3/_5$
      $= ^{10}/_{35} + ^{21}/_{35} = ^{31}/_{35}$
   f $^1/_9$ and $^3/_4 = ^4/_{36} + ^{27}/_{36}$
      $= ^{31}/_{36}$

3 a $^2/_3$ of $750:
      $750/3 = 250$
      $250 \times 2 = 500$
   b $^3/_4$ of 160:
      $160/4 = 40$
      $40 \times 3 = 120$
   c $^5/_6$ of 72:
      $72/6 = 12$
      $12 \times 5 = 60$
   d $^2/_9$ of 81:
      $81/9 = 9$
      $9 \times 2 = 18$
   e $^3/_5$ of 620:
      $620/5 = 124$
      $124 \times 3 = 372$
   f $^2/_7$ of 91:
      $91/7 = 13$
      $13 \times 2 = 26$

4 a $^1/_2 = 100$:
      $100 \times 2 = 200$
   b $^1/_4 = 100$:
      $100 \times 4 = 400$
   c $^1/_3 = 50$:
      $50 \times 3 = 150$
   d $^2/_3 = 50$:
      $^1/_3 = 50/2 = 25$
      $25 \times 3 = 75$
   e $^3/_4 = 120$:
      $^1/_4 = 120/3 = 40$
      $40 \times 4 = 160$
   f $^1/_7 = 10$:
      $7 \times 10 = 70$
   g $^2/_7 = 10$:
      $^1/_7 = 10/2 = 5$
      $5 \times 7 = 35$

h $4/5 = 20$
 $1/5 = 20/4 = 5$
 $5 \times 5 = 25$

5 a $1/2 \times 1/2 = 1/4$
b $1/2 \times 1/4 = 1/8$
c $1/4 \times 1/4 = 1/16$

d $1/3 \times 1/3 = 1/9$
e $1/3 \times 1/2 = 1/6$
f $2/3 \times 1/2 = 2/6 = 1/3$

Calculating percentages from fractions: 1 (page 299)

a $4/8 = 50\%$
b $44/88 = 50\%$
c $19/56 = 33\%$
d $76/145 = 52\%$
e $9/11 = 81\%$
f $196/567 = 34\%$

g $11/91 = 12\%$
h $128/256 = 50\%$
i $117/327 = 35\%$
j $67/84 = 79\%$
k $87/181 = 48\%$
l $12/96 = 12\%$

m $667/713 = 93\%$
n $19/38 = 50\%$
o $765/999 = 76\%$
p $65/230 = 28\%$

Calculating percentages from fractions: 2 (page 299)

a 6 of the 11 plants are deciduous: 54.5% are deciduous; 45.5% are not. (54.5 + 45.5 = 100%.)

b 41 out of 230 children in the school have reading difficulties: 17.8% have reading difficulties; 82.1% do not have reading difficulties. (17.8% + 82.1% =

99.9%: The numbers are rounded down slightly.)

c 23,456 of the town population went to see the movie out of a population of 234,560: 10% percentage of the town saw the movie; 90% did not. (10% + 90% = 100%.)

d 873 of 9,786 participants took part in the competition online, 2,314 by texting, the rest by phone-in: 8.9% took part online; 23.6% by texting. 8.9% + 23.6% = 32.5%. The percentage who took part by phone-in is 100% − 32.5% = 67.5%.

Rounding up and down (page 300)

a $41.34675 \rightarrow 41.3$
b $912.172 \rightarrow 912.2$
c $22.222 \rightarrow 22.2$

d $99.88 \rightarrow 99.9$
e $1.714 \rightarrow 1.7$
f $10.08 \rightarrow 10.1$

g $66.55 \rightarrow 66.6$
h 6.1098

Calculating averages: the mean (page 302)

a $1 + 2 + 3 + 5 + 6 + 7 + 8 + 9 + 11 + 15 + 17 = 84$
Mean = $84/11 = 7.6$

b $234 + 19 + 1 + 66 + 2002 + 7 = 2329$
Mean = $2329/6 = 388.2$

c $7 + 7 + 6 + 8 + 9 + 8 + 11 + 7 + 6 + 11 + 2 + 14 + 5 = 101$
Mean = $101/13 = 7.8$

d $11 + 22 + 33 + 44 + 55 + 66 + 77 + 88 + 99 + 111 = 606$
Mean = $606/10 = 60.6$

e $7 + 14 + 19 + 8 + 6 + 11 + 21 + 32 + 8 + 19 + 21 + 5 = 171$
Mean = $171/12 = 14.3$

f $23 + 36 + 42 + 56 + 57 + 58 + 59 + 59 + 59 + 69 + 69 = 587$
Mean = $587/11 = 53.4$

Calculating averages: the median (page 303)

a 1, 2, 3, 5, 6, 7, 8, 9, 11, 15, 17
Median = 7

b 234, 19, 1, 66, 2002, 7
$19 + 66 = 85$
Median = $85/2 = 42.5$

c 7, 7, 6, 8, 9, 8, 11, 7, 6, 11, 2, 14, 5
Median = 7

d 11, 22, 33, 44, 55, 66, 77, 88, 99, 111
55 + 66 = 121
Median = 121/2 = 60.5

e 7, 14, 19, 8, 6, 11, 21, 32, 8, 19, 21, 5
11 + 14 = 25
Median = 25/2 = 12.5

f 23, 36, 42, 56, 57, 58, 59, 59, 59, 69, 69
Median = 58

Comparing means, medians, and modes (page 304)

a 1, 1, 1, 3, 3, 4, 7, 7, 10
Mean = 37/9 = 4.1
Median = 3 (mid-point)
Mode =1
Note the impact of a small minority of scores of 1 on the mode and on the mean.

b 28, 14, 21, 28, 26, 62
Mean = 179/6 = 29.8
Median = 27
Mode = 28
The extreme value (62) makes little noticeable difference.

c 19, 170, 17, 19, 19, 16, 20
Mean = 280/7 = 40
Median = 19
Mode =19
The extreme value (170) makes no difference to the mode or median but distorts the mean.

Using five-number summaries (page 306)

a Set of class scores: 10, 31, 39, 45, 46, 47, 48, 55, 56, 57, 58, 59, 61, 63, 64, 65, 66, 67, 68, 69, 71
Five-number summary:
10; 46.5; 58; 64.5; 71.

b Number of pets per household: 0, 0, 0, 0, 0, 0, 0, 0, 1, 1, 1, 1, 1, 1, 1, 2, 2, 2, 2, 2, 2, 2, 3, 3, 4, 4, 5,17
Five-number summary:
0; 0; 1; 2; 17.

c Life expectancy for males in sample families (in years): 32, 39, 41, 56, 58, 64, 65, 67, 69, 70, 71, 71, 73, 73, 73, 73, 74, 77, 77, 78, 81, 84, 89, 92
Five-number summary:
32; 64; 71; 77; 92.

Interpreting graphs (page 308)

a What was the average salary for Aremian men in October?
Answer: $40,000.

b In which quarter did Aremian women's earnings rise above $20,000?
Answer: July–October.

Interpreting charts: 1 (page 310)

Group A's scores are closer to those of the university as a whole, so are more representative than those for group B. The pattern of scores is also more similar for group A and the university overall. In group B, men's scores are relatively higher than the women's. This is not typical of the university overall.

Interpreting charts: 2 (page 310)

The 24 students in the two groups are not representative of the whole university in that the pattern of subject choices is very different. For example, none of the students in these groups study nursing and medicine, whereas these are the main subjects studied overall. On the other hand, geology is the main subject studied in the two groups (25%), but a small proportion in the university overall. Of students in Groups A and B, 12.5% studied Film compared to only 5% for the university overall.

Chapter 14

Research projects, reports, and case studies

This chapter offers you opportunities to:

- understand what is required for undergraduate research projects, reports and case studies

- understand the role of independent study in such assignments

- make negotiated independent study work for you

- clarify the similarities and differences among research papers, reports and research projects

- develop a research strategy for your project

- identify the main sections of reports and research projects

- identify the different kinds of writing style required for various sections of a report.

reliance. Because of this, you may find that a successful outcome in these is all the more satisfying.

A bachelor's essay, capstone or research project is a larger-scale project that, depending on your institution, may be optional or compulsory. It will almost certainly be the largest piece of work you undertake as an undergraduate. It combines some aspects of report writing and some aspects of writing research papers. Because they combine so many skills, research projects and larger assignments are likely to be set towards the *end* of your program. Earlier smaller-scale projects will allow you to develop the skills and approaches you will need for research projects and larger assignments, and also to develop more general project-management skills.

As a student, you may be asked to undertake a variety of assignments, such as reports, case studies or larger-scale study projects. If there are opportunities to pursue an independent or group project, such as a bachelor's essay, a capstone or research project related to your major, consider them seriously. Although they can be demanding, they give you practice in applying a range of research, computer and people skills (as covered in other chapters). They also help you to develop a range of writing, numerical, organizational and project management skills.

Research projects and report-based assignments often require you to work more independently than when writing papers. They are a good test of your problem-solving skills, resourcefulness and self-

The key advantages of these kinds of assignments are outlined below, along with strategies for addressing some of the potential pitfalls. This chapter looks at ways of gathering different kinds of evidence, managing the task and writing up a project of your own. It suggests strategies for managing independent study successfully. Your instructors are likely to inform you of any further discipline-specific requirements for your project, for example, in relation to structure or methodology.

What is a project?

Characteristics of projects

Projects share the following characteristics.

- *Unique* A project is always unique. Each project has a specific purpose or brief.
- *Informed* A project is based on research.
- *Focused* A project focuses on one topic in depth.
- *Set apart, yet relevant* A project is usually outside of the usual patterns of study or work.
- *Time-bound* A project must be completed within a given time.
- *Managed* Carrying out a project will require good organization, planning and time management.

Unique

In each project, there will be some aspect—the subject matter, the client group, the data or the finished product—that will make this project different from everybody else's. Your instructors will be looking to see that your work is *original*. This may simply mean that you:

- tested out other people's findings for yourself
- conducted a questionnaire or survey so that you could work from your own data
- applied existing research to a new area.

Informed

Although your project will be "unique" in the ways described above, your instructors will want to see that you have used previous research to inform your own project. Your project report should indicate how you drew upon previously published materials and well-tried methods in shaping your own project. It should make clear how your own project has built on previous research or projects.

Focused

Make sure that your project brief is manageable. Choose a subject that can reasonably be researched and completed within the set time and page limits. If necessary, narrow down the topic to make the workload more realistic. Avoid large subjects that can only be covered in a superficial way within the time limit.

Identify your key questions, so that you have a clear goal. Your instructors will want to see that you can design a manageable, focused project, using an appropriate methodology. Avoid collecting and including material that, though interesting, is not directly related to the project goal.

Set apart yet relevant

Projects are usually one-time pieces of work, related to the overall program or major but covering ground chosen by the student. Make clear to your instructor how the subject you have chosen is relevant to your program: to work covered in class and to class texts.

Time-bound

Projects are often larger pieces of work than research papers, with higher word or page limits and taking more time to complete. The time allocations for projects tend therefore to be greater than for papers. However, there is usually more work to do than with a paper, so the work must be carefully planned and managed.

Managed

Projects usually require that you think and plan ahead. You will need to pay attention to small details. For example, you may need to book rooms or resources well in advance, ensure that participants are available, design materials and so on. These tasks are not necessarily difficult, but they require time and good planning.

Typically, projects require you to:

- make a good choice of subject
- identify appropriate methods, including ways of recording your data
- identify the people, places and materials to use
- break the project down into manageable tasks
- produce a report
- complete the project brief on time.

What is a "research project"?

A bachelor's essay, capstone or research project is an extended piece of writing based on broader reading and research than is typical of individual research papers or reports. A research project is an opportunity for you to:

- undertake a substantial piece of independent academic study
- pursue in much greater depth a relevant topic that interests you
- develop a personal specialism
- put your personal stamp on a piece of work
- explore the literature on your chosen topic
- refine and extend your skills in finding, selecting and critically analyzing information
- refine your skills in decision-making, task management and problem-solving
- refine skills in summarizing and presenting findings.

Differences between research projects and other academic tasks

- *Independence* You have more control over the nature and scope of your project.

- *Personal involvement* A research project requires a high level of personal commitment. You will probably become very involved in the task and take pride in the finished product. Choose a topic that really interests you.
- *Time* As this is a major piece of writing, all of your time may be dedicated simply to the research project. Your study time may be structured differently than for other aspects of your program.
- *Self-management and motivation* You are likely to work more on your own. You will need strategies to keep you motivated and on time with your schedule.
- *Literature search* This is more extensive than for other academic work. You need to read more and to summarize it concisely. As you read, make accurate and well organized records so that later you do not waste time searching for details or references you want to use.
- *Presentation* Your research project should be carefully proofread and attractively finished, ready for the library shelf. You may also be asked to give a formal oral presentation on your project.

Chapter 14

Similarities between research projects and other academic tasks

Research papers	Project work	Reports
Like a research paper, a research project: - follows the basic procedure for writing assignments (Chapters 11 and 12) - adheres to academic conventions (see pages 265–6) - involves research skills (Chapter 5) - includes continuous prose within most sections - requires analytical and critical reading and writing skills.	Like project work, a research project: - requires strategy and management - requires a systematic methodology - uses data you have collected yourself - is unique—nobody else will have covered exactly the same ground or be using the same data - is a one-time, time-bound task - uses new material or approaches that you have devised, to test out theories, hypotheses or methodologies from your subject discipline.	Like a report, a research project: - includes an abstract (see page 331) - has many of the features of a report (see page 327) - is structured in sections (page 328).

Independent study: benefits, challenges, risks

Benefits	Challenges	Risks
More control over your study time	■ To manage time effectively. ■ To meet deadlines.	Losing a sense of time. Wasting time. Underestimating how long study tasks take. Forgetting things that must be done. Missing essential deadlines.
More control over your free time	■ To use free time effectively in building your personal profile. ■ To recognize the difference between free time and independent study time. ■ To put time aside to relax, rest and enjoy yourself.	Using all your free time for study. Mistaking time not spent in taught sessions as "free time." Missing opportunities to develop a wider personal profile that will benefit you later when applying for jobs.
More choice about when and where to study	■ To create structures for your day. ■ To organize a place to study. ■ To work out the best places and times for you for different kinds of study activity.	Not getting down to study. Not creating a place that allows you to study without interruption.
More choice about how you study	■ To identify your learning style for different types of tasks. ■ To take responsibility for your learning and achieving your goals.	Not bothering to explore and develop your learning style. Doing what you enjoy most rather than what works best for you, if these are different.
More responsibility for your own successes	■ To identify barriers to your learning and to address these. ■ To identify ways of improving your own performance. ■ To make effective use of feedback and to learn from mistakes.	Failure to understand previous barriers to learning. Not addressing weaknesses in your performance. Giving up too easily. Ignoring feedback. Becoming despondent at early failures rather than using these to guide improvement.
More choice about how much energy you devote to topics that interest you	■ To find the right balance between a broad set of interests at a superficial level and too much depth in a narrow range of topics. ■ To broaden your range of interests.	Devoting too much time to topics that interest you at the expense of those needed to complete the program. Becoming specialized in too narrow a range of topics.
There isn't a teacher looking over your shoulder all the time	■ To keep on target with little guidance. ■ To keep yourself motivated. ■ To take responsibility for pursuing solutions to problems on your own. ■ To recognize when you need help and to ask for it.	Letting things slip. Falling behind in your work. Losing motivation. Losing a sense of what you are supposed to do. Not asking for help, not finding out what help is available or not using it. Running for help too soon instead of trying to solve the problem yourself.
More control over choice of topics	■ To create a coherent program of study that interests you and meets your goals.	Choosing topics that do not fit together well or that do not contribute towards your goals.

Managing projects and other independent study

Higher education provides opportunities for demonstrating that you have the intellectual and personal maturity to take charge of an area of academic study alone or with other students. This requires good management skills.

Manage the scale

- Choose a manageable project (see page 320).
- Ensure a clear focus. When working independently, it is all the more important to identify what is *core* to the assignment, and what are interesting but *peripheral* issues.
- Check the level descriptors and/or grading criteria to ensure that your planned assignment will meet these.
- Choose your topic to reflect the scale of the project (see page 320 and Chapter 11).

Manage your time (see also Chapter 4)

- A key risk with independent study is to assume there is plenty of time to settle into the project.
- Start early—don't wait to get started.
- Consider your options, but choose your subject quickly. Don't wait until you have done the research: Narrow your focus early, then conduct your research in line with your selected focus.
- Once you have chosen a topic, stay with it unless serious problems arise.

Contact your research advisor

You will have access to a research advisor or faculty mentor to support you.

- Don't wait for them to contact you: Make contact at agreed, regular intervals.
- If you feel you are getting into difficulties, ask to see your advisor.

Your advisor will probably have only a small allocation of time for each student, so you need to plan how to make best use of the time available:

- Do as much as you can before contacting your research advisor.
- If you find something difficult, experiment with solving the problem before contacting your research advisor. Be prepared to talk through what has and hasn't worked so far.
- Prepare a list of questions in advance. Put these questions in order of priority.
- Your advisor knows the field: use her or him for advice on the best resources.
- Listen to what your research advisor says, and follow the advice or guidance you are given.

Draw on existing academic skills

Use the skills you have acquired through other kinds of assignment, which will carry you a long way:

- Maintain high motivation (page 86).
- Read in a focused, strategic way (Chapter 5).
- Collect, select and organize information, applying effective search skills (Chapters 5 and 6).
- Apply number skills as needed (Chapters 13 and 14).
- Analyze your material in a critical way (Chapters 5, 6 and 7).
- Apply your writing skills, acknowledging your source materials, and compile a list of references (Chapters 5, 11, 12).

Maintain contact; use support

- Maintain contact with other students.
- Organize a support group (page 225).
- Contact other students, even if they are not studying by independent study; share ideas and experiences.
- Check if there are lectures relevant to your assignment that you could attend. These might provide valuable background information and also fire your interest and imagination.

Choosing the topic

Choosing the *subject* is the most important aspect of project and research project management. The larger the project, the more important it is to decide an appropriate *topic* early on.

Advancing knowledge and understanding

Reports and research projects are expected to advance, in some small way, knowledge and understanding of an issue, methodology or application. When choosing your topic, be prepared to answer this question: "In what way will this research add to what is known about this subject?" It takes time, thought and research to identify a new angle.

Small is beautiful

Some students have difficulties with reports and research projects because they choose a subject which:

- is too broad and that might take years to complete well
- lacks a research basis—you need to build upon what has gone before
- is too ambitious in attempting new ground—you need to be realistic: A topic is "original" even if it is a replication of previous research or varies in just one aspect.

Spot the niche

Brainstorm an initial list of potential topics. After some initial research, narrow this down to what is feasible. Select a topic:

- that interests you
- for which there are some gaps in the research (indicated by professors or your own reading)
- that relates to your town, your background, your year group or some other area you know well or can access easily
- that will be advantageous to your academic or career prospects.

Build on what has gone before

Select a topic:

- that is already well researched
- in which your professors have expertise
- in which there are well-established research methodologies and techniques
- to which you can bring a slightly different perspective (for example, where you might replicate a piece of research using a new client group or in a related area, or with a small modification)
- in which there are limited ethical and financial considerations.

Start early on a list of potential topics

Specify your research question

- As you research the literature, narrow down your focus until you settle on the exact topic about which you will write. Do this as early as you can.
- Clarify one or two main questions that your research project will address. What kind of answers are you looking for?

Although you will still focus on addressing key questions, your title may be more open-ended than for a research paper. It may sound more like a statement than a question. For example:

- "The effects of local flooding on small businesses in Smalltown."
- "The application of ABC techniques to stimulate nitrogen fixation in leguminous plants."
- "Using XYZ software to improve athletic performance."

Developing a research strategy

Aspects of a research strategy

A research strategy consists of:

- planning
- a literature search
- the research hypothesis
- a literature review
- research design or methodology
- collecting, collating and analyzing data
- drawing conclusions
- writing a report.

Planning

Research projects require good management.

- Draw up an action plan (pages 16 and 334–335).
- Set clear targets and milestones (page 69).
- Get support—find people who will motivate you and share ideas (page 225).
- Leave lots of time for editing, printing, copying and binding the final report.

Read the assignment brief carefully

Your instructors will guide you on how to approach the project. Check:

- the word or page length required
- the deadline
- any restrictions on what topics can be covered
- if you need approval from your college's institutional review board (IRB) or other ethics committee to conduct the research
- guidance on useful source materials and methods
- how the final draft must be presented.

Use your research advisor effectively

Research advisors or faculty mentors are there primarily to guide you.

- Check early on that you are on the right track: A large project is harder to turn around later.
- Take advice about the topic.
- Take advice on appropriate reading.
- Take advice on the methods to use.
- Find out what software is available to analyze data and where you can learn to use this.
- Check that you are working to the right scale. Is your project too ambitious? Is it challenging enough?

Literature search

- Allocate time to browse titles in the library catalogs. Check that there is sufficient relevant and up-to-date material that you can obtain easily.
- Browse through student research projects in your college library or online. Develop a feel for what is a suitable project for your subject, taking account of the page limit.
- Read the abstracts of a range of journal articles. Identify which would be most relevant to read later in full.
- Identify key articles, chapters of books, conference papers, websites and other materials.
- Look for ideas on methods you could adapt.
- Gradually focus your reading on a specific topic. Take clear notes. Keep a list of details for your reference list (pages 112–114).

The research hypothesis

Most academic reports include a "hypothesis." Your hypothesis, formed *before* you start the research, states what you *expect* will happen. It is useful in giving you a clear focus when deciding exactly what to read, measure and report. See page 329.

Literature review

- Read selected information, critically evaluating what you read (Chapter 7).
- Look for "chains": How does one piece of research or set of ideas give rise to the next? Trace briefly how a subject developed over time.
- Write brief notes about the development of the research on that topic until now. Note the key 5–10 pieces of research that have had most influence on the subject. Chart briefly how each piece of research influenced others in the chain.
- Identify how your project will follow on from what has gone before. What will it add to knowledge about the topic or methods?
- Write this up in your introduction.

Research design or methodology

The research design refers to the way in which you will conduct your research. This includes matters such as:

- the information and data you need
- ways of collecting this
- if relevant, the number and type of people you want to interview or to take part in experiments
- what, exactly, you want those people to do
- how you will design questions to achieve only the exact data you need.

Most research projects use data that you have generated or collected yourself, through observation, experiment, questionnaire or similar. Alternatively, however, you may use printed materials (such as government data or historical sources) and consider these from a new perspective.

Each subject has its own conventions about acceptable research methods. Your instructors will give you details of these. Journal articles will give you a good feel for how material and data are generated and analyzed in your subject. However, basic principles—of being accurate, as objective as possible and avoiding distortion—are common to most subjects (see page 245 and Chapter 7).

Collecting, collating and analyzing data

Plan to collect enough data to achieve convincing and reliable results. Collecting and analyzing data are time-consuming tasks, however, so take advice on what is the acceptable minimum for your subject. Having too much data is not helpful for student projects: It simply means that time is wasted in collecting, sorting and selecting from information that you cannot use.

Design forms to collect information in a way that helps you collate it quickly (pages 323–324). Once you have collected your information, organize it into charts or tables so that you can interpret it. Look for patterns and trends. Make relevant comparisons. Your instructors will be looking to see how well you make sense of your findings.

Drawing conclusions

Identify whether the research hypothesis was supported or not. If not, are there any evident reasons for this? Make recommendations, if these are required.

Writing a report

Write sections of the report as you complete each set of related tasks. Different sections of reports require different writing styles—further details are given on pages 329–331.

Designing questionnaires

Designing questionnaires

Many student projects involve questionnaires or surveys. Well-worded questions are at the heart of good research. Different kinds of questions are useful for research based on *quantitative* research, for which precise numbers are required, and for *qualitative* research. (For the difference between these two types of research, see pages 269–272.)

Questions for quantitative research

For quantitative research, a small number (2–5 simple questions), if asked of a large number of people (at least 30), can deliver manageable but significant results.

To get useful answers:

- Set short, clear, unambiguous questions.
- Set a small number of key questions, carefully chosen to deliver the information you actually need.
- Avoid personal questions or questions that might embarrass or distress the interviewee.
- Check that each question is a single question. (Avoid asking "two questions in one.")
- Use closed questions that give "yes/no" answers or a response that you can count. This will make it easier for you to record and analyze the answers.
- Ensure that questions cannot be misinterpreted. To check, try them out on friends or family first.
- Select a representative sample of people, appropriate to the project brief.
- Use controlled conditions, so you know exactly how the questions were delivered and who answered them.

Examples of well-structured questions

- Which font style do you prefer? *Answer "sample 1," "sample 2" or "no preference."*
- Are you a member of staff? *Yes/No*
- How often do use this bus?
  a) Every day   b) About once a week
  c) About once a month   d) Hardly ever

Activity

Poor questionnaire technique

What is wrong with the following questions?

1 How old are you? Please circle one of the following: *0–20 20–40 40–60*

2 Do you know who is the current government secretary?

3 Do you believe in capital punishment? *Yes/No*

4 Do you like coming onto campus and eating in the café?

(For feedback, see page 338.)

Using scales

One way of collecting data is by giving participants a list of statements and asking them to circle the responses they prefer. Alternatively, you can ask participants to rate responses on a scale, such as the Likert-type scale in the example below.

Example of a scaled question

Please indicate your opinion of this vacation resort on a scale of 1–5, where 1 is very poor and 5 is very good.

	Very poor				Very good
Quality of hotels	1	2	3	4	5
Local transport	1	2	3	4	5
Cleanliness	1	2	3	4	5
Things for children to do	1	2	3	4	5
Shopping	1	2	3	4	5

Alternatively, each of your questions could be followed by a scale that people check. For example:

Strongly agree	Agree	Neither agree nor disagree	Disagree	Strongly disagree
☐	☐	☐	☐	☐

Chapter **14**

Preparation

If you wish participants to complete the questionnaire themselves, then plan carefully how it looks on paper or electronically.

- Leave lots of space to answer questions.
- Include a maximum of five questions.
- Bear in mind that most people will respond only to "yes/no" or "check the box" questions. (Very few people write comments.)
- Postal surveys attract a very low response rate—and you do not know who has actually completed the returned surveys.
- SurveyMonkey is a useful tool for developing quantitative surveys that participants can easily access and complete online.

Record responses

- Keep accurate records.
- Order your findings into tables.
- Devise a simple tool to collect your responses.

The following table would allow a researcher undertaking face-to-face surveys to record quickly and clearly which font style is preferred, according to status and gender, for each participant.

Preferences for samples of font style		
	Female	Male
Sample 1		
Sample 2		
No preference		✓
Staff (student)		

(This answer is from a male student with no preference.)

If you are using SurveyMonkey, responses will be recorded automatically and you will be able to access a detailed overview of the results.

Questions for qualitative research

In qualitative research, typically only one or two people or items can be included in a student project. However, a good questioning technique will usually encourage interviewees to express themselves in detail.

Prepare prompts that politely encourage the interviewee to return to the subject you want to discuss. For example:

- I'd like to ask you more about a point you mentioned earlier …
- That's very helpful. Thank you. I'd also like to ask you about …

A few open-ended questions will usually deliver a lot of material. This material will take considerable time to analyze. For qualitative research:

- *Good questions are open-ended.* Most encourage a response other than a simple "yes" or "no."
- *Good questions are focused.* They encourage the interviewee to respond on the issue you are researching.
- *Good questions invite respondents to consider an issue from different angles.* For example, "What were the advantages of taking part in the pilot study?" and "What were the disadvantages?"
- *Good questions are free of bias.* They do not lead the interviewee to a particular answer (as do "I suppose you think taking part was a bad idea?" or "I hear you are glad you took part?")

Evaluate your questionnaire

- ☐ How long will it take to complete?
- ☐ Is that time reasonable?
- ☐ Will it give the exact data I need?
- ☐ Is every question necessary?
- ☐ Is every question a single question?
- ☐ Will people understand the questions?
- ☐ Could any question be interpreted in a way other than the one I intended?
- ☐ Are there any leading questions?
- ☐ Are there sufficient options to enable people to make accurate responses?
- ☐ Will the layout of the questionnaire encourage people to complete it?
- ☐ Will responses be easy to record?
- ☐ Will responses be easy to analyze?

Interview techniques

Prepare for the interview

Good preparation helps to ensure that you remain in control of the interview, keeping it focused and limited to a reasonable length.

- Prepare your questions in advance.
- Consider how you will introduce yourself at the start of the interview. This must be clear but brief: You must state that this is a student project or name any company involved.
- You need to let participants know what happens to the data. How will you ensure confidentiality?
- If responses are to be held on an electronic database, participants must know this and agree to it.
- Decide how will you close the interview.

Consistency

It is usually important that you carry out all of your interviews in near-identical conditions, to ensure consistency.

- Prior to the interview, make a list of questions, with possible prompts for each.
- If there is another interviewer, agree questions, prompts and any other words in advance. Practice so that you phrase questions and record responses in the same way.
- Conduct the interview just as you practiced it. Interview each person in the same way.

Conducting the interview

- Know your questions well so that you do not have to read them. This will engage participants better.
- Sit at right angles to the interviewee.
- Use eye contact, and smile occasionally.
- Be confident but polite.
- Keep it short: Don't impose on people's time.
- Thank people for participating.

Pilot the process

- Practice the whole interview. Check that it will work the way you want.
- Adapt your interview so that it is easy to conduct.
- Check that you can record the answers easily. If not, is this because the questions are too complex, or do you need a better chart to record answers?
- Analyze the answers from the pilot. Are they yielding the kind of data you want? If not, design new questions.

Blah blah blah blah blah blah blah...

Ground rules and boundaries

Where there are a number of interviews with a single person, such as for a case study, the interviewer may become too involved. Take steps to ensure that you remain interested but detached.

- Be clear with participants what you expect.
- Explain what will happen during and after the interview, and how long it will take.
- Specify your requirements for interview space or privacy. Negotiate acceptable alternatives. If there are any risks to you, do not proceed.
- Do not make promises.
- Do not get drawn into sharing personal experiences, as this can lead to unforeseen consequences. It can also distort the kind of information you receive in answer to your questions.

After long interviews

- Write up your notes as soon as possible.
- If you are required to transcribe the interview, write down exactly what was said, indicating pauses, coughs, "ums" and "ahs" and so on.
- Go through your notes with colored pens or pencils, marking all sections that refer to similar themes.
- Write a list of the themes and where you can find these in your notes.

Presenting and analyzing the data

Presenting information

Decide which method of presentation will show your results most clearly. You may wish to use a table, chart or graph (see Chapter 13).

Tables

Add up responses for each question. If you divide the responses—by age, gender, location, job or similar—state this clearly in the title of the table.

Table 1: Preferences for samples of font style, by gender

	Women	Men	Totals
Sample 1	8	15	23
Sample 2	13	5	18
No preference	9	10	19
Totals	30	30	60

Tables are useful for setting out information in clear categories. For example, Table 2 indicates preferences (three options) by gender (two options) and occupation (two options).

Table 2: Preferences for samples of font style, by gender and occupation

	Sample 1	Sample 2	No pref.	Totals
Male staff	13	2	0	15
Female staff	4	6	5	15
Male students	2	3	10	15
Female students	4	7	4	15
Totals	23	18	19	60

Bar charts

When presenting information in bar charts, select two things that can be compared against each other. Label the horizontal line (axis) with the details of what is being compared. In the following example, the horizontal axis refers to sample preferences. Label the vertical axis with the difference that is being measured. In the example here, this is the number of people who indicated a given preference.

Figure 1: Preferences for samples of font style, by sample

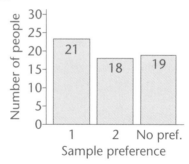

Pie charts

Pie charts are useful for presenting information in a way that the eye can take in at once.

Figure 2: Preferences for samples of font style, by occupation

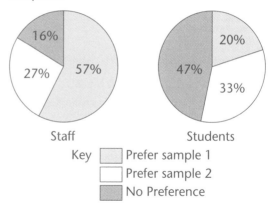

Analyze the data

It is easier to look for patterns and to draw conclusions when you have organized your data according to categories, as in the charts and tables above. It is important to organize results in different ways and to compare the results.

- Analyze your data. What does it tell you? Is this what you expected?
- How do your findings compare with those in the research literature?
- What questions are you not able to answer because of the way you designed your research? Could the design be improved?
- What questions are raised by your research?

Characteristics of reports

What is a "report"?

A report is the formal writing up of a piece of research or project work. Reports are usually written in a concise style, giving precise detail.

Although there are many different kinds of reports, they are usually structured in similar ways so that readers can find information quickly. Reports are not the same as research papers or essays.

Reports	Research papers
1 Reports originate from outside an educational context: They are typical of writing required for the world of work.	1 Papers originate in academic settings: They are rarely used anywhere else.
2 Reports present research data and findings that you have collected yourself—through a laboratory experiment, a survey, a questionnaire or a case study, or by applying theory to your work placement or some other situation.	2 Papers focus on analyzing or evaluating theory, past research by other people and ideas. They seldom present the findings of new research.
3 Papers and reports have different structures. Reports are structured as on page 328.	3 Papers are structured as on page 248.
4 A report is divided into separate sections.	4 Papers do not have sections; they flow as a continuous piece of writing.
5 A report contains tables, charts, and appendices.	5 Papers do not include tables or appendices.
6 Each section of the report is given a heading (see page 328). Each point is numbered (see the diagram on page 332).	6 Papers do not include section headings or numbering. (If these are used during drafting, remove them before handing in the paper.)
7 Reports contain a mixture of writing styles, depending on the section (see below).	7 Papers use a consistent writing style throughout.
8 Reports include descriptions of the methods used.	8 Papers should not refer to the method used in arriving at conclusions.
9 The description in a report should include a brief comment on how the research could have been improved and what gaps remain for further research.	9 Papers do not do this. Papers are not usually reflective about the process of researching and writing the paper itself.
10 Reports often include recommendations for for action.	10 Papers do not include recommendations.

Different goals

The style and content of your report should be appropriate to the readers for whom you write.

- If you make recommendations for action, evaluate different options.
- For business reports, include details of costs, losses and potential profits for each option.
- For a report based on an experiment, describe the experiment and the conditions under which it took place.
- If you are writing for a client (such as a work placement employer), tailor your report to the client's own requirements.

Structuring reports

Check if your subjects use a particular structure for reports. If not, then include the following, in this order.

Title   Write this on its own in the center of the first page, with your name, class, and the date.

Acknowledgments   List people you wish to thank for help given.

Abstract   Give a brief summary or overview of your report, including the research hypothesis and your conclusions. Restrict this (usually) to one paragraph. Omit details or examples, except main experimental data.

Report abstracts may be reproduced and read separately from the rest of the report, so they often contain information also included in other sections.

List of contents   List the main sections of the report and the page on which each begins (including any appendices).

List of tables and illustrations   List any illustrations, charts, maps and so on, giving the page number for each.

Introduction   Briefly discuss what the research is about—why is it important or significant? State your proposals or hypotheses briefly: What are you going to show or prove?

Review of the literature   Discuss briefly some of the most important writings on the subject, discussing other researchers' main findings. Do you agree or disagree with them? Focus on how previous research connects with and leads up to your research. Introduce your experimental hypothesis, if you have one.

Method   How did you conduct your research? What methods did you use? Did you replicate methods used by other researchers? Even if your instructors told you what methods to use, include these in the report.

Exactly what were the conditions of the experiment? How many people or items were included? How did you select them? What instructions did you give to participants?

Measurement criteria   Discuss the kinds of data you gathered. How did you analyze them? How reliable or accurate are your data?

Present the results   Present your main findings briefly, under headings if appropriate. Give results in the order in which you conducted any experiments, or start with the most important. Be honest about your results.

Discuss the results   This is a longer section. Analyze and explain your findings. Were they what you had expected? Were they consistent with your hypothesis? Did they fit the theory or seem to disprove it? How are they significant? It is more important that you show that you understand the results than that your hypothesis was proved right or wrong.

How could the research have been improved? What follow-up research would be useful?

Conclusions   In some subjects, a conclusion is inappropriate. Otherwise, summarize your key points and show why your hypothesis can be maintained or rejected.

Recommendations   In subjects such as social policy or health, you may be asked to give a numbered list of suggestions for action to resolve problems.

References   List all your sources, in alphabetical order.

Bibliography   If required, list relevant further reading, again in alphabetical order.

Appendices   Present together any essential extra material, such as instructions to participants, copies of materials used or tables and graphs of data. Number each item. Do not include items unless they are mentioned in the report.

Writing the report: opening sections

Different kinds of writing are used in each section of a report.

Introduction

The introduction:

- states the problem or issue covered by the report
- summarizes the main themes in the research literature, drawing out the main points and showing how each piece of research builds on previous work
- shows how your project uses and builds upon previous research.

In the example below note that, as a rule, only a few words can be devoted to any one piece of previous research. This should influence your note-taking: Select only key details. Notice, too, how the chosen items are organized so that they "lead up to" the student's project. The final paragraph then shows how the student will "take the research forward."

The following introduction would suit a report of 1500–2000 words or 5–6 pages double-spaced. A longer report or research project might refer to more sources but would not usually include more about each, unless some were very highly significant.

Example: an introduction to a report

It has been argued (Ayer 2004, Bea 2006) that diet can be affected by the color of food. For example, Bea found that 15% of participants in a series of six experiments showed strong aversions to certain food color combinations. People were less likely to eat food if they disliked the color combination. Dee (2008) found that food color preferences are affected by age, with green being the least popular food coloring among children. However, Evans challenged Dee's results. Evans (2010, 2011) found that children's preferences for color only applied to certain types of food. For sweet foods, for example, children showed a strong preference for red products, but chose green as frequently as other color options.

Jay extended this area of research to nonnatural food colors. Early indications (Jay 2012a) suggest children are likely to select blue colored food even though these do not occur naturally. This research was replicated by Kai (2011). Similar results were also found for adults (Jay 2012b). However, Jay's research included only sugar-based products. As Evans has shown that there are different color preferences for sweet and salty produce, Jay and Kai's findings may not hold true across all food products, especially for salty foods.

Jay's research (2012b) indicated strong adult preferences for sweet food colored blue; Jay argued this was probably due to its "novelty value." The aim of the current research was to see whether adults showed the same preferences for blue food coloring when presented with salty food options. The research hypotheses were that ... [see section below]. It was assumed that the "novelty effect" would hold true for salty products.

Other types of introduction

If your report was commissioned by a business or agency, the introduction would usually give more background about:

- who commissioned the report
- why the report was commissioned
- the scope of the report: what it will cover
- definitions of any terms
- the methodology
- an overview of findings and recommendations.

The research hypothesis

The hypothesis must be worded very clearly and precisely. It usually states that something will or will not happen.

Example: research hypothesis

The research hypothesis was that adults would show a preference for salty food colored blue over salty food colored with food dyes simulating natural colorings. The second hypothesis was that there would be no significant difference in the preferences of men and women.

Writing the report: the body of the report

Methodology or "research design"

The methodology section gives the details that the reader needs in order to know how you gained and analyzed your data. You should provide sufficient explanation that readers could repeat your research for themselves if they wished to. The writing is descriptive, and follows the order of your own actions: "First this was done, then that was done ..."

Example: methodology

> **Participants**
> The research participants were 32 adult students, all aged over 25. There were equal numbers of men and women.
>
> **Materials**
> Four types of food were prepared (potato salad, chapatti, rice, couscous) and each was divided into 4. Four different food dyes were used; three were dyes used in the food trade designed to look like a "natural" food color; the fourth dye was pale blue. A quarter of each of the four food types was dyed a different color so that all foods were available in each color, to give 16 possible options.
>
> **Method**
> First, participants were told that all of the food was colored using artificial dyes. Each person was then allowed to choose three items to eat. This meant they could not select one of each color. A record was kept of the colors selected by each person. The results were then calculated according to food color preference overall and preferences by gender.

Results

Reports usually include a table of key results. Other data and tables are attached as an appendix. The results section simply *presents* the data: The data are not discussed here. Keep this section short; include only relevant and representative data.

State whether or not your results support your research hypothesis. Often results do *not* support the hypothesis: This is neither "good" nor "bad."

Example: results

> 24 of the 32 participants (75%) did not select a blue food item. The findings do not support the first research hypothesis. However, 7 of the 8 participants who did select a blue option were women. 44% of women selected a blue option compared to 6.25% of men. This does not support the second research hypothesis.

Discussion

Critical, analytical writing is used in the discussion section. The discussion section analyzes the data and draws out interesting findings. It includes:

- the significance of your results and whether these confirm or differ from previous research
- your conclusions, and the evidence for these
- a note of whether or not the research hypothesis was supported
- any improvements that could be made to the research method, and further research that is needed
- how your results could be applied elsewhere.

For the research described above, for example, the discussion might include an analysis of:

- *The sample* Was it representative? Could the ethnic mix or age range, or asking students only, have made a difference?
- *The method* Could this have been improved? Did the blue food look unpleasant rather than simply "unnatural"? Would there have been a different response to an unnatural-looking green?
- *Future research* What research is needed to clarify these results further? For example, do color preferences apply to all foods or only to some? How long does the "novelty factor" last?

Example: part of the discussion section

> The research indicated that even when participants were told that all food options were artificially colored, they still choose salty food that looked "natural" rather than food dyed blue. This suggests that adults have a preference for natural colors in salty food. However, the blue dye was streaky; this might have distorted the results.

Chapter **14**

Writing the report: conclusions, recommendations, abstracts

Conclusions

Conclusions sum up your research, setting out its significance and your findings. No new information or references are included. The conclusions are also included in the abstract, the introduction and the discussion.

For the research mentioned above, the conclusions might include:

- a note that your research findings are not consistent with previous research findings
- a brief summary of *why* your results may be different (for instance, adult participants rather than children, and salty food rather than sweet)
- notes of any shortcomings of the research (the streakiness of the blue coloring might have distorted results).

Example: Conclusions

The research suggests that adults do not select salty foods dyed blue, if given the choice of other options of dyed food. The "novelty effect" of blue products, suggested by previous research, did not hold true for salty foods. The research suggests that people choose salty food on a different basis from sweet food. However, this hypothesis would need to be tested further by researching the choices made for sweet and salty products by a single group of participants (etc.).

Recommendations

The purpose of recommendations is to suggest ways forward. They might propose how to improve current ways of working or action that needs to be taken. They are numbered. For example, if you were undertaking research for an agency, your recommendations might be:

1 Undertake further research using a larger sample.
2 Avoid use of blue food dyes in the manufacture of salty food products for adults.

Research undertaken from an academic or scientific perspective, rather than a marketing one, does not usually include recommendations.

Abstracts

The abstract is placed before the contents page of the report. Although it is presented at the beginning, it is usually easiest to write if you leave it until last. Leave lots of time to write it—it usually takes a lot longer than expected.

The abstract sums up your aims, your research hypothesis, your methodology, your findings and your conclusions. You may be set a small word limit, such as 50–100 words. An abstract needs to be both brief and concise.

Example 1: Abstract (50-word limit)

This report suggests that research into truancy has neglected the critical role of school play-time. In-depth interviews with 6 former truants, now college students, highlight the pivotal role of group dynamics within the playground. The interviews suggest that "feeling like an outsider" at playtime encourages initial acts of truancy.

Example 2: Abstract (100-word limit)

This report presents an analysis of adult responses when given the choice of foods dyed blue or foods dyed with traditional colorings. The initial hypothesis, based on research by Jay (2012b), was that adults would show a preference for food dyed blue over foods that looked more natural. This project replicated the methods used by Jay, but substituted salty for sweet foods. 32 adults, all aged over 25, were asked to select three items from a selection of 16 possible choices. Their responses indicate that adults are less likely to select blue food for salty items. The results were statistically significant.

Summaries

Some subjects require a summary rather than an abstract. This is usually longer than an abstract, but still no more than a page.

The summary contains the aims and objectives, a brief outline of the research problem, the methodology, the key findings, the conclusions and the main recommendations.

Reports: layout, presentation, and style

Numbering headings

Give each section a heading, to indicate what the section covers (see **Structuring reports**, page 328). Use brief subheadings to introduce different kinds of subject matter. Number each section and subsection in a logical way, so that the reader can tell easily when the report is moving on to a new section.

The following table indicates one way of numbering sections and subsections.

9	**Results**
9.1	*Results of experiment A*
9.1.1	In experiment A, none of the participants completed …
9.1.2	On the second attempt, 4% of participants completed …
9.1.3	On the third attempt, 17% of participants completed the …
9.2	*Results of experiment B*
9.2.1	In experiment B, 33% of the participants completed …
9.2.2	On the second attempt, 64% of participants completed …
9.2.3	On the third attempt, 97% of participants completed the …

Levels of heading

Headings are organized into levels: "A," "B," "C," "D," and so on. The "A" heading stands out the most: This is the title. Avoid using more than three or four levels or the report and its numbering may become confusing. For example:

A Main headings: in large print and bold type.
B Section headings: in a slightly larger font than the text, and in bold type.
C Subheadings: may be in italics or bold.
D Other lesser headings: should stand out clearly.

Whatever method you use to organize your headings, use it consistently throughout the report.

Presenting the text

- Number the pages in order. On the contents page, give the page number for each section.
- Use fonts that are easy to read.
- Leave clear margins at each side.
- Avoid fancy graphics, unless the project brief requires these.
- Use a clear layout. Avoid cluttering the report with tables and diagrams unless these are essential. Place most tables, data and examples of materials (if these are needed) in the appendices at the end of the report.

Writing style

All writing in a report is:

- *formal*—avoid slang and abbreviations
- *focused*—address only the project brief
- *concise*—avoid tangents and unnecessary examples
- *subject-specific*—follow the style appropriate to your subject.

Writing for a purpose

The content will depend on the purpose of the report. For example, the report on pages 329–331 is written about research undertaken on campus. However, if you undertook similar research for a company wanting to launch a range of picnic food, the research and the report would reflect those different purposes. For example:

- The introduction would state briefly what the company wanted the research to achieve.
- The sample would be bigger, focusing on members of the public rather than students.
- If the sample were bigger, the method should be simpler. For example, you could offer a choice of only two food items, one dyed and one not, followed by fewer questions.
- The discussion would focus on the implications of the results for the proposed range of new foods.
- You would probably make a recommendation—in this case, not to use blue colorings.

Project checklist

Item	Checked	Any further action needed
1 Clarify the goal or purpose of the research project.		
2 Write a project hypothesis, if one is required.		
3 Select a precise and clear topic.		
4 Undertake a literature review, and write this up.		
5 Decide on a research method, and write this up.		
6 Check with the instructor or research advisor that the project is suitable in terms of subject matter and scale.		
7 Book any rooms, participants and equipment. If necessary, get permission to use materials or to interview participants.		
8 Book facilities for binding the project report, if required.		
9 Develop forms to collect and record data accurately.		
10 Collect and record the data, following the selected methodology.		
11 Analyze the data. Write up "Results" and "Discussion" sections.		
12 Complete the report. Does the whole report address the project topic?		
13 Have all required sections been completed and included?		
14 Are there clear headings for all sections?		
15 Is the right material included in each section?		
16 Does the report meet the page or word limit?		
17 Do readers have all the information they need? Is all information relevant?		
18 Write the abstract, and place this after the title page.		
19 Number all pages (allowing for a "Contents" page).		
20 Write a "Contents" page, including page numbers.		
21 Is the right style of writing used for each section?		
22 Is the report clear and easy to read?		
23 Has the report been proofread?		
24 Is the final report neat, presented as required and bound if necessary?		

Chapter **14**

Research projects, reports, and case studies   **333**

PLANNER

Research project action plan

Project title:

Completion date:

Target	Milestones (steps to be taken)	Notes	By (date)	Done (✓)
1 Organization and planning	1 Read the project brief carefully.			
	2 Plan each step. Write all tasks in your planner.			
	3 Plan to work effectively with your research advisor.			
	4			
2 Select the subject of your research	1 Browse previous research projects in the library.			
	2 Brainstorm a list of potential topics.			
	3 Browse the literature for ideas and identify gaps.			
	4			
	5 Specify the research question.			
3 Literature search and review	1 Read and take notes on key research literature for the topic.			
	2 Trace the way existing research "leads up to" your own project.			
	3			
	4			
	5 Write up the literature review.			

Target	Milestones (steps to be taken)	Notes	By (date)	Done (✓)
4 Methodology	1 Decide on a possible methodology. What information do you need? How can you collect this?			
	2 Discuss this with an instructor or check it against journal articles for your subject.			
	3 Select the right scale: enough data but not too much.			
	4 Design your materials.			
	5 If necessary, book access to rooms, people, or collections of papers, etc., well in advance.			
	6			
	7			
	8 Write up the methodology section.			
5 Collect data	1 Plan time for this in your planner or organizer.			
	2 Keep accurate records.			
	3			
	4			
6 Analyze data and discuss findings	1			
	2			
	3			
7 Writing the research project	1 Write up the research project.			
	2 Edit and proofread.			
	3 Bind the research project?			
8 Submit the research project	Hand in the research project—and celebrate your success!			

Research projects, reports, and case studies

Case studies

A case study is an in-depth study of a single example. It offers a chance to analyze one case—such as a single person, group, company, event, or geographical area—as an example of a general type. It allows you to look at something in much more detail than is typical of other research methods.

Characteristics of a case study

A case study allows you to test out techniques or theory in a real-life or simulated situation.

- It involves detailed analysis of a single example of an issue, a technique, a member of a client group or the like.
- It is factual and is usually based on a real-life subject.
- It brings an issue vividly to life.
- You must relate the case study to a theoretical framework and show how it either illustrates or contradicts the theory.
- You must show how your case study either illustrates or contradicts previous related research.
- You may be required to use the case study to analyze a problem and to make recommendations.

Advantages of case studies

- Case studies are useful in illustrating a point.
- They allow more investigation into small details; these details can throw new light on how something really works in practice.
- As they are drawn from "real life," case studies may show up complexities that do not emerge under controlled conditions such as experiments.

- They can be used to test out a theory.
- The level of detail considered can be helpful in advancing the theoretical framework.
- Case studies may open up new lines of inquiry for research.
- They are useful in identifying how rules, theory or work practice should be adapted to meet the needs of special cases.
- They can draw out examples of good or bad practice in the workplace.

Limitations of case studies

- Case studies may not be representative of what happens in general.
- Care must be taken in drawing up general rules from only one case study or from only a small number of case studies.
- Case studies are time-consuming, so only a few can be undertaken.

Case studies as qualitative research

Case studies are examples of *qualitative* research. (Differences between qualitative and quantitative research are discussed on pages 270–271.) A research strategy for a case study would include some or all of the following:

- *Identifying the purpose.* Is the study undertaken in order to understand an issue? To test out theory? To trial a product? To recommend change?
- *Reading background information.* Read the history of the case until you know it thoroughly.
- *Identifying relevant theory and research methods.*
- *Observing or questioning.* This is usually open-ended in the early stages, so that you do not prejudge the outcomes.
- *Analyzing early data* for emerging themes.
- *Focusing further observation or questions* on specific themes or on gaps in the information. Check that what you have been told is accurate.
- *Identifying probable causes of problems.*
- *Evaluating or testing potential solutions.*
- *Making recommendations* for action.

Writing a case study

Structuring a case study

Introduction

The introduction outlines why the case study was undertaken, and gives a brief overview.

Background

As a student, you may be expected to include in your case study a summary of related research on the issues raised by your study.

Sections of the case study

The body of the report organizes issues raised by the case study into sections under appropriate headings. Likely sections include:

- background information
- research methods used (if relevant)
- a statement of the problem, issue or focus
- early action or intervention, if any
- current action or intervention
- client responses to any action or intervention
- other people's responses
- an overall evaluation of the intervention or action
- any outstanding issues or problems
- probable causes of any outstanding problems
- possible solutions to outstanding problems
- an evaluation of these possible solutions.

Conclusions

Draw together your main findings. How far does this case study illustrate or contradict previous research and existing theory? How typical is it of other cases?

Recommendations

List any recommendations suggested by the case study. Good recommendations are:

- *based on real needs*
- *reasoned*—they make a good case, based on the evidence, for what action is needed, and state what outcomes can be expected if that action is taken

- *clear about alternatives*
- *suitable*—they fit the culture of the organization or the situation of the individual
- *realistic*—they can reasonably be afforded and carried out, within relevant time scales and with the expertise available
- *specific*—it is clear exactly what must be done, by whom and when.

Writing style

Example: case study writing

> Rabina was then referred to an educational psychologist, who told her she was dyslexic. The psychologist's report describes her as "very bright," with the "cognitive ability to succeed in college."
>
> Rabina had also been referred to several ear specialists as she appeared to have difficulties with listening and processing spoken information. The results suggested her hearing was within normal range. This surprised Rabina and her parents. However, research has shown that dyslexic people often show hearing differences when given a wider range of hearing tests. For example, the Baltic Dyslexia Research Laboratory has found associations between dyslexia and left ear dominance and other auditory processing anomalies (Johansen 1991, 1994). The tests undertaken at the Baltic Center were not available for Rabina so she may have hearing difficulties that have not yet been identified.
>
> Rabina reported that as a child, she had thought she was "going crazy" when words "fell off the edge of the page." It is not unusual for people to attribute aspects of dyslexia to a range of reasons that "make sense" to them as children. Usually, these are associated with events that caused them extreme embarrassment and shame. Edwards (1994) has shown that the scars can last well into adulthood. In Rabina's case, this was manifested in being withdrawn and reluctant to join in classroom activities. She …

Note in this example how the writing:

- focuses on a particular individual
- gives more detail than is typical of research papers
- links Rabina's experience to wider research
- brings out what is particular about Rabina's experience.

Review

Projects can be very varied. The purpose or goal of a project will influence the way you approach the research and how you write it up. Most student projects and reports will be of an academic nature, written mainly for your instructor. You may use other students as participants, so that you can collect data.

The main reason such project or report work is assigned is to acquaint you with the techniques of researching a subject and managing the overall process for yourself. It is not usually expected that you will make major discoveries.

The best student projects are clear and well defined. They are carefully thought through, so as to be manageable within the time limits. The objectives may seem very small. This is not a problem as long as the project is well managed, has clearly written outcomes and is linked to previous research.

It is often a good idea to apply previous research to a small sample that has not been researched before. For example, you could use examples from your own age group, from a minority ethnic group, from a local area or similar. This could make the project more interesting and relevant for you, and it would add to the overall body of knowledge about the subject.

Once you have learned how to do projects and write papers and reports, a research project should be a manageable task. Research projects are challenging because you are more in control. You have to make more decisions and to manage the process for yourself. A research project is a larger-scale project: It requires more reading; it requires the collection of a larger set of data (in some cases); and it takes more time to analyze and present.

Research projects require good management skills, forward planning and attention to detail. However, by the time you are given a research project to do, the basic procedures should be familiar to you.

Research projects provide opportunities to cover a subject that really interests you, so they can be extremely rewarding and enjoyable.

Answers to activity on page 323

1 It is not clear which box should be completed by a person who is 20 or 40. The text should read "0–19 20–39 40–60" or "0–20 21–40 41–60." Also, there no provision has been made for people older than 60.

2 The question does not capture accurate information. Government secretary? If they say "yes," how do you know if they really do? It should read:

> Who is the current United States Secretary for … [named Department, such as Agriculture]?

3 This question does not capture the variety of positions people might hold on the issue. It could read:

> Which of the following positions is nearest to your own?

and then list several numbered options.

4 This contains two questions. The person might like coming onto campus but not eating in the café, or vice versa. These two issues should be separated out. If the question is about whether people like eating at the café on campus, it could be worded:

> Do you like eating at the café on campus?

Chapter 15

Planning your next move

LEARNING OUTCOMES

This chapter offers you opportunities to:

- identify your study achievements so far

- evaluate your achievements

- understand what is meant by "personal development planning"

- identify your personal planning to date

- identify the next set of targets for your own progress.

This chapter is an opportunity to take stock of what you have achieved so far. If you have worked through one or more chapters of the book already, then the *Study skills achievements* chart on pages 340–345 is one place where you can record your evaluation of your achievements.

To make an accurate judgment about what you have achieved—neither understating it nor overstating it—you will need to consider a number of points:

- What do you *believe* you have achieved? What can you do now that you could not do before?
- What is the *evidence* of your achievement—how do you *know* that you succeeded?
- What is the *significance* of your achievement—what does it mean, and how does it help?
- What is still *left* to do? There is always room to fine-tune skills so that you can work more creatively, more effectively, with less stress and so forth. In addition, you may lose skills if you do not make use of them. Plan opportunities to *practice* your skills.

- What new challenges do you wish to set yourself? How can you broaden your range of skills or your perspectives on life and open up new opportunities?

Study skills are part of a developmental process. This book suggests study strategies and concepts that can be applied to *most* aspects of study. They have been used effectively by students at all levels, including graduate students.

However, successful study also benefits from a range of additional skills not traditionally linked with the term "study skills." These skills are more commonly associated with the concepts of "personal development" or "continuous professional development." Developing your skills and experience on a broad front can have a positive impact on academic work, on career outcomes and on personal well-being.

This chapter introduces the concept of personal development planning. It maps out personal development already addressed through this book and begins the process of setting targets towards a wider set of personal goals.

SELF-EVALUATION

Study skills achievements

Name:

Program:

Use the chart below to identify study skills or milestones that have been met, and on what date. Clarify the basis of your evaluation: How do you know you have improved? If you feel there is still work to do, return to the relevant pages in this book using the index on page 363.

Achievement	Typical milestones	How I know I have improved at this study skill	Date
Being prepared for study (Chapter 1)			
Very good ☐ Good ☐ OK ☐ Weak ☐ Very weak ☐	☐ I have identified and addressed anxieties about being a student ☐ I have identified my personal resources ☐ I have identified my readiness for study ☐ I understand the teaching methods employed in college ☐ I understand what is expected of me as a student ☐ I am organized for the start of the year ☐ I understand the importance of attending orientation events		
Understanding my own learning (Chapters 3 and 4)			
Very good ☐ Good ☐ OK ☐ Weak ☐ Very weak ☐	☐ I understand how my attitudes to learning and intelligence can affect my study success ☐ I am aware of optimal conditions for learning ☐ I adopt optimal learning conditions for myself ☐ I am aware of my own learning style and what I need in order to learn best ☐ I use my preferred learning style to help me study ☐ I am aware of study habits that may hinder my learning ☐ I am aware of how I could sabotage my own success ☐ I adopt effective study habits and strategies		
Organization and planning for study (Chapter 4)			
Very good ☐ Good ☐ OK ☐	☐ I have organized a suitable study space ☐ I have organized my files and papers ☐ I have organized my computer folders		

Achievement	Typical milestones	How I know I have improved at this study skill	Date
☐ Weak ☐ Very weak	☐ I am able to find information easily when I need it ☐ I use planners to organize study tasks ☐ I have the resources I need for effective study ☐ I prepare effectively in advance for classes		
Time management (Chapter 4) ☐ Very good ☐ Good ☐ OK ☐ Weak ☐ Very weak	☐ I am aware of how I use time ☐ I make effective use of small pockets of time ☐ I make effective use of my planner or organizer ☐ I know when I study best and organize my time to enable me to study at those times ☐ I organize my work well so that I meet deadlines ☐ I am aware of appropriate time-saving strategies ☐ I am able to identify personal priorities		
Reflective and creative thinking skills (Chapter 4) ☐ Very good ☐ Good ☐ OK ☐ Weak ☐ Very weak	☐ I am aware of the value of reflective thinking ☐ I put time aside regularly for structured reflection ☐ I maintain a regular reflective journal ☐ I use a reflective journal to monitor progress ☐ I use strategies to develop creative thinking ☐ I am confident in using creative thinking strategies ☐ I evaluate my personal progress ☐ I take good use of instructor or peer feedback so as to improve performance		
Reading and note-taking (Chapter 5) ☐ Very good ☐ Good ☐ OK ☐ Weak ☐ Very weak	☐ I apply a strategy for reading tasks ☐ I am confident about finding the resources needed for assignments ☐ I select the right kinds and amounts of information needed for papers and reports ☐ I am able to select the right kinds and amounts of required information for research projects ☐ I use library and other resources effectively ☐ I take notes that are easy to use ☐ I use lecture time effectively		

Chapter **15**

Planning your next move

Achievement	Typical milestones	How I know I have improved at this study skill	Date
Referencing skills; plagiarism (Chapter 5)			
Very good ☐ Good ☐ OK ☐ Weak ☐ Very weak ☐	☐ I know what is meant by "plagiarism" ☐ I know how to avoid plagiarism ☐ I understand how to reference source materials ☐ I reference work appropriately on a consistent basis ☐ I know how to produce a list of references ☐ I know how to produce independent work when working in groups		
E-learning and using technology (Chapter 6)			
Very good ☐ Good ☐ OK ☐ Weak ☐ Very weak ☐	☐ I am confident in using the computer to produce my assignments ☐ I understand basic health and safety for computer use ☐ I can find and use Internet resources effectively ☐ I can conduct advanced searches in databases ☐ I know how to use e-communications well ☐ I know how to manage an e-group project		
Critical and analytical thinking skills (Chapter 7)			
Very good ☐ Good ☐ OK ☐ Weak ☐ Very weak ☐	☐ I know what is meant by "analytical" ☐ I can critically evaluate the main line of reasoning in a text ☐ I am able to evaluate evidence presented in texts ☐ I can identify bias and distortion in texts and source materials ☐ I can evaluate if the evidence presented by other people supports their conclusions ☐ I apply critical thinking skills when using evidence to support my own line of reasoning ☐ I apply critical analytical skills to my own writing		
Memory (Chapter 8)			
Very good ☐ Good ☐ OK ☐ Weak ☐ Very weak ☐	☐ I use a range of practical memory strategies ☐ I have a basic awareness of how the brain works and how to use this knowledge to help my memory ☐ I know which memory strategies suit me best ☐ I apply strategies to remember essential information ☐ I organize information to make it easier to remember		

Achievement	Typical milestones	How I know I have improved at this study skill	Date

Studying for tests and test-taking (Chapter 9)

Very good · Good · OK · Weak · Very weak

- I understand the purpose of revisiting my work
- I review work on a regular basis
- I look for themes that run through my program
- I regularly identify areas of difficulty and address these
- I regularly check my own understanding
- I know which study strategies work best for me
- I use a good study schedule
- I practice answers using test files or likely questions
- I read test questions and instructions carefully
- I know which kinds of questions I answer best
- I schedule time to ensure all questions receive enough attention according to the points they gain
- I structure essay-based answers with a clear line of reasoning
- I answer all test questions as required
- I check my answers before handing in the test

Group work (Chapter 10)

Very good · Good · OK · Weak · Very weak

- I listen to other people without interrupting
- I put across my own point of view effectively
- I encourage other people to speak
- I am aware of prejudice or when other people are being treated unfairly
- I help to ensure that everyone is included and treated well
- I am aware of factors that make groups work well
- I contribute to making groups work effectively
- I make effective use of a study support group

Making a presentation (Chapter 10)

Very good · Good · OK · Weak · Very weak

- I know how to prepare for a talk or verbal presentation
- I am aware of the needs of my audience and that these change while they are listening to a presentation
- I can plan material to fit the presentation time available
- I can use audio-visual aids appropriately

Achievement	Typical milestones	How I know I have improved at this study skill	Date
☐	I sound confident when making a presentation, even when I don't *feel* confident		
☐	I make suitable eye contact with the audience		
☐	I keep to time without rushing the talk		
☐	I respond well to questions		

Writing skills (Chapters 11, 12, 14)

Very good ☐ Good ☐ OK ☐ Weak ☐ Very weak ☐	Typical milestones	How I know I have improved at this study skill	Date
☐	I am confident about getting started on writing tasks		
☐	I break writing tasks down into manageable steps		
☐	I focus writing on the question or assignment prompt		
☐	I understand the requirements of academic writing (style, layout, conventions, etc.)		
☐	I write in an analytical way		
☐	I organize and structure my ideas clearly		
☐	I order information so that it follows a clear line of reasoning		
☐	I meet the word or page requirements		
☐	I meet writing deadlines		
☐	I proofread my writing so that it reads well and is free of errors		

Writing for assignments (Chapters 11, 12, 14)

Very good ☐ Good ☐ OK ☐ Weak ☐ Very weak ☐	Typical milestones	How I know I have improved at this study skill	Date
☐	I am aware of what is required for writing a research paper		
☐	I write papers that receive the grades I want		
☐	I am aware of the differences between various kinds of written assignment		
☐	I can design good assignment questions, if required		
☐	I know what is required for writing a report		
☐	I write reports that receive the grades I want		
☐	I know what is required for writing a case study		
☐	I know what I need to do to improve my assignment writing skills		

Achievement	Typical milestones	How I know I have improved at this study skill	Date
Research projects (Chapter 14)			
Very good ☐ Good ☐ OK ☐ Weak ☐ Very weak ☐	☐ I know what is required for dissertations ☐ I can identify a good project topic ☐ I can organize and plan my time so that all project tasks are clearly managed ☐ I can apply research skills to larger-scale projects such as research projects ☐ I know how to write up the research project		
Confidence with numbers (Chapter 13)			
Very good ☐ Good ☐ OK ☐ Weak ☐ Very weak ☐	☐ I can add, subtract, multiply and divide fractions ☐ I can calculate percentages ☐ I can round numbers up and down to the decimal point required ☐ I can calculate a "mean" average ("equal share") ☐ I can calculate the "median" ("middle number") ☐ I can calculate the "mode" ("most frequent") ☐ I can calculate five-number summaries, including quartiles ☐ I can interpret raw data ☐ I can interpret information presented in tables and charts ☐ I can present my own data as a table or chart		
Independence and self-reliance as a student (Chapters 1 and 14)			
Very good ☐ Good ☐ OK ☐ Weak ☐ Very weak ☐	☐ I understand what is meant by independent study as an aspect of all college study ☐ I know how specific programs of independent study differ from traditional taught programs ☐ I am able to design my own assignments in line with given criteria ☐ I know how to work effectively without constant supervision ☐ I know how to work effectively with an academic or research advisor ☐ I am strongly self-motivated to complete an assignment well ☐ I can manage study time over a semester		

Evaluating achievement

Identify one study skill achievement that particularly pleases you or of which you are proud. You can use the following table to analyze your achievement in more detail and evaluate your progress. When you have completed this sheet, you might like to repeat the process with another of your achievements.

Prompt	Evaluation
What I have achieved What has changed? (For example, what can I do now that I couldn't do before?)	
How I know I have achieved this What is the evidence for my achievement? (For example, how I feel, comments from other people or changes in my grades.)	
What I did to achieve this What steps did I take? (Did I change my attitudes, habits or behavior? Did I have a good strategy? Did I ask for support? Did I practice skills? Did I reflect on my performance?)	
The significance or relevance of the achievement What is significant or meaningful about this achievement? (Why is it relevant or important? Why am I pleased or proud about it?)	
Taking it further What can I do to build upon this success? (How can I fine-tune my skills further? Could I apply these skills to a new situation? What is my next step?)	

Planning your future

Personal planning

Study skills activities are part of a wider process of personal development. Personal planning is not something you do once and then forget: Rather, it is an attitude towards your future. It has no limits; it does not come to an end.

Personal planning is a process that:

- deepens your understanding of yourself
- makes you more aware of your motivations
- helps you formulate what you really want for your life and career
- helps you to face up to your own limitations and to address these realistically
- helps you see yourself as other people see you
- assists you to plan over the longer term towards goals that are important to you
- helps you make more effective use of work-based processes such as performance appraisals or reviews.

What does PDP involve?

Personal development planning (PDP) involves:

- *Reflection* The focus of your reflection will change over time but will include thinking deeply about issues such as who you are, who you want to be, what you want, why you want it, what your alternatives are in life and what kind of life journey you want.
- *Increasing self-awareness* PDP requires you to be aware of your individual strengths, interests, inspirations, preferences, qualities and ambitions—and of your own weaknesses and shortcomings.
- *Being informed* You can find out about opportunities and choices that are open to you, and broaden your perspective.
- *Taking personal responsibility* As an adult, you can take responsibility for your own education, training, choices and forward planning.
- *Developing a strategy to get where you want to be* PDP helps you plan, set targets, take action, develop skills and review your position.

Seven benefits of personal development planning

Many colleges offer personal development planning or similar initiatives, so that students are better prepared for life and work once they have completed their degree.

There are many benefits from PDP. Here are just seven of them.

1 PDP gives you a clearer sense of your direction and purpose. Many students are unclear about which major to pursue or what they want to do after college, and may make the wrong choices early on, for example, by not taking the classes required for a particular career path.

2 Direction and purpose make study more meaningful. This builds motivation, which you can direct to achieve your academic goals.

3 The reflective, strategic, analytical and creative thinking skills associated with PDP are relevant to academic study and are useful in most life contexts.

4 PDP will give you a better sense of who you are in the world and what you want: This in turn will give you more control over your future.

5 Typically, PDP activity will spur you on to develop skills and to take on activities that give you a broader range of experience when you leave college. This will enable you to compete for better jobs and to cope in the wider world.

6 PDP can increase your self-confidence, based on better knowledge of yourself and your opportunities, and advance planning.

7 You will receive more than just a degree from your education.

Activity

Personal development planning

- What other benefits of personal development planning would you add to the list?
- Which three benefits are the most important to you?
- Which aspects are *not* very important to you?

Personal development already undertaken

Personal development in this book

Earlier sections of this book have already introduced aspects of personal development planning. Below are some examples.

- Understanding skills development in relation to different contexts:
  - identifying skills and personal qualities (Chapter 2)
  - understanding personal learning styles (Chapter 4).
- Planning:
  - setting goals and targets so that you can measure your progress (pages 69 and 358)
  - clarifying what you want from college in order to increase your focus (Introduction and Chapter 2).
- Developing a strategy:
  - using desired outcomes to guide strategy (Chapter 4).
- Monitoring and evaluating performance:
  - self-evaluations (pages 30, 57–58 and 346).

Your personal development history

Even before you came to college, you were engaged in processes of personal planning. For example, you may have selected qualifications in high school, chosen part-time work for experience, picked the most suitable college or moved away from home.

- In what ways are you using personal planning now, to make choices that affect your future—for example, how you choose to spend your time, how you make subject choices, how you choose work experience, any volunteering you do and any other extracurricular activities?
- What do you hope to achieve through these choices?
- How could you improve your personal planning so as to prepare better for your future and to broaden your horizons?

Activity

Personal development history

Check which types of personal planning you have already undertaken.

- ☐ Researching and planning in order to complete a qualification or program in high school or college.
- ☐ Researching and planning a major life event (such as a birth in the family or a change of address).
- ☐ Researching and planning an occasion (such as a party, a vacation, or a festival).
- ☐ Researching and planning to inform your choice of college.
- ☐ Research and planning to inform your choice of college program.
- ☐ Research and planning to find a part-time or full-time job.
- ☐ Planning a student project or work project.

- ☐ Thinking through how to give someone bad news.
- ☐ Balancing a busy schedule.
- ☐ Planning how you will develop a skill over time (such as driving, using a computer, or learning to skate).
- ☐ Thinking long-term when making choices.
- ☐ Taking specific courses to develop personal awareness (such as courses in management, counseling, or facing personal challenges or career awareness).
- ☐ Taking courses to develop your personal interests.
- ☐ Traveling in order to challenge your ideas and broaden your perspective.

Planning towards a career

Plan ahead

If you wish to gain a good job as a graduate, the process of preparation cannot begin too soon. By themselves, your major and grade will not usually be enough to impress employers. They will also be looking to see how well you can demonstrate skills and attributes they value. They will be looking, for example, for people who can:

- take responsibility for themselves, for other people and for the work they will be given
- plan ahead to address future needs
- spot and create opportunities
- make the best use of opportunities that arise
- demonstrate an understanding of the employer's needs
- take responsibility for personal development and for improving performance.

Ideally, planning should start in your first year of college, so that by the time you apply for jobs as a college graduate, you are in a strong position.

Develop a "rounded portfolio" of skills

When you apply for a job, the subjects and extracurricular activities you have been engaged in will count. When you make job applications, you will be asking:

- "How have I used my time … ?"
- "What have I done that will make my application stand out?"
- "What will make this company consider me rather than somebody else?"
- "What evidence have I got that I can deliver the skills they are asking for?"
- "What experience can I offer … ?"

Your time in college is an investment. Obviously, it is important to spend time on gaining your degree. However, you do not have to invest *all* your time in study. There are "smart" ways of using your time and putting a degree together, so that you leave college with a rounded portfolio of skills.

Typically a rounded student portfolio will contain "investment" in at least three of the following:

- the academic degree
- complementary courses
- skills development
- unusual technical expertise
- work experience
- volunteer activity
- contributing to the community
- a position of responsibility
- a broad set of skills that could be transferred to the workplace.

Activity

Personal skills portfolio

- In which of the nine areas listed above have you invested already?
- Realistically, what else could you undertake in the next six months to develop your personal skills portfolio?

Career readiness

Below are suggestions of steps you can take now to develop your readiness for later when you apply for college graduate jobs.

Visit your Career Center

It is never too early to use the Career Center. Choices made in the first year and early in the second year can have long-term effects. Most career advisors would prefer that students visit the Career Center in their first year. An early chat about your aspirations and goals can point you in the right direction, help you make good decisions and save you time and money later.

Your Career Center will have a library of up-to-date information about employers and different professions. Find out the full range of career and academic choices that are open to you as a result of the classes you are taking—many graduates enter careers that have little obvious connection with their major. On the other hand, if you have identified your preferred career path, career and academic advisors will tell you which classes you have to take to qualify for this career.

What the Career Center can offer

The Career Center can advise you on how to make the best use of your time while you are a student, so that you:

- develop your ideas about the kinds of jobs you really want
- choose the right subject options and classes for careers that interest you or suit you best
- are aware of the skills and qualities employers want in the fields of work that interest you
- make the best use of opportunities open to you as a student
- prepare well in advance for the kinds of jobs that interest you
- are aware of the range of opportunities available to you, through college and beyond.

College Career Centers often have a job search or similar facility to help you gain student jobs or work placements while you are studying.

Prepare questions for the career advisor

It may help to ask the career advisor:

- What kinds of jobs are open to me because of my major?
- What kinds of jobs do most students with my major enter?
- What further training would I need for the career I have in mind?
- What competition is there for that career?
- What additional things will employers be looking for, apart from my degree?
- What can I do while in college to improve my chances of getting a good job in the area that interests me?

Labor market trends

Ask career advisors about current trends in the labor market and how these may affect you. What opportunities are there?

Find out what kinds of jobs college graduates enter when they leave your program. Decide whether these interest you. If so, how can you put yourself in a good position to compete for them?

If those jobs do not interest you, there is no cause for alarm. A very wide range of jobs are open to graduates from any discipline.

Decide what is important to you

Many students find it useful to talk with a career advisor about what is involved in pursuing a certain career. Before you commit yourself to a particular route, make sure that you know what the job would entail.

Beware of the apparent glamour of some jobs: Search below the surface for details of what day-to-day work would be like, and think if this would suit you. For example:

- Are long hours expected of employees in these kinds of jobs? If so, would you be prepared to work those hours?
- Would you be willing to work for many years on a training wage until you were fully qualified?

- Would you be prepared to take more qualifications in order to pursue your chosen career?
- Can you afford the further training?
- Would you like the kind of people who are usually attracted to this kind of work?
- Would a lot of travel be required? If so, would this be acceptable to you?
- Would you be likely to be moved to different parts of the country, or to other countries? Would you mind?
- How stressful is the job? How much stress would you be prepared to put up with?
- Are there any health and safety risks associated with this kind of work?
- What would be the effects of this kind of job on family life? Would you be prepared to accept these?
- Would you be expected to socialize regularly with colleagues? Is that something that would appeal to you?

Your answers to these questions are not simply about the type of *work* you think you would like but about the kind of *life* you want to lead, the sort of *person* you want to be and the *people* with whom you wish to mix.

Career plan
18 Shop assistant
25 Manager
30 Director
35 U.S. President
45 Take over the World
50 ?

Choices of study options

It pays to consider the full range of subject options open to you. Consider if you could:

- take a class that would give you an unusual but marketable range of expertise
- develop new skills or languages
- develop an international perspective
- develop business skills
- develop relevant professional skills
- create an opportunity for work experience.

However, bear in mind that there will be many learning opportunities throughout your life when you could catch up in areas that you have missed.

Stand out from the crowd

Consider what opportunities you can make use of now so that later, when competing with others for jobs or academic places, you stand out as "distinctive."

Gain work experience

There is no substitute for work experience—it builds a range of skills and attitudes that are hard to learn through study. Work experience need not necessarily be in a relevant area. If you want to enter a career quickly after graduating, it can pay to have *any* kind of work experience during your time in college—especially if you have not been in paid work before.

There is a wide range of choices:

- paid work
- voluntary work schemes
- work-based learning programs or work placements
- high school mentoring programs
- artists in residency (for arts students)
- student organizations.

Stand out from the crowd

Write a resumé

Write a resumé and keep it up-to-date. Maintain good records and keep track of experience, jobs, dates and addresses of employers. You may need to send out a resumé at short notice, so update it regularly.

Update your personal records

Keep a good portfolio of your personal records.

Every six months, write a thumbnail sketch about yourself. Include the following.

- What inspires you most at present?
- How have you used existing skills in new contexts?
- What personal qualities have you developed out of recent experience?
- What are your long-term goals now?
- What are your immediate goals and targets?

Broaden your life experience

Identify ways of broadening your outlook, your range of skills and your ability to deal with a wider range of people. Build your confidence in coping with a wider set of circumstances and situations.

Give serious attention to undertaking a range of activities *apart* from study. Take on positions of responsibility so that you can develop and demonstrate your ability to cope with difficulties and show leadership skills.

If you work, see if you can take a work-related study option to make the most of the experience—many colleges offer these. Consider undertaking community work, get involved with student organizations, drama, music or political activity—there is usually a wide range of activities offered in college.

Develop your resumé

When you apply for a job, you will probably be asked to send in a resumé. On this, you list your educational and work history, your interests and other activities you have undertaken. Your academic qualifications form only one part of a resumé. If you do nothing but study while in college, you may have very little to write on your resumé or to discuss at interview.

You can expect employers to ask for examples of:

- where you have demonstrated certain skills
- how you dealt with certain kinds of situation typically encountered in the workplace (such as dealing with the public)
- voluntary work or public service.

It is worth planning ahead to ensure that you build up at least some experience upon which you can draw for application forms and interviews. This may be through work experience, performing, putting on an exhibition or some other activity.

Lifelong learning?

What is lifelong learning?

The rapid rate of change in knowledge, technology and society means that it is now essential to keep updating skills and expertise. In addition, there are far more opportunities, today, to change career or to develop specialisms long after leaving college. Increasingly, employers expect graduates to demonstrate personal commitment to continued personal development (CPD) and to show an appreciation of lifelong learning.

Universities and colleges contribute to lifelong learning, providing opportunities for graduates to develop expertise in new areas. This can be very useful if you did not make ideal academic choices the first time around.

Developing skills as a student

As you reach the end of this study skills book, you may feel you know all you want to know about skills development! It may indeed be time for a break. However, the challenge of continued personal development will remain.

- No one person is likely to have a perfect set of skills and strategies that will meet every eventuality. There is always something that can be improved or updated.
- At each level of study in high school and then college, the skills needed will be more sophisticated than at the previous level. At each new level, more will be expected. You will need new strategies and ways of thinking.

New opportunities for personal advancement

Many colleges now offer opportunities for a wide range of additional learning, including the following:

- *Graduate or higher-level programs.*
- *Continuous professional development programs.*

- *Short courses* at various levels, including courses to update skills.
- *Additional classes*—the chance to take a few classes to suit your needs rather than an entirely new degree.
- *Lifelong learning awards, or other, shorter programs*—these are typically the equivalent of half a year's undergraduate study, but usually taken over a longer period.
- *Credit accumulation*—this enables students to build up academic credits over a long period of time to suit their work and life circumstances.
- *Extramural studies*—these "continuing education" programs enable people to follow up on interests either before or after their degree.
- *Work-based learning*—programs offered in the workplace, or with workplace assignments.
- *Work-related learning*—at college, but centered on work.

Even while you are taking your degree, it is worth finding out about the range of future study options on offer. This may help you now, as you make subject choices. For example, you may prefer to leave some specialist areas relevant to your career interests to a future part-time program, after you have completed your degree.

Activity

Identifying opportunities

- What opportunities are open to you for adapting your degree program or for taking options that develop unusual skills?
- If there are aspects of your program that do not interest you now, can they be studied in the future instead?
- Are there opportunities for gaining credit for work-based learning?

Where next? Skills for success

This book has taken a broad approach to academic development. For example, it has offered opportunities to:

- develop your understanding of a range of concepts that can assist the learning process
- undertake reflective activities that can increase your awareness of your own learning development
- learn how to study successfully while working with other people
- develop skills of prioritizing, action planning and self-evaluation.

Most of these developmental skills will remain important in advancing your academic, personal and professional success. The next step is to identify which of these skills would be usefully developed further.

The following questionnaire will help you explore your experience and skills at a more advanced level than that covered by this book. This should help identify your next set of personal targets.

Knowledge, skills, qualities and experience	Already experienced	Want to know more	Want to develop further	Order of importance
Understanding success - Understanding personal approaches to success - Using sources of inspiration - Using personal values as sources of motivation - Being aware of the ingredients of success - Coordinating your efforts				
People skills - Developing rapport - Listening skillfully - Developing mutual trust - Contributing to teamwork - Using "action sets" for group work - Offering constructive criticism - Receiving criticism with openness - Being assertive - Dealing with difficult people				

Knowledge, skills, qualities and experience	Already experienced	Want to know more	Want to develop further	Order of importance
People skills *(continued)* <ul><li>Negotiating skills</li><li>Exercising leadership</li></ul>				
Creative thinking <ul><li>Using the brain effectively to improve performance</li><li>Thinking with the whole brain</li><li>Developing confidence in personal creativity</li><li>Using creative thinking strategies</li><li>Creative problem-solving</li><li>Generating ideas</li><li>Creativity and risk-taking</li></ul>				
Problem-solving and task management <ul><li>Elaborating a problem</li><li>Basic approaches to problem-solving</li><li>Applying strategy to complex problems</li><li>Identifying solutions to problems</li><li>Drawing up an action plan</li><li>Becoming a good self-starter</li><li>Following through an action plan</li><li>Managing tasks</li><li>Managing projects successfully</li><li>Finishing jobs</li><li>Using performance indicators (PI)</li><li>Evaluating personal competitiveness</li></ul>				
Self-management <ul><li>Using your life story to understand yourself better</li><li>Making the best use of learning styles, habits and preferences</li><li>Applying areas of personal expertise to new problems</li><li>Evaluating your own emotional intelligence</li><li>Managing change, confusion and uncertainty</li><li>Identifying barriers to personal success</li></ul>				

Chapter **15**

Knowledge, skills, qualities and experience	Already experienced	Want to know more	Want to develop further	Order of importance
Self-management *(continued)* ■ Developing constructive attitudes to achieve personal goals ■ Managing "goal inertia" ■ Working at your "personal edge"				
The art of reflection ■ Understanding more about "reflection" ■ Understanding what is meant by the "reflective practitioner" ■ Being aware of different methods of undertaking reflection ■ Being aware of different ways of recording reflection ■ Presenting reflective work to other people				
Successful job applications ■ Choosing a graduate job ■ Knowing what you want from an employer ■ Using progress files and personal records ■ Preparing good job applications ■ Writing good cover letters ■ Making good competence-based applications ■ Writing a good resumé ■ Using the Internet to find a job ■ Applying for jobs if you have a disability ■ Preparing for job interviews ■ Effective interview techniques ■ Starting a new job				
Recording achievement ■ Developing effective personal records ■ Recording evidence of competence for college graduate jobs				

Clarifying personal targets

Look at the previous activity (pages 354–356), and note the skills you wished to pursue further. Of those you identified, which *three* are your top priorities? To focus your thinking on these, complete the boxes below for your three chosen targets.

	Target 1	Target 2	Target 3
1 What is the target?			
2 What is the point of developing this skill? (What are the benefits to you?)			
3 How will you make time to do this?			
4 What support or guidance will you need? Where will you go for this, and when?			
5 What would demonstrate that you had achieved your aim?			

Chapter **15**

PLANNER

Action plan for personal development planning goals

Goal:

Main things to do (targets)	Steps to take (milestones)	What indicates successful completion?	Start date	Target completion date	Done
1	a				
	b				
	c				
2	a				
	b				
	c				
3	a				
	b				
	c				

What now?

Although this is the end of the book, it is not the end of your development as a student.

Using the *Study Skills Handbook* after a first reading

The *Study Skills Handbook* is not designed to be worked through a single time. As you develop as a student, you will find things of benefit that you missed the first time around. Browse through the text from time to time—you may be surprised at what catches your eye.

Monitoring your progress

As the *Handbook* has emphasized, as an adult student you are ultimately responsible for monitoring your own progress. If you keep a study journal, read back over it and note changes in your ideas. Return to the self-evaluation questionnaires and complete these again. Compare your current answers with your earlier responses. What changes do you note? How have you changed as a person? What did you identify for improvement and then forget all about? Does this still need attention?

Need help?

If you feel you are not making the progress you would like, make an appointment to see your academic advisor. When you meet, take evidence of your difficulties as well as your attempts to resolve them. Advisors can help you best if they see how far you can manage on your own, what you have already tried and where they need to focus the support. If you turn up empty-handed, there may be very little they can do to help.

Looking backwards, looking forwards ...

In this chapter you have returned, in some ways, to the starting point of the book. The book began by inviting you to review your skills and to identify your own priorities. In this chapter you have reviewed your achievements and evaluated some that are most important to you. You have also begun to identify next steps forward in your own personal development.

Having been through different levels of study in high school and now in college, you will have become aware that where one stage of learning ends, another begins. Increasingly this process of personal development is a feature of professional life. Many jobs you may enter as a college graduate will expect you to take responsibility for this process of:

- evaluating your own performance
- identifying areas to improve
- identifying your training needs
- developing a strategy and an action plan to address these
- monitoring your own progress
- evaluating successful achievement.

Whereas the book has focused mainly on study skills, this chapter has encouraged you to consider your skills development in the wider context of your life and career ambitions. The final activities, on pages 353–358, encouraged you to think about different, often more advanced, aspects of skills you have already developed. It is up to you whether you take this further.

Good luck!

Enjoy your learning and succeed with your studies.

References

Bower, G. H., Clark, M., Lesgold, A. and Winzenz, D. (1969). "Hierarchical retrieval schemes in recall of categorised word lists," *Journal of Verbal Learning and Verbal Behaviour* **8**, 323–43.

Bowlby, J. (1951). *Maternal Care and Mental Health.* Report to the World Health Organization. New York: Shocken Books.

Bowlby, J. (1969). *Attachment and Loss: Attachment.* New York: Basic Books.

Butterworth, G. (1992). "Context and cognition in models of cognitive growth." In Light, P. and Butterworth, G. (eds). *Context and Cognition.* London: Harvester.

Buzan, T. (1993). *The Mind Map Book.* London: BBC.

Buzan, T. and Keene, R. (1996). *The Age Heresy: You Can Achieve More, Not Less, As You Get Older.* London: Ebury Press.

Clarke, A. M. and Clarke, A. D. B. (1976). *Early Experience: Myth and Evidence.* London: Open Books.

Clarke-Stewart, A. (1988). "The 'effects' of infant day care reconsidered: risks for parents, children and researchers," *Early Childhood Research Quarterly* **3**, 292–318.

Colon, J. (1982). *A Puerto Rican in New York and Other Sketches,* 2nd edn. New York: International Publishers.

Cottrell, S. M. (2010). *Skills for Success: Personal Development and Employability,* 2nd edn. Basingstoke: Palgrave Macmillan.

Cottrell, S. M. (2011). *Critical Thinking Skills: Developing Effective Analysis and Argument,* 2nd edn. Basingstoke: Palgrave Macmillan.

Cottrell, S. M. (2012). *The Exam Skills Handbook: Achieving Peak Performance,* 2nd edn. Basingstoke: Palgrave Macmillan.

Cottrell, S. M. and Morris, N. (2012). *Study Skills Connected: Using Technology to Support Your Studies.* Basingstoke: Palgrave Macmillan.

Donaldson, M. (1978). *Children's Minds.* Glasgow: Fontana.

Flanagan, K. (1997). *Maximum Points, Minimum Panic: The Essential Guide to Surviving Exams,* 2nd edn. Dublin: Marino.

Freeman, R. and Mead, J. (1991). *How to Study Effectively.* Cambridge: National Extension College.

Fuhrman, J. A., McCallum, K., Davis, A. A. (1992) "Novel major archaebacterial group from marine plankton." *Nature* **356**:148–149.

Gardner, H. (1993). *Frames of Mind: The Theory of Multiple Intelligences,* 2nd edn. London: Fontana.

Glaser, E. (1941). *An Experiment in the Development of Critical Thinking.* New York: Teachers' College, Columbia University.

Harris, J.E. and Sunderland, A. (1981). "Effects of age and instructions on an everyday memory questionnaire." Paper presented at the British Psychological Society Cognitive Psychology Section Conference on Memory, Plymouth, 1981.

Karmiloff-Smith, A. (1992). *Beyond Modularity: A Developmental Perspective on Cognitive Science.* Cambridge, Mass.: MIT Press.

Keane, M., Kahney, H. and Brayshaw, M. (1989). "Simulating analogical mapping difficulties in recursion problems." In Cohn, A. G. (ed.) (1989). *Proceedings of the Seventh Conference of the Society for the Study of Artificial Intelligence and Simulation of Behaviour.* Morgan Lauffman. (Cited in Kahney, H. (1993). *Problem Solving: current issues,* 2nd edn. Buckingham: The Open University.)

Mackintosh, N. J. and Mascie-Taylor, C. G. N. (1985). "The IQ question." In *Report of the Committee of Inquiry into Education of Children from Ethnic Minority Groups.* London: HMSO, pp. 126–63.

O'Connor, J. and McDermott, I. (1996). *Principles of NLP.* London: Thorsons.

Oke, A., Keller, R., Mefford, I. and Adams, R.N. (1978). "Lateralization of norepinephrine in human thalamus." *Science* **200**:1411–1413.

Reed, S. K., Dempster, A. and Ettinger, M. (1985). "Usefulness of analogous solutions for solving algebra word problems," *Journal of Experimental Psychology; Learning, Memory and Cognition* **11**(1), pp. 106–25.

Resnick, L., Levine, J. and Teasley, S. D. (eds) (1991). *Perspectives on Socially Shared Cognition.* Washington, D.C.: American Psychological Association.

Rose, C. (1985). *Accelerated Learning.* Aylesbury: Accelerated Learning Systems Ltd.

Simon, H. (1974). "How big is a chunk?" *Science* **183**, 482–8.

Spearman, C. (1927). *The Abilities of Man.* London: Macmillan.

Springer, S. P. and Deutsch, G. (1981). *Left Brain, Right Brain.* San Francisco: W. H. Freeman.

Sternberg, R. J. (1984). "Facets of intelligence." In Anderson, J. R. and Kosslyn, S. M. (eds). *Tutorials in Learning and Memory: Essays in Honor of Gordon Bower.* San Francisco: W. H. Freeman.

Sternberg, R. J. (1985). *Beyond IQ: A Triarchic Theory of Human Intelligence.* Cambridge: Cambridge University Press.

Terman, L. M. (1975, first published 1916). *The Measurement of Intelligence.* New York: L. L. Arno Press.

Thompson, A. (1996). *Critical Reasoning: A Practical Introduction.* London: Routledge.

Thurstone, L. L. (1960). *The Nature of Intelligence.* Littlefield: Adams.

Tizard, B. (1991). "Working mothers and the care of young children." In Woodhead, M., Light, P. and Carr, R. (eds). *Growing Up in a Changing Society.* London: Routledge.

Vygotsky, L. (1978). *Mind in Society.* Cambridge, Mass.: Harvard University Press.

Wilkinson, G. (1997). *Understanding Stress.* London: British Medical Association ('Family Doctor' Series).

Wilson, P. (1997). *Calm at Work.* London: Penguin.

Woese, C. R. (1994). "There must be a prokaryote somewhere: Microbiology's search for itself." *Microbiological Reviews* **58**, 1–9

Appendix 1

Quick multiplier

Use the grid below to see what number results when you multiply a number from the top row with a number from the left-hand column. The diagonal shaded row shows each number multiplied by itself.

Spend time seeing if you can detect any patterns in the numbers. For example, look at the final digits in the *4* column, the *5* column, the *9* column and the *11* column.

0	1	2	3	4	5	6	7	8	9	10	11	12	13	14	15	16	17	18
1	1	2	3	4	5	6	7	8	9	10	11	12	13	14	15	16	17	18
2	2	4	6	8	10	12	14	16	18	20	22	24	26	28	30	32	34	36
3	3	6	9	12	15	18	21	24	27	30	33	36	39	42	45	48	51	54
4	4	8	12	16	20	24	28	32	36	40	44	48	52	56	60	64	68	72
5	5	10	15	20	25	30	35	40	45	50	55	60	65	70	75	80	85	90
6	6	12	18	24	30	36	42	48	54	60	66	72	78	84	90	96	102	108
7	7	14	21	28	35	42	49	56	63	70	77	84	91	98	105	112	119	126
8	8	16	24	32	40	48	56	64	72	80	88	96	104	112	120	128	136	144
9	9	18	27	36	45	54	63	72	81	90	99	108	117	126	135	144	153	162
10	10	20	30	40	50	60	70	80	90	100	110	120	130	140	150	160	170	180
11	11	22	33	44	55	66	77	88	99	110	121	132	143	154	165	176	187	198
12	12	24	36	48	60	72	84	96	108	120	132	144	156	168	180	192	204	216
13	13	26	39	52	65	78	91	104	117	130	143	156	169	182	195	208	221	234
14	14	28	42	56	70	84	98	112	126	140	154	168	182	196	210	224	238	252
15	15	30	45	60	75	90	105	120	135	150	165	180	195	210	225	240	255	270
16	16	32	48	64	80	96	112	128	144	160	176	192	208	224	240	256	272	288
17	17	34	51	68	85	102	119	136	153	170	187	204	221	238	255	272	289	306
18	18	36	54	72	90	108	126	144	162	180	198	216	234	252	270	288	306	324
19	19	38	57	76	95	114	133	152	171	190	209	228	247	266	285	304	323	342
20	20	40	60	80	100	120	140	160	180	200	220	240	260	280	300	320	340	360

Appendix 2

Online research tools

General help sites and academic search engines

IngentaConnect

Access to online journal abstracts and articles, many free of charge:
- www.ingentaconnect.com

Find Articles

Access to articles from magazines, journals, trade publications and newspapers:
- http://findarticles.com

Google Scholar

A specialist branch of the main Google search engine that focuses searches on "scholarly" material such as peer-reviewed articles:
- http://scholar.google.com

Questia

A large online library with a broad selection of complete books and journal articles in the humanities and social sciences. There is no charge for searching the library, but a subscription is required to access publications:
- www.questia.com

Internet tutorials

Several sites provide tutorials on using the Internet, and some teach basic research strategies. You can choose tutorials on general Internet skills or skills specific to your subject:
- www.sc.edu/beaufort/library/pages/bones/bones.shtml
- www.internettutorials.net

Social science resource databases

- http://infomine.ucr.edu
- www.ipl.org/div/subject/browse/soc00.00.00

Other subject sites

Arts and humanities

- http://vos.ucsb.edu

Biology

- www.academicinfo.net/biology.html

Biomedical and pharmaceutical

- www.embase.com

Chemistry

- http://chemweb.com

Computing

- http://arxiv.org/corr/home

Education

- www.eric.ed.gov

Engineering

- www.efunda.com

Geography

- http://education.nationalgeographic.com

History

- www.besthistorysites.net
- www.fordham.edu/Halsall/mod/modsbook.asp

Law

- www.lexisnexis.com/hottopics.lnacademic

Mathematics

- http://mathforum.org/library
- www.khanacademy.org

Nursing and health

- www.cinahl.com

Psychology

- www.apa.org/pubs/databases/psyinfo/index.aspx

Subject directories

Websites for finding lists of subject directories:
- www.ipl.org
- www.about.com
- www.digital-librarian.com
- http://library.sau.edu/bestinfo
- www.khanacademy.org

Index

work-based learning (*Continued*)
   managing study leave 82
   managing work-based projects 81
   workplace mentors 81
work placements 8
writing 31, 231, 288
   academic writing 231, 245
   analysis 149–51, 158–66, 243, 245, 275, 277–8
   argument *see* reasoning, line of
   compare and contrast 243, 245, 277–9
   on computer 122, 236–8, 255, 260, 262

conclusions 157, 242, 248–9, 259
drafts 122, 234, 238, 241, 249–50, 254–5, 259
evaluation of writing skills 232, 261, 263
from experience 280
getting started 20, 59, 233–4, 236–7
introductions 204, 242, 248, 261, 274
linking ideas 232, 259
organizing tasks 64–5, 234, 240–1, 246–7, 249–54, 276, 279
paragraphs 256–9

plans 241, 247–50, 276, 278–9
self-evaluation 232
speed 201
structure 203, 239, 245–6, 248, 281
style 239, 245, 261, 265–8, 273–80, 288
sub-skills 232
writer's block 236–7
see also report-writing; research papers; research projects